CATHOLIC REVIVAL IN THE AGE OF THE BAROQUE

This book is a study of Catholic reform, popular Catholicism, and the development of confessional identity in Southwest Germany. Based on extensive archival study, it argues that Catholic confessional identity developed primarily from the identification of villagers and townspeople with the practices of Baroque Catholicism – particularly pilgrimages, processions, confraternities, and the Mass. Thus the book is in part a critique of the confessionalization thesis which currently dominates scholarship in this field.

The book is not, however, focused narrowly on the concerns of German historians. An analysis of popular religious practice and of the relationship between parishioners and the clergy in villages and small towns allows for a broader understanding of popular Catholicism, especially in the period after 1650. Local Baroque Catholicism was ultimately a successful convergence of popular elite, lay and clerical elements, which led to an increasingly elaborate religious style.

MARC R. FORSTER is Associate Professor of History, Connecticut College.

NEW STUDIES IN EUROPEAN HISTORY

This is a new series in early modern and modern European history. Its aim is to publish outstanding works of research, addressed to important themes across a wide geographical range, from southern and central Europe, to Scandinavia and Russia, and from the time of the Renaissance to the Second World War. As it develops the series will comprise focused works of wide contextual range and intellectual ambition.

CATHOLIC REVIVAL IN THE AGE OF THE BAROQUE

Religious Identity in Southwest Germany, 1550–1750

MARC R. FORSTER

PUBLISHED BY THE PRESS SYNDICATE OF THE UNIVERSITY OF CAMBRIDGE
The Pitt Building, Trumpington Street, Cambridge, United Kingdom

CAMBRIDGE UNIVERSITY PRESS
The Edinburgh Building, Cambridge, CB2 2RU, UK http://www.cup.cam.ac.uk
40 West 20th Street, New York, NY 10011–4211, USA http://www.cup.org
10 Stamford Road, Oakleigh, Melbourne 3166, Australia
Ruiz de Alarcón 13, 28014 Madrid, Spain

First published 2001

Printed in the United Kingdom at the University Press, Cambridge

Typeset in Baskerville 11/12.5pt [VN]

A catalogue record for this book is available from the British Library

Library of Congress Cataloguing in Publication data

Forster, Marc R.
Catholic revival in the age of the baroque: religious identity in southwest Germany, 1550–1570 / Marc R. Forster.
p. cm. – (New studies in European history
Includes bibliographical references (p. 245).
ISBN 0 521 78044 6
1. Catholic Church – Germany, Southern – History – 16th century. 2. Germany, Southern – Church history – 16th century. 3. Catholic Church – Germany, Southern – History – 17th century. 4. Germany, Southern – Church history – 17th century. 5. Catholic Church – Germany, Southern – History – 18th century. 6. Germany, Southern – Church history – 18th century. I. Title. II. Series.
BX1537.G3 F67 2001
282'.434'0903 – dc21 00-036305

ISBN 0 521 78044 6 hardback

For my parents

Contents

Maps

Acknowledgments

The Alexander von Humboldt Stiftung and the National Endowment for the Humanities funded extended visits to German archives. Further support came from the German Academic Exchange Service (DAAD), the R.F. Johnson Faculty Development Fund, and the President's Office at Connecticut College. The Ecole des Hautes Etudes en Sciences Sociales in Paris gave me the opportunity to spend a month testing out my ideas on French colleagues. The staffs of the Generallandesarchiv Karlsruhe, the Hauptstaatsarchiv Stuttgart, the Erzbischöfliches Archiv Freiburg, and the Tiroler Landesarchiv in Innsbruck were always generous with their time and professional expertise.

Many people provided indispensable advice and support at various stages of this project. I would like to thank my colleagues in the History Department at Connecticut College for providing me with the time to research and write this book. Frederick S. Paxton, Jeffrey Lesser, Lisa Wilson, Anthony Crubaugh, Sarah Queen, and Catherine McNicol Stock all read and commented on various sections of this book. Discussions with other Connecticut College colleagues, especially Charlotte Daniels, Robert Gay, David Patton, MaryAnne Borelli, Stuart Vyse, Candace Howes, Ursula Love, Geoffrey Atherton, and Gerhard Hufnagel have widened my intellectual horizons and made this a better book.

It is impossible to name everyone who helped me during the ten years this project took to complete. Louis Bergeron, Thomas A. Brady Jr., Richard Goldthwaite, Olof Hirn, R. Po-chia Hsia, Benjamin J. Kaplan, David Martin Luebke, H.C. Erik Midelfort, Jason Nye, John O'Malley, Steven Ozment, Wolfgang Reinhard, James Tracy, Peter Wallace, Lee Palmer Wandel, and Wolfgang Zimmermann all contributed in important ways. The anonymous readers for Cambridge University Press made many invaluable suggestions.

My wife Tina and my daughters Sara and Jenny have been part of this book from the beginning. By the time Sara was eight years old, she was talking about being a historian, and at age 18 months Jenny knew that the proper answer to the question "Where is Daddy?" was "Daddy archives!" My aunt and uncle, Gisela and Horst Cyriax, continue to be my most important mentors in the German language as well as rigorous editors of my writing in any language.

This book is dedicated to my parents, Elborg and Robert Forster. From my earliest childhood they gave me a sense of the excitement and wonder of history and the value of being both a scholar and a teacher. Their support and advice have always been invaluable; they are wonderful editors and the most engaged and knowledgeable critics of my work. Much more importantly, in observing and following their professional and personal lives I have found the best role models and unending inspiration.

Abbreviations

Archives

EAF	Erzbischöfliches Archiv Freiburg
GLAK	Badisches Generallandesarchiv Karlsruhe
HStASt.	Hauptstaatsarchiv Stuttgart
TLA	Tiroler Landesarchiv (Innsbruck)

Journals

FDA	*Freiburger Diözesan Archiv*
ZGO	*Zeitschrift für die Geschichte des Oberrheins*
RJfKG	*Rottenburger Jahrbuch für Kirchengeschichte*

Secondary works

Ebner, *Birndorf*	Jakob Ebner, *Aus der Geschichte der Ortschaften der Pfarrei Birndorf (bei Waldshut am Hochrhein)* (Karlsruhe, 1938)
Ebner, *Engelwies*	Jakob Ebner, *Geschichte der Wallfahrt und des Dorfes Engelwies bei Meßkirch* (Meßkirch, 1923)
Ebner, *Görwihl*	Jakob Ebner, *Geschichte der Pfarrei Görwihl im Hotzenwald* (Wangen: Selbstverlag des Verfassers, 1953)
Ebner, *Hochsal*	Jakob Ebner, *Geschichte der Ortschaften der Pfarrei Hochsal* (Wangen: Selbstverlag des Verfassers, 1958)
Ebner, *Niederwihl*	Jakob Ebner, *Geschichte der Ortschaften der Pfarrei Niederwihl (Niederwihl, Oberwihl und Rüßwihl)* (Wangen: Selbstverlag des Verfassers, 1956)
Ebner, *Unteralpfen*	Jakob Ebner, *Aus der Geschichte des Hauensteiner Dorfes Unteralpfen*, 2nd edn. (Karlsruhe, n.d.)

Introduction

One may try to distinguish for the common man the essentials of Christianity [*das Wesentliche des Christentums*] as clearly as one wishes, but he still does not like to be disturbed in his longstanding outward devotional practices. If this happens, then he believes (although unjustly) himself justified in throwing over all remaining devotional practices and permits himself indifference in worshipping God, diversion, and carelessness.

Ludwig Haßler, the *Stadtpfarrer* of Rottenburg am Neckar, 1793[1]

Pfarrer Haßler knew his parishioners well. They were staunch Catholics who faithfully attended church services and participated in a wide range of devotional practices. At the heart of popular devotional life were pilgrimages, processions, church festivals, and the Mass – what Haßler called "outward devotional practices" but which we might call aspects of a public and communal religiosity. This commitment to the religious practices of Roman Catholicism was essential for the formation of a strong Catholic identity among the people of Southwest Germany between 1550 and 1750.

The creation of religious identities occurred in Southwest Germany and throughout the Catholic and Protestant territories of Germany in the early modern period. Southwest Germany was a region of beautiful churches and wealthy monasteries, elaborate processions and dramatic pilgrimages, and Catholic confessional identity made it the heartland of Baroque Catholicism.[2] The Catholic confessionalism of the population was profound and lasting. In the nineteenth century the population was still known for its *Kirchlichkeit*, its churchliness or loyalty to the Roman Church, and in the twentieth century these people frequently supported Catholic political parties.

[1] HStASt. B467/769. See chapter 2.

[2] The Duchy of Württemberg and Margraviate of Baden-Durlach were the only important Protestant territories in the region.

The origins of this strong Catholic identity and the character of its accompanying churchliness are the subjects of this study. In the middle of the sixteenth century boundaries between Catholics and Protestants were still unclear, especially for the common people. In fact, Protestants and Catholics mingled easily in the villages and towns of the Southwest. By the middle of the seventeenth century, however, this was no longer the case, and by 1700 an "invisible frontier" divided Protestant from Catholic Germany.[3] All groups in Catholic society had acquired a confessional identity and were relatively immune to the lure of Protestantism. Across Germany, as well as in the Southwest, the confessional boundary was not just political, but personal, as it came to be internalized by the population as a whole. What had brought about this dramatic change in the two centuries after 1550?

Generations of church historians have argued that the development of churchliness and confessionalism was a consequence of the success of the reform program initiated by the Council of Trent. In fact, a number of trends in Southwest Germany must have pleased Catholic reformers of the sixteenth and seventeenth centuries. Rural Catholicism became "clericalized" as the population increasingly accepted the indispensable role of the priest in the sacraments and devotions of Catholic life. Furthermore, by the first decades of the eighteenth century, the long effort of church reformers, especially the Jesuits and Capuchins, to encourage more intense and individual devotion appeared to be bearing fruit, in rural parishes as well as in the towns and cities.

The development of confessional identity was also a goal of many state officials, and Southwest Germany experienced "confessionalization" as well as Tridentine reform. The notion that there was a process of confessionalization, in which state and Church cooperated successfully to enforce religious conformity and inculcate religious identity, has dominated the discussion of religious and cultural developments in this period.[4] This "confessionalization thesis" is by no means universally accepted but, together with the older argument that credits Tridentine reform with bringing new elements to Catholicism, it has led scholars to emphasize the role of the clerical elite and the state in bringing about religious change.

The present study is in part a critique of the confessionalization thesis.

[3] The term "the invisible frontier" (*die unsichtbare Grenze*) comes from Etienne François, *Die unsichtbare Grenze. Protestanten und Katholiken in Augsburg, 1648–1806* (Sigmaringen, 1991).

[4] Marc R. Forster, "With and Without Confessionalization: Varieties of Early Modern German Catholicism" *Journal of Early Modern History* 1,4 (1998), esp. pp. 325–329.

It is also an examination of popular religious practice and a study of Baroque Catholicism as a dynamic complex of religious practices. A focus on the daily experience of Catholicism shows clearly that peasants and townspeople did not passively accept an identity imposed by the elite. Instead, the population played a major role in the creation of Catholic confessionalism and consequently the churchliness of the common people often developed in directions unforeseen by the Church. In fact, many episcopal officials, Jesuit fathers, and educated Catholic lay people were quite unhappy with the state of popular Catholicism, even at the peak of the popular revival in the early eighteenth century. Some trends, for example the explosion of pilgrimage piety between about 1680 and 1750, the continued role of rural communes and town councils in administering parishes, or the growing diversity and variety of the sacral landscape, contradicted centralizing and rationalizing tendencies within the Church. Other trends, for example the development of devotions such as the cult of the Rosary, occurred in directions the church leadership neither anticipated nor desired.

Despite such elite concerns about aspects of popular religiosity, one of the strengths of the Catholic Church was its willingness to accommodate popular desires and thus meet many of the religious needs of the population. Especially after 1650, this tolerant policy, together with the active role of the people in everyday religion, gave rise to a Catholic identity with strong popular roots, rather than a sense of imposed religious loyalty or an unenthusiastic accommodation to religious norms imposed from above.

Baroque Catholicism, conceived of as a complex of religious practices, is not well understood. In the first place, historians have left the term "Baroque" to scholars of literature and art history, who distinguish between the seventeenth-century Baroque and the eighteenth-century Enlightenment. In Germany the *Volkskundler*, the folklorists, have dominated the study of popular religion in the seventeenth and eighteenth centuries, and their use of the concept of Baroque is rather different from that used by the humanists. The dean of the "religious folklorists," Wolfgang Brückner, has lamented the imprecision that comes from referring to a wide range of religious practices, such as pilgrimage and the Rosary, as elements of "Baroque piety" (*Barockfrömmigkeit*) even in their twentieth-century manifestations.[5]

[5] Wolfgang Brückner, "Zum Wandel der religiösen Kultur im 18. Jahrhundert. Einkreisungsversuche des 'Barockfrommen' zwischen Mittelalter und Massenmissionierung" in Ernst Hinrichs and Günter Wiegelmann (eds.), *Sozialer und kultureller Wandel in der ländlichen Welt des 18. Jahrhunderts* (Wolfenbüttel, 1982), p. 65.

Brückner also points to the limited amount of research on Baroque Catholicism in Germany, especially in comparison with the work on both the preceding period (late medieval Christianity) and the following period (the Enlightenment and "secularization").[6] The only real survey of the period remains Ludwig Veit and Ludwig Lenhart's *Kirche und Volksfrömmigkeit im Zeitalter des Barocks*, which was published in 1956.[7] Brückner points out that *Volkskundler* have studied various Catholic practices, such as pilgrimages, new cults of saints, for example that of St. John of Nepomuk, and the Rosary, and criticizes historians for neglecting to incorporate this research into their understanding of the period 1650–1750.[8] Yet Brückner also recognizes that even the *Volkskundler* have a limited grasp of Catholic practice in this period, especially in the first half of the eighteenth century.

This study seeks to fill some of these gaps in the study of early modern Germany. The historiographical focus at one end of the period on the Reformation of the sixteenth century and, at the other end, on the secularization and "modernization" of the Enlightenment, often produces a caricature of Baroque Catholicism. Descriptions of popular Catholicism in the two centuries after 1550 vary from the crude – it was emotional and superstitious – to the general and vague – "a sensuous Baroque Catholicism with its extroverted manifestations of faith."[9] The realities of life in the Catholic Southwest were both more complex and more concrete.

As one examines Catholicism at the local level in this region and period, certain features of religious practice and clerical–lay relations stand out. Particular practices, especially pilgrimages, processions, and participation in the liturgy, became central features of popular Catholicism and an integral part of the Catholic identity of the population. A kind of clericalism, by which I mean a respect for the special status and powers of the clergy, especially parish priests, increasingly characterized

6 Brückner, "Zum Wandel der religiösen Kultur im 18. Jahrhundert," pp. 66–67.

7 Ludwig Veit and Ludwig Lenhart, *Kirche und Volksfrömmigkeit im Zeitalter des Barocks* (Freiburg, 1956). This book is in fact even more dated than its publication date would suggest, since it is essentially based on research completed before World War Two. Several collections of articles about the Baroque in Southwest Germany came out at the time of an exhibition in Bruchsal in 1981: Badisches Landesmuseum Karlsruhe (ed.), *Barock in Baden-Württemberg. Vom Ende des Dreißigjährigen Krieges bis zur Französischen Revolution.* Ausstellung des Landes Baden-Württemberg: Vol. I, Katalog, Vol. II, Aufsätze (Karlsruhe, 1981); Volker Himmelein, Klaus Merter, Wilfried Setzler and Peter Ansett (eds.), *Barock in Baden-Württemberg* (Stuttgart, 1981).

8 Brückner, "Zum Wandel der religiösen Kultur im 18. Jahrhundert," pp. 72–73.

9 Quoted from Eva Kimminich, *Religiöse Volksbräuche im Räderwerk der Obrigkeiten. Ein Beitrag zu Auswirkung aufklärerischer Reformprogramme am Oberrhein und in Vorarlberg* (Frankfurt, 1989), p. 59: "den sinnenfreudigen Barockkatholizismus mit seinen extrovertierten Glaubensmanifestationen . . ."

the relationship between the Catholic population and the clergy. Priests were indispensable for many vital religious services, but their power was restrained by the communalism of local Catholicism, which left village communes and town councils with considerable power over the administration of parishes and the organization of devotional life.

Baroque Catholicism developed within the framework of the historical traditions, political realities, and institutional particularities of Southwest Germany. This was one of the classic landscapes of the old Reich. A geographically diverse and fragmented region, it contained most of the political and religious institutions so peculiar to the Holy Roman Empire. Southwest Germany was the heartland of the imperial Church, the *Reichskirche*, where wealthy monasteries and convents and the old military orders, the Teutonic Knights and the Knights of St. John, ruled clusters of villages and thousands of subjects.[10] It was also the home of many imperial counts and free imperial knights, rulers of tiny territories, as well as somewhat larger principalities, such as those ruled by the Dukes of Fürstenberg and the Margraves of Baden-Baden.

The geography of the region varied from the vineyards of the Rhine valley to the high mountains and narrow valleys of the Black Forest and the rolling hills of Upper Swabia and the shores of Lake Constance. The inhabitants of this agricultural region made their living from farming and animal husbandry. As the population exploded in the eighteenth century, rural industry also grew in importance.[11] Southwest Germany was not economically or culturally isolated. Served by the Rhine, Neckar, and Danube rivers, this part of Germany was firmly integrated into the commercial world of early modern Europe.

Despite political fragmentation and socio-economic diversity, there were several unifying factors. The first was the fact that this part of Germany was part of the "individualized country" made famous by Mack Walker's study of "German home towns."[12] Urban centers could

[10] This book deals with the Catholic regions of the modern German state of Baden-Württemberg which lay south of the Protestant Duchy of Württemberg. It does not deal with the Catholic regions of northern Baden, which were part of Franconia in the early modern period. For a geographical overview: Anton Schindling and Walter Ziegler (eds.). *Die Territorien des Reichs im Zeitalter der Reformation und Konfessionalisierung. Land und Konfession*, Vol. V, *Der Südwestern* (Münster, 1993) and Die Kommission für Geschichtliche Landeskunde in Baden-Württemberg (ed.), *Historischer Atlas von Baden-Württemberg* (Stuttgart, 1972–).

[11] Sheilagh Ogilvie (ed.), *Germany. A New Social and Economic History*, Vol. II, *1630–1800*, (London, 1996); Robert S. DuPlessis, *Transitions to Capitalism in Early Modern Europe* (Cambridge, 1993); David Sabean, *Property, Production, and Family in Neckarhausen, 1700–1870* (Cambridge, 1990).

[12] Mack Walker, *German Home Towns: Community, State, and General Estate, 1648–1871* (Ithaca, 1971).

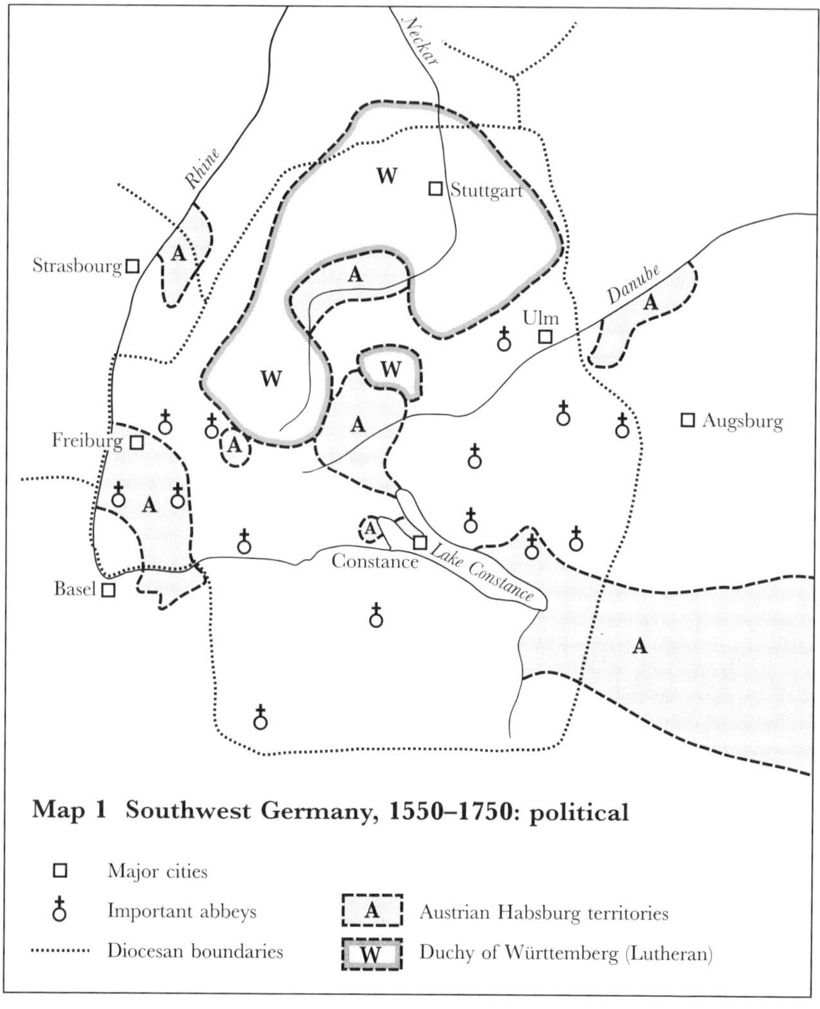

Map 1 Southwest Germany, 1550–1750: political

be found everywhere. Some, such as Rottweil and Überlingen, Biberach and Ravensburg, held the status of free imperial cities; others, such as the Austrian cities of Villingen and Rottenburg am Neckar, were integrated into the surrounding states. Most towns were small, with 2,000–3,000 inhabitants, and their populations were heavily engaged in agriculture, but an exceptionally large proportion of the overall population lived in urban settings. The largest Catholic cities in Southwest

Germany were Freiburg im Breisgau and Constance, both Austrian possessions, while the largest cities overall, Strasbourg, Basel, Augsburg and Ulm, were Protestant or biconfessional and lay on the edges of the region.

A second unifying feature of the region was the omnipresence of Austrian Habsburg power. It is easy for a modern observer to forget that the Habsburgs had extensive possessions in this part of Germany. *Vorderösterreich*, or Outer Austria, was a fragmented but significant territory governed until the Thirty Years' War from the town of Ensisheim in Alsace, and after the war from Freiburg.[13] The Habsburgs had dispensed patronage and cultivated clients, exerted influence and strong-armed friends and enemies in this region for centuries. Monasteries depended on the protection of Austrian armies and many of the regional elite, whether noble or patrician, made careers in Austrian service. These ties were strong enough to keep most of the region's princes, nobles, and cities Catholic during the Reformation. They also made the whole region a military bulwark against French armies in the seventeenth century.

Finally, the Catholic territories and *Landschaften* of Southwest Germany were almost all part of the vast Bishopric of Constance.[14] Although the bishops, who resided in the town of Meersburg, across the Lake from Constance, were chronically impoverished, they provided important leadership to the Catholic Church. Together with the Habsburgs, with whom they constantly clashed, the Bishops of Constance came to personify the Catholic Church of the region. As the inhabitants' confessional identity grew, Catholicism itself became an important regional characteristic. As we shall see, however, one should be careful not to overstate the unifying role of Catholicism. There were considerable differences in the religious styles of different parts of Southwest Germany, for example between the Catholicism of wine farmers in the Rhine valley and that of sheep and cattle herders in the Black Forest.

From Freiburg to Lake Constance, from the Rhine valley to Upper Swabia, religious unity distinguished a region fragmented by particularism, political division, and institutional and geographic diversity. Both in its diversity and in the variety of its institutions, Southwest Germany

[13] Freiburg was occupied for long periods by the French (particularly between 1679 and 1697), during which time Constance served as the administrative capital of Outer Austria. Austrian officials in Innsbruck also played a regular role in the administration of these territories. See Hans Maier and Volker Press (eds.), *Vorderösterreich in der frühen Neuzeit* (Sigmaringen, 1989).

[14] *Landschaften* are sub-regions within Southwest Germany which, given the political fragmentation of the region, often had a social and economic unity that transcended political boundaries.

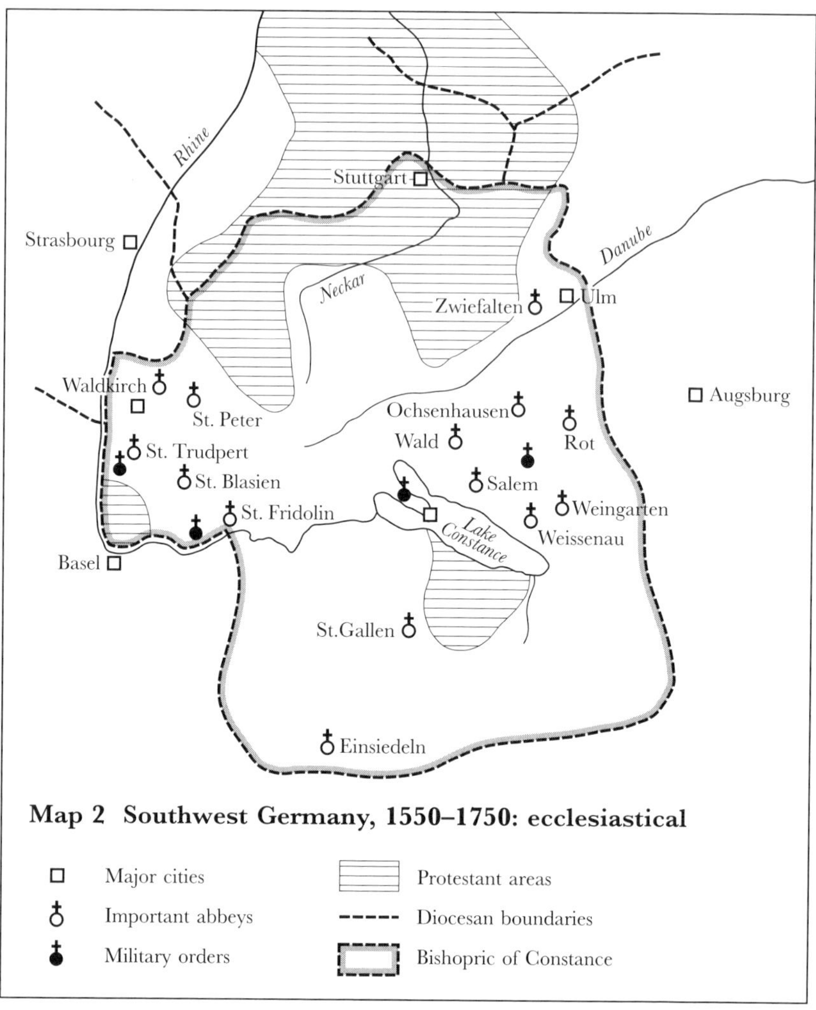

Map 2 Southwest Germany, 1550–1750: ecclesiastical

was a microcosm of the long-settled regions of the Holy Roman Empire. Understanding the creation of Catholic identity in this corner of the old Reich, in its local and regional variety, brings us a greater understanding of the development of confessional cultures in Germany as a whole.

In the two centuries after 1550, Catholics all across this part of Germany participated in recombining religious forms into the new religious synthesis known as Baroque Catholicism. Some ideas and practices were obviously the result of elite innovation, sometimes imposed against popular resistance, but more often requiring wide participation to have any staying power. Other Catholic practices were clearly popular and traditional, survivals or revivals of practices dating back to the fifteenth century and before. Ultimately, however, in order to understand the evolution of Catholicism in this period, it is necessary to move beyond the simple contrast between traditional Catholicism favored by the population and modern Catholicism supported by the elite. Religious change came both from above and from below, and new perspectives are needed to understand this process. This study investigates the evolution of Catholicism by examining the negotiations between different groups about the nature of religious practice and by evaluating the role of intermediaries, particularly the parish clergy, in the development of Baroque Catholicism.

Certainly, elite initiatives in the form of Tridentine reform and the process of confessionalization energized Catholicism in the late sixteenth century. Thus in looking at continuity and change in the Southwest German religious experience we have to analyze the reception of the reformers' program. If Tridentine reform was episodic in nature in Southwest Germany, it nevertheless left significant traces in Catholic life. The related process of state-sponsored confessionalization also left its mark, although in this part of Germany the absence of a single dominant state significantly reduced its impact.

Certain social groups and institutions served as intermediaries in the process of religious change. These groups included of course the parish priests, who found themselves trapped between the demands of the Church and the needs of their parishioners on a daily basis. Monasteries, convents, collegiate chapters, and military orders formed another important group of intermediaries. As patrons of rural parishes, secular lords, and religious centers, they often played a significant part in religious life.

Changes in religious life, ranging from the development of new devotions to the revival of old practices and new emphases within traditional rites, all required negotiation between the above groups. Such negotiations took place within the framework of a traditional society and within the context of existing institutions. The unusually complex institutional setting of Southwest Germany produced a considerable diversity of religious practice, as in political and cultural life more generally. Diversity and particularism characterized this part of

Germany, but did not give Catholicism an exclusively local character. Instead, forms of religious experience varied from place to place, depending on the particular constellation of institutions, social groups, and religious traditions.

All the groups and institutions that played a role in the creation of Catholic life and culture in Southwest Germany also had to operate within a finite set of discourses about religion. Certain religious options, or even certain kinds of religious language, were not available to German Catholics, most obviously ideas and practices associated with Protestantism (salvation by faith alone, communion in both kinds, divorce with remarriage). The laws and theology of the international Church provided another set of restrictions, especially for the elite, although in practice these were often more open to negotiation than we may recognize today. The religious traditions of the region, exemplified by particular religious practices and by the structure of the sacral landscape, formed a very powerful discourse, which all Catholics had to respect. Change could and did occur, but the range of options was by no means unlimited.

The continuities in the Catholic experience in Southwest Germany are just as important as the changes. Certain basic characteristics of Baroque Catholicism were important aspects of pre-Reformation Christianity, and especially after 1650 one can hear strong echoes of late medieval religion. These were deep structural aspects of rural religion and included the communal domination of much of parish life and the drive to provide more diverse and intense religious experiences, as well as the revival of particular practices, such as pilgrimage and the cult of the saints. In some ways, the Reformation, the Counter-Reformation, and Catholic reform in the period 1520 to 1650, by attempting to simplify and rationalize religious practice, interrupted the long-term elaboration of a diverse religious experience that had begun in the High Middle Ages.[15] After 1650, at least in Catholic areas, this intense religiosity once again flourished.

Such religious and ecclesio-political structures interacted frequently with initiatives to reform and change Catholicism. Chapter 1 shows how, between 1550 and 1650, Tridentine reform came to dominate the policies of both the Church and the most important Catholic state in the

[15] Eamon Duffy, *The Stripping of the Altars. Traditional Religion in England, 1450–1580* (New Haven, 1992); Robert Scribner, "Ritual and Popular Religion in Catholic Germany at the Time of the Reformation" in *Popular Culture and Popular Movements in the Reformation* (London, 1987).

region, Austria. The Council of Trent and its decrees energized the Catholic elite and led to some important changes, particularly with respect to the clergy. Church reform is an integral part of the history of Catholicism, even if in the end it was not as effective as its proponents wanted or later church historians have claimed.

Catholicism evolved and confessional identity developed as popular Catholicism flourished between 1650 and 1750. The central chapters of this book analyze, first of all, the active role of the population in elaborating the sacral landscape of the region and extending pilgrimage piety (chapter 2). It is also important to understand the less dramatic, but equally significant rituals of the liturgical year, weekly and daily church services, and common devotional practices. In the century after 1650, a prodigious creativity, flexibility, and diversity characterized popular Catholic practice (chapter 3). The renowned vitality of Baroque Catholicism is not a myth.

Churchliness, *Kirchlichkeit*, was rooted in part in an attachment to Catholic practices. It was also a consequence of the ways in which Baroque Catholicism came to incorporate the ecclesio-political traditions of this part of Germany. Chapter 4 shows how certain views that were common before the Reformation, such as the desire for more resident priests and the demand that priests focus their attention on their religious duties, converged with a Tridentine emphasis on pastoral work to create a kind of popular clericalism. Clericalism meant that the common people accepted the special status of priests, but it did not mean that they obeyed them unquestioningly.

In fact, clericalism was closely linked to communalism. Chapter 5 argues that the "communal church" (*gemeinde Kirche*), which historians have identified as so important in this region in the fifteenth and early sixteenth centuries, was alive and well in Catholic villages and towns in the century after 1650.[16] Communalism meant that communes managed the administration of parishes and supervised the work of parish priests, whom villagers and townspeople considered servants of the community, albeit indispensable for providing the sacraments. Communes did not just oversee the parishes; they also initiated and organized processions and pilgrimages, founded new confraternities, and encouraged new devotions.

Baroque Catholicism was not a perfect expression of popular needs

[16] On the pre-Reformation communal church: Peter Blickle, *Communal Reformation: The Quest for Salvation in Sixteenth-Century Germany* (New Jersey, 1992); Rosi Fuhrmann, *Kirche und Dorf: Religiöse Bedürfnisse und kirchliche Stiftung auf dem Lande vor der Reformation* (Stuttgart, 1995).

and desires. Instead it was a compromise, or rather a convergence, between these and the elite ideal. Even in the late seventeenth century the Catholic elite, in particular the clerical elite, continued to want, at least in theory, an austere and intellectualized religiosity as formulated by the Council of Trent. The popular goal was a flexible religious experience, provided and served by a diligent clergy subservient to local needs.

After 1650, the Catholic elite sought to revive the reform impulse (chapter 6). This effort never really succeeded, as the Thirty Years' War had weakened the confessional militancy of the elite. After 1650, church reform programs increasingly took a back seat to popular religious initiatives. When clerics, whether episcopal officials, parish priests, or members of the religious orders, took a role in the devotional life of the wider Catholic population, they did so as intermediaries and facilitators, not as leaders. If the elite, particularly the Jesuits and the monasteries, played a role in shaping the diversity of Catholic religiosity, the common people certainly dominated Catholic practice.

This study brings the religious life of lay people back to the center of the discussion of confessionalization, that is, the origins and nature of confessional identity. No one would deny that German princes sought to use religion to cement the loyalty of their subjects. The Catholic Church also pursued its own agenda, a program designed to guide popular religion into carefully prescribed paths. Yet when one leaves the rarefied air of council chambers and episcopal assemblies for the messier worlds of town squares and parish churchyards, one finds people who had their own ideas about the place of religion in their lives, people who knew how to pick and choose from the dictates coming from above. When they identified themselves as Catholics, they did so because Catholic practices, rituals, and devotions were important to them and because they understood them to be their own creations. When they expressed their identity as Catholics, they did so by bringing their child to be baptized, by going on a pilgrimage, by attending Mass, and by confessing their sins on their deathbed. Confessional identity was created from daily experience and was lived out in the everyday world of the peasants and townspeople of Southwest Germany.

The priest [*Pfaff*] must be gotten rid of . . . It is not up to him to bring new practices into the church, the church is ours, not his. (The people of Burkheim, 1585)[17]

[17] GLAK 229/16206, p. 27v. This case is discussed in detail in chapter 1.

The people of Burkheim made it clear that they would take an active role in the local parish. Their attitude makes it likely that they made it difficult, if not impossible, for their parish priest to dominate local religious life. Like the priest in Burkheim, modern historians should be careful not to over-emphasize the elite role in determining religious practice and creating confessional identities. Scholarship on both the "success and failure" of Tridentine reform and the "confessionalization" thesis has tended to do just this.

Tridentine reformers certainly played an important role within the Catholic Church and they often took credit for developments within popular Catholicism.[18] By about 1700, reformers supported the clericalization of rural Catholicism, the churchliness of Catholic life, and the growth of more intense and individual devotion, in rural parishes as well as in the towns and cities. Yet confessional identity cannot be closely linked to Tridentine reform; reformers were most active and most aggressive in the decades around 1600, but popular confessionalism and churchliness only developed after 1650, becoming most intense after 1700. In Southwest Germany, weak episcopal institutions and the fragmentation of ecclesiastical authority further hindered Catholic reform. The Council of Trent and the reform program it unleashed are part of the history of Catholicism in this part of Germany, but they do not sufficiently explain the origins or nature of Catholic identity.

Confessionalization means little to historians unfamiliar with the recent historiography of early modern Germany.[19] Confessionalization has both a broad and a more specific meaning. Broadly, it designates the process through which the people subject to each of the three German "confessions," Lutheran, Reformed, and Catholic, developed a religious identity. In its narrower meaning, as formulated by Heinz Schilling and Wolfgang Reinhard, this "consolidation of official religions" was a

18 For bibliography: Forster, "With and Without Confessionalization," esp. p. 317 and R. Po-chia Hsia, *The World of Catholic Renewal. 1540–1770* (Cambridge, 1998), pp. 217–218.

19 Wolfgang Reinhard and Heinz Schilling (eds.), *Die katholische Konfessionalisierung* (Heidelberg, 1995); R. Po-chia Hsia, *Social Discipline in the Reformation: Central Europe, 1550–1750* (London and New York, 1980); Heinz Schilling, "Confessionalization in the Empire: Religious and Societal Change in Germany between 1555 and 1620" in *Religion, Political Culture and the Emergence of Early Modern Society. Essays in German and Dutch History* (Leiden, 1992), pp. 205–245; Wolfgang Reinhard, "Gegenreformation als Modernisierung? Prolegomena zu einer Theorie des konfessionellen Zeitalters" *Archiv für Reformationsgeschichte* 68 (1977), pp. 226–252; Heinrich Richard Schmidt, *Konfessionalisierung im 16. Jahrhundert* (Munich, 1992). For a critique of the "confessionalization thesis", see Heinrich Richard Schmidt, "Sozialdisziplinierung? Ein Plädoyer für das Ende des Etatismus in der Konfessionaliserungsforschung" *Historische Zeitschrift* 265 (1997), pp. 639–682.

program driven by an educated elite with power in both ecclesiastical and state institutions, and had the long-term effect of modernizing society by its "promotion of rationalization, growing bureaucracy, social discipline, [and] individualism . . ."[20]

The "confessionalization thesis" was founded on a synthesis of studies of Catholic reform, on the one hand, with studies of the institutionalization of Protestantism after 1555 on the other. The ambitions of its proponents were considerable. As Reinhard himself states: "In 1980/81 Heinz Schilling and I independently decided to elevate Ernst Walther Zeeden's 'confessional formation' [*Konfessionsbildung*] now known by the richer and more complex social science term 'confessionalization' [*Konfessionalisierung*], from an event in Church history to a fundamental process in the social history of the early modern period . . ."[21] Schilling has been just as explicit: "'confessionalization' constitutes the most important historical process of the epoch. The interpretive category of 'confessional formation' . . . which sheds new light on ecclesiastical and cultural history of this era has been recast into a paradigm of societal history, i.e. 'confessionalization'."[22]

The confessionalization thesis has had a number of salutary influences on the study of Catholic Germany. By insisting on the close parallels between developments within Catholicism and Protestantism, Schilling and Reinhard transcended the simple contrast between Reformation and Counter-Reformation. The thesis also gives Catholic Germany a new importance. No longer marginalized as traditional and even reactionary, the Catholic Church became a confessionalizing institution and thus part of what many historians consider the essential development in the early modern period: the rise of the modern state. Reinhard hammered this point home by calling his path-breaking article on confessionalization "Counter-Reformation as Modernization" ("*Gegenreformation als Modernisierung*").

Yet the value of this concept for the study of Southwest Germany is limited. The development of confessional identity was a goal of many state officials and Southwest Germany did experience some kind of "confessionalization." Austrian officials periodically attempted to enforce religious uniformity as a way of strengthening the state, particu-

[20] Robert Bireley, "Early Modern Germany" in John O'Malley (ed.), *Catholicism in Early Modern Europe* (St. Louis, 1988), p. 12.

[21] Wolfgang Reinhard, "Was ist katholische Konfessionalisierung?" in *Die katholische Konfessionalisierung*, p. 420.

[22] Schilling, "Confessionalization in the Empire," p. 207.

larly in the period between 1570 and 1620 (chapter 1). However, such a policy was never really instituted in the smaller Catholic territories and after the Thirty Years' War it is hard to identify anything that can be called confessionalization, even in the Austrian territories (chapter 6).

This book presents three basic criticisms of the confessionalization thesis. The first is perhaps the simplest. By the late seventeenth century most people living in Southwest Germany developed a confessional identity in the absence of strong states and without being subjected to a sustained policy of confessionalization. Confessional identity could be found in monastic territories, small principalities, and villages governed by imperial knights and military orders, as well as in Habsburg Austria.

Secondly, the local experience of Baroque Catholicism bears few marks of an elite-sponsored program of social discipline or modernization. The elaboration of religious services, the popularity of pilgrimages and shrines, and the local nature of much Catholic devotion had nothing to do with the rationalizing tendencies attributed to confessionalization. There is clear evidence across the two centuries of this study that religious change promoted "from below" was more important than elite initiatives.

Finally, an analysis of religious practice at the local level reveals that the origins of Catholic identity were not political but in fact popular. Baroque Catholicism appealed to the population because it was generally adapted to local and communal needs and desires; it was not exclusively, or even primarily, a tool of the elite. This conclusion is not really so surprising if one puts the study of German Catholicism in a wider perspective.

Because of the central importance of the religious division of Germany since the Reformation, German historians have been particularly concerned with the development of confessional identity. This issue is of less concern to scholars of Catholicism in other parts of Europe.[23] Studies of popular Catholicism in Italy or Spain, for example, are not concerned with the discontinuities caused by the Reformation and focus instead on Catholic reform. Furthermore, such studies increasingly seek to move beyond an analysis of the "success and failure" of Tridentine policies by focusing on the reception of reform measures, especially popular resistance to reform.

[23] For a survey of this material, see Hsia, *The World of Catholic Renewal.*

The idea that religious practices developed through a negotiation between elite and popular classes and between ecclesiastical elites and local communities has also become common in local studies outside Germany. David Gentilcore, in his study of popular religion in Southern Apulia, argues that conflicts over religious practice "give us the impression that there were tensions between the ruling and subordinate classes, centre and periphery, resulting in change and compromise on both sides." Gentilcore uses the concept of negotiation to analyze this process of religious change at the local level, "since it implies a separation and distinction between cultures, without making the gulf too great, which would render the dialogue impossible."[24]

Studies of Spanish Catholicism, following the lead of William Christian, have focused on the development of religious practice at the local level.[25] Henry Kamen, in his study of Catalonia, emphasizes that "the community dimension was fundamental to Christianity . . . the practice of religion coincided almost wholly with the functioning of the community." Furthermore, "devotions, like loyalties, were rooted in the local communities, and were as volatile as they were."[26] This local perspective is just as essential for an understanding of Baroque Catholicism in Germany as it is for Italy or Spain.

Louis Châtellier's wide-ranging studies also have much to offer scholars of German Catholicism.[27] On the one hand, Châtellier shows how the Jesuits engaged in Europe-wide programs to revitalize Catholicism, first among the elite and then among the common people. Germany was very much a part of Catholic Europe and shared, for example, in the development of elite Marian sodalities. Châtellier recognizes, however, that there was considerable national and local variation in the reception of Jesuit devotions.

Châtellier also shows that the Jesuits were intermediaries between the Church and believers. The concept of religious or cultural intermediaries has been important in many studies of local Catholicism. Timothy Tackett, for example, has shown how important local priests were for

[24] David Gentilcore, *From Bishop to Witch. The System of the Sacred in Early Modern Terra d'Otranto* (Manchester and New York, 1992), p. 4.

[25] William Christian, *Local Religion in Sixteenth-Century Spain* (Princeton, 1981); Sara T. Nalle, *God in La Mancha: Religious Reform and the People of Cuenca, 1500–1650* (Baltimore, 1992); Henry Kamen, *The Phoenix and the Flame: Catalonia and the Counter Reformation* (New Haven, 1993).

[26] Kamen, *The Phoenix and the Flame*, pp. 29, 43.

[27] Louis Châtellier, *Europe of the Devout. The Catholic Reformation and the Formation of a New Society* (Cambridge, 1989); Louis Châtellier, *La Religion des pauvres: les missions rurales en Europe et la formation du catholicisme moderne, XVIe–XIXe siècles* (Paris, 1993).

the ability of the French Catholic Church to command the loyalty of the population.[28] Where curés were local and where they attempted to accommodate and guide popular religion rather than dominate and control it, a strong sense of popular clericalism developed in the countryside. Rather than simply considering them a part of the clerical elite or "agents of the Counter-Reformation," this perspective allows for a more sophisticated understanding of the role of the parish priest.

All these perspectives – the importance of the popular role in religious practice, the focus on local and communal religion, and use of concepts such as reception, negotiation, and intermediaries – have not been absent from the study of German Catholicism. Because of the dominance of the confessionalization thesis, however, they have often been pushed into the background. By incorporating the study of German Catholicism into the wider study of European Catholicism, it should be possible to employ a wider range of methods and perspectives.

In the end, an analysis of popular Catholicism in Southwest Germany must steer between two extremes. On the one hand, this was (and is) a region in the middle of Europe and it shared in developments that affected the whole Catholic Church. The Roman Catholic Church was not, however, monolithic, and there were important and significant differences between German, Italian, French, and Spanish forms of Catholicism, to say nothing about those of Latin America or Asia. What was peculiar and special about Southwest German Catholicism is one part of the story; what this region tells us about the development of popular religion and religious identity in general is equally important.

[28] Timothy Tackett, *Religion, Revolution, and Regional Culture in Eighteenth-Century France: The Ecclesiastical Oath of 1791* (Princeton, 1986); Tackett, *Priest and Parish in Eighteenth Century France. A Social and Political Study of the Curés of the Diocese of Dauphiné, 1750–1791* (Princeton, 1977). See also Keith Luria, *Territories of Grace. Cultural Change in the Seventeenth Century Diocese of Grenoble* (Berkeley, 1991); Philip Hoffman, *Church and Community in the Diocese of Lyon, 1500–1789* (New Haven, 1984); Alain Lottin, *Lille, Citadelle de la Contre-Réforme (1598–1668)* (Lille, 1984); Alain Croix, *La Bretagne au 16e et 17e siècles. La vie – la mort – la foi* (Paris, 1981).

CHAPTER I

The Counter-Reformation offensive, 1550–1650

Southwest Germany, like the rest of Catholic Europe, experienced the Counter-Reformation in the form of measures taken by both the Church and Catholic states to combat the spread of Protestantism. Catholic leaders in this part of Germany also worked to implement the reforms of the Church, the clergy, and religious practice advocated by the Council of Trent.[1] Tridentine reforms came to the Southwest in the later sixteenth century as Catholic officials pursued reforms of the clergy and made tentative efforts to reform popular religious practice. Tridentine reform was slowed by the conservative and traditional nature of many powerful ecclesiastical institutions, especially the great monasteries, and by the relatively late arrival of the Jesuits in the region, but it left an indelible mark on the Church.[2]

The period from 1550 to the end of the Thirty Years' War was the era most marked by Tridentine reform and the related processes of Counter-Reformation and confessionalization, although the decrees of the Council of Trent remained a blueprint for church reform into the eighteenth century. Yet even during these decades of reform, an analysis of the successes and failures of reform measures does not do justice to the complex interplay of social groups that created Catholic religiosity and culture. As one moves back and forth between the "top-down" analysis of reforms and the reception of such measures at the local level, two characteristics of Southwest German Catholicism become apparent. Firstly, the Catholic elite instituted Tridentine reforms tentatively and in a limited way, and the reforms were not universally welcome, even within the clergy. Secondly, people at the local level, whether it

[1] For an overview of Catholicism in Germany, see R. Po-chia Hsia, *The World of Catholic Renewal. 1540–1770* (Cambridge, 1998), pp. 73–79.

[2] For a discussion of these issues and for extensive bibliography: Marc R. Forster, "With and Without Confessionalization: Varieties of Early Modern German Catholicism" *Journal of Early Modern History* 1,4 (1998), pp. 315–343.

was the local population, parish priests, or local officials, actively engaged these reform measures, supporting some, altering some, and rejecting others. For such measures to have any lasting impact on local religious practices, they had to be embraced at the local level.

Thus even at the height of the Counter-Reformation, religious change took place through a process of negotiation and exchange involving state officials, bishops and their officials, local clergy, city and village leaders, and the common people. Reformers could claim some successes. Most significantly, by the beginning of the seventeenth century, firm confessional boundaries had been created, clear norms of official Catholic practice put in place, and the most public abuses of the clergy, especially concubinage, eliminated. Popular religiosity, however, changed little, and there is little evidence of a revival of popular Catholicism; this revival would occur after 1650.[3] Tridentine reform in the "Age of Confessionalism," as the period from 1550 to 1650 is known, was a prelude to the full flowering of Baroque Catholicism, not its direct cause.

In the decades after the Council of Trent there were two groups of reformers active in Southwest Germany. The first was found among state officials, especially in the upper levels of the Austrian state. These men were "confessionalizers," for they advocated a close cooperation between the state and the Catholic Church for the purpose of creating religious unity in the population. Within both the lay and the clerical Catholic elite were also many church reformers who, inspired by the decrees of the Council, pushed for an extensive reform of the clergy which, in their view, would lead to a full-scale popular religious renewal.

The Austrian Habsburgs, rulers of Outer Austria (*Vorderösterreich*), the largest state in the region, were the early leaders of the Catholic cause within this part of Germany. Beginning in the 1560s Austrian authorities moved aggressively to suppress Protestantism in their territories and advocated church reforms along the lines encouraged by the Council of Trent. Austrian religious policy emphasized obedience to state authorities, linking loyalty to the Catholic Church with loyalty to the Habsburgs. In practice, this policy led to a focus on the external markers of religious loyalty. Austrian officials moved rapidly to bring the clergy into line. In an effort to counter the most obvious abuses of the clergy, they favored monastic reform and efforts to eradicate clerical concubinage.

[3] Hsia, *The World of Catholic Renewal*, p. 75: "the revival of popular Catholicism took off slowly in the 1660s and reached its climax between 1700 and 1760."

Somewhat later, Austrian reformers attempted to require priests to perform more uniform religious services.

These state-sponsored reform policies brought the Austrian *Regierung* into a more intense relationship with the bishops of the region, particularly the Bishop of Constance. At times state and church authorities cooperated to institute and enforce reform measures, but at other times Austrian officials lamented the hesitancy and inefficiency of episcopal leaders.[4] Reformist bishops and their officials supported Austrian policies that were intended to reform the clergy and they even took the lead in this endeavor in the non-Austrian parts of the region. The Bishops of Constance also gave considerable support to the Tridentine-inspired effort to strengthen episcopal authority, which on more than one occasion caused conflict with secular authorities and the great monasteries of the diocese. However, although several activist bishops attempted extensive reforms, the lack of unity among important Catholic powers in the region meant that Tridentine reform in the Bishopric of Constance proceeded sporadically, as it did elsewhere in Catholic Germany.

Tridentine reform and confessionalization were promoted not just by the Habsburgs and the bishops. Catholic cities, smaller principalities, and some monasteries also embraced elements of the reform agenda. The town councils of Catholic imperial cities such as Rottweil and Überlingen instituted important reforms, especially of the clergy. The monastery of Weingarten, notably under the leadership of Abbot Georg Wegelin (abbot from 1586 to 1627), was a powerful force for church reform, both among the many monasteries of the Southwest and in the villages governed by Weingarten.

The most effective reforms were often those that were embraced at the local level, by local officials, the local clergy, or the local people. If at times reformers could discipline the clergy and force public obedience to Catholicism, they could not force changes in religious practice on villagers and townspeople. Even in those areas, such as the Habsburg territories, where officials pursued an aggressive reform program, Catholic practice developed out of the interplay of popular and elite notions of the role of religion. This negotiation of Catholic practice can be seen in the story of the small Austrian town of Burkheim in the 1580s.

[4] Austrian officials turned at times to papal nuncios when they pursued a more thoroughgoing reform of the clergy, for example in the city of Constance: Wolfgang Zimmermann, *Rekatholisierung, Konfessionalisierung und Ratsregiment. Der Prozeß des politischen und religiösen Wandels in der österreichischen Stadt Konstanz 1548–1637* (Sigmaringen, 1994), p. 132.

CONFESSIONALIZATION UNDER AUSTRIAN LEADERSHIP

The case of Burkheim, 1585–1587

In 1585 relations deteriorated between the city fathers of Burkheim and their priest, Jacob Hornstein.[5] Trouble began with disputes over the tithe, escalated when the priest reported the presence of Protestants in the town, and ultimately led the townspeople to refuse to confess to their pastor. The bundle of issues that concerned the parties in this small Austrian town in the Kaiserstuhl, as well as the ways in which the disputes were resolved, reveals much about the way state-sponsored confessionalization played out at the local level.

There were several different actors in this little drama. The Burkheimer were represented by the *Obervogt*, the mayor, and the town council of the town. In this group the *Obervogt*, the representative of the Austrian state in the town, was the most important and most active. Although probably a local man, the *Obervogt* was the chief law enforcement officer and had considerable power, as well as direct access to Austrian officials in the capital Ensisheim, just across the Rhine. The *Obervogt* was not unwilling to use this authority and provoked some of the conflict by arresting the priest's servant and throwing him in jail.

Pfarrer Hornstein had come to Burkheim in 1583 and clearly considered himself a representative of a new kind of clergyman. "Out of duty to my priestly office, I will pay attention to their [the Burkheimer's] public violation of Christian Catholic [*Christlicher Catholischer*] ordinances, statutes, and practices, perhaps more diligently than has happened before."[6] In addition to this enthusiasm for disciplining his parishioners, Hornstein was very concerned with his "clerical honor" (*Priesterliche Ehre*) which he could assert quite aggressively. "During this past Christmas time," he wrote in January 1586, "out of pressing need, I brought out and showed from the pulpit my investiture, the synod statutes, and all sorts of relevant Church ordinances. [I did this] with proper modesty."[7] Hornstein's parishioners clearly did not find any modesty in this assertive display of authority and superiority.

The priest and the town leaders aired their grievances to the University of Freiburg, which held the patronage of the village. University officials had appointed Hornstein and considered him exemplary. In their view the *Pfarrer* was dedicated and especially good in theology. The university had, of course, little relationship with the inhabitants of

[5] GLAK 229/16206. [6] GLAK 229/16206, p. 28r. [7] GLAK 229/16206, p. 27r.

Burkheim, and tended to side with Hornstein. The rector and regents of the university, however, did not approve of the kind of aggressiveness that led Hornstein to wave his documents from the pulpit. The university's letters to the priest regularly admonished him to "behave modestly" and to try to get along with his parishioners.[8]

Austrian officials in the Alsatian town of Ensisheim, the administrative capital of Outer Austria in this period, were the final arbitrators of the disputes in Burkheim. State officials initially responded to reports of conflicts in Burkheim by insisting that local officials enforce recent decrees forbidding Protestants from living in Austrian territory.[9] Austrian officials also equated obedience to the priest with obedience to the state. In a letter in July 1585 they wrote to the inhabitants of Burkheim:

> ... In the name of His Majesty ... it is our earnest decision, opinion, and order that you, neither in word nor deed, plan, say, or act with impertinent arrogance [*ungeburliches anmassen*] toward your pastor. Rather you should completely let all such things go and treat him according to Christian commandments and behave in such a way that you give no reason for more serious [investigation] ... [10]

Official concern about Protestants in Burkheim came from a May 1585 report from *Pfarrer* Hornstein.[11] The priest stated that the *Stadtschreiber* (town secretary) and his wife openly identified themselves as Lutherans and refused to take communion from him. Hornstein also denounced the local miller and several servants as Protestants. Hornstein's report goes even further, for he also claimed that the church was almost empty at Easter and that the *Obervogt*, the mayor, and the whole town council refused to confess to him or receive communion from him. The *Pfarrer* clearly implied that the whole town was suspiciously lukewarm toward Catholicism.

The Austrian state concentrated its attention on the threat of Protestantism, which was an issue of obedience to the state. Secondarily, officials insisted that local people obey their priest, who was after all a kind of local official. The people of Burkheim denied the charge that they were Protestants and worked hard to show that they were loyal subjects, even if they disobeyed the priest. The town council insisted, for example, that "we will neglect nothing to uphold the ancient, true, Catholic religion." The mayor and the *Rat* assured Ensisheim that they had publicized all the church ordinances that had come

[8] GLAK 229/16206, pp. 2r, 31r.

[9] GLAK 229/16206, pp. 4r–v, 6r.

[10] GLAK 229/16206, p. 16r.

[11] GLAK 229/16206, pp. 9r–v.

from the central authorities and that they would punish any transgressors.[12]

The tension between obedience to the Austrian state and obedience to the *Pfarrer* came into starker outline during Hornstein's sermon on Palm Sunday 1585. On this occasion the priest accused the Burkheimer of attending services in a neighboring town without permission, of eating meat during Lent, and of failing to properly pay the tithe.[13] Here again, he implied that the townspeople who ate meat and those who went elsewhere for services were Protestants. The latter accusation was not unreasonable, since it was not uncommon in confessionally divided regions for people to travel to other towns and villages for Protestant services.[14] The town council recognized which of these issues were most important in Ensisheim and denied that any Burkheimer were going to Protestant services. The council also repeated that it would keep an eye open for Protestants and would deal severely with anyone who did not tithe properly. The Burkheimer did not, however, admit that they must also obey Hornstein in the same way they obeyed the *Herrschaft*. In fact, they clearly considered him a servant of the village, not an authority figure.

> The priest [*Pfaff*] must be gotten rid of. He has not yet been confirmed and the citizens must place him on the altar [*uff den altar setzen*], before it [his appointment] takes effect. It is not up to him to bring new practices into the church, the church is ours, not his. We deal with the church warden [about the tithe] and the sacristan [about church services], not with him . . . [15]

The relationship between Hornstein and local luminaries such as the *Obervogt* went downhill rapidly. During the Christmas season of 1585, the *Pfarrer* attacked town officials from the pulpit, stating that they had violated his clerical immunity by arresting his servant, who had been caught climbing the town walls after the gates had been closed and locked.[16] Hornstein rejected a proposed compromise which would have released his servant from jail and then attacked his main opponent, the *Obervogt*, who reported:

> He said that I had better pay good attention to him for he is certainly going to pay sharp enough attention to me. [He also] . . . said he wanted to have nothing

[12] GLAK 229/16206, pp. 17v–18r. [13] GLAK 229/16206, pp. 17r–v.

[14] People who ate meat during Lent were also commonly accused of being secret Protestants. See below for a case in Rottenburg (TLA Ferd. 178(1), 178(3) (*Visitations Handlungen*)). Perhaps this issue was particularly important in Southwest Germany and Switzerland, since Zwingli began his attack on the Catholic Church by eating sausages during Lent.

[15] GLAK 229/16206, p. 27v. [16] GLAK 229/16206, pp. 24r–v.

to do with me, which really was too much for me to take [*mir über die mass wehe gethan*] with the *Rat* right there witnessing. So I said to him, from now on I will do as a good Christian person should and go to church, and if he does not like to see me, that is too bad for him.[17]

When the town council made another effort to meet with Hornstein, he let them cool their heels for four hours in an unheated room of the parsonage. Such behavior led the town council to appeal to the university and to Ensisheim for the appointment of a new priest, with whom they hoped they would never fall into such conflict.[18]

During the Easter season of 1586 *Pfarrer* Hornstein continued to berate his parishioners from the pulpit. According to town officials, the things he said about the commune were so terrible that they could not be written down. By this time it was apparent to all parties that the disputes would erupt at each high point of the liturgical year, especially at Easter and Christmas. Furthermore, the issues had become clearer. Hornstein no longer accused the townspeople of being Protestants, and now focused his complaints on problems with the payment of the tithe. In rebuttal the Burkheimer referred to the priest's "stubborn stinginess" as the source of all their problems.[19]

At some point in the spring of 1586 Austrian officials sent a commission to investigate conditions in Burkheim. Already at the beginning of the conflict, both the university and officials in Ensisheim had written about the need for peace in Burkheim.[20] Austrian officials supported the idea of an agreement (*Vergleich*) or treaty (*Vertrag*) between *Pfarrer* Hornstein and the Burkheimer, and the 1586 commission managed to negotiate such an agreement. Although no copy of the *Vertrag* exists, the general outline of its provisions can be gleaned from the correspondence between Ensisheim and Burkheim.[21] The town agreed to pay all tithes and fees properly and promised not to resist a "renovation" of parish income.[22] In exchange, Hornstein gave up his insistence that the Burkheimer come to him at Easter for their annual confession and communion. At Easter 1586 the majority of the townspeople went to a nearby Catholic church in Rotweil to fulfill their annual obligations.

Austrian officials had engineered a solution to a difficult problem. Disputes over the tithe, exacerbated by the *Pfarrer*'s attacks on the religious loyalty of the Burkheimer, and his abrasive sermons led

17 GLAK 229/16206, p. 25r.
18 GLAK 229/16206, pp. 25r, 26r.
19 GLAK 229/16206, pp. 34v–35v.
20 GLAK 229/16206, pp. 13r–v, 20r, 21r, 31r–32r.
21 GLAK 229/16206, pp. 40r–41v, 43r, 44r–v, 49r, 52r–v, 56r–57r.
22 A renovation was a renewal of account books and probably a reassessment of property. It was, of course, a method of raising the income from church property.

prominent townspeople to refuse to confess their sins to him. Secular officials were not particularly interested in the problem of confession and saw no reason to force their subjects to confess to the parish priest. On this issue, the state did not support a key aspect of church reform. Allowing the parishioners to go elsewhere to confess clearly undermined the authority of the priest and hindered the development of the parochial conformity so central to Tridentine reform.[23] For episcopal officials, confession was a central way of reforming popular behavior. In 1570 they criticized Austrian officials for allowing unapproved priests to hear confessions, stating that "confession is nothing other than a court of souls and the confessor a judge of consciences."[24] Austrian officials probably had little interest in giving Hornstein this sort of power, especially after he criticized the Burkheimer for appealing to secular authorities and not the bishop.[25]

In Burkheim we can see the limits of confessionalization. The Austrian regime wanted a loyal Catholic population that would obey trustworthy, energetic, and celibate priests. Such a policy had an element of "social disciplining" and even cultural hegemony. Yet such concepts do not capture the day-to-day practice of *Herrschaft* or the relationship between the rulers and the ruled.[26] Austrian officials in Ensisheim wanted the people of Burkheim to demonstrate their obedience by attending church and paying the tithe; what happened during confession and communion was of much less concern. In fact, Hornstein was dangerously heavy-handed, perhaps arrogant, and certainly immodest. He even demonstrated a disturbing loyalty to episcopal authority and concern for his clerical rights and privileges. These various attitudes might have weakened Austrian rule in Burkheim. The university shared this practical view, fearing that conflicts could hurt its income from the tithe. There was cooperation between Church and state in Burkheim, but *Pfarrer* Hornstein did not receive the unconditional support of higher authorities. Ultimately, Austrian authorities could, and did, pick and choose from those parts of the Tridentine program that fit their needs, and resist those parts which threatened the state's domination of the Church in Austrian territories.

[23] John Bossy, "The Counter-Reformation and the People of Catholic Europe" *Past and Present* 47 (1970), pp. 51–70. On confession, see W. David Myers, *"Poor, Sinning Folk." Confession and Conscience in Counter-Reformation Germany* (Ithaca and London, 1996).

[24] TLA Ferd. 178(1), 1570, 24 July.

[25] GLAK 229/16206, p. 28v.

[26] David Sabean, *Power in the Blood. Popular Culture and Village Discourse in Early Modern Germany* (Cambridge, 1984), esp. Introduction.

The people of Burkheim, led by the town council, were not helpless victims of reform and confessionalization, nor did they simply resist outside forces. Like the Austrians, they supported some aspects of reform and rejected others. Most of all, they used the jurisdictional disputes among their various lords to hinder those aspects of church reform which they found most noxious, in this case the effort of *Pfarrer* Hornstein to use the sacrament of confession to discipline his parishioners. Church reforms could be implemented if villagers found them attractive; they could not be imposed against the opposition of an organized local community.

State-led reform

Protestantism had some appeal in Outer Austria in the early sixteenth century, as it did throughout Southwest Germany.[27] By the 1550s and 1560s, however, Austrian officials faced few serious threats to the Catholic Church in either the major towns of the region or the countryside. Urban elites in Habsburg-dominated areas found loyalty to the old Church a great benefit to their families. Because most of the nobility had *Reichsunmittelbar* status and were only subject to the emperor, there were no significant territorial nobility within *Vorderösterreich*. This situation left Protestantism weaker here than in Lower and Inner Austria where a self-conscious nobility led the Protestant party. Bavarian influence in Upper Swabia, together with the wealth and power of the great monasteries, was another force that helped stabilize Catholicism.

The vital social and political place of church institutions, particularly the patronage network they possessed and employed for the political benefit of the Habsburgs, helped prevent the growth of a widespread Protestant movement after the 1520s.[28] Repression was also important in the Habsburg lands. Already in the 1520s Austrian officials moved aggressively against Anabaptist communities, especially in the Hohenberg district around Horb and Rottenburg am Neckar. After the Schmalkaldic War (1546–1547) Habsburg officials instituted a thorough and mostly successful recatholicization of the imperial city of Gengen-

[27] Dieter Stievermann, "Österreichische Vorlande" in Anton Schindling and Walter Ziegler (eds.), *Die Territorien des Reichs im Zeitalter der Reformation und Konfessionalisierung. Land und Konfession*, Vol. V *Der Südwesten* (Münster, 1993), pp. 265–268.

[28] Volker Press has emphasized that Habsburg influence in the Southwest from the fifteenth century depended to a large extent on interlocking state and church clientage systems: Volker Press, "Vorderösterreich in der habsburgischen Reichspolitik des späten Mittelalters und der frühen Neuzeit" in Hans Maier and Volker Press (eds.), *Vorderösterreich in der frühen Neuzeit* (Sigmaringen, 1989), pp. 1–41, esp. p. 21.

bach and the surrounding *Reichslandvogtei* Ortenau, a region that had returned to Austrian rule after some twenty years under a Protestant prince.[29] By the 1560s confessional lines in Southwest Germany had stabilized and Outer Austria was firmly Catholic.

Despite the strength of Catholicism, the Austrian regime based at Ensisheim in Alsace and at Innsbruck in the Tyrol continued to stress the threat of Protestantism. In the later sixteenth century, officials focused their attention on those individuals who practiced Protestantism secretly or who took advantage of confessional fragmentation to visit Protestant services in neighboring jurisdictions. Officials in the headquarters of the *Regierung* reacted energetically to any sign of Protestant activity. In 1578 officials in Innsbruck, responding to a letter from several clergymen of Rottenburg am Neckar, wrote to local officials in the Austrian district of Hohenberg, insisting that they suppress "sectarian" activities in their jurisdiction. Officials in Innsbruck spoke of a group of non-Catholics who ate meat during Lent, possessed Protestant books, and were generally "suspect in their religion." The regime told local officials to uphold the Catholic religion "diligently and not sleepily [*schläfferig*]." They should do everything in their power to make sure that "the sectarian religion should not move in there (Rottenburg) and their area of administration," and if necessary imprison people suspected of attending Protestant services.[30]

Officials both at the regional level and in the town of Rottenburg had a different perspective and denied that there were any Protestants under their jurisdiction. The highest official in the area, the *Statthalter*, claimed that all the inhabitants were good Catholics. Although he admitted that "eight or nine years previously several people had somewhat suspiciously eaten [meat]," they had since proved themselves good Catholics. In the opinion of officials in Rottenburg, the whole issue stemmed from an old dispute between the parish priest and several citizens. The priest had refused to allow the eating of meat at a wedding feast held on the day of an official church holiday, an order the wedding party had publicly disobeyed. The *Pfarrer* was upset that only the innkeeper had been punished and that his punishment was not very severe since he served his prison term drinking wine with the local constable (the *Stadtknecht*).[31]

29 Stievermann, "Österreichische Vorlande," pp. 266–268; Wolfgang Müller, "Die kirchlichen Verhältnisse" in *Vorderösterreich. Eine geschichtliche Landeskunde* (Freiburg, 1967), p. 228.

30 TLA Ferd. 178(1), esp. 1578, 30 April, Oberösterreichische Regierung in Innsbruck to Erzherzog Ferdinand; 1578, 30 June, Rottenburg to Innsbruck; 1578, 30 August, Oberösterreichische Regierung in Innsbruck to Erzherzog Ferdinand.

31 TLA Ferd. 178(1), 1578, 8 April, Statthalter zu Hohenburg (and others) to Erzherzog Ferdinand; 1578, 30 June, Rottenburg to Innsbruck.

This exchange between local officials and somewhat distant state officials indicates, on the one hand, how important religious unity, or even uniformity, was to the central government. On the other hand, local officials recognized a more complicated set of problems. In the first place, there was the sometimes fractious relationship between the clergy and the laity. Secondly, at the local level it was not always easy to distinguish between devout Catholics, loyal but traditional Catholics, and Protestant sympathizers. The definition of what it meant to be a "good Catholic" was not completely clear even in 1578, making it possible for some people to express loyalty to the Church without obeying all its rules and regulations.

Austrian religious policy toward the city of Constance is instructive.[32] In 1548, after the Austrian army captured this predominantly Protestant imperial city, it was forcefully incorporated into the Habsburg territories. The Austrian policy of recatholicization proceeded slowly, but the regime showed no interest in a compromise with the Protestant population. Efforts in the 1550s by city leaders to negotiate a special religious status for Constance with the aim of separating loyalty to the prince from loyalty to Catholicism failed utterly. In 1555, King Ferdinand was explicit. He informed Constance that he would not tolerate Protestants in the city because such special standing would undermine the religious uniformity of his territories.[33] The Austrian regime was willing to risk difficulties with the large Protestant population of Constance; it had no toleration for the small numbers of Protestants in the rest of *Vorderösterreich.*

Beginning in the 1560s, the Austrian state made it even clearer that being a good Catholic was an essential characteristic of a loyal subject. In 1567 Archduke Ferdinand took control of the Tyrol and Outer Austria and began a forceful policy of Catholic confessionalization. In the Tyrol, Ferdinand's regime required professions of faith from government officials, worked to install better educated priests and improve their incomes, and at the same time promulgated mandates against religious "innovations."[34] The Habsburgs brought the Jesuits

[32] Zimmermann, *Rekatholisierung, Konfessionalisierung und Ratsregiment*; Wolfgang Zimmermann, "Konstanz in den Jahren von 1548–1733" in Martin Burkhardt, Wolfgang Dobras, Wolfgang Zimmermann (eds.), *Konstanz in der frühen Neuzeit. Reformation, Verlust der Reichsfreiheit, Österreichische Zeit*, Vol. III *Geschichte der Stadt Konstanz* (Constance, 1991).

[33] Zimmermann, *Rekatholisierung, Konfessionalisierung und Ratsregiment*, pp. 87–95.

[34] On Tyrol, Jürgen Bücking, *Frühabsolutismus und Kirchenreform in Tirol (1565–1665). Ein Beitrag zum Ringen zwischen "Staat" und "Kirche" in der frühen Neuzeit* (Wiesbaden, 1972); Heinz Noflatscher, "Tirol, Brixen, Trient" in Anton Schindling and Walter Ziegler (eds.), *Die Territorien des Reichs*, Vol. I *Der Südosten* (Münster, 1989), pp. 86–101.

and later the Capuchins to the Tyrol and pressured the bishops to conduct visitations and reform the clergy.

Ferdinand's policies in the Austrian territories in Southwest Germany were similar to those in the Tyrol. The intense interest of the Habsburgs in church affairs is exemplified by the career of Andreas von Österreich (1558–1600), Ferdinand's son by his marriage to the commoner Philippine Welser. Ineligible for a princely inheritance, Andreas pursued an ecclesiastical career. Named cardinal in Rome at the age of twenty-two, Andreas became coadjutor in Brixen (1580, Bishop of Brixen 1591), abbot of several important monasteries, and in 1589 Bishop of Constance. In 1579 Ferdinand also made Andreas governor of Upper and Outer Austria, a job he tended to prefer to his episcopal duties. The accumulation of ecclesiastical and secular posts allowed Andreas to follow an intensive policy of strengthening the Catholic Church.[35]

The Austrian state promulgated a series of ordinances designed to create religious uniformity. A 1585 mandate ordered all Protestants to emigrate and in 1586 an oath of loyalty to the Church was required of all government officials. Although the latter requirement ran into opposition from the nobility, it was effective in making Protestantism less attractive to urban elites.[36] These policies left no doubt about the close identification of the Austrian state with Catholicism. By the 1580s, there was no longer room for negotiation on this issue. These edicts were also important steps in a policy of confessionalization, that is, a cooperative effort by state and Church to create both religious uniformity and a wider popular identification with Catholic beliefs and practices.

Austrian officials agreed with Tridentine reformers that the most public failings of the Church should be corrected first. For this reason, initial efforts aimed at reforming the monasteries. Pressure from the Austrian regime on the Bishops of Constance led in 1571 to a visitation of monasteries and convents by a combined Austrian/episcopal commission.[37] Although this inspection can, in part, be traced to the episcopal synod of 1567, the impulse clearly came from the Austrians. Cardinal Mark Sittich von Hohenems's instructions to the episcopal visitors

[35] Like many aristocratic and princely bishops in Germany, Andreas never took higher clerical orders: Stievermann, "Österreichische Vorlande," pp. 269–271; Erwin Keller, "Bischöflich-konstanzische Erlasse und Hirtenbriefe. Ein Beitrag zur Seelsorgsgeschichte im Bistum Konstanz" *FDA* 102 (1982), p. 17.

[36] Stievermann, "Österreichische Vorlande," pp. 270–271. Protestant nobles with *Reichsunmittelbar* status had sometimes pursued careers in Habsburg service.

[37] Moritz Gmelin, "Aus Visitationsprotokollen der Diözese Konstanz von 1571–1586" *ZGO* 25 (1873), pp. 154–173; Hugo Ott, "Die Benediktinerabtei St. Blasien in den Reformbestrebungen seit 1567, besonders unter Abt Kaspar II. (1571–1596)" *FDA* 84 (1964), pp. 151–155.

reflected the leading role of the secular authorities. In this document, the cardinal reminds his representatives to uphold episcopal rights, but accepts the participation of Austrian commissioners in the visitation and even instructs the visitors to turn to secular authorities for advice and protection when episcopal authority is too weak. The Austrian commissioners were indispensable to the 1571 visitation. In Villingen, for example, the town council did not want to allow episcopal visitors to inspect the monasteries there, claiming that town officials had recently inspected the several monasteries. The visitors' argument that "the Council of Trent has given their lord [the bishop] the duty of visiting all monasteries once a year" did nothing to convince the city fathers to change their view. Instead, they stated "because their lord and territorial prince [*herr und landsfürst*] has said so, they will allow it [the visitation] to happen and will no longer oppose it."[38]

The 1571 visitation of the monasteries in Austrian territories began in August in Villingen, where the combined Austrian and episcopal visitors inspected the *Vettersammlung*, a convent affiliated with the Dominicans, the St. Clara convent, and the Franciscan monastery. The visitors also investigated the secular clergy in Villingen, although almost as an afterthought.[39] The rest of their work was exclusively in monasteries and convents, and proceeded slowly. In the fall of 1571 several more monasteries were visited, followed in 1572 by the monastic establishments in Freiburg and the monastery of St. Trudpert in 1573.[40] Monastic reform was a goal of episcopal as well as Austrian officials, but no such visitations took place outside the Austrian territories. Without Austrian initiative, the bishops were in no position to enforce Tridentine decrees about monastic reform.

Austrian influence over monasteries was most important in cities and towns such as Villingen and Freiburg. Habsburg officials could put considerable pressure on the smaller and poorer urban establishments of the Franciscans and Dominicans, especially since many of these had suffered severe recruitment problems in the aftermath of the Reformation. The large and wealthy rural abbeys in Austrian territories, the most prominent being the Benedictine house of St. Blasien, had stronger defenses against state interference. Nevertheless, from the 1560s on even the monks at St. Blasien felt the influence of the Austrian regime. Abbot

38 Gmelin, "Aus Visitationsprotokollen der Diözese Konstanz," pp. 155–156, 162.
39 Gmelin, "Aus Visitationsprotokollen der Diözese Konstanz," pp. 166–170.
40 Gmelin, "Aus Visitationsprotokollen der Diözese Konstanz," pp. 136–139; Ott, "Die Benediktinerabtei St. Blasien," p. 155.

Kaspar I was appointed one of the episcopal visitors for the Austrian-dominated visitation of 1571–1573 and the visitation may have come to St. Blasien at some point.[41] Extensive reforms both within the abbey and in the parishes it governed would, however, have to wait until the 1590s.

Clerical concubinage was a further focus of the Austrian regime. The Habsburgs took the lead on this issue because they believed that episcopal authorities, who had ultimate responsibility for disciplining priests, moved too slowly. In a letter of 1588, the *Regierung* in Innsbruck complained to the Bishop of Constance that there were many priests with concubines in the Austrian county of Hohenberg and that "such unpriestly lifestyle and behavior [both] takes place and is permitted . . ."[42] In the name of Archduke Ferdinand, the regime demanded that priests who "were stained with such attachments [*anhenngen*]" should be removed from their posts immediately. By the 1580s the effort to end concubinage had been underway for several decades, although with limited success.

Some Austrian parish priests defended concubinage, even in the immediate aftermath of the Council of Trent and the episcopal synod of 1567 in Constance, both of which expressly forbade such a lifestyle. In a 1568 letter, the clergy of the Breisgau, a predominantly Austrian region, "tacitly criticized the prohibition against concubines," as a marginal comment by an episcopal official put it.[43] According to the priests, the poor incomes of their benefices made celibacy financially impossible. In order to perform their clerical duties and maintain a proper house, priests needed the help of loyal servants, presumably ones who worked without having to be paid. Other priests in Southwest Germany made similar arguments, claiming they needed "maids" to take care of the cattle.[44] The Breisgauer clergy defended concubinage as financially necessary, trying to use a practical argument that church reformers and state officials would have a hard time countering. In the long run they failed and the moralizing discourse of the Tridentine Church carried the day.

There were practical problems in identifying and expelling concubines, but this "abuse" was susceptible to reform from above. Episcopal visitors quite easily located those priests who had concubines and listed

[41] Ott, "Die Benediktinerabtei St. Blasien," pp. 151–156.

[42] GLAK 82a/273. [43] EAF A1/684.

[44] Jörn Sieglerschmidt, "Der niedere Klerus um 1600. Eine vergleichende Untersuchung am Beispiel des Landdekanats Engen" in Elmar Kuhn, Eva Moses, Rudolf Reinhardt and Petra Sachs (eds.) *Die Bischöfe von Konstanz*, Vol. I *Geschichte* (Friederichshafen, 1988), pp. 116–117.

them in their reports. These visitation reports show a steady decline in concubinage by the 1590s. In 1590 in the Rural Chapter of Stockach, an area where Austrian authorities had considerable power, only two priests are identified as *concubinarii*, and several others are listed as suspect.[45] The vast majority of *Pfarrer* had mothers, sisters, or other family members managing their households. The transition to a celibate clergy was clearly underway. Johann Helderlein, the priest in Liggaringen, like several colleagues, explained that he had "sent his family away" and was living honestly. In the area around Freiburg, where Austrian officials were very active, the visitors in 1590 found only one concubine, which was considerably fewer than the eight concubines identified a decade earlier.[46]

The success of the attack on concubinage was uneven. Because it was led, at least in the last decades of the sixteenth century, by Austrian officials, this effort succeeded in areas where Austrian authority was relatively undisputed. These areas were few. In the district around Stockach, Austrian influence over appointments was strong, but even here the emperor appointed only seven of the twenty-seven priests.[47] Patronage rights reflected the fact that this part of Germany was the heartland of the *Eigenkirche*, the privately owned and founded churches of the Middle Ages, together with the political fragmentation of the region. As if the scattered nature of the Austrian territories was not sufficient problem, confessionalization was further hindered by the fact that the Habsburg emperor actually held the patronage of only a small percentage of the parishes in his territories.[48]

When Austrian officials could control appointments, they put celibacy at the top of their list of attributes for a good priest. Officials in far-away Innsbruck kept close track of appointments in the small town of Binsdorf, where the town council had the *jus nominandi*, the right to nominate the parish priest. In 1568 their primary concern was that the suggested priest be Catholic and "not stained with any sect."[49] By 1587 the regime was only interested in concubinage. The town had

[45] EAF A1/725.

[46] 1590: EAF A1/684. 1581: Gmelin, "Aus Visitationsprotokollen der Diözese Konstanz," pp. 181–86. Concubinage was eradicated rather later in non-Austrian territories. See Sieglerschmidt, "Der niedere Klerus um 1600," pp. 122–123. After 1600 there was " . . . eine sichtbare Verbesserung gegenüber der Zeit vor 1600 . . ."

[47] EAF A1/725. Parish patrons in the Rural Chapter of Stockach: Austria, seven parishes; nobles (four different ones), eight parishes; the city of Überlingen, two parishes; the Teutonic Knights, four parishes; the Cathedral Chapter in Constance, five parishes; the Knights of St. John, one parish.

[48] GLAK 79/828. [49] TLA Ferd. 10(1) (*Benefizia*).

nominated Jacob Armbruster, who, they admitted, had a concubine, but who was otherwise good at his duties and a fine singer.[50] Officials in Innsbruck demanded that he get rid of his concubine and made no reference to his other qualifications. Armbruster served for three years. In 1590 Johan Hurmann was appointed, a young man who had studied in Freiburg and lived with his parents. He had no concubine and, according to the Binsdorfer, was good at "preaching, singing, and other church services." The clergy of Binsdorf, as elsewhere in Catholic Germany, were transformed in the 1580s and 1590s. A priest such as Armbruster, who openly admitted to concubinage, could still be appointed, but the future belonged to Hurmann and his generation. The difference between the two priests had nothing to do with commitment to the duties of their position; it was purely a matter of celibacy.

Concubinage was the decisive factor in the appointment in 1588 of Matthias Schreiber to the parish of Deilingen.[51] The other candidate for this position, Christopf Bregenzer, had the support of the commune of Deilingen, who said that he had performed well as chaplain in a nearby village. Officials of the Austrian district of Hohenberg confirmed that Bregenzer was an experienced priest and was "not stained with any other sect and is well enough qualified to serve such a parish." This was faint praise, however, since they also reported that Bregenzer was a former monk who had left his monastery because of his concubine. He continued to live with this woman and their two children and over the previous years had bounced from post to post. The Austrian state was too well organized to appoint such a priest; instead Schreiber, who had studied with the Jesuits and had no concubine, became *Pfarrer* in Deilingen. Bregenzer passed the "loyalty to Catholicism" test, which would have been sufficient for appointment to an Austrian parish in the middle decades of the sixteenth century. In the last decades of the century, however, celibacy defined a clergyman's commitment to the true Church.

Both the local priests and the state authorities understood that the crusade against concubinage had several aims. The primary goal, of course, was to enforce celibacy and emphasize the special sexual status of the clergy. A secondary, but important goal was to change the way of life of the peasant-priest. The Council of Trent had endeavored to create a better-trained and morally upright clergy. Parish priests were supposed to stand apart from local society, in their behavior and their

50 HStASt. B37a/134. See a similar case in Hirrlingen (1594): HStASt. B37a/288.
51 HStASt. B37a/147.

lifestyle.[52] Austrian officials agreed, at least implicitly, with the priests who argued that their meager incomes did not allow them to live in a proper priestly manner. An effort to improve clerical incomes was thus an integral part of the Austrian-led church reform.

There were relatively few ways to improve clerical incomes. One option was to convince patrons to turn over larger portions of the tithes and property of a parish to the clergymen who served it. This alternative was of course difficult to implement, given both the independence and the legal protections enjoyed by patrons, especially wealthy monasteries.[53] A second method, and the one Austrian officials turned to in the late sixteenth century, was to give smaller additional benefices (chaplaincies, primissaries, etc.) to parish priests.[54] This solution led to pluralism, something Tridentine reformers sought to prevent, but it could be justified as a necessary expedient. Parish priests needed sufficient income in order to provide proper pastoral services.

The idea of combining benefices for the purposes of improving the income of parish priests appears to have come from local officials, rather than from state officials in Innsbruck and Ensisheim. Episcopal officials resisted such endeavors. As early as 1565 officials in Stockach proposed hiring only one priest for the neighboring parishes of Schwandorf and Holzach.[55] Episcopal officials did not like the idea, but accepted it, citing their great respect for the Habsburgs. Austrian officials may have taken this 1565 agreement as an opening to "unite" more benefices. In 1570 there were further discussions between officials of the Austrian *Landvogtei* Nellenburg (the district around Stockach) and representatives of the Bishop of Constance about a broad effort to combine clerical posts.[56] In these discussions, episcopal officials argued that combining benefices in this way was only a stop-gap solution to a problem caused by the siphoning off of resources to monasteries and lay church patrons. They further pointed out that more benefices might be good for pastoral care, a viewpoint that was almost prophetic. In the century after 1650, communities would need and demand more priests and would put considerable effort into reviving secondary bene-

[52] Hsia, *The World of Catholic Renewal*, pp. 114–121.

[53] Sieglerschmidt, "Der niedere Klerus um 1600," pp. 120–121.

[54] Similar strategies were used in the Bishopric of Speyer: Marc R. Forster, *The Counter-Reformation in the Villages. Religion and Reform in the Bishopric of Speyer, 1560–1720* (Ithaca and London, 1992), pp. 87–89.

[55] TLA Ferd. 178(1) (*Visitations Handlungen*), 1565, 20 December.

[56] TLA Ferd. 178(1) (*Visitations Handlungen*), 1570, 20 July, letter from Constance officials to Archduke Ferdinand in Innsbruck; subsequent letter from *Amtleute* in Stockach to regime in Innsbruck.

fices which had been absorbed into parishes in the later sixteenth century.[57]

By the 1590s, however, church and state officials were working together to improve clerical incomes. Tridentine reform focused on creating a rational and orderly benefice system, particularly by strengthening parishes at the expense of other structures.[58] In 1590, Johann Pistorius, vicar general of the Bishop of Constance, investigated vacant benefices in the county of Hohenberg.[59] It is a sign of the congruence of state and church interests that he submitted his final report both to the bishop and to Archduke Ferdinand. Pistorius tried to balance the interests of the bishop, such as a concern for the conditions of the original endowment and the maintenance of episcopal authority, with the pastoral needs of the people, which secular officials tended to emphasize. The vicar general recommended combining several benefices and suggested giving some chaplaincies to parish priests. At the same time, he favored "renovations," that is, the renewal of accounts, hoping to mobilize more money for the poorer benefices. Pistorius was reluctant, for example, to allow organist benefices to disappear. He pointed out that communes had created these positions and that "since having an organ is most necessary for praising and honoring God, they should be improved and built for the beautification of churches." In the first decades of the seventeenth century, all indications were that clerical incomes had improved, even if there remained pockets of impoverished priests.

Despite these efforts, the complexity of the benefice system throughout this part of Germany made it difficult to improve clerical incomes. Even the relatively powerful Austrians had trouble mobilizing resources in their territories. The Rhine valley village of Herbolzheim provides a good example of the complexity that could confuse efforts to find money for priests. There were eight different parties that contributed to some aspect of the local church.[60] When local officials tried to assemble funds in 1624 to build a new parsonage, they faced, not surprisingly, an administrative nightmare. While officials could itemize the legal obligations of the different parties, actual practice might be different. In 1580

[57] See below, chapters 4 and 5.

[58] Bossy, "The Counter-Reformation and the People of Catholic Europe."

[59] HStASt. B37a/15. On Pistorius: Konstantin Meyer, "Zu den Generalvikaren in der Neuzeit" in Kuhn et al. (eds.), *Die Bischöfe von Konstanz*, Vol. I *Geschichte*, p. 86.

[60] GLAK 229/42370, GLAK 229/42371. The eight parties were Austria, the Bishop of Strasburg, *Junker* Philip Jacob von Seebach, the Monastery of Schuttern, the Monastery of Ettenheimmünster, the parish priest, the parish church endowment, and the Commune of Herbolzheim.

an effort to improve the income of the priest in Herbolzheim ran into the opposition, not of monasteries or noblemen, but of local peasants, some of whom had leased tithes from the titheholders. On this occasion the commune protested the attempt by the *Pfarrer* to collect tithes on calves and pigs, which the villagers considered an "innovation." This conflict was of course a typical one between a priest who felt his legal rights had been either frittered away by incompetent predecessors or chipped away by unscrupulous peasants. This situation was repeated across Southwest Germany in the four decades after 1580.

As a result of the financial reforms favored by Austrian officials, by the 1620s there were fewer clergymen overall in the countryside, but parish priests were better paid. In fact, by the middle of the seventeenth century many benefices were forgotten, the result of course of the destruction of the Thirty Years' War as well as the reorganization brought about by the reformers. In 1588 episcopal visitors identified fifty-five benefices served by thirty-seven priests in the Rural Chapter of Breisach. In 1666, visitors listed thirty-seven benefices, held by thirty-seven priests.[61] Later seventeenth-century visitors tended to think in terms of priests, not benefices, which explains the absence from their reports of vacant or incorporated benefices. It also appears that secondary benefices, once absorbed into parishes, were forgotten. The priest in Wasenweiler in 1666, perhaps hoping for help serving his parish, commented that there once had been a chaplaincy in his village.[62] Church reform had certainly helped bring about a simplification of the benefice system in Southwest Germany. The trend toward a plainer and more basic ecclesiastical structure would be reversed after 1650.

TRIDENTINE REFORM IN THE BISHOPRIC OF CONSTANCE

The Bishops of Constance and their officials enacted a reform program inspired by the Council of Trent. Episcopal reform began in 1567 with a diocesan synod, and then continued with visitations of rural parishes and the creation of a Clerical Council (*Geistliche Rat*) in 1594. Tridentine reformers of course understood church reform as a top-down process, in which their leadership would result in a reform of the clergy and eventually a reform of popular religion.

Conditions in the Bishopric of Constance caused bishops and their officials to emphasize the jurisdictional reforms of the Council of Trent.

[61] EAF Ha 63, pp. 431–451, 583–756. [62] EAF Ha 63, p. 625.

In the middle of the sixteenth century, important practical and political problems undermined the authority of the bishops. Although the vast majority of the diocese remained Catholic after the Reformation, Protestantism had captured several important states, especially Württemberg, and influential cities such as Ulm and Zurich. The existence of strong Protestant states hindered Tridentine reformers, especially when Protestant states had jurisdictional rights in Catholic territories. The vast size of the diocese of Constance caused further practical problems and made it impossible for the impoverished bishops to create an effective episcopal bureaucracy. Most dramatically, by the late sixteenth century the Swiss part of the diocese had basically broken away from the authority of the bishops, a development favored by the papal nuncio in Lucerne, who acted in effect as bishop for Catholic Switzerland.[63]

Even within the staunchly Catholic parts of Southwest Germany, privileges and exemptions held by both secular princes and church institutions limited episcopal authority. Secular princes, such as the Habsburgs, were not inclined to give authority to bishops, and bishops were not in a good position to assert such power. The Church so needed the support of the Habsburgs in the confessionally divided empire that bishops tolerated considerable Austrian interference in their jurisdiction. Smaller Catholic states followed the Austrian lead and refused to recognize episcopal authority.[64]

Monasteries and military orders claimed extensive exemptions from episcopal jurisdiction and tenaciously defended their privileges against any new episcopal claims based on the decrees of the Council of Trent. These institutions had an ambiguous attitude toward Trent. On the one hand, they opposed the decrees that increased episcopal authority over monasteries. On the other hand, the leading monasteries of the region, such as the Benedictine houses of Weingarten and St. Blasien and the Cistercian house of Salem, responded positively to the call for reform of order, discipline, and morality within monastic walls. The most important monasteries supported Tridentine reform, at least where it promised a moral and religious renewal of the Church. However, since the bishops

[63] Rudolf Reinhardt, "Frühe Neuzeit" in Kuhn et al. (eds.), *Die Bischöfe von Konstanz*, Vol. I *Geschichte*, pp. 34–35; Beat Bühler, "Hochstift und Diözese Konstanz im Jahre 1587" *FDA* 107 (1987), pp. 35–44.

[64] Rudolf Reinhardt argues that episcopal authorities asserted "clerical immunity, the idea of the freedom of the Church, and the independence of the clergy" more aggressively in the eighteenth century than in the period directly after the Council of Trent. Rudolf Reinhardt, *Die Beziehungen von Hochstift und Diözese Konstanz zu Habsburg-Österreich in der Neuzeit: Zugleich ein Beitrag zur archivalischen Erforschung des Problems "Kirche und Staat." Beiträge zur Geschichte der Reichskirche in der Neuzeit*, Vol. II (Wiesbaden, 1966), esp. Introduction.

tended to emphasize jurisdictional issues, there were also clashes between forces at the highest levels of the ecclesiastical hierarchy.

Given all these impediments to church reform, it is surprising that the Bishops of Constance were able to enact any reform program. Yet as Rudolf Reinhardt has shown, there was a new spirit abroad in the Catholic elite, and the five bishops who ruled from 1589 to 1644 considered themselves "the bishops of reform."[65] Most importantly, these bishops improved the administration of their diocese, dividing the episcopal council (*Rat*) into three smaller councils, the *Weltliche Rat*, which dealt with political matters, the *Kammerrat*, which managed the property and finances of the bishop, and the *Geistliche Rat*, the Clerical Council. The Clerical Council, founded in 1594, was responsible for ecclesiastical matters and took the lead in instituting Tridentine reforms. Most significantly, between 1590 and the 1620s the *Geistliche Rat* organized visitations of many of the rural parishes of the diocese. These inspections not only led to the "reform" of "abuses" such as concubinage, but also exposed episcopal officials to the realities of religious life in the countryside. In the long run, the massive volume of minutes gathered by the visitors must have led episcopal officials to a realistic understanding of the possibilities and limits of Tridentine reform.

In the last decades of the sixteenth century, important elements of the Catholic elite were committed to Tridentine reform. At the same time, there was also skepticism in many circles, among the clergy as well as the common people. Overall, however, reforms received a mixed reception, which led at the local level to their piecemeal adoption and frequent modification. The story of Tridentine reform also reveals much about the variety and diversity of Catholicism in Southwest Germany, a diversity that the rationalizing tendencies within Tridentine Catholicism could not overcome. After 1650, diversity and variety would become increasingly characteristic of Catholic culture.

Synods

The first step in implementing Tridentine reform was to organize a synod of the clergy. Cardinal Mark Sittich von Hohenems (Bishop of Constance, 1561–1589) demonstrated his commitment to church reform (and belied his reputation as a worldly bishop) by organizing a large

[65] Reinhardt, "Frühe Neuzeit," pp. 30–35.

diocesan synod in 1567. The cardinal was explicit about the connection between this synod and reform of the clergy:

It is inevitable [and] of the greatest necessity, that we begin the implementation of reformation of the clergy [ordered by] the holy council. [We must] end their bad behavior, drunkenness, gambling, suspicious domestic relations, and other such disorderly things . . . and institute more God-fearing discipline and order [*Disciplin und Zucht*] . . . [As a result, the bishop plans] to hold a synod or gathering of all prelates and clergy of the Bishopric of Constance, to the extent that they are required to attend a synod, in order to publish and publicize the decrees of the council, and in addition, to implement the punishments and ordinances found therein.[66]

The importance von Hohenems attached to synods reflected the influence of Carlo Borromeo, Archbishop of Milan, who held seven provincial councils and eleven diocesan synods in the two decades after the Council of Trent. Like Borromeo, von Hohenems was a cardinal-nephew and "a creature of the Roman curia," gaining his high position in the Church because of the patronage of his uncle, Gian Angelo de Medici, who was elected Pope Pius IV in 1559. Unlike Borromeo, Mark Sittich never developed a personal commitment to the life and work of a reform bishop. Yet, at the Synod of 1567 he set in motion a significant reform of the clergy of the Bishopric of Constance.[67]

The Synod of 1567 was well attended. The Abbot of Salem attended personally and all the great monasteries sent high-level representatives, fearing their absence would imply a lack of interest in Tridentine reform. The lower clergy attended in great numbers, including a large delegation from the Swiss part of the diocese. There was real enthusiasm for church reform. The assembled clergymen supported new statutes regulating clerical behavior, outlawing heretical books, and establishing a clear profession of faith. The spirit of reform did not, however, create an enthusiasm for new financial obligations or a strengthening of episcopal authority. Both the Swiss clergy and the monasteries objected to the financing of an episcopal seminary. Further disputes erupted over questions of legal jurisdiction, reforms of tithe collection, and new regulations for patronage of churches. The cardinal-bishop finessed these problems by assuring the assembled

[66] Konstantin Maier, "Die Konstanzer Diözesansynoden im Mittelalter und in der Neuzeit" *RJfKG* 5 (1986), pp. 63–67, quote pp. 63–64.

[67] Maier, "Die Konstanzer Diözesansynoden," p. 63; Reinhardt, "Frühe Neuzeit," p. 31. On Borromeo and the concept of the cardinal-nephew, see Hsia, *The World of Catholic Renewal*, pp. 106–110.

clergy that many proposed reforms were really long-term goals. Furthermore, he claimed that only the statutes relating to morality and belief would go into effect immediately. Von Hohenems further stated that he had no interest in attacking the privileges of the clergy or of the prelates, and that disputed issues, such as the funding of the seminary, would be dealt with at a later date.[68]

In April 1568 the cardinal-bishop promulgated, from his distant residence in Rome, an impressive set of synod statutes. He ignored many of the concessions he had made the previous year in Constance. The statutes publicized most of the key reform decrees of the Council of Trent, emphasizing the education of the clergy, the attack on concubinage, and the institution of regular episcopal visitations. Yet as Konstantin Maier has argued, von Hohenems quickly dissipated the authority and reputation he had gained from the synod.[69] The cardinal's real interest in reform was limited, and in 1569 he moved permanently to Rome. It then took several decades for the first visitation to get off the ground, and the dispute over the funding of a seminary also continued for decades. Finally, in 1589, after the payment of a large sum of money, von Hohenems resigned his see in favor of Cardinal Andreas von Österreich.[70]

Even when the bishop tried to enforce them, many of the reform statutes had little effect, especially in the short term. Problems began at the highest level of the bishopric. Although the bishop hoped they would set a good example, the canons and chaplains of the Cathedral Chapter in Constance vigorously resisted the decrees requiring them to send away their concubines (and all women under forty years old).[71] When the canons finally agreed to these rules "after long consultation," they made no effort to enforce them. The cardinal had to concede that he could not reform the cathedral clergy and asked the secular arm, in this case the Austrian authorities, to arrest the clergy's concubines in the city of Constance. As Wolfgang Zimmermann has pointed out, in the 1570s episcopal authority eroded rapidly, especially in Switzerland, and the initiative in church reform shifted to the Habsburgs and the papal nuncios based in Lucerne.

68 Maier, "Die Konstanzer Diözesansynoden," pp. 64–66; Hugo Ott, "Die Benediktinerabtei St. Blasien," pp. 144–146.

69 Maier, "Die Konstanzer Diözesansynoden," p. 67.

70 Stievermann, "Österreichische Vorlande," pp. 269–270.

71 Zimmermann, *Rekatholisierung, Konfessionalisierung und Ratsregiment*, pp. 127–132.

Visitations

Tridentine reform in the Bishopric of Constance peaked between 1590 and about 1630. During this period there was a general convergence of interests, especially between the bishops and the Habsburgs.[72] The Catholic elite, lay and clerical, agreed that the Church itself, and in particular the clergy, needed reform. Yet even this consensus was fragile. In the first place, Cardinal-Bishop Andreas von Österreich demonstrated only sporadic interest in an active reform policy. Secondly, the most important episcopal institution dedicated to reform, the Clerical Council, invested much time and political capital in jurisdictional disputes, sacrificing momentum and enthusiasm for reform in a concerted effort to strengthen episcopal authority.

On October 1, 1591 Andreas issued an extensive "*Charta visitatoria*," a set of instructions for the clergy of his diocese. This *Charta* has earned Andreas the reputation of "the first Tridentine reform Bishop of Constance."[73] In fact, the *Charta* reflects the central dilemma for Tridentine reform in the diocese. This document emphasizes two issues: the strengthening of episcopal jurisdiction and the improvement of pastoral services to be brought about by a reform of the clergy. From the perspective of episcopal officials these two goals were complementary. In reality the first goal gave rise to conflict with secular authorities and many ecclesiastical institutions whose cooperation was necessary for a successful reform of the clergy.

The *Charta* can be read as a clear commitment to the Tridentine reform program. The second part requires priests to improve the quality of pastoral services by performing church services diligently, teaching catechism classes, and providing all the sacraments. Section three of the *Charta*, entitled "*De vita parochorum*," contains the standard rules against concubinage, excessive drinking and socializing, and unseemly dress. Part five even moves from the reform of the clergy to proposals for the reform of religious life in the parishes. Episcopal authorities sought greater uniformity in church holidays, wanted the people to obey the rules for fasting more diligently, and demanded adherence to the new Tridentine marriage regulations.

[72] Bishops in neighboring dioceses, especially Basel, Strasbourg, Speyer, and Augsburg, also experienced Tridentine inspired reforms in this period.

[73] Erwin Keller, "Bischöflich-konstanzische Erlasse und Hirtenbriefe. Ein Beitrag zur Seelsorgsgeschichte im Bistum Konstanz" *FDA* 102 (1982), pp. 17–30; Reinhardt, *Die Beziehungen von Hochstift und Diözese Konstanz zu Habsburg-Österreich*, p. 39; Reinhardt, "Frühe Neuzeit," pp. 30–35.

Yet the pastoral concerns of the *Charta* were balanced, and even perhaps outweighed, by the concern for "the restitution of episcopal jurisdiction along the lines of the Council of Trent." Thus the whole of the first section of the *Charta* aims at enhancing episcopal control of the appointment and removal of priests and seeks to limit the power of secular authorities and parish patrons. Episcopal officials were obsessively concerned with such jurisdictional issues, particularly because the Bishops of Constance had such difficulty asserting their rights, especially against the opposition of the Austrian state, the monasteries, and the Swiss cantons.[74]

Although episcopal authority remained weak, between the 1570s and the 1620s episcopal officials in Constance managed to organize extensive visitations of their diocese. Like all aspects of Tridentine reform, the visitations were sporadic and by no means universal in this enormous diocese. Nevertheless, more visitation reports have survived from the Bishopric of Constance than from any other German diocese except Würzburg and Augsburg.[75] The amount of paper produced by episcopal officials is one indication of their interest in reform.

As we have seen, the first visitations in the 1570s took place because of pressure from the Austrian regime and they were limited in their extent.[76] In the 1590s, Cardinal Andreas von Österreich instituted what Peter Thaddäus Lang has called a "lavishly complex visitation system." Andreas appointed a "special visitor" for each of the four districts of the diocese (Swabia, Allgäu, Breisgau, Switzerland). These visitors were to supervise annual visitations in their districts and report the results to the two "general visitors" in Constance. In theory at least, each rural chapter was inspected directly by its dean, and indirectly by the special visitor and a general visitor.

This "system" of course depended on the interest and engagement of individual visitors. The central role of the deans, who were local priests themselves, meant that the visitations were imperfect instruments of reform. Episcopal officials tried to guide visitations with instructions, like the *Charta visitatoria* of 1591. The Clerical Council also sought out reform-minded priests for the position of visitor, generally appointing

[74] The *Charta* declares *reversales litteras* illicit and contrary to canon law. Such oaths obligated clergymen to perform certain duties and were considered a kind of simony. Keller, "Bischöflich-konstanzische Erlasse und Hirtenbriefe," pp. 20, 30.

[75] Peter Thaddäus Lang, "Die Erforschung der frühneuzeitlichen Kirchenvisitationen. Neuere Veröffentlichungen in Deutschland" *RJfKG* 16 (1997), pp. 192–193.

[76] Peter Thaddäus Lang, "Die Visitationen" in Kuhn et al. (eds.), *Die Bischöfe von Konstanz*, Vol. I *Geschichte*, pp. 103–109, esp. pp. 104–106.

priests from the towns of the region.[77] The visitation reports indicate that central control was limited and that visitors often followed their own interests. In contrast to visitations in better organized dioceses like Würzburg, visitors in Southwest Germany often strayed from their list of questions and dealt with whatever pressing problem turned up in the parish they were visiting.[78]

The concerns of visitors also evolved over time. Just like Austrian officials, in the 1570s to 1590s, visitors were obsessed with concubinage. Unlike secular officials, however, visitors also wanted to know if priests had received proper investiture from the bishop and if they had paid all fees owed to him.[79] The Dean of the Rural Chapter of Rottweil in 1574 had similar interests. His report about the parish priest in Kappel, although an extreme case, gives the flavor of these early visitations:

> Capell: Collator [Patron] is the nobleman von Falckenstein. D. Antonius Mieg, invested pastor, of legitimate birth. He is a scandalous [*ärgerlich*] person, has one maid, who hits him, scolds him, and curses at him. She is also old and he has lived with her for eight years . . . He preaches badly, so that the people [*underthonen*] only laugh at his sermons. Immodest and thoughtless in speaking to women and men. He has three children by a prior concubine. He blasphemes with the concubine.[80]

This report caused Mieg to be called before the vicar general in Constance. He was forced to resign one of the three parishes he held, and ordered to get rid of the concubine and to improve his sermons and his behavior. The visitation clearly could lead to disciplinary action, but Mieg seems to have been let off rather easily given the extent of his crimes.

The new impetus that Andreas von Österreich, the Clerical Council, and reforming officials gave to Tridentine reform was reflected in the visitations from the 1590s on. Especially during the extensive visitation of 1608–1609, officials investigated the financial condition of the benefices, including chaplaincies and other smaller benefices, demanded to know how often and effectively the priest preached and taught catechism, asked about weekly church services, and even investigated the ornaments of churches.[81] The 1608 report about Hochsal, a parish in

[77] See discussion of appointment of visitors in 1594: EAF Ha 207, p. 18.

[78] Lang, "Die Erforschung der frühneuzeitlichen Kirchenvisitationen," p. 193.

[79] See for example EAF A1/725 (*Landkapitel* Stockach, 1590) and EAF A1/684 (*Landkapitel* Freiburg, 1590).

[80] Moritz Gmelin, "Aus Visitationsprotokollen der Diözese Konstanz," p. 176. See also Johan Kraus, "Aus den Visitationsakten des ehemaligen Kapitels Trochtelfingen 1574–1709" *FDA* 73 (1953), esp. pp. 146–148.

[81] Lang, "Die Visitationen," p. 106.

the southern Black Forest, contains a detailed explanation of the church services performed by the priest and the endowed masses he had to read.[82] The visitors also reported on the nature of wedding and funeral services in Hochsal, and on the condition of local confraternities, as well as on the resources of both the parish church and a chapel in the village. The 1608–1609 reports give the general impression that the most dramatic clerical abuses, particularly concubinage, were no longer a big problem, and that visitors (and church reformers) had shifted their focus to somewhat more mundane issues.[83]

There were many gaps in this "visitation system" in the Bishopric of Constance.[84] The monasteries and the military orders stubbornly resisted allowing episcopal visitations in their incorporated parishes. The leaders of these institutions correctly interpreted visitations as attempts to expand episcopal authority, as well as an effort to reform the clergy and religious life in the parishes. The city fathers of Catholic cities in Southwest Germany had the same concerns, and very few episcopal visitations took place in urban parishes. Both the jealous defense of privilege and the tendency of the episcopal administration to use the decrees of the Council of Trent to reassert episcopal rights weakened visitations as tools of reform.

Even when visitors were able to visit parishes, they depended on the cooperation of church patrons. In 1608 the visitors identified problems with two parish priests who had been appointed by the noble convent of St. Fridolin in Säckingen.[85] The bishop asked the nuns to deal with the two priests. The *Pfarrer* in Stetten, who had a concubine, was told to get rid of her.[86] The second priest, in Zell, neglected services, drank heavily, and "asked women inappropriate questions in confession."[87] The nuns treated him leniently as well, accepting his promise to improve his behavior in the future. The reform of the clergy depended on more than simply episcopal efforts.

The Abbey of St. Blasien provides a good example of the monastic attitude toward visitations and, by extension, toward episcopal authority. At one level, all monasteries did what they could to prevent episcopal officials from inspecting conditions within monasteries themselves.

[82] EAF Ha 62, pp. 362r–363r.

[83] EAF Ha 62, pp. 324, 326r–327v (*Landkapitel* Saulgau, 1608); EAF Ha 62, pp. 362r–371v (*Landkapitel* Waldshut, 1608).

[84] Lang, "Die Visitationen," pp. 108–109.

[85] On St. Fridolin, see David M. Luebke, *His Majesty's Rebels. Communities, Factions, and Rural Revolt in the Black Forest, 1725–1745* (Ithaca and London, 1997), pp. 35–48.

[86] GLAK 61/10498, p. 269r.

[87] GLAK 61/10498, pp. 271v–272r.

In an attempt to avoid such episcopal involvement, many monasteries in the Southwest asked the papal nuncio Felician Ninguarda to conduct a visitation of their houses in 1579.[88] In 1591 the Bishop of Constance's vicar general came to St. Blasien, but left the abbey before completing his inspection, perhaps due to resistance from the monks. Later that year, two professors from the University of Freiburg, appointed by episcopal officials but apparently acceptable to the abbot, inspected conditions in the monastery and sent a report both to St. Blasien and to the bishop. This report, along with a visit from another nuncio, led St. Blasien to produce a "reform charter" in 1594. This charter provided a blueprint for a fairly effective internal reform at the monastery.

Monasteries also sought to limit the impact of a Tridentine decree which gave bishops the right to "visit monasteries to which is annexed the cura of seculars . . . "[89] As most monasteries had incorporated a number of parishes, this decree made it possible for episcopal officials to break into the jurisdiction of monasteries. St. Blasien had more parishes under its control than any other monastery in the diocese and had appointed monks as parish priests in many places. Although the Benedictines at St. Blasien, like those at Weingarten, were interested in improving the quality of the parish clergy, they wanted to do it themselves, without interference from Constance. As a result, St. Blasien became a test case for visitations in monastic territory.

Throughout the 1580s and 1590s, Bishop Andreas, represented by his vicars general, attempted to end St. Blasien's practice of using monks to serve as parish priests in the parishes incorporated into the monastery.[90] Vicar General Johann Pistorius, who had a well-deserved reputation as a militant church reformer, caused great consternation in St. Blasien when he stated in 1593 "that all religious belong in the monastery."[91] The visitations in this period revealed the extent to which St. Blasien used monks in rural parishes and made it clear to episcopal officials how little control the bishop had over these priests. Despite the new Tridentine decrees, it was difficult for bishops to discipline monk/priests, since their persons were protected by monastic privileges. Pistorius asserted during one meeting with monastic representatives that because of monastic privileges the bishop "had almost

88 Ott, "Die Benediktinerabtei St. Blasien," pp. 156–160.

89 Twenty-fifth session, Reform of Regulars, Chapter IX. Rev. H.J. Schroeder, *Canons and Decrees of the Council of Trent* (London, 1941), pp. 224–225.

90 On vicars general, see Konstantin Maier, "Zu den Generalvikaren in der Neuzeit" in Kuhn et al. (eds.), *Die Bischöfe von Konstanz*, Vol. I *Geschichte*, pp. 85–89, esp. p. 86, 108–109.

91 GLAK 99/363, p. 46r.

or barely half a diocese to administer in the Breisgau, Alsace, the Black Forest, and Switzerland."[92]

The dispute over monks serving in parishes was, then, about jurisdiction and not about pastoral services, which were rarely brought up in the discussions. In 1588, in one of the few exchanges about the quality of work done by monk/priests, the Abbot of St. Blasien denied a report that he changed priests often in the parishes and appointed "idiots" as parish priests.[93] Otherwise, the issues were jurisdictional and financial. The bishop wanted to examine all parish priests and collect all relevant fees. The abbot was concerned that such fees would come from the monastery's coffers and that the appointment of secular priests would be very expensive. Interestingly, the abbot also argued that if all the monks who worked and lived outside the monastery, including the parish priests, came to live at St. Blasien, it would not only be prohibitively expensive but also difficult to have so many monks live together in peace and friendship.[94]

The conflict came to a head with a 1597 episcopal ordinance that drew on the Tridentine decrees and explicitly forbade the use of monks as parish priests.[95] As was always the case, this decree was open to negotiation, which took place over the next several years. By early 1599, monastic officials had presented enough documents to the bishop's representatives to convince them that St. Blasien could indeed appoint monks to serve as parish priests.[96] At the same time, the abbot agreed to appoint secular priests to parishes further away from the monastery. He also conceded to the bishop the right to examine new priests, although only in their capacity as pastors. Further compromises were reached about the fees monk/priests would pay the bishop. The parties negotiated these issues more or less as equals. Tridentine decrees may have caused bishops to reassert their rights, but they did not ensure the success of their claims.

[92] GLAK 99/378, p. 6. The reference to Alsace is surprising, since the Bishop of Constance had no jurisdiction there.

[93] GLAK 99/363, p. 29r. It appears that St. Blasien had an extensive network of contacts in Constance and in Meersburg, at the episcopal court. The abbot received frequent reports about reform plans and other policy decisions made by the episcopal administration.

[94] GLAK 99/378, pp. 8r–v, 26r–31r. The abbot also argued that St. Blasien was in an inhospitable location in the Black Forest which was poorly suited to a larger population of monks.

[95] GLAK 99/363, p. 64.

[96] GLAK 99/378, pp. 40r–47v. The monastery appeared to have a better archive than the bishops, which gave it an advantage in disputes that hinged on documentation about privileges and exemptions.

St. Blasien parishes remained difficult for episcopal officials to inspect during visitations. In 1608 the monastery protested that it did not like the form of the impending episcopal visitation and that the monks serving as parish priests should not be visited by the Dean of the Rural Chapter of Waldshut.[97] Abbot Martin told episcopal officials that monastic officials inspected the parishes every two or three years and insisted that he had every interest in promoting "reform." The monastery got its way, and the dean sent a note with his visitation report indicating that he had not visited the St. Blasien parishes and that they would be visited from the monastery.[98]

There were other gaps in the visitation system. In 1608 the Order of Teutonic Knights told the priests serving in the parishes incorporated by the order to deal very carefully with episcopal visitors.[99] The priests were only to discuss the condition of churches, pastoral care, and the administration of sacraments with the visitors. Under no circumstances should they, or the churchwardens, give episcopal representatives any information about the Knights' property, including the salaries the order paid its priests or even the condition of parsonages. The Teutonic Knights had a deserved reputation for giving few resources to parishes, and thus had reason to worry about the results of a visitation. When visitors did inspect the order's parishes, they found priests poorly paid, parsonages in ruins, churches lacking ornaments and badly in need of repair, and pastoral services neglected.[100]

Visitations could be a powerful tool for church reform, especially with respect to the clergy. Episcopal officials in the Bishopric of Constance used them with some effect, especially in their campaign against concubinage. Visitations alone were, however, not sufficient to bring about permanent reform of the clergy and of popular religion in Southwest Germany. The bishops therefore attempted to create the institutions, especially the Clerical Council and an episcopal seminary, that would give stability and permanence to the reform of the clergy. These efforts achieved only limited success.

[97] GLAK 99/363, pp. 69r–v, 70r–72v. [98] EAF Ha 62, p. 369v.

[99] EAF Ha 62, pp. 370r–371v. The Knights tried to prevent their priests from joining rural chapters: EAF Ha 207, p. 95. Priests in the Knights' parishes sometimes refused to allow visitations even in the early eighteenth century: GLAK 93/253.

[100] Even monasteries complained about the Knights. In 1590 the monastery of Schussenried asked the bishop to force the Knights to give more of the tithe from the parish of Michelwinnaden to the church there: HStASt. B466a/209. Episcopal officials also produced a scathing report in 1623, most of which the order's commandary in Beuggen could not deny. The priest in Minseln was accused of concubinage, which was very unusual by this date: GLAK 86/90, GLAK 86/91.

The Clerical Council and the episcopal seminary

The Clerical Council (*Geistliche Rat*) was founded by Cardinal Andreas von Österreich in 1594 to manage the spiritual administration of the Bishopric of Constance.[101] This council was to advise and assist the vicar general and the suffragan bishop (*Weihbischof*), who had handled most of these duties until this time. The creation of the Clerical Council of course signaled an episcopal commitment to reform. The council discussed all aspects of church reform, including the organization of visitations and the punishment of priests, as well as clerical appointments. The councilors, who came partly from the Cathedral Chapter and partly from the episcopal administration, guided reform policy. Among these responsibilities were regular discussions of the organization of visitations, the publication of liturgical books, the funding of a seminary, and the role of the Capuchins in pastoral work.[102] Since "reform bishops" such as Andreas were often absent from the diocese, the council played a real leadership role.

The council was also immersed in the day-to-day administration of the diocese. It was its job, for example, to respond to letters sent to the bishop from and about local clergymen. In 1595, one priest asked for a reaffirmation of an episcopal dispensation which had allowed him to succeed his father as parish priest. Apparently his parishioners had raised new objections to his serving the parish. In another case, an elderly chaplain requested a remission of half of his fine for concubinage, claiming that he could not afford to pay it from his meager retirement funds.[103]

The *Geistliche Rat* was very active, especially in the 1590s.[104] In addition to responding to problems and petitions coming from the local level, the councilors dealt with requests that originated with secular authorities. Such requests came from counts and smaller lords, as well as some town councils, but never from the Austrian authorities or from the great monasteries, which took a dim view of episcopal authority. Thus in 1596 the Count of Hohenzollern asked the bishop to punish three

[101] Georg Weiland, "Die geistliche Zentralverwaltung des Bistums" in Kuhn et al. (eds), *Die Bischöfe von Konstanz*, Vol. I *Geschichte*, pp. 69–72.

[102] Visitations: EAF Ha 207, pp. 18, 79–80, 146, 167. Seminary: EAF Ha 207, pp. 220–222. Liturgical books: EAF Ha 207, pp. 26–27, 209–210. Capuchins: EAF Ha 207, p. 15.

[103] EAF Ha 207, pp. 26, 87.

[104] The council met between twenty-five and thirty-five times a year, mostly in Constance at the episcopal palace. In 1615 it met forty-eight times, a record. Weiland, "Die geistliche Zentralverwaltung des Bistums," pp. 71–72.

priests, two of whom he charged with concubinage and one with abandoning his parish.[105] The council ordered the three priests to be brought to Constance for trial and punishment.

Despite its engagement with clerical reform, a review of the minutes of the council in the 1590s indicates that jurisdictional disputes occupied much of its time.[106] Conflicts over jurisdiction with the monasteries, especially St. Gallen and Einsiedeln in Switzerland, and with the Catholic Swiss cantons, illustrate once again how even the most reform-minded officials saw Tridentine reform as an opportunity to expand episcopal jurisdiction.[107] Furthermore, in the period from its founding until about 1650, the level of activity of the *Geistliche Rat* varied considerably depending on location. The councilors dealt with local issues in the small principalities in the region around Constance itself and, as we have seen, punished priests from smaller principalities such as Hohenzollern. Further away from the episcopal see, the council was less active and could at most attempt to guide policy. In Austrian territories it had little chance of guiding Church reform at the local level.

Nor was the Clerical Council able to raise the funds for a seminary in the Bishopric of Constance.[108] The Council of Trent had clearly ordered bishops to found a seminary to educate parish priests, and Cardinal von Hohenems made the seminary a major topic at the Synod of 1567. Strong opposition from all parties developed immediately, since a seminary required new financial contributions from the whole clergy. The secular clergy complained about existing taxes, especially the *Türkensteuer*, the imperial tax collected to help fund the wars against the Ottomans.[109] The clergy from Switzerland wanted to fund a seminary for Catholic Switzerland, and did not want to support an episcopal seminary. Conflict erupted between the bishops and the Habsburg regime over the location of the seminary and the role of the Jesuits in its administration. Perhaps most importantly, the monasteries, whose financial support was essential to the project, resisted it at every turn.

105 EAF Ha 207, pp. 137–139.

106 Weiland, "Die geistliche Zentralverwaltung des Bistums," pp. 69–70.

107 Conflicts with Catholic Switzerland: EAF Ha 207, pp. 255–257.

108 Peter Schmidt, "Die Priesterausbildung" in Kuhn et al. (eds.), *Die Bischöfe von Konstanz*, Vol. I *Geschichte*, pp. 135–142; Georg Föllinger, "Zur Priesterausbildung in den Bistümern Köln, Paderborn und Konstanz nach dem Tridentinum" in Walter Brandmüller, Herbert Immenkotter and Erwin Iserloh (eds.), *Ecclesia Militans. Studien zur konzilien- und Reformationsgeschichte. Remigius Bäumer zum 70. Geburtstag gewidmet*, Vol. I *zur Konziliengeschichte*, (Paderborn, Munich, Vienna, and Zurich, 1988), pp. 392–397; Rudolf Reinhardt, "Die frühe Neuzeit," p. 32; Zimmermann, *Rekatholisierung, Konfessionalisierung und Ratsregiment*, pp. 133–154.

109 EAF Ha 207, pp. 220–222; Schmidt, "Die Priesterausbildung," pp. 135–136.

The reluctance of monasteries to contribute resources to the seminary was part of a general unwillingness to pay for improvements in pastoral care.[110] Financial considerations were of course central to this refusal, but issues of jurisdiction and control were also factors. Monasteries found the haphazard and fragmented training of priests quite convenient, for it gave parish patrons more flexibility in appointing priests and allowed them to exert influence, play favorites, and manipulate the process to their advantage. A seminary would turn over full control of the education of parish priests to the episcopal administration. Monasteries, the Swiss cantons, and many secular lords feared that a seminary would undermine their influence over the local clergy. After an episcopal seminary was founded in 1735, this fear proved to be well founded.[111]

The achievements of episcopal reform in Southwest Germany were limited. The practical, political, and geographic constraints on Tridentine reform were considerable in this part of Germany, and the expectations of reformers far too great to be achieved in a few short decades. The character of Tridentine reform added to the difficulty. Reformers focused their efforts, whether in synod statutes and episcopal decrees, during visitations, or in the decisions of the Clerical Council, on strengthening episcopal jurisdiction. This emphasis undermined cooperation between Church and state, both at the highest levels and in local communities. The concern with jurisdictional issues also meant that Tridentine reformers had a limited interest in religious practice and the reform of popular religion. Episcopal as well as state officials left the Catholic people to practice their religion as they wished. Popular religion was affected only when town councils, local state officials, or parish priests embraced Tridentine reform.

CATHOLIC REFORM UNDER LOCAL LEADERSHIP

Episcopal officials, like distant princes and their officials, could only sporadically affect religious conditions at the local level. In Burkheim, Austrian officials played a decisive role at a time of crisis in the relations between the town council and the town priest. Yet even then they had to operate through local authorities such as the *Vogt*, who was also a party

110 On monasteries' attitude toward pastoral care: Marc R. Forster, "Kirchenreform, katholische Konfessionalisierung und Dorfreligion um Kloster Salem, 1650–1750" *RJfKG* 16 (1997), pp. 93–110.

111 See below, chapter 5.

in the dispute. Once the crisis ended, Burkheim probably disappeared from the discussions in Ensisheim and Innsbruck. The Clerical Council in Constance also became involved in local problems, but was even less able to follow up its decisions. By the late sixteenth century the Austrian state had built up some regular administrative structures, but the episcopal bureaucracy remained quite *ad hoc* until the eighteenth century.

Local governments, especially town councils in Catholic imperial cities, were in a better position to impose and enforce church reform than were large states or bishops. Monasteries such as Salem and Weingarten, despite their resistance to episcopal jurisdiction, also moved to reform conditions in the parishes of their territories, as did some of the counts and lords of small secular territories. One must really look at the smaller territories to find a close and effective involvement of the secular authorities in religious matters. As a result, Catholic reform took on a local flavor. Town councils, abbots, and other such *Obrigkeiten* were interested in improving the behavior of the clergy and strengthening religious practice at the local level; they did not generally conceive of church reform as a renewal of the international Church.

The Catholic cities

Scholars have long recognized that Tridentine reform in the decades before the Thirty Years' War had its greatest impact in urban areas.[112] The Catholic imperial cities in Southwest Germany, particularly the two most important ones, Rottweil and Überlingen, confirm this point.[113] Catholic reform in Rottweil follows a typical pattern. Threatened by a Protestant movement in the 1520s and 1530s, the clerical establishment almost collapsed in the 1540s and 1550s, as the

[112] Louis Châtellier, *Europe of the Devout. The Catholic Reformation and the Formation of a New Society* (Cambridge, 1989); Hsia, *The World of Catholic Renewal*, pp. 73–79, 117–118; R. Po-chia Hsia, *Social Discipline in the Reformation: Central Europe 1550–1750* (London and New York, 1989), ch. 5; Wilfried Enderle, "Die katholischen Reichsstädte im Zeitalter der Reformation und Konfessionsbildung" *Zeitschrift der Savigny-Stiftung für Rechtsgeschichte, Kanonistische Abteilung* 106 (1989), pp. 228–269.

[113] Wilfried Enderle, "Rottweil und die katholischen Reichsstädte im Südwesten" in Schindling and Ziegler (eds.), *Die Territorien des Reichs*, Vol. V *Der Südwesten*, pp. 215–230. The two largest Catholic cities, Freiburg im Breisgau and Constance, were Austrian territorial cities. The Catholic imperial cities were quite small and included, in addition to Rottweil and Überlingen, four cities in Upper Swabia (Buchau, Buchhorn, Pfullendorf, and Wangen), and three in the Ortenau (Gengenbach, Offenburg, and Zell am Harmersbach). There were two biconfessional cities in Upper Swabia, Ravensburg and Biberach. See Paul Warmbrunn, *Zwei Konfessionen in einer Stadt: Das Zusammenleben von Katholiken und Protestanten in den paritätischen Reichstädten Augsburg, Biberach, Ravensburg, und Dinkelsbühl von 1548–1648* (Wiesbaden, 1983).

number of Dominican monks declined and the town council found it difficult to hire competent Catholic priests.[114] Yet the presence of the imperial *Hofgericht* (Aulic Court) in Rottweil gave the city a special relationship with the Habsburgs. These ties, along with a pragmatic political analysis of Austrian power in the region, led the town council to suppress Protestantism and keep the city firmly Catholic.

After 1550, the town council and the local clergy led a reform of traditional Catholicism in Rottweil. *Pfarrer* Johannes Uhl was a key figure, serving the city for over forty years, beginning in 1559.[115] Uhl promoted the official acceptance of Canisius's catechism and a reform of the city's Latin school. In 1627 the *Rat* organized the founding of a Capuchin house in Rottweil. Underlying such Tridentine measures was the revival of traditional institutions and forms of devotion. Around 1600 the city's elite began once again to give financial support to the Dominican monastery. During the same period the wider population demonstrated growing enthusiasm for processions, pilgrimages, and the veneration of relics. Already before the Thirty Years' War then, Catholic reform in Rottweil involved both Tridentine reform and a "restoration" of traditional Catholicism.

The same pattern can be seen in the staunchly Catholic city of Überlingen on Lake Constance.[116] Although the town council's original reasons for keeping the city Catholic were political, Wilfried Enderle argues that beginning in the 1580s the *Rat* followed a conscious policy of *Konfessionsbildung* or confessional formation. Responding in part to the spirit of reform coming from Trent and from the bishops, and in part to the local desire to improve the quality of pastoral services, the city fathers reorganized the clergy into a chapter (*Stift*). The *Stift* brought the town's clergy together into a carefully regulated corporate body and allowed for improved clerical discipline and better use of financial resources. This reorganization improved clerical incomes and encouraged sons of prominent families to choose careers in the local clergy, which further improved the status of the clergy. By 1618, the secular clergy was firmly entrenched as part of the elite of Überlingen society. Parish priests in the countryside would only gain such status in the late seventeenth and the eighteenth centuries.

114 Enderle, "Rottweil und die katholischen Reichsstädte im Südwesten," pp. 221–225.

115 Enderle, "Rottweil und die katholischen Reichsstädte im Südwesten," pp. 224–225.

116 Enderle, "Rottweil und die katholischen Reichsstädte im Südwesten," pp. 221–229; Wilfried Enderle, *Konfessionsbildung und Ratsregiment in der katholischen Reichsstadt Überlingen (500–1618)* (Stuttgart, 1990), esp. pp. 377–384.

Enderle also demonstrates how the Überlinger *Rat* took a large role in promoting certain religious practices, including processions and the veneration of relics: "The *Rat* undertook a systematic restoration of late medieval devotional forms or [of devotions] neglected at least since the Reformation."[117] He further points out that Catholic reform in the city was "Janus-like" in that it included both the restoration of traditional types of devotion and an openness to religious innovation. Throughout this process, the town council was careful and moderate. On the one hand, it strongly supported elements of Tridentine reform, such as the reform of the clergy. On the other hand, Überlingen prevented the expansion of episcopal authority, and even increased its control of the clergy in the city. Even the reform of the clergy was traditional in its use of the corporate organization of the *Stift*. Church reform in the cities was based on local interests and concerns.

Monasteries and reform

Rudolf Reinhardt has shown how the Council of Trent caused a series of reforms in the Benedictine monastery of Weingarten.[118] A visitation of a papal nuncio from Lucerne and a new commitment to internal discipline and the traditional vows of poverty, chastity, and obedience, led to the election of Abbot Georg Wegelin in 1586. Having studied with the Jesuits at Dillingen, Wegelin promoted the expansion of Jesuit influence in his house, as well as in the other Benedictine abbeys of the region. Eventually, Wegelin's influence spread to all the important Southwest German monasteries, all of which sent monks to study with the Jesuits at Dillingen. Trent inspired German monasteries to reform monastic life, in part by demanding a renewed dedication to the rules of the orders, but also by inspiring monks to emulate the asceticism, rigorous educational standards, and religious commitment of the Jesuits. Monasteries such as Weingarten, Salem, St. Blasien, Ochsenhausen, and Rot an der Rot were not isolated from developments within the Catholic Church.[119]

Tridentine reforms were, however, problematic for all monasteries.

[117] Enderle, *Konfessionsbildung und Ratsregiment*, pp. 372–374, quote p. 372.

[118] Rudolf Reinhardt, *Restauration, Visitation, Inspiration. Die Reformbestrebungen in der Benediktinerabtei Weingarten von 1567 bis 1627* (Stuttgart, 1960), esp. pp. 5–30; Armgard von Reden-Dohna, "Weingarten und die schwäbischen Reichsklöster" in Schindling and Ziegler, (eds.), *Die Territorien des Reichs*, Vol. V *Der Südwesten*, pp. 246–247.

[119] Marc R. Forster, "Kirchenreform, katholische Konfessionalisierung und Dorfreligion," pp. 93–110.

The decrees of the Council certainly threatened the privileges and independence of the abbeys, especially by reinforcing episcopal authority. By emphasizing the centrality of pastoral care, Tridentine reform also marginalized monastic life in important ways. Indeed, monasteries and convents were very conscious of the threat posed by many of the institutional reforms envisaged by Trent.[120]

Monks and abbots in monasteries such as Salem responded ambiguously to Trent and Tridentine reforms for a number of other reasons as well. The emergence of new orders, especially the Jesuits, gave the old orders what Reinhardt has called "inferiority complexes."[121] The spirit of Tridentine reform, including the emphasis on centralization, discipline, and rationalization, could easily be applied within monasteries and even within monastic orders. But such attitudes were more difficult to reconcile with the local, regional, and particularistic traditions in German abbeys.[122] The Tridentine critique of secular activities of clerics also did not play well in Germany, where the monasteries had a political and constitutional role in the Reich, as well as a special place within the imperial Church. Ultimately, the culture and attitudes of monks and abbots in Salem did not mesh easily with the "spirit of the Counter-Reformation."[123]

The ambiguous attitude of abbots, abbesses, monks, and nuns toward Tridentine reforms deepened when they considered the reform of their parishes and of popular religion. Trent had assigned this project to the bishops, without clearly resolving the longstanding tension between episcopal authority and monastic privilege. Monastic establishments did not oppose the reform of the secular clergy or the effort to discipline and reform popular religion. On the other hand, they did resist any loss of income, or any increased costs reform might engender.

In general, abbots and monks were primarily concerned with moral and economic conditions inside the monasteries themselves. Their interest in religious practice and belief in the surrounding villages was limited. The example of St. Blasien is instructive. The reform charter produced at St. Blasien in 1594 consisted of 101 *puncta*, of which only six dealt in any

[120] Marc R. Forster, "The Elite and Popular Foundations of German Catholicism in the Age of Confessionalism: The Reichskirche" *Central European History* 26 (1994), pp. 311–325.

[121] Reinhardt, *Restauration, Visitation, Inspiration*, p. 23.

[122] Forster, "The Elite and Popular Foundations of German Catholicism," 311–325; Peter Hersche, "Intendierte Rückständigkeit: Zur Charakteristik des geistlichen Staates im alten Reich" in Georg Schmidt (ed.), *Stände und Gesellschaft im alten Reich* (Stuttgart, 1989).

[123] In 1599 the Imperial Knights complained about monastic reform, prompting the Clerical Council in Constance to point out that monasteries were religious institutions and did not belong to the nobles: EAF Ha 207, pp. 592–594.

direct way with the many parishes incorporated into the monastery.[124] There is no indication that the Cistercians at Salem, the Premonstratensians at Rot, or the Benedictines at Ochsenhausen were more interested in their parishes than were the Benedictines at St. Blasien.

The Cistercians at Salem supported reform efforts aimed at improving the personal morality and pastoral performance of parish priests. In 1594 the monastery issued a very Tridentine set of regulations governing the work of the assistant priest in Leutkirch, an incorporated parish of the monastery.[125] The *collaborator* or *Helfer* was ordered to assist the parish priest in all ways, including preaching, administering the sacraments, and reading mass. Monastic officials stressed that the priest was to behave in a dignified manner in public and in his home, should dress in priestly attire, and should only speak to people with a good reputation. The Cistercians were quite aware of the reform of the clergy and what it meant for parish priests.

Salem's support for reform was always held in check by the monastery's financial interests. A 1616 *Revers* (a kind of employment contract signed by a newly hired priest) contains two parts.[126] The first section outlines the monastery's expectations of the priest. He was to reside in the parish, serve the parish in person, and behave properly. If he converted to any "new sect" he was immediately to give up the parish. The second half of the *Revers* was designed to protect Salem's property in Leutkirch. The priest was forbidden to sell or alienate parish property in any way and could only rent land with the permission of monastic administrators. Most bluntly, the priest had to promise to be happy with his income, not to ask for an increase (an *Addition*), and to show proper "reverence" for Salem. The parish priest was an employee of the Cistercians.

Salem's policy of protecting its income worried episcopal officials and secular lords with an interest in improving the quality of the clergy. Austrian officials claimed that Salem had a lack of interest in "the wide planting of the correct God-pleasing religion."[127] Above all, reformers suspected the monastery of underpaying parish priests. In the 1620s, for example, episcopal officials were willing to allow Salem to incorporate the parish of Griesingen, but only if the priest there was given "an honorable upkeep." The bishop's men suspected that Salem would take the parish income for the monastery's use without paying the *Pfarrer* a sufficient income.

[124] Ott, "Die Benediktinerabtei St. Blasien," p. 184. [125] GLAK 98/3377.
[126] GLAK 98/3376. [127] GLAK 98/758. This was in 1640.

In the late sixteenth century, the Cistercians at Salem, as rulers of a principality of twenty-five villages, fourteen hamlets, and twenty-two isolated farms, also acted to reform the religious lives of their subjects.[128] Responding to complaints from parish priests, the monastery issued a church ordinance (*Kirchenordnung*) specifying fines for swearing and blasphemy, absence from church services, and failure to confess and take communion during Lent.[129] Much of the ordinance attempts to correct the behavior of the peasants during services. According to the priest in Leutkirch: "there are people in the community who when they want to come to church services arrive at the church when the service is half over, or they leave during the service and stand outside the church gossiping and laughing so that they bother those praying in the church yard . . ."[130] Such behavior was typical of Catholic villages in this period, as parishioners went in and out of the church, perhaps avoiding overly long sermons, but making sure they witnessed the elevation of the host. Salem's response, ordering fines for those who did not show proper devotion during services, was also typical.

Salem's interest in improving the religious behavior of its subjects reflects more than a concern for the villagers' salvation. The church ordinances included a clear assertion of the monastery's right to judge violations of these rules. As the *Niedergerichtsherr*, the holder of the right to adminster lower justice, Salem did in fact punish blasphemy, failure to attend church services, and other religious and moral crimes. The 1574 ordinance states that punishments are needed to end the "immorality that takes place in churches" and to improve the popular "fear of God." The monastic archive contains a listing of people punished by the *Niedergericht*, which was probably created to support Salem's claim to such legal jurisdiction.[131] The records show that monastic officials punished peasants for blasphemy throughout the sixteenth century, with no increase in cases after the onset of Tridentine reform. The records are

[128] On Salem: Erika Dillman and Hans-Jürgen Schulz, *Salem. Geschichte und Gegenwart* (Salem, 1989); Erika Dillman, *Stephan I. Fundamente des Barock. Salem an der Wende zum 18. Jahrhundert* (Tettnang, 1988); Erika Dillman, *Anselm II. Glanz und Ende eine Epoche. Eine Studie über den letzten großen Abt der Reichsabtei Salem* (Salem, 1987); Hermann Baier, "Die Stellung der Abtei Salem in Staat und Kirche" *FDA* 35 (1934). An early eighteenth-century description of Salem's secular holdings: GLAK 98/2315.

[129] GLAK 98/804. No date, although the handwriting indicates it is from the later sixteenth century. A very similar ordinance was issued in 1574: GLAK 98/3071.

[130] GLAK 98/804. Peasants in the Bishopric of Speyer also behaved this way: Forster, *The Counter-Reformation in the Villages*, p. 115.

[131] GLAK 98/3071.

very fragmentary for other crimes, but failure to attend church appears to have been punished more regularly in the 1580s and 1590s. In any case, Salem's enforcement of church ordinances was a way of asserting the monastery's legal jurisdiction and rights as a secular lord, as much as a sign of commitment to Tridentine reform.

Salem, St. Blasien, and Weingarten were the richest and most prestigious monastic institutions of Southwest Germany. Monks at these abbeys had international connections and met papal nuncios, high-ranking Jesuits, and leaders of their orders. Such monasteries were wealthy enough to send young monks to the best Catholic educational establishments, including the secondary schools and universities staffed by the Jesuits. Weingarten was even the leader of Tridentine-inspired monastic reform in the region and throughout Catholic Germany. Yet the abbots and monks of even these monasteries were reluctant to expend additional resources in the parishes they controlled. As secular lords, monasteries could discipline their subjects, as Salem did. As Catholic reformers, their engagement did not go far beyond the walls of the *Klöster*. In the less wealthy and less well-connected monasteries, and especially in the commandaries of the military orders, enthusiasm for Tridentine reform was even more restrained.

Smaller princes and lords could be engaged in religious matters. Wilhelm Heinrich von Truchsess, the brother of the Count von Waldburg, wrote several letters to episcopal officials outlining pastoral problems in the village of Wolfartsweiler. In 1614, von Truchsess claimed to have personally investigated villagers' complaints about the lack of a priest.[132] He then suggested a series of financial manipulations designed to raise money to pay a resident priest, claiming everything was arranged except for episcopal approval. The Clerical Council expressed concern that there were insufficient resources in Wolfartsweiler to support a resident priest. In this case, episcopal officials hesitated to institute the kind of project that should have been dear to the hearts of Tridentine reformers. The involvement of princes such as the von Waldburgs in church reform depended on the personal inclinations of individuals. Especially in the three or four decades after 1580, Catholic princes, even in deepest Swabia, developed a commitment to Catholic reform.

[132] HStASt. B466a/418 (two letters, from 1614 and 1616).

CONCLUSION

The Counter-Reformation episode came to an end during the Thirty Years' War, although Tridentine ideals remained influential into the eighteenth century. The war provided Catholic powers with little opportunity to convert conquered Protestant territories to the old faith, as occurred in Bohemia, the Upper Palatinate, or some areas on the Rhine. The destruction caused by marauding armies, however, ended efforts to reform the clergy, build a seminary, or reorganize parish finances. In the war's second and third decades, churches, parsonages, and other church buildings were destroyed or fell into ruin, priests fled the countryside and were not replaced, and monks and nuns abandoned monastic houses. When episcopal visitors returned to the countryside in the early 1650s, they found vacant benefices and ruined buildings.[133] Yet the visitations were also essential for rebuilding the infrastructure of religious life in the Catholic countryside. The ability of the Church to use its archives to reach back to a time before the war allowed it to reclaim resources that had been lost for decades. As the countryside recovered economically, the benefice system was recreated in the form that had existed before the war.

It was not quite so easy to restore the reforming spirit that had driven confessionalizers and Tridentine reformers in the period after the Council of Trent. For the secular and clerical Catholic elite, the Counter-Reformation period had been a time of great ambitions and real militancy. After 1650 militancy gave way in Southwest Germany to a sense of triumph, which manifested itself in the massive Baroque building program undertaken by bishops, monasteries, and secular princes. Tridentine reform did not disappear, but it lost its central place for most church leaders.

Part of the change in tone was a result of the disaster of the Thirty Years' War, which gave a bad name to militancy in the name of religion. Furthermore, Tridentine reform and confessionalization had not been very successful. There are several reasons for this. In one sense, church reformers had not been aggressive or organized enough. Neither the Jesuits nor the Capuchins were directly active in the region before 1620. The Jesuits, in particular, might have stoked the fires of militancy as they had done in Bavaria, Westphalia, and Franconia. Yet such a scenario was unlikely, given the strength of traditional ecclesiastical institutions

[133] For example, the report from the Linzgau in 1651: EAF Ha 70, pp. 442r–462r.

in the Southwest. In fact, the Cathedral Chapter in Constance was an important force in obstructing the founding of a Jesuit house in Constance.

The creation of a Jesuit college in Constance had also been delayed for decades until 1604 by disputes between the Bishop of Constance and the Austrians.[134] Such conflicts were an integral part of Catholic politics in this part of Germany. Episcopal officials understood Tridentine reform as an opportunity to restore episcopal jurisdiction, while Austrian officials saw it as a chance to strengthen the state. Such different aims led to disputes with the Austrians and with powerful ecclesiastical institutions. As a result, Church–state relations were always tense, and secular and ecclesiastical officials only sporadically cooperated to institute reform policies.

Church reform was in any case sporadic and uneven. Episcopal policy depended on the personality and commitment of individual bishops and their officials. The Clerical Council did give reform an institutional home, but few other Tridentine institutions were created. Some princes, town councils, and monasteries in this politically fragmented region consistently pursued church reform, but others did so only sporadically, and some had little or no interest in reforming the clergy or "improving" popular religion.

What is striking about the Counter-Reformation is the supreme confidence of all authorities that reform from above would change religious practice at all levels of society. From this hierarchical and elitist perspective, decrees from above would lead to a reform of the clergy. On fairly short notice this reformed clergy would bring their loyal and obedient parishioners to a more disciplined and orderly religious practice. Needless to say, such a program was unrealistic, and it is not hard to demonstrate that church reformers failed to realize it.

Whatever its realistic chances for complete success, just such a program was instituted by Catholic reformers in Southwest Germany, as elsewhere in Germany. Much of the clerical elite in fact embraced Tridentine reform, seeing themselves as part of what Louis Châtellier has called "The Europe of the Devout."[135] Clergymen, whether monks or secular priests, gave up their concubines, increasingly studied with the Jesuits, and took up their pastoral duties with a new vigor. Before the 1620s these "new priests" were scattered across Southwest Germany, but the religion of the people of the villages and hamlets was not

[134] Zimmermann, *Rekatholisierung, Konfessionalisierung und Ratsregiment* pp. 134–154.
[135] Louis Châtellier, *Europe of the Devout.*

Tridentine. As the people of Burkheim said, "It is not up to him [the parish priest] to bring new practices into the church, the church is ours, not his."

After 1650, many churchmen who had frequent contact with the Catholic population, especially parish priests, Jesuit fathers, and Capuchin friars, lost confidence in the effectiveness of decrees and ordinances to change religious practice. Priests who took the Tridentine concern for pastoral care seriously struggled to accommodate to popular needs and desires. At the same time, the everyday experience of the local clergy influenced their reception of reform measures and the way in which they sought to implement them in the villages and towns.[136] Meanwhile, peasants and townspeople were not passive recipients of new ideas, but remained adamant about the kinds of practices, devotions, and services they wanted. As the Church became more receptive of popular initiative, there developed increased religious innovation, popular enthusiasm, and churchliness. After 1650, the population developed its Catholic identity in the context of the flowering of Baroque Catholicism.

[136] This could be called the beginning of what Châtellier has dubbed "the religion of the poor." Louis Châtellier, *La Religion des pauvres: les missions rurales en Europe et la formation du catholicisme moderne, XVIe–XIXe siècles* (Paris, 1993).

CHAPTER 2

The sacral landscape and pilgrimage piety

It is possible to identify a number of fundamental characteristics of popular religious practice in the Catholic villages and towns of Southwest Germany. Throughout the early modern period, but particularly in the century after 1650, popular Catholicism centered around public and often dramatic practices, especially pilgrimage, processions, and the festivals of the liturgical year, many of which were associated with the immensely popular cult of the Virgin Mary. This dramatic religious style, which we tend to associate with Baroque Catholicism, was complemented by a commitment to regular daily and weekly church services which fed the popular appetite for the other central cult, that of the Eucharist.

Much of popular Catholicism remained communal and public. In the eighteenth century there was, however, a trend toward more individual and private religious devotion. Such devotions were part of pilgrimage piety, included in regular parish services, and could be found within confraternities. The prayers of the Rosary, most often practiced by women in small groups or individually, spread quickly and widely in this part of Germany and served as a kind of benchmark of more individualized devotional practices.

Despite the growing popularity of individual devotional practices, which were generally promoted by the clergy, popular Catholicism never succumbed to the other efforts by lay and clerical elites to regularize, systematize, and simplify religious practice. Instead, Catholic practice in Southwest Germany became ever more diverse and elaborate after 1650. Peasants and townspeople built more churches and chapels, they went on new pilgrimages, supported additional holidays and new saints, embraced additional devotions, and attended more frequent church services. When "Josephine" and "enlightened" reformers complained in the late eighteenth century about the great quantity of church services and the time people needed to participate in them, they were not necessarily exaggerating.

The Catholic people of Southwest Germany also practiced their religion in a series of concrete places. Regular services, communal practices, and individual devotions took place in parish churches, local chapels, and monasteries and convents, at pilgrimage shrines and at roadside crosses. A dense network of sacred buildings and sites already covered the countryside in the sixteenth century, and between 1650 and 1750 this complex became increasingly dispersed, complicated, and diverse.

The buildings and sites literally entrenched Catholicism in the landscape and further linked the Church to the traditional religion of the people who lived there.[1] Simultaneously, the sacred spaces helped to perpetuate and strengthen the local character of Catholicism. Sacred places were, however, never entirely local in character. Parish churches, for example, gained their status partly from a bishop and from the Church itself, and partly from their saintly patrons. Furthermore, a parish church was linked, both historically and in practice, with its ecclesiastical patron, whether the bishop, a monastery, or a secular lord. Chapels might be more strictly local, but they were also dedicated to a saint, or more often Mary, and thus depended on the wider context for meaning. Shrines could also be very local, but many of them became known in a wide range of villages in the region, and some, like Triberg, Birnau, or Todtmoos, became shrines of regional significance.[2] Sacred places, then, reflected the dynamic tension between local religion, regional Catholicism, and the international Church.

The sacral landscape of Southwest Germany evolved during the early modern period. New churches and chapels were built, while others were abandoned. New pilgrimage shrines became popular and ancient sites were revived, while other sites were forgotten and unused. This evolution was not uniform, however. The parochial structure, for example, was remarkably stable, as was the number of monasteries in the region. The number of chapels and shrines varied across the period, with a large

[1] William Christian, *Local Religion in Sixteenth-Century Spain* (Princeton, 1981); Marie-Hélène Froeschlé-Chopard, *Espace et Sacré en Provence (XVIe–XXe siècle)*(Paris, 1994).

[2] Shrines: Lionel Rothkrug, "Popular Religion and Holy Shrines. Their Influence on the Origins of the German Reformation and their Role in German Cultural Development" in James Obelkevich (ed.), *Religion and the People, 800–1700* (Chapel Hill, 1979); Rothkrug, "Holy Shrines, Religious Dissonance, and Satan in the Origins of the German Reformation" *Historical Reflections/Réflexions Historiques* 14 (1987), pp. 143–286; Rothkrug, "German Holiness and Western Sanctity in Medieval and Modern History" *Historical Reflections/Réflexions Historiques* 15 (1988), pp. 161–249; Philip Soergel, *Wondrous in His Saints. Counter-Reformation Propaganda in Bavaria* (Berkeley, 1993).

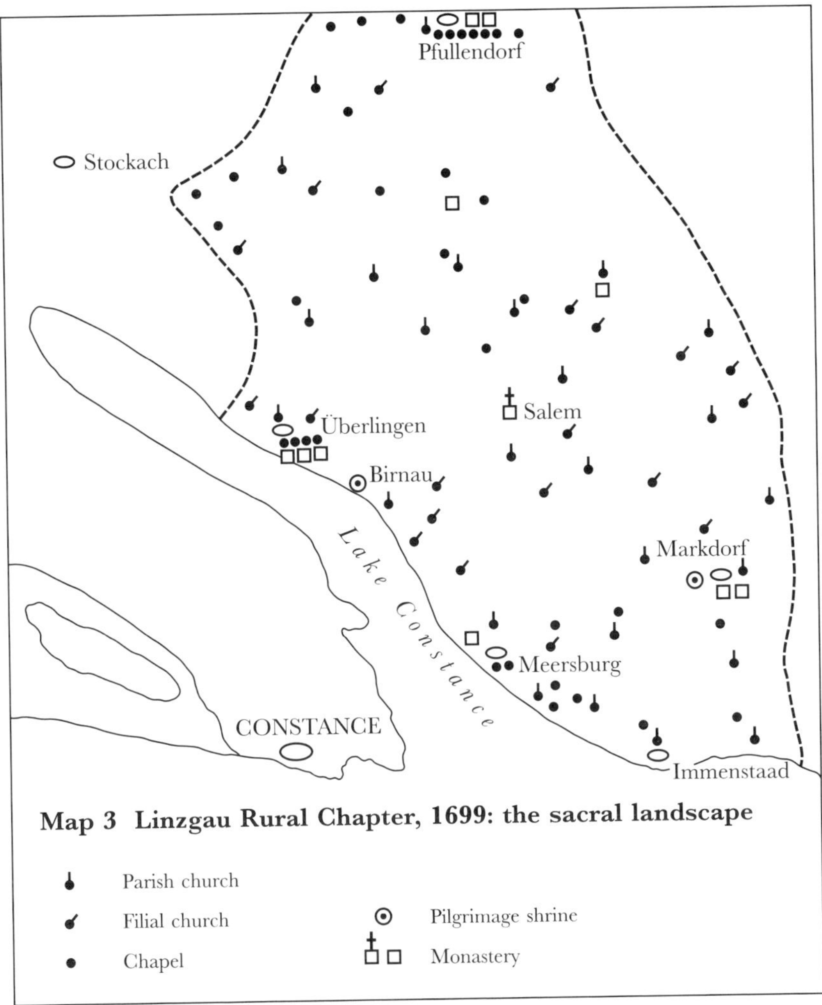

Map 3 Linzgau Rural Chapter, 1699: the sacral landscape

number of new ones founded and built in the sixty to seventy years after 1680. Significantly, the kinds of sacred sites did not change dramatically. A framework that was in place in the sixteenth century was expanded and made more detailed and diverse over time, but few new forms were added. This stability contributed to the traditional nature of local Catholicism. The importance of "ancient" churches, chapels, and sites reinforced the autonomy of popular religion and undermined the sporadic efforts of church reformers to regularize and confine religious practice.[3]

A discussion of the sacral landscape of any Catholic region cannot easily be detached from a discussion of the religious practices that occurred there. Indeed, an analysis of sites and buildings magnifies the ways in which the practices and places played off and influenced each other. This was particularly the case for Catholicism in the early modern period, since many important ceremonies and devotions occurred outside church buildings themselves. If the Church could, to some extent, prescribe proper religious practice, it neither could nor wished to prevent believers from taking these practices into the villages, up local mountainsides, or to isolated chapels. This was, then, one of the ways in which the practices and beliefs of an international institution maintained ties to local and popular religion.

THE SACRAL LANDSCAPE

Parish churches

The number of parish churches in Southwest Germany changed very little between the late sixteenth and the early eighteenth centuries. Episcopal visitation reports from various regions of the Bishopric of Constance show that few new parishes were added before 1700 (see table 2.1). More general overviews of sacred sites are scarce in Southwest German sources. Episcopal visitation reports, for example, focused on the persons of the priests and on the financial resources of the parishes, rather than on the buildings. The broadest trends, however, are clear. We know, for example, that many parish churches were destroyed during the Thirty Years' War. The parish church at Assmanshardt was destroyed in the 1630s and had still not been rebuilt in 1661.[4] This delay was unusual, for village communes and parish patrons gave priority to repairing parish churches in the 1650s. In 1651 the finances of the parish of Siggingen were, according to the episcopal visitor, in a miserable state. Still, even though there had been no resident priest for thirteen years, the church itself was in reasonable condition, although the parsonage was falling down.[5] Inhabitants of villages with parish churches apparently worked to keep them in good repair.

[3] Froeschlé-Chopard, *Espace et Sacré en Provence*, p. 153.
[4] EAF Ha 63, p. 59.
[5] EAF Ha 70, p. 454v.

Table 2.1. *Number of parishes in each rural chapter, Bishopric of Constance*

Rural Chapter of Biberach[a]		Rural Chapter of Linzgau[b]		Rural Chapter of Stockach[c]		Rural Chapter of Waldshut[d]	
Year	No.	Year	No.	Year	No.	Year	No.
1583	17	1620	23	1590	26	1608	10
1588	17	1661	23	1665	23	1681	14
1625	17	1699	25	1685	28	1695	15
1640	17			1708	30		
1661	17						
1696	18						

Sources: [a] EAF Ha 63, pp. 7–9, 13–17, 19–28, 37–41, 42–48, 51–72, 185–201, 267–270, 279–281.
[b] EAF Ha 70, pp. 233r–265r, 269r–292v, 555r–571v. Hermann Schmid, "Die Statuten des Landkapitels Linzgau von 1699 als historisch-statistisch-topographische Quelle" *FDA* 111 (1991), pp. 194–198.
[c] EAF A1/725.
[d] EAF Ha 62, pp. 362r–369v; EAF Ha 78, pp. 249v, 283r–288v, 343r–345v. The smaller number in 1608 reflects the fact that the monastery of St. Blasien refused to allow episcopal officials to investigate the parishes served by its monks.

The network of parish churches, quite dense in the Rhine valley, Upper Swabia, and around Lake Constance, more scattered in the mountains, provided a basic structure of sacred sites. Episcopal authorities also worked to expand the parishes' administrative importance. To be sure, parish churches, along with the monasteries, had status as the oldest sacred sites in the region. Patron saints such as St. Martin, St. Germanus, St. Vedastus, St. Ulrich, and St. Afra even linked some parish churches to the original christianization of the region.[6] Ancient parishes sometimes benefitted from the financial donations of many generations of parishioners. The parish of Seefelden, for example, dated from the twelfth century, but by the seventeenth century few parishioners lived near the church. The parish, however, was huge, encompassing at least eight villages, and providing a nice income for the parish priest. The parish church also reflected the wealth of the parish and in 1620 the episcopal visitors commented enthusiastically on its beauty.[7]

The parish structure, then, was quite old and very stable. There were a number of reasons for this stability, and for the very slow growth in the number of parish churches. Monasteries, military orders, and other ecclesiastical institutions were invariably unwilling to support the creation of new parishes, despite constant pressure from rural communes for more churches and priests. Furthermore, there were few large secular states engaged in organizing a more developed parish system, and wartime disruption hindered major reforms. Villagers, on the other hand, clearly wanted more churches, as shown by their enthusiastic response in the 1770s and 1780s to the efforts of Josephine reformers to fund more parishes.[8] Village communes and the rural population did not, however, privilege the parish church either as a sacred site or as a site for services. The population considered chapels and shrines acceptable, and sometimes preferable, alternatives.

[6] *Zu Fuss, zu Pferd . . . Wallfahrten im Kreis Ravensburg* (Biberach, 1990), p. 8. See also Froeschlé-Chopard, *Espace et Sacré en Provence*, p. 87.

[7] Hermann Schmid, "Aus der älteren Geschichte der Pfarrei Seefelden. Ein Überblick unter besonderer Berücksichtigung des Pfarrurbars von 1629" *FDA* 111 (1991), pp. 171–185; EAF Ha 70, 257v–258v.

[8] Some examples: GLAK 79/825, no. 26, no. 92 Survey of 1777; 79/823.

Chapels

Rural chapels were an important part of the sacral landscape of Southwest Germany, as they were everywhere in Catholic Europe.[9] In fact, because of the rigidity of the parish structure, many villages did not have their own parish church. As a consequence, chapels were often the primary locus of religious practice and performed an important role in linking local communities to the Church. Chapels were frequently administered by local communities, and church officials often had only a shaky grasp of their number, location, and importance. In this sense, as in a number of others, chapels were closer to popular religion than the parish churches.

Parish churches comprised somewhat less than half of the churches in Southwest Germany, especially in the eighteenth century. This is borne out for those places where officials conducted extensive and apparently complete investigations. Linzgau appears to have been especially well equipped with chapels. In 1699, officials counted twenty-five parish churches, twenty-four filial churches, twenty-nine rural chapels and fourteen "urban" chapels. In the Rural Chapter of Stockach in 1708, episcopal visitors found thirty parishes and sixty consecrated (*consecratas*) churches and chapels. There were fewer sacred sites in the less populated mountains. In Hauenstein episcopal visitors identified eight parishes, one filial parish, and six chapels. When the Austrian government undertook a detailed survey of all religious establishments in its territory in the 1770s and 1780s, it found 132 filial churches and chapels.[10]

By the mid-eighteenth century, Southwest Germany was covered with an extensive and diverse network of filial churches and chapels. The filial churches often resembled parish churches, were located in the center of villages, and filled many of the roles of a parish church. Filial churches also shared attributes of chapels, especially in that many of them were managed, repaired, and decorated by village communities. Indeed, most filial churches were originally built as chapels and grew in importance along with the village around them.

[9] Christian, *Local Religion in Sixteenth Century Spain*, esp. ch. 3. See also Sara T. Nalle, *God in La Mancha. Religious Reform and the People of Cuenca, 1500–1650* (Baltimore, 1992), pp. 154–156, 174–179.

[10] Linzgau 1699: Schmid, "Die Statuten des Landkapitels Linzgau von 1699 als historisch-statistisch-topographische Quelle" *FDA* 111 (1991), pp. 194–198. The "urban chapels" were located in the small cities of Überlingen, Pfullendorf, and Meersburg. Stockach 1708: EAF A1/725. Visitation of 1608: EAF Ha 62, pp. 362r–369v. The numbers are similar for 1681 and 1685: Ha 78, pp. 249v, 283r–288v, 343r–345v. 1780s: GLAK 79/837.

Chapels came in all sorts of sizes and shapes.[11] Many were small and poorly equipped. The chapel at Schmidhofen had no property or income, and was the setting for only one Mass a year. In 1781, it was reported that the St. George Chapel at Kenzingen had no income and, as far as anyone knew, had never possessed any property. In the Austrian *Amt* of Altdorf, the villages of Baind and Sulbach each had a small unendowed chapel where Mass could be said. The chapel in nearby Hindermoos was even more modest and was not outfitted, large enough, or properly consecrated to be a setting for Mass. The chapel did, however, have a bell "which could be rung." The local village communes maintained all three chapels.[12]

Many chapels were located outside villages. As names such as *Kapelle St. Anton auf dem Schönenberg* and *Unsere Liebe Frau auf den Totnauberg* attest, chapels were often built on hillsides on the edges of parishes. Their isolated locations made them ideal for private devotion, or as alternative places for the faithful to attend Mass on special occasions. Church officials and villagers also appreciated the way in which hillside chapels could be seen. One parish priest, for example, spoke approvingly of the distance from which one could see the proposed site for a chapel in Riedböhringen.[13]

Many chapels traced their beginnings to a communal or individual vow. In Herlazhofen, the commune had built a small "field chapel" (*Veldkapellen*), dedicated to Saints John and Paul.[14] The villagers went in procession from the village to the chapel every fourteen days in the summer, "in order to ward off thunderstorms," and to ask for protection from damaging hail. In Spaichingen in 1713 a miller vowed to build a new chapel, causing the episcopal authorities to wonder whether he had enough resources to provide a permanent endowment. Still other chapels were built at the initiative of local princes and nobles, as was the chapel in Henighofen, proposed in 1711 by the Count of Montfort.[15]

The majority of chapels had some sort of endowment. In many cases it was quite modest. The chapel in the village of Giesenweiler (in the Austrian *Amt* of Bergatreute) had an annual income of 1fl. A local official (*Amtmann*) had endowed the chapel in Tauttenhofen, apparently in a modest way. By contrast, the *Laienkapelle* in Bergatreute, founded, like

[11] The *Kurzkataloge der volkstümlichen Kult- und Andachtsstätten der Erzdiözese Freiburg und der Diözesen Limburg, Mainz, Rottenburg-Stuttgart und Speyer* (Würzburg, 1982) lists 356 *Kult- und Andachtsstätten* ("places of cults and devotions") for the contemporary Diocese of Freiburg, and 222 for the Diocese of Rottenburg-Stuttgart. These two modern dioceses encompass approximately the area of this study. A vast majority of the sites listed were in place in the early modern period.

[12] GLAK 79/837; HStASt. B61/199.

[13] EAF Ha 218, pp. 382–383 (1712).

[14] HStASt. B61/199; HStASt. B61/213.

[15] EAF Ha 218, pp. 214–217, 402–403, 458.

Table 2.2 *Summary of ecclesiastical property, debts, income, and expenses (in Gulden) in the Austrian Landschaften of Frickthal, Möhlinbach, and Rheinthal, 1781*

In Gulden	Property	Debts	Income	Expenses
Landschaft Frickthal				
Frick, parish	>17,907	>1,347	>806	>689
Giph chapel	>535		>27	>26
Herznach, parish	>20,407		>898	>706
Zeyhen Kapelle	>122		>5	>6
Wölflinswihl, parish	>9,498		>424	>355
Hurnussen chapel	>128		>6	>6
Weittnau, parish	>4,952	>500	>234	>221
Eiken, parish	>5,430		>255	>204
Münchwilen chapel	>906		>356	>187
Landschaft Möhlinbach				
Möhlin, parish	>10,475		>503	>415
Chapel in Möhlin	>762		>39	>30
Ayburg chapel	>502		>25	>18
Wallbach chapel	>583		>28	>26
Helliken chapel	>488		>24	>19
Zeiningen, parish	>7,429	>1,454	>347	>592
Magden, parish	>4,952		>225	>202
Augst, parish	>6,033	375	>280	>422
Landschaft Rheinthal				
Wyhlen, parish	>3,744		>176	>160
Herthen, parish	>6,722		>320	>230
Chapel in Herthen	>331		>16	>11
Degerfelden chapel	>1,082		>51	>29
Eichsel, parish	>8,853	>91	>436	>328
Miniselen, parish	>20,460	>134	>875	>769
Filial Nordschwaben	>559	>172	>26	>60
Nollingen, parish	>4,881	>72	>236	>246
Wannbach, parish	>894	>32	>45	>52

Source: GLAK 79/837.

many chapels, by the *Gemeinde*, had an annual income of over 115fl., with expenses of around 7fl. The St. Anthony Chapel in the town of Laufenburg had an annual income of over 86fl., with expenses of about 72fl.[16] Taking the example of one Austrian-governed district, table 2.2 gives some indication of the relationship between the resources of parish

[16] HStASt. B61/213; HStASt. B61/199; GLAK 79/837.

churches and the endowments of chapels. As a rule, parish churches had larger endowments and higher expenses, but chapels could be blessed with considerable resources.

By the later eighteenth century Southwest Germany was covered with a dense network of churches and chapels. Even compact parishes in the Rhine valley had several churches. In 1781, for example, the parish of Scherzingen contained a parish church, a filial church, two other churches (probably chapels), and the chapel "*auf der schwarzen Eich.*" In Kenzingen there were a parish church and two smaller churches. The appropriately named Kirchhofen had a parish church and three chapels, dedicated to Mary, St. Anton, and St. Nicolaus. Some larger parishes had even more chapels. The density of chapels more closely resembles sixteenth-century Spain or seventeenth-century Provence than it does the neighboring Bishopric of Speyer in this period.[17]

The picture so far of the place of chapels in the sacral landscape of Southwest Germany is a static one, based on mid-eighteenth-century sources. In fact, of course, the religious buildings and locations existing in the 1760s, 1770s and 1780s had been put in place in the previous centuries. If the administrative rigidity of the Catholic Church tended to create stability in the parish structure, population changes, frequent warfare, and, above all, the religious needs of the population made for constant building, destruction, and reconstruction of chapels and filial churches.

Many chapels and other smaller ecclesiastical buildings (and their attached benefices) fell into disuse or were abandoned in the sixteenth century. The Protestant critique of shrines, saints, and pilgrimage certainly contributed to this trend, as did the widespread disorganization of the Church.[18] A 1593 report from the Austrian County of Hohenberg laments that rural chapels were "vacant," that is, without priests, and that local officials had diverted the endowments for the salaries of schoolteachers and organists.[19] It is not clear how this development affected the chapel buildings themselves, though the diversion of funds must have hindered their maintenance. Other chapels, especially those associated with local pilgrimages, sometimes disappeared in the second half of the sixteenth century. The *Severinskappelle* in Buchholz was built

[17] GLAK 79/837. Christian, *Local Religion in Sixteenth Century Spain*: Froeschlé-Chopard, *Espace et Sacré en Provence*; Marc R. Forster, *The Counter-Reformation in the Villages. Religion and Reform in the Bishopric of Speyer, 1560–1720* (Ithaca and London, 1992).

[18] See Soergel, *Wondrous in His Saints*, ch. 2, for discussion of the decline of pilgrimage and abandonment of shrines.

[19] HStASt. B37a/15.

before 952 and rebuilt in 1497. In the late fourteenth century it became a pilgrimage destination, but by 1575 the pilgrims had stopped coming.[20] Chapels were also destroyed during the Thirty Years' War. In 1656 the chapel in Hummertsried had been in ruins since the war, and it took the commune eighty years to convince the Abbey of Rot an der Rot to help pay for repairs. Similarly, the St. Anna Chapel in Uttenweiler, founded in 1621, was destroyed in the war and only repaired in the early eighteenth century.[21] The crisis of the sixteenth century and the destruction of the Thirty Years' War hindered any extensive building programs. After 1650, and especially after 1700, however, the sacred landscape of the region was extended and elaborated.

Most commonly, the late medieval chapels and local shrines that had fallen into disuse and disrepair in the sixteenth century were rebuilt and revived after 1650. The church and shrine at Laiz were originally built in the twelfth century and rebuilt in 1426. Then, after 1650, they were redecorated and rebuilt several times, receiving a new altar in 1667, expanding in 1687, and undergoing a major reconstruction in 1765–1768. Still other chapels were built new. The *Wallfahrtskapelle auf dem Giersberg*, near Kirchzarten, was built between 1700 and 1710 and then rebuilt in 1737.[22] One could easily multiply the examples of this major building program from all across Southwest Germany.

The initiative for building chapels often came from the villagers themselves. A certain Blasi Vetscher, from Hof bey Illwangen, built a chapel near his farm in the early eighteenth century.[23] The inhabitants of Mühlhausen in Upper Swabia were very attached to their chapel, which from the 1630s was without a resident priest. In 1678 the commune negotiated an agreement with the Abbey of Rot to maintain the chapel and its benefice, an agreement that the two parties renegotiated in 1713.[24] At other times ecclesiastical authorities took the initiative in constructing new chapels. In 1741 the Abbot of Rot was distressed to see the poor condition of the chapel at Eichenberg, which had originally been built by the villagers. The abbot, expressing an attitude typical of eighteenth-century churchmen, offered not only to contribute to the necessary repairs, " . . . but also to have it decorated on the inside, [so as to encourage] greater devotion." The abbot's enthusiasm for the chapel

[20] Buchholz: *Kurzkataloge der volkstümlichen Kult- und Andachtsstätten*, p. 22 (# 1.038).

[21] HStASt. B486/483: EAF Ha 218, pp. 319–320. Other examples of ruined chapels: EAF Ha 63, p. 46 (St. Mauritius Chapel, Schemmerberg) and *Kurzkataloge der volkstümlichen Kult- und Andachtsstätten*, p.24 (# 1.047).

[22] *Kurzkataloge der volkstümlichen Kult- und Andachtsstätten*, pp. 41 (# 1.142), 42 (# 1.149).

[23] GLAK 61/13465, pp.228–230.

[24] HStASt. B486/510.

was, however, limited, in that he carefully avoided committing the abbey to any long-term obligations. When repairs were needed again in the 1780s, the *Gemeinde* alone paid.[25]

Church patrons, such as the military orders, generally resisted building chapels. The Teutonic Knights at Mainau were skeptical about the project of the village of Egg to rebuild the "ruinous" St. Joseph Chapel, and seemed downright queasy about the suggestion that the chapel might even need to " . . . be rebuilt from the foundation up."[26] As a general rule, most chapels were repaired or built upon the urging of and with the financial contribution of the population. In the mid-eighteenth century, however, many of the monasteries willingly contributed to the construction of chapels. This willingness of course reflected the abbots' and abbesses' desire to demonstrate power, wealth, piety, and artistic good taste. At the same time, however, the combined efforts of people and abbey, as in the case of Eichenberg, indicate a religious culture, a kind of local Catholicism, shared by prelates and the population.

Shrines, roadside crosses, and holy trees

Churches and chapels were the most obvious sacred sites in any early modern landscape. More difficult to locate in the sources, but of considerable importance to the population, were a variety of small, unofficial sacred places. These included obscure local shrines, roadside crucifixes and crosses, statues of saints, and even trees and springs credited with healing powers.[27] These sites, perhaps even more than the chapels, escaped the oversight of the official Church; at the same time they provided a vital bond between the people in their village, and the official cult.

Many roadside crucifixes, crosses, and statues were both sites of local devotion and markers for pilgrims and processions headed to the larger shrines of the region. Thus the roadside cross at Gwigg had a picture of the *Gnadenbild* from Bergatreute, and indicated the road to this important shrine. On the other hand, a votive picture near Waldsee was dedicated to St. Walpurga and did not refer to any particular shrine.[28] Similarly, in the late seventeenth century, a Herr Stegelin from Owingen had a painting of the crucifixion posted along the road between Owingen and Pfaffenhausen. He also provided a small fund for the

[25] HStASt. B486/272. [26] GLAK 93/252.
[27] *Zu Fuss, zu Pferd . . . Wallfahrten im Kreis Ravensburg*, p. 50.
[28] *Zu Fuss, zu Pferd . . . Wallfahrten im Kreis Ravensburg*, p. 52–53.

upkeep of the picture. In 1701, Stegelin's grandson, Johan Stegelin, the *Statthalter* and *Amman* (i.e. *Amtmann*) in Owingen, provided an additional donation of 40fl. for the upkeep of this *Strassenbild*. Between 1706 and 1722 the endowment was managed by the monastery of Salem. It received regular donations of 1–2fl. a year from people worshipping there and earned interest on the capital. During these years, the managers of the fund spent 25fl. on various repairs, including building a new roof over the painting and hiring a painter to come and repaint the picture.[29] This roadside picture, like many crucifixes, was probably unknown to all except those who passed by it, yet it was sufficiently beloved that a family of important villagers provided for it financially.

Crosses, crucifixes, and statues were ubiquitous. There were crosses on all the routes out of Mettenberg (near Biberach), on the roads to Laupertshausen, Ellmansweill, and Warthausen.[30] There were statues and paintings of traditional saints, such as St. Walpurga near Waldsee, and of new "Counter-Reformation saints," such as St. John of Nepomuk, who could be found on a bridge between Birndorf and Görwihl and in the fields outside Oggelshausen.[31] Crucifixes and statues of saints were objects of devotion, but they were also a mark of Catholic identity. They may have had a special resonance in places were Catholics came into direct contact with Protestants and they often marked the boundaries between Catholic and Protestant villages.[32]

As one moves through the hierarchy of sacred spaces, from large man-made structures, such as monasteries, cathedrals, and parish churches, to smaller buildings (chapels and shrines), to crucifixes and

[29] GLAK 98/3512. See also GLAK 61/13463, pp. 309r–v.

[30] EAF A1/1418, *Landkapitel* Biberach. On crosses, see also Jakob Ebner, *Aus der Geschichte des Hausensteiner Dorfes Unteralpfen*, 2nd edn (Karlsruhe, n.d.) (hereafter Ebner, *Unteralpfen*), p. 124.

[31] Jakob Ebner, *Aus der Geschichte der Ortschaften der Pfarrei Birndorf (bei Waldshut am Hochrhein)* (Karlsruhe, 1938) (hereafter Ebner, *Birndorf*), p. 114; Ebner, *Geschichte der Pfarrei Görwihl im Hotzenwald* (Wanger, 1953) (hereafter Ebner, *Görwihl*), p. 118. It is not clear whether there was one Nepomuk statue or two. Ebner says that the Görwihler went on procession to a statue on the "Tiefensteiner Brücke," while the Birndorfer went to the "Steinbacher Brücke." Bridges were a favored location for Nepomuk, who was martyred by being thrown off a bridge in Prague. Oggelshausen: EAF A1/1418, *Landkapitel* Biberach.

[32] Compare Forster, *The Counter-Reformation in the Villages*; Etienne François, *Die unsichtbare Grenze. Protestanten und Katholiken in Augsburg, 1648–1806* (Sigmaringen, 1991); Peter Zschunke, *Konfession und Alltag in Oppenheim. Beiträge zue Geschichte von Bevölkerung und Gesellschaft einer gemischtkonfessionellen Kleinstadt in der frühen Neuzeit* (Wiesbaden, 1984); Paul Warmbrunn, *Zwei Konfessionen in einer Stadt: Das Zusammenleben von Katholiken und Protestanten in den paritätischen Reichstädten Augsburg, Biberach, Ravensburg, und Dinkelsbühl von 1548–1648* (Wiesbaden, 1983). Confessional conflict was important in the Breisgau and the Rhine valley, where there were significant Protestant territories, as well as in the region of the Austrian County of Hohenberg, which was surrounded by Protestant Württemberg.

statues under an open sky, one finally reaches a whole category of "natural" sites of sacred significance. These sites included wells, springs, and trees that were considered to have special powers. The most famous and important of these sites became important shrines and a chapel or church was built. Others remained sites for local devotion and eventually disappeared from view.

A number of important Southwest German shrines began as holy trees. The most famous of these was *Unser Liebe Frau in der Tanne zu Triberg*, which first became popular in the 1640s, when a man found a picture of Mary painted on parchment and embedded in a tree.[33] Trees were the focus of several other shrines. Around 1700, a young shepherd found a picture of Mary in a tree on the Giersberg near Kirchzarten. Ten years later, as thanks to Mary for saving them from cattle disease, the Kirchzartner built a wooden chapel next to the tree to house the picture. The shrine at Ottersweier is known as *Maria Linden* because of the grove of linden trees that surround the chapel with its miraculous statue of Mary. The *Bildeich-Kapelle* at Esseratsweiler was built in 1748 on the site of an oak tree with an attached statue of Mary. As Kristiane Schmalfeldt points out in reference to Triberg, the icon and the trees were inseparable; the cult of Mary was part of nature and fixed (quite literally) in the local landscape.[34]

Springs and wells could have sacred significance as well. An interesting example is the *Verenabrunnen* near the important Marian shrine of Engelwies.[35] The legend is that the spring was created when a shepherd, fearing that he and his flock would die of thirst, had his prayers answered by Mary and St. Verena, who sprinkled water, producing a new spring. A medieval chapel at the site was destroyed in the fifteenth century and devotions there took place in open air until the nineteenth century. Another holy spring was located near the monastery and shrine in St. Ulrich. In 1771 an *Ulrichs-Brunnenkapelle* was built over the spring and was more closely integrated into existing devotions to the saint.[36] Springs and wells, then, often supplemented existing sacred sites; one might argue that they gave (fairly obscure) saints such as

[33] On Triberg: Kristiane Schmalfeldt, "Sub tuum praesidium confugimus. Unser Liebe Frau in der Tanne zu Triberg" *FDA* 108 (1988), pp. 1–302. See also Hermann Brommer (ed.), *Wallfahrten im Bistum Freiburg* (Munich and Zurich, 1990), pp. 173–177.

[34] Brommer (ed.), *Wallfahrten im Bistum Freiburg*, pp. 67–69, 123–124; *Zu Fuss, zu Pferd . . . Wallfahrten im Kreis Ravensburg*, pp. 158–159; Schmalfeldt, "Sub tuum praesidium confugimus" *FDA* 108 (1988), pp. 43–44. Other examples of holy trees: EAF Ha 216, p. 184.

[35] Brommer (ed.), *Wallfahrten im Bistum Freiburg*, p. 223. Jakob Ebner, *Geschichte der Wallfahrt und des Dorfes Engelwies bei Meßkirch*, (Meßkirch, 1923) (hereafter Ebner, *Engelwies*), pp. 32–33.

[36] Brommer (ed.), *Wallfahrten im Bistum Freiburg*, p. 137.

St. Ulrich and St. Verena a more effective tie to landscape in which they resided.

Monasteries and convents

Monasteries and convents were, and still are, a particularly visible part of the sacral landscape of southern Germany. Monasteries, however, had an ambiguous place in this region, for they were centers of *Herrschaft*, that is, of power and authority, as well as sacred sites. The great abbeys of the German Southwest were all very old, which gave them a certain status in a traditional society. Abbesses and abbots carefully used the power of history and tradition, especially as it favored Catholicism over Protestantism. Monastic institutions were also all local centers of devotion and most abbeys had important collections of relics and active shrines.

Many monasteries purchased and brought new collections of relics to Southwest Germany in the eighteenth century.[37] Relics no longer attracted popular devotion as they had in the fifteenth century, but they contributed to the diversity and variety of the sacral landscape. The relics of obscure saints and martyrs – the Convent of Wald, for example, acquired the remains of Saints Bonifacius, Dioscurus, and Candidus in 1701, and in 1726 Rot an der Rot acquired Saints Renatus and Domitia – surely did not replace Mary at the center of popular devotion.[38] It is also hard to imagine that a piece of the True Cross (surely the most common relic in Catholic Europe), such as the one acquired by the Abbey of Ochsenhausen for the church at Rottum in 1761, had much resonance in the population.[39] On the other hand, relics provided a further alternative and a further locus of sacred power. Since many of the relics came from Rome itself, these new devotions further connected local practices and local monastic institutions to the Catholic Church as a whole.

Relics had considerably more popular appeal if they were of local origin. The best example of the role of relics in the sacral landscape is the development of the shrine to the *Gute Beth* at Reute.[40] This shrine

37 *Zu Fuss, zu Pferd . . . Wallfahrten im Kreis Ravensburg*, pp. 19–21.

38 Maren Kuhn-Rehfus, *Das Zisterzienserinnenkloster Wald* (= *Germania Sacra*, n.s. 30) (Berlin and New York, 1992), pp. 327–337.

39 HStASt. B481/78.

40 *Zu Fuss, zu Pferd . . . Wallfahrten im Kreis Ravensburg*, pp. 189–202. Lionel Rothkrug links local shrines and local saints to the strength of Catholicism in Bavaria and southern Germany during and after the Reformation. See Rothkrug, "Popular Religion and Holy Shrines" in James

held the body of Elisabeth Achler (died 1420), a nun who had possessed a variety of magical powers. The cult of *Gute Beth* thrived in the fifteenth century and in the early modern period received new impulses on two occasions. In 1623 the grave was opened, prompting a new outburst of miracles. In 1767 Beth was canonized, bringing (it is reported) 150,000 people to Reute for the month-long celebrations. The Church and local secular authorities clearly promoted the shrine at Reute, but it developed an important place in popular religion as well.

Monasteries and convents led a boom in church building and decoration in the eighteenth century. Famous architects and designers, such as the Zimmermann brothers, the brothers Asam, Johann Georg Fischer, and Peter II Thumb, rebuilt all the great monasteries of the region in dramatic style. The rebuilt abbeys dominated the landscape as never before, and the lavish decoration of the church interiors displayed the wealth and power of the monasteries in new ways. The Baroque and Rococo monasteries, such as Salem, Zwiefalten, and Ochsenhausen, not only marked the landscape themselves, but influenced the architecture and decoration of churches and shrines in the surrounding countryside.[41]

The interior of churches and their decoration

R. J. W. Evans points out that the monasteries and the village churches and chapels of southern Germany were part of the same religious world.

> This *Wieskirche* [a shrine in Upper Bavaria] may stand for dozens of evocative sites, obscure village churches and rustic monasteries decorated in the mid-eighteenth century in the deep countryside of Bavaria, Swabia, and Franconia, their very names a litany: Ottobeueren and Weingarten, Osterhofen and Neresheim, Vierzehnheiligen, Diessen am Ammersee and Steinhausen bei Schussenried, Gössweinstein and Marktoberdorf, Rott am Inn and, most mellifluous of all (if correctly pronounced), Rot an der Rot.[42]

Many of the same architects, builders, and decorators who worked on the great monasteries also built parish churches and local pilgrimage

Obelkevich (ed.), *Religion and the People*, esp. p. 56. It is, however, also necessary to trace changes and developments between the Middle Ages and the period after 1650.

41 Thomas DaCosta Kaufmann, *Court, Cloister, and City. The Art and Culture of Central Europe. 1450–1800* (Chicago, 1995), ch. 15; Henry-Russell Hitchcock, *Rococo Architecture in Southern Germany* (London, 1968); Hitchcock, *German Rococo. The Zimmermann Brothers* (London, 1968); Karsten Harries, *The Bavarian Rococo Church. Between Faith and Asceticism* (New Haven, 1983); R.J.W. Evans, "Kings and the Queen of the Arts" *The New York Review of Books*, 43, 9 (May 23, 1996), pp. 21–24.

42 Evans, "Kings and the Queen of the Arts," p. 24.

shrines. There was no clear boundary between the art and architecture patronized and appreciated by the Catholic elite and by Catholic peasants. The careers of the architect Dominikus Zimmermann (1685–1766) and his brother Johann Baptist Zimmermann illustrate this quite well.[43] The Zimmermanns were very prolific, and worked all across southern Germany. Both Zimmermanns of course worked for great monasteries and even the Dukes of Bavaria. At the same time, however, they decorated and designed parish churches and pilgrimage shrines. In the Southwest, the most important of these was the church at Steinhausen, a regional shrine designed and built by Dominikus between 1728 and 1733, with ceiling frescos by Johann Baptist. Modern art historians greatly appreciate Steinhausen as a classic example of the rococo church; in the eighteenth century tens of thousands of pilgrims came to Steinhausen to see the *Gnadenbild*, and they too experienced the expansive design of the little church.

Dramatic new churches such as Steinhausen were only part of the building boom in the eighteenth century. Churches and chapels also received new altars, statues, and paintings. Redecorating, like all construction projects, required a complicated process of negotiation between village communities and parish patrons over the financial ramifications. This negotiation, in turn, often brought the parish priest and sometimes episcopal authorities into the mix, either to act as facilitators, or to approve the religious aspects of the design.

There is evidence that the interiors of many churches and chapels fell into disrepair in the sixteenth century. Episcopal visitations from the 1570s and 1580s regularly refer to the poor quality of ornaments or the need for repairs. In some cases, as in Engeratshofen in 1576, "the ornaments are very bad, due to the poverty of the parish."[44] The church in Bombach was in bad shape in 1588, and both the patron of the parish (the Abbot at Schüttern) and the secular authority (the Austrian *Amtmann* in Kenzingen) agreed on the need for repairs, although they could not agree on who was responsible for paying.[45] In general, though, the churches in Southwest Germany were in good condition, probably because the Reformation had disrupted the ecclesiastical system less there than in some other regions. The visitors complained most frequently about the lack of respect accorded the vestments and ornaments

[43] Hitchcock, *German Rococo*.

[44] Moritz Gmelin, "Aus Visitationsprotokollen der Diöseze Konstanz von 1571–1586. Ein Beitrag zur Geschichte des Klerus" *ZGO* 25 (1873), p. 180.

[45] EAF Ha 63, pp. 1144–1145.

used in the sacraments and about the unwillingness of churchwardens (*Kirchenpfleger*) to maintain a perpetual light in front of the Eucharist.[46] These complaints reflect the lesser emphasis placed on ornaments by the communities, but parishioners, priests, and church officials all agreed on the need to keep church buildings in good repair.

Visitation reports from the early seventeenth century indicate no general problems with church buildings and decoration. In the Linzgau in 1620 churches and chapels were almost all in "decent" or "satisfactory" condition.[47] Some churches even impressed the visitors, who found the church in Linz "well-decorated," and the parish church in Seefelden "beautiful." There were some problems in Frickingen and Fischbach. In both places the utensils were poorly polished, and in Frickingen the altar and sacrarium had insufficient furnishing.[48] Frickingen also lacked a confessional, as did the parish church in Siggingen, but apparently by this early date all the rest of the churches did have confessionals.[49]

Many churches needed new furnishings in the aftermath of the Thirty Years' War. All the visitations conducted in the 1650s, and even the 1660s, focused on the need to use resources to replace utensils, pictures, and statues lost and stolen during the war.[50] The recovery from the war was followed by a wave of redecorating and redesigning which began in the last two decades of the seventeenth century.

In many ways, developments inside churches and chapels mirrored the development of the sacral landscape itself. As the number of churches and sacred sites increased after 1650, so too did the number of altars, the quantity and quality of furnishings, the number of statues and paintings, and the general density of decorations in the churches.[51] The effect of denser furnishings was also to provide a greater variety of settings for religious practice.

[46] Gmelin, "Aus Visitationsprotokollen der Diöseze Konstanz," pp. 185, 187; EAF Ha 63, p. 1151.

[47] EAF Ha 70, 233r, 234v, 237r, 238v, 239r, 245r, 251r.

[48] EAF Ha 70, pp. 242r, 258r (Seefelden); 247v, 258r (Frickingen).

[49] The visitors commented that the confessional in Weildorf was in a poor location. EAF Ha 70, 251r. On confessionals: Henry Kamen, *The Phoenix and the Flame. Catalonia and the Counter-Reformation* (New Haven, 1993), pp. 125–127; John Bossy, "The Counter-Reformation and the People of Catholic Europe" *Past and Present* 47 (1970), pp. 63–64. In Kurköln the first confessionals were installed after the Thirty Years' War: Thomas Paul Becker, *Konfessionalisierung in Kurköln. Untersuchungen zu Durchsetzung der katholischen Reform in den Dekanaten Ahrgau und Bonn anhand von Visitationsprotokollen 1583–1761* (Bonn, 1989), pp. 57–60.

[50] See for example the visitations of *Landkapitel* Biberach, 1650 and 1661, EAF Ha 63, pp. 43–48, 51–72.

[51] Froeschlé-Chopard, *Espace et Sacré en Provence.* Becker has traced the same development for Kurköln: Becker, *Konfessionalisierung in Kurköln*, ch. 2.1.

The Catholic population, church patrons, and secular authorities all supported the adornment of churches. The driving force appears to have been the village community, especially in the late seventeenth century. In 1669 the *Gemeinde* of Schönau, in the Black Forest, rebuilt the interior of the chapel at Schönenbuch, removing St. Blasien as the patron and replacing him with St. John the Baptist, probably to the displeasure of the local lord, the Abbey of St. Blasien.[52] In 1683 the *Gemeinde* of Mindersdorf asked its parsimonious lords, the Teutonic Knights in Mainau, for help in paying for new bells for the parish church.[53] The Knights were never enthusiastic about such expenditures, and the Mindersdorfer had to engage in the typical long process of appeal, especially to the bishop, to try to squeeze some money out of the parish patron. Such disputes had been the pattern since the sixteenth century, and probably before. While parish patrons often had some obligation to pay for the upkeep of parish churches, village communities frequently were the only ones willing to pay for the decoration of chapels.

Beginning around 1700, however, many parish patrons, especially the monasteries, became active, and even enthusiastic, about decorating village churches and chapels. Not surprisingly, of course, abbots and abbesses preferred dramatic projects such as the construction of the new shrines at Steinhausen and Birnau. At the same time, however, the constant need to refurbish parish churches and local chapels provided further opportunities to patronize the arts. Although ecclesiastic patrons always sought to avoid new financial obligations, in the eighteenth century they often responded positively to requests for new decorations. The cooperation between villagers and church institutions reflects the unity of rural Catholicism, as well as the desire for self-promotion and religious representation that characterized the world of the Catholic elite.

The interplay of popular pressure and monastic reaction in the decoration of church interiors is best illustrated with concrete examples. By 1708, when the commune of Bachhaupten wanted to put a new *Mater Dolorosa* statue in its parish church, the patron of the parish, the Abbey of Salem, was already engaged in an extensive building program.[54]

[52] GLAK 229/94046. [53] GLAK 93/248.

[54] Between 1708 and 1718, Abbot Stephan I of Salem sponsored the building of the Maria Victoria Chapel at Stephansfeld, and the rebuilding of chapels in Oberuhldingen and Gebhardsweiller. Erika Dillman, *Stephan I. Fundamente des Barock. Salem an der Wende zum 18. Jahrhundert* (Tettnang, 1988), p. 47 and GLAK 98/3590.

Appeals from the commune and from the Count von Truchsess caused Abbot Stephan to help pay for the statue. The inscription placed on the statue read: "This statue was placed in memorial of the pledge, vow, and devotion of the community and transferred here on the feast of St. Agneta, virgin and martyr, 1708. Stephanus 35th Abbot in Salem, in the 10th year of his reign."[55] Although the statue in Bachhaupten was placed in the church purely at the initiative of the local parish, Abbot Stephan, with only a small outlay from Salem's well-stocked treasury, was able to assert his piety and authority and link himself and his monastery to a local religious devotion.[56]

As elsewhere in Catholic Europe, confraternities frequently sponsored the construction of new altars and the redecoration of chapels and churches. In Mainwangen in 1710, a new confraternity (probably a confraternity of the Rosary) organized new devotions and brought more people to services.[57] The confraternity, fearing the collapse of the roof over the choir of the church, asked Salem to help pay for major repairs, while also proposing the construction of several new altars. Local officials supported this proposal and allowed building to begin without consulting Salem. The confraternity offered to contribute wood, stones, and labor for the construction. Monastic officials were more skeptical, fearing that the confraternity would not remain active enough in the long run to maintain the new altars, saddling the parish and the monastery (as parish patron) with new expenses. The monks at Salem, although inclined to put off this project until peacetime (this was during the War of Spanish Succession), were also embarrassed that neighboring lords had recently funded new churches. The monastery approved repairs on the roof, but allowed the building of three new altars only if the confraternity funded them. Here again, the initiative for new construction and decoration came from the local parish. Salem, however, had a variety of reasons to contribute to the projects, some having to do with a desire to support local religious devotion, others having to do with a need to assert itself as a local center of power and devotion.

Ecclesiastics were very conscious of the importance of high-quality decorations in churches. As noted before, in 1741 the Abbot of Rot an der Rot commented not only on the repairs of the chapel at Eichenberg,

[55] GLAK 98/3693: *Hanc Statuam ex Paciscentium communi voto et devotione in monumentum posuit, qui Anno MDCCVIII transegit in festo S. Agnetis Virg. et Mart. STEPHANUS ABBAS in Salem XXXV Anno Reg: X.*

[56] See Christian, *Local Religion*, for comparison.

[57] GLAK 61/13465, pp. 458–460, 566–475. Froeschlé-Chopard, *Espace et Sacré en Provence*, Part III; *Zu Fuss, zu Pferd . . . Wallfahrten im Kreis Ravensburg*, pp. 61–64.

but also an appropriate decoration for the interior.[58] In the eighteenth century, even the Teutonic Knights, who were generally less willing to fund church repairs than were monasteries, took a new interest in the interior of churches. In 1719, the Knights in Mainau apparently asked for a report on the condition of the altars and the liturgical apparatus in all the parishes under their patronage. The priest in Mindersdorf submitted a long report, emphasizing the poor quality of the linen, chalices and other decorations in the church.[59] In this very period the Knights began to improve the decoration of the churches. In 1712, for example, the House in Mainau agreed to pay for perpetual lights to be placed in front of the Eucharist in the parish churches under the order's patronage.[60]

Parish priests often clearly grasped the interplay of popular initiative and the need of abbots and lords to patronize the population. Two letters from Carl Joseph Schwickart, *Pfarrer* in Sulmingen, to Abbot Anselm II of Salem illustrate this interaction very well. In a fawning letter from October 1774, Schwickart thanked Anselm for commissioning a painting for his church:

> The painting of our church patron Dionysius by Herr Brugger was finished in time for his feast day. It shows his life and is as incomparably beautiful as it is artistically made. We and everyone in the church praised this, and everything about it, [saying] not that it is too luxurious or so costly, but rather that it is appropriate for the location.[61]

Three years later Schwickart wrote to the abbot for permission to install stations of the cross in his church and upgrade several reliquaries. Several parishioners had agreed to pay for these new decorations, and Schwickart only needed permission to proceed from the abbot. Diplomatically, however, the *Pfarrer* credits Anselm for setting a good example in church decoration, probably in reference to the painting. The abbot gave permission, as long as the project did not lead to any cost to the monastery. Schwickart, it seems, cleverly recognized Abbot Anselm's desire to set the tone and style of religious art, even in parish churches.[62] The priest also knew, however, that ideas and projects sometimes came from his parishioners, and it was his job to coordinate the two groups, which he did with some success.

58 HStASt. B486/272. 59 GLAK 93/248. 60 GLAK 93/249.

61 GLAK 98/4033, p. 11r.

62 Given Salem's massive patronage of the arts during Anselm II's reign, it would have been hard for an informed priest to miss this interest. See Erika Dillman, *Anselm II. Glanz und Ende eine Epoche. Eine Studie über den letzten großen Abt der Reichsabtei Salem* (Salem, 1987).

The decoration of churches was one aspect of the extensive elaboration of sacred places in Southwest Germany after the Thirty Years' War. More altars, more paintings, more statues, and more elaborate decorations were built into churches in this period. Outside the churches, villagers, abbots, Catholic lords and town councils, and officials of the larger states all supported the construction of more churches and chapels. This building boom led to a further sacralization of the landscape itself.

The Catholic elite and the peasantry shared the sacral landscape of Southwest Germany. Especially during the century after 1650, great lords and peasant communities participated in the construction of the sites, and both groups incorporated them into their devotions. The ways in which Baroque art and architecture penetrated into the villages illustrate this particularly well. Nowhere else in Europe can one find as many and as beautiful *Barocklandkirchen*.[63] The elite brought the Baroque and Rococo styles to the region, but they clearly resonated with wide groups in the population as well.

People recognized the importance of place in religious life. Many pilgrimage sites came to be located in a place chosen by the miraculous picture or statue itself. The villagers of Sasbach carried a *Gnadenbild* up the Litzelberg and allowed it (in an unknown way) to choose the exact location for the chapel.[64] The priest in Riedböhringen understood the importance of place when he proposed that a chapel in his parish be built in a location that was "*weitsichtig*," that is, easily seen from far away and with a good view.[65] Episcopal officials recognized the importance of both decoration and locale when they ordered that a picture of Mary that had attracted undue devotion be stripped of its decorations and be moved to a dark side altar in the church.[66] They suggested further that the picture eventually be removed from the church and placed in a monastery for safekeeping.

The sacral landscape was, as we have seen, constantly changing. The sacred spaces and places were alive in another sense as well. The people of the region heard the Mass, listened to sermons, and practiced their devotions in the churches and chapels.[67] But they also constantly moved

[63] Ludwig Veit and Ludwig Lenhart, *Kirche und Volksfrömmigkeit im Zeitalter des Barock* (Freiburg, 1956), pp. 37–38.

[64] Brommer (ed.), *Wallfahrten im Bistum Freiburg*, p. 138.

[65] EAF Ha 218, pp. 382–384.

[66] EAF Ha 216, pp. 190–191, 193.

[67] Werner Freitag, "Konfessionelle Kulturen und innere Staatsbildung" *Westfälische Forschungen* 42 (1992), pp. 164–166.

through the landscape, in procession and as pilgrims, often linking together sacred sites, and even sacralizing the fields and hillsides themselves by taking the liturgy out of the churches. The landscape provided a setting and a framework for the public practice of Catholicism, but the practice itself transformed the setting. By turning our attention now to the practice of Catholicism, and particularly to pilgrimage piety, we can further examine the interplay of the place and experience of German Catholicism.

PILGRIMAGE PIETY

In the Christian tradition pilgrimage was often an extraordinary experience. In seventeenth- and eighteenth-century Germany, however, pilgrimage piety was an integral part of everyday religious practice.[68] After collapsing in the wake of the Reformation, pilgrimages regained some popularity in the late sixteenth century. Popular enthusiasm for pilgrimage really peaked after 1650, in Southwest Germany as in all of Catholic Germany. Protestant critics and Catholic apologists, Enlightenment reformers and defenders of local traditions, romantic folklorists and modern scholars have all recognized the important place of pilgrimage in Baroque Catholicism.[69]

In Southwest Germany, pilgrimage was both central and unremarkable. For this reason, an analysis of pilgrimage piety provides a valuable window on many aspects of Catholicism. The characteristic features of pilgrimage, the centrality of popular initiative, the diverse function of shrines, the ambivalent attitude of the official Church, and the ways in which pilgrimage was embedded in daily life, were important aspects of Catholic confessionalism more generally. The constantly changing world of pilgrimage piety demonstrates the dynamism of Catholicism in this period, while the nature of pilgrimage piety sheds light on the people's loyalty to the Church itself. Grasping the nature of this "churchliness" involves understanding the interlocking popular identification with the local church, particularly the parish and local shrines,

[68] Alphonse Dupront, "Pilgrimage and Sacred Places" in Jacques Revel and Lynn Hunt (eds.), *Histories. French Constructions of the Past* (New York, 1995); Victor and Edith Turner, *Image and Pilgrimage in Christian Culture. Anthropological Perspectives* (New York, 1978), esp. ch. 1, "Pilgrimage as a Liminoid Phenomenon."

[69] Veit and Lenhart, *Kirche und Volksfrömmigkeit im Zeitalter des Barocks*, esp. Part II, ch. 2; Michael Pammer, *Glaubensabfall und wahre Andacht. Barock Religiösität, Reformkatholizismus, und Laizismus in Oberösterreich, 1700–1820* (Munich, 1994), pp. 6–7; Richard van Dülmen, *Kultur und Alltag in der frühen Neuzeit*, Vol. III. *Religion, Magie, Aufklärung, 16–18 Jahrhundert* (Munich, 1994), pp. 75–78.

and regional structures, such as major shrines, monasteries, mendicant orders, and the episcopacy. Not surprisingly, in the seventeenth and eighteenth centuries, popular German Catholicism had many ties to the local and regional Church, but few to international Catholicism or its representatives, such as the Jesuits.

Pilgrimages and shrines

Pilgrimage piety was an important structural aspect of early modern German Catholicism, but it also had a history; the role and significance of pilgrimage changed over time. In the decades immediately after the Council of Trent, the clergy promoted pilgrimage, primarily as an assertion of Catholic identity, even in regions without significant Protestant populations.[70] This Counter-Reformation program did not resonate strongly with the population. The crisis of the Thirty Years' War prompted a new upsurge in pilgrimages and the creation of new shrines. The greatest explosion of pilgrimage piety came in the century after 1650 and included the foundation of a large number of new shrines and pilgrimages, as well as the revitalization and expansion of existing sites. The vitality of pilgrimage piety was primarily fueled by popular enthusiasm, especially after 1700, just when clerical and elite attitudes toward shrines and miracles moved from uneasiness to skepticism.[71]

The meaning and function of pilgrimage piety varied, even in the same time and place. Pilgrims turned to the important practices and devotions of everyday Catholicism at the shrines, including communal processions, prayers, confession, and communion. The prevalence of these practices indicates the extent to which popular religion was practiced within the framework of official church liturgy. Yet at the same time, Catholic peasants and townspeople experienced shrines as places where miracles could and did happen on a regular basis. The miracles themselves, the vast majority credited to the intercession of the Virgin Mary, were sometimes dramatic and more often mundane, occasionally widely reported, but mostly local in importance. Pilgrimage piety was part of the diverse and dispersed world of local Catholicism.

[70] Bavaria, a purely Catholic territory from the late sixteenth century, was a major pilgrimage region, and pilgrimage was clearly part of the Wittelsbach Counter-Reformation program. See Soergel, *Wondrous in His Saints* and Rothkrug, "Popular Religion and Holy Shrines."

[71] Rebekka Habermas, *Wallfahrt und Aufruhr: Zur Geschichte des Wunderglaubens in der frühen Neuzeit* (Frankfurt, 1991); Werner Freitag, *Volks- und Elitenfrömmigkeit in der frühen Neuzeit. Marienwallfahrten im Fürstbistum Münster* (Paderborn, 1991); Freitag, "Konfessionelle Kulturen und innere Staatsbildung," pp. 75–191.

If we go to the shores of Lake Constance (Bodensee) in the middle of the eighteenth century, we can obtain a glimpse of the world of pilgrimage piety. In September 1749, a monk at the Cistercian Abbey of Salem put his pen to paper. The abbot had given him the task of describing the wonders and benefits (*Wohltaten*) performed by a picture of Mary, which had resided in the monastery since 1747. This report reflects many of the issues that made pilgrimage so important in Southwest Germany.[72]

The "*wunderbares Bildnis unserer Lieben Mutter*" at the monastery of Salem was neither a new object of devotion nor a new source of supernatural power. The monks had moved it from its traditional resting place in a small chapel in the nearby village of Birnau, which had given the picture its name: Our Lady of Birnau. The Cistercians from Salem were building a new church for the picture much closer to the monastery. Although the monks did not admit it openly, they were clearly motivated in part by financial gain in this transfer. Financial issues were certainly behind the outcry from the nearby imperial city of Überlingen, which held considerable rights in the original shrine at Birnau, and stood to lose money from the shrine's relocation to a site further from the city.[73]

In fact, the *translatio* of the icon clearly made the monks nervous, and they needed to show potential pilgrims (and perhaps themselves) that it was the picture and not its traditional location that exerted power. Our monk's report was a public relations measure; it sought to provide evidence of the picture's continued value to local pilgrims: "We profess that Our Dear Lady, who has been so compassionate for so many centuries, has not changed in the least because of the change of place. Indeed, within the wall of the monastery of Salem, she has not only frequently blessed us [the monks] but the whole surrounding area as well with her charity." The monks of Salem were, however, a tad defensive about promoting this shrine. Perhaps whiffs of the Enlightenment critique of the clerical exploitation of popular credulity had reached the Catholic heartland of Germany: "We do not want to canonize the [benefits] as miracles, but rather want to report them as they happened. We leave the correct interpretation [*rechten Verstand*] of them to the Church . . . with devotion and submission." This was not the sixteenth century when the open promotion of shrines had been a

[72] The report is in GLAK 98/3262.

[73] Salem claimed that an inn, built on Überlingen territory near the original shrine, was an important reason for the relocation of the icon. The monks argued that the drinking and frivolity at the inn undermined the sanctity of Birnau.

standard feature of Catholic polemics. On the other hand, our monk's audience was not the *République des Lettres* but rather the surrounding population, the local clergy, and neighboring monasteries. For this reason, the report moved on to publicize the sacred power still manifested by the picture of Mary.

The benefits and minor miracles manifested by the picture were in many ways fairly mundane. An expectant mother in serious danger gives birth to a healthy child. A stonemason working on the new shrine survives a serious fall without injury. A three-year-old boy who cannot walk comes to the shrine and starts walking the next day. A woman with a seriously injured foot is cured. The Abbot of Salem prays to Mary and, unexpectedly, is able to solve the serious financial problems of the monastery. The same abbot survives several serious illnesses by offering masses to the Marian picture. A monk comes uninjured through a serious carriage accident by appealing to Mary for help. Finally, for two years running the harvest in the surrounding region is saved by votive processions to "Our Lady of Birnau at Salem." The picture of Mary protected and aided a cross-section of the local population: men and women, adults and children, stonemasons and abbots, monks and peasants.

The public position of the monastery was that the picture of Mary was powerful, but that the faithful needed the support and mediation of the clergy to appeal to it properly and effectively. Thus the author emphasized that each person who received Mary's help had certified it by reporting the miracle to a priest. Salem's view coincided with the Church's ongoing effort to control and channel popular access to the sacred; in the local context the abbey wanted to avoid trouble with the local parish priests and the bishop.[74] By the middle of the eighteenth century, the population accepted the role of the clergy at shrines, an indication of the clericalization of popular religion and the links between popular devotion and the institutional church.

Pilgrimage and confessionalism in the late sixteenth century

Pilgrimages contributed to the creation and strengthening of Catholic confessionalism. In the late sixteenth and early seventeenth centuries, Jesuits, reforming bishops, and other Catholic leaders promoted pilgrimage as a potent anti-Protestant measure, as "spiritual medicine for

[74] Salem was engaged in serious jurisdictional disputes with the Bishops of Constance throughout the eighteenth century. Marc R. Forster, "Kirchenreform, katholische Konfessionalisierung und Dorfreligion um Kloster Salem, 1650–1750" *RJfKG* 16 (1997), pp. 93–110.

heretical poison."[75] This "Counter-Reformation" aspect of pilgrimage peaked in the decades around 1600, particularly in areas bordering on Protestant territories, before fading in the period after 1650. Even in the eighteenth century, Protestants considered pilgrimages and communal processions a form of Catholic aggression, particularly within biconfessional cities.[76] The need to combat Protestantism was less direct in the Catholic countryside, but religious polemic remained part of the culture of pilgrimage piety.

Pilgrimage piety in the Southwest revived in the late sixteenth century, as it did elsewhere in Catholic Germany. This revival proceeded slowly and shrines did not benefit as directly from elite sponsorship as they did in Bavaria or Franconia. There were no Catholic princes in the Southwest who promoted pilgrimages as did Duke Albrecht of Bavaria or Prince-Bishop of Würzburg Julius Echter von Mespelbrunn in the 1570s and 1580s. More common in the Southwest was the pattern of the great Franconian shrine of Walldürn, which revived under the leadership of an energetic and imaginative local priest.[77]

Some new pilgrimages in Southwest Germany were true "Counter-Reformation" cults, arising from the crisis caused by the progress of Protestantism in the sixteenth century. The shrine at Maria Sand outside Herbolzheim dates from the second half of the sixteenth century. According to legend, in the 1550s the inhabitants of a village near Herbolzheim, which had recently converted to Protestantism, threw a terracotta statue of Mary into a stream. Despite its weight, the one-meter tall statue washed up on shore several kilometers away in Herbolzheim, where it became the focus of an important shrine.[78]

In 1615, pilgrims began to come to the Austrian town of Endingen, not far from Herbolzheim, to pray at the *Wallfahrt zur weinenden*

[75] Soergel, *Wondrous in His Saints*, esp. ch. 6. See also R. Po-chia Hsia, *Social Discipline in the Reformation. Central Europe, 1550–1750* (London and New York, 1989); Louis Châtellier, *Europe of the Devout. The Catholic Reformation and the Formation of a New Society* (Cambridge, 1989). On the decline of pilgrimages in the early sixteenth century, see Erwin Keller, "Bischöflich-konstanzische Erlasse und Hirtenbriefe. Ein Beitrag zur Seelsorgsgeschichte im Bistum Konstanz" *FDA* 102 (1982), p. 29.

[76] Such processions, which often went to shrines, caused considerable conflict in biconfessional cities. Forster, *The Counter-Reformation in the Villages*, pp. 228–230; Etienne François, *Die unsichtbare Grenze*, p. 239.

[77] Wolfgang Brückner, *Die Verehrung des Heiligen Blutes in Walldürn* (Aschaffenburg, 1958), pp. 45–59. On Bavaria, see Soergel, *Wondrous in His Saints*, esp. ch. 3. On Würzburg, Hans Dünninger, *Maria siegt in Franken. Die Wallfahrt nach Dettelbach als Bekenntnis* (Würzburg, 1979), pp. 19–37.

[78] Brommer (ed.), *Wallfahrten im Bistum Freiburg*, pp. 120–122. Herbolzheim bordered on several Baden-Durlach villages which became Lutheran in the 1550s. "Swimming" (or even "surfing") Madonnas were not unusual. See Soergel, *Wondrous in His Saints*, pp. 222–223.

Gottesmutter. The report compiled by episcopal commissioners sent to investigate the foundation miracle indicates that this was also an anti-Protestant shrine. The story itself was not unusual. Shortly before Ascension Day a wooden Madonna statue in the St. Martin Chapel started to sweat or weep. This miracle quickly drew a crowd of local people, who all testified that the statue continued to sweat after being dried, that other pictures and statues in the church remained dry, as did the altar on which the statue stood. Furthermore, both Mary and the baby Jesus appeared to grow pale and weep, "looking [according to a butcher] like nothing other than persons on their death bed."[79]

The commissioners, the local clergy, and many of the local people were perplexed by this miracle. Why did Mary and Jesus sweat or weep?[80] The statue belonged to a journeymen's confraternity, four members of which carried it every year in the Ascension Day procession. Otherwise, this Madonna had not previously excited any special devotion. When pressed, however, a number of people mentioned that a journeyman knife-grinder (*Scherer*), an outsider from Meßkirch, had insulted the statue. One witness reported that this young man had commented that "Our Lady is prettily dressed, [and that] he had been here a long time and would never be so well dressed." According to a different witness, he had "flippantly said that people decorate this picture, but not him, and he has to live very poorly."[81]

Journeymen were a religious problem in confessionally fragmented Germany, since they traveled from town to town and Protestant apprentices and journeymen worked in Catholic towns and vice versa. If a Protestant journeyman, or even a disrespectful Catholic journeyman, had insulted the statue of Mary on the eve of the Ascension Day procession in which the journeymen played an important role, the whole community's salvation was at stake. The Endinger initially responded with fear or sadness to the miracle, indicating a concern that Mary's weeping might be the result of some sacrilege in their town. Only later did the miracle lead people to prayer and greater devotion. The commissioners concluded that "this event has given many people belief and no one any doubts, [and] many people were badly frightened [*übell erschrocken*], wept, and were unusually sad."

[79] Brommer (ed.), *Wallfahrten im Bistum Freiburg*, pp. 113–114 and EAF A1/1420. The *Pfarrer* claimed to have been especially skeptical and diligent in checking the veracity of the miracle.

[80] Although now referred to as the *Tränenmirakel*, the original report refers to "*ein Bild zu Unserer Lieber Frau daß geschwitzt haben soll*" ("a picture of Our Dear Lady that is supposed to have sweated").

[81] EAF A1/1420.

The Endingen *Tränenmirakel* played out in an atmosphere of heightened confessional consciousness. Caspar Freyschmidt, possibly a journeyman himself, testified that "he thanked God that he was born of Catholic parents, and had stayed Catholic until this time, and that he had seen this miracle." Another man testified that four or five Lutheran traveling journeymen (*Wandergesellen*) had been skeptical of the miracle and had wiped off some of the tears, which reappeared immediately. The parish priest himself also wiped off the tears, with the same result. Finally, this miracle, for all its typicality, was in its early stages created by the common people of Endingen, who came in large numbers to view the statue before the local clergy became involved. Once established, however, local priests and the town magistrates all adopted the shrine and they all played an important role in the investigation by the episcopal commission.[82]

Other shrines and pilgrimages revived during the late sixteenth century. The shrine at Maria Lindenberg, near the Benedictine monastery of St. Peter, was founded around 1500, but apparently went through a rebirth after about 1580, when the chapel was expanded and an endowment fund for a new high altar created. This program, probably led by the monks at St. Peter, was crowned in 1601 when the suffragan Bishop of Constance came to consecrate the new altar.[83] Similarly, another late medieval pilgrimage destination, the chapel on the Hörnleberg, received clerical promotion in the first decades of the seventeenth century, when the Bishop of Constance secured new indulgences for a confraternity affiliated with the shrine.[84]

The story of the shrine at Reute provides a more dramatic example of the Church's promotion of pilgrimage. In 1623, the nuns at Reute opened the grave of the saintly founder of the convent, Elisabeth Achler, known at *Die gute Beth*.[85] The open grave led to further miracles and a dramatic increase in pilgrims. The shrine received a further impulse when Archduke Leopold, brother of the Emperor Ferdinand II, came in 1629 to inaugurate a new church at the shrine. Reute was clearly a case where the population responded positively to the Counter-Reformation effort to promote pilgrimage.

The widespread effort to promote pilgrimages did not always

[82] The *Burgermeister*, *Stadtschreiber*, and two priests all testified. EAF A1/1420. Weeping or sweating statues and pictures were common. See especially the shrine of Maria Steinbach, discussed below.

[83] Brommer (ed.), *Wallfahrten im Bistum Freiburg*, pp. 132–133.

[84] Brommer (ed.), *Wallfahrten im Bistum Freiburg*, pp. 142–143.

[85] *Zu Fuss, zu Pferd . . . Wallfahrten im Kreis Ravensburg*, pp. 189–202.

succeed. The Marian shrine at Todtmoos in the southern Black Forest was a major pilgrimage destination in the fifteenth century, under the patronage of the Abbey of St. Blasien.[86] The shrine declined so dramatically after the Reformation that the ruined church had to be razed in the early seventeenth century. St. Blasien had the church rebuilt in 1627, but the shrine only gained popular support in the 1640s. Church reformers promoted Todtmoos, as they did other pilgrimage destinations, but their efforts only came to fruition after the Thirty Years' War, when the population itself took the lead in pilgrimage piety.

Pilgrimage and the Thirty Years' War

The Thirty Years' War loomed large in the popular imagination in the late seventeenth and the eighteenth century, and played a role in the explosion of pilgrimage piety in the region. Many shrines arose, or received new life, as the result of what we might call the "Swedish soldier legend." This legend usually involved a sacrilege perpetrated by a (Protestant) Swedish soldier against an object venerated by Catholics. The shrine at Geisingen is exemplary.[87] This pilgrimage destination revolved around a life-size crucifix with a bullet hole in Jesus' head. According to the foundation legend, in 1633 a Swedish soldier fired on the crucifix, after which the bullet hole began to bleed. The soldier died soon after. A small local pilgrimage developed in the seventeenth century, and Geisingen became a major regional shrine in the 1730s, after the local priest recorded and published this story.

There are other examples of "Swedish soldier legends" in Southwest Germany. The *Mariazell* shrine near Hechingen originated in a story similar to that of Geisingen.[88] In 1631 the Swedes destroyed this isolated church, but when a soldier attempted to toss a Madonna statue into the flames, Mary lifted herself out of the fire. The soldier died later that same day and was buried in a field next to the shrine, where a stone cross, called the *Sühnekreuz* (cross of sins), was then erected. The *Frauenbergkapelle* at Bad Waldsee grew in status when, during the war, Mary protected the town from Swedish soldiers by causing a light to shine in the chapel; this led passing soldiers to believe that the town was already on fire, and thus not worth plundering. The sitting Madonna at Betenbrunn has a nick on its head, supposedly caused in 1632 by a Swedish

[86] Brommer (ed.), *Wallfahrten im Bistum Freiburg*, pp. 156–158.
[87] Brommer (ed.), *Wallfahrten im Bistum Freiburg*, p. 168.
[88] Brommer (ed.), *Wallfahrten im Bistum Freiburg*, pp. 219–221.

soldier attempting (unsuccessfully) to destroy the statue. In 1643 a statue of Mary at the monastery of Salem wept during the Swedish siege of nearby Überlingen, causing it to become an important shrine in the second half of the seventeenth century.[89]

Perhaps the most obvious example of an "anti-Protestant" shrine with origins in the war is the Loretto Chapel outside the city of Constance.[90] During the Swedish siege of Constance in the fall of 1633, the population put itself under Mary's protection and renewed an earlier vow to build a chapel in her honor if the city was spared destruction. After the successful defense of the city, the Jesuits and their Marian sodality sponsored the project, but enthusiasm among the wider population was limited. Indeed, the city council did not participate in the project and the Jesuits completed the project themselves in 1637/1638. The *Lorettokapelle* owed more to clerical promotion than popular enthusiasm.

The Swedish soldier legend is clearly part of the world of confessional conflict and was promoted by the counter-reformers who dominated Catholic Germany in the first half of the seventeenth century. Many, if not most, of the shrines which trace their origins to the war did not become popular pilgrimage destinations until the early eighteenth century. In this respect the shrine of the *Heilig Kreuz* at Geisingen was typical. The pilgrimage dates to the Thirty Years' War, but pilgrims only began to come there in large numbers in the 1730s. During the height of pilgrimage piety, especially in the first half of the eighteenth century, people returned to shrines with links to the Thirty Years' War. The appeal of such places was not their anti-Protestant message but rather the sense of social crisis invoked by memories of the 1630s. A shrine that had manifested power in such a dark time could surely solve the problems of a later period.

The heyday of pilgrimage

Even a cursory examination of modern shrines of Southwest Germany show that the vast majority of them were either founded or experienced their heyday between 1650 and the middle of the eighteenth

[89] Brommer (ed.), *Wallfahrten im Bistum Freiburg*, pp. 189–202, 206. Another example of a trigger-happy soldier comes from Pfullendorf. See Brommer (ed.), *Wallfahrten im Bistum Freiburg*, p. 227.

[90] Wolfgang Zimmermann, "Konstanz in den Jahren von 1548–1733" in Martin Burkhardt, Wolfgang Dobras and Wolfgang Zimmermann (eds.), *Konstanz in der frühen Neuzeit. Reformation, Verlust der Reichsfreiheit, Österreichische Zeit*, Vol. III *Geschichte der Stadt Konstanz* (Constance, 1991); Brommer (ed.), *Wallfahrten im Bistum Freiburg*, pp. 194–195. The Jesuits promoted Loretto shrines throughout Catholic Europe in this period.

century.[91] In some cases, the explosion of pilgrimage piety involved the revival of late medieval shrines, but in many cases whole new shrines were founded. The Clerical Council (*Geistliche Rat*) of the Bishops of Constance struggled to cope with reports of new miracles, shrines, and pilgrimages, particularly in the years around 1700.[92] The council's minutes give the impression that the popular enthusiasm for pilgrimages had left episcopal officials in Constance behind.

The widespread enthusiasm for pilgrimage piety bears all the marks of a popular movement, particularly in contrast to the clerical promotion of the period 1580–1620.[93] Clerical encouragement did not disappear, however, as the examples of both Geisingen and Birnau attest. The shrine at Geisingen needed the publication of a miracle report by the local priest to gain a wider reputation. Birnau had always been under the protection of the Cistercians at Salem, and the transfer to Neu-Birnau represents the final victory of the abbey in its struggle with the city of Überlingen for control of the shrine. In the wider context of pilgrimage after the Thirty Years' War, however, clerical patronage fades in comparison with popular initiative.

Indeed, clerical promotion of shrines could fail, as the example of the shrine at Weggental outside Rottenburg am Neckar attests. In 1653, the Austrian government entrusted the management of the shrine to the Jesuits, and in the 1660s several episcopal decrees confirmed this situation. In 1670, however, the city government of Rottenburg took oversight of the finances of Weggental back from the Jesuits and reported that the shrine had declined under Jesuit control. The Jesuits continued to serve as preachers and pastors at Weggental and took credit for the popularity of the shrine in the mid-eighteenth century, when the shrine shared in the general enthusiasm for pilgrimage in this period.[94]

Pilgrimages required popular enthusiasm to become established (or "reestablished"). The pilgrimage to *Maria in der Tanne* at Triberg im Schwarzwald, for example, experienced two periods of popular

[91] Brommer (ed.), *Wallfahrten im Bistum Freiburg* and *Kurzkataloge der volkstümlichen Kult- und Andachtsstätten* provide surveys of shrines in the modern-day diocese of Freiburg.

[92] EAF Ha 216, pp. 69, 74, 92, 99–100, 121, 135, 153, 175, 182, 183, 184, 185, 190–191, 193, 323–324, 344–345.

[93] Klaus Guth, "Geschichtlicher Abriß der marianischen Wallfahrtsbewegungen im deutschsprachigen Raum" in Wolfgang Beinert and Heinrich Petri (eds.), *Handbuch der Marienkunde* (Regensburg, 1984), esp. p. 804; Veit and Lenhart, *Kirche und Volksfrömmigkeit*, pp. 174–180; Wolfgang Brückner, *Walldürn*, has the most sophisticated discussion of this issue, eg. pp. 98, 112.

[94] Bernhard Duhr, *Geschichte der Jesuiten in den Ländern deutsche Zunge von 16. bis 18 Jahrhundert* (4 vols., Freiburg im Breisgau, 1907–1921), Vol. III, p. 144, Vol. IV Part III, p. 289; HStASt. B466a/324, Report from 1673 and HStASt. B38/172.

enthusiasm before attracting support from the clergy.[95] This Marian shrine, where a parchment painting of Mary was found embedded in a tree, was first popular in the 1640s. A small statue of Mary was soon installed and a period of miracles and local popularity followed. The shrine, however, soon fell into disuse. In 1692, a young soldier, Gabriel Maurer, rediscovered the statue and the tree, and was cured of lameness. This miracle initiated a new explosion of local devotion. By the time an episcopal commission came to Triberg in 1697 to investigate the shrine and its associated miracles, the pilgrimage was in full bloom. Large numbers of pilgrims were coming to the shrine, reporting many miracles, Maurer had joined the Capuchin order and was installed as a "*Wallfahrtsbruder*," and the local people had built a stone chapel next to the tree. The commission expressed concern that the popularity of the shrine would be short-lived, and feared the criticism of Protestants in such a case. They were, however, persuaded to give official episcopal sanction to the Triberg shrine. "Developments in Triberg had already created a kind of fait accompli, and could not be turned back without great difficulty."[96] Popular initiative created the shrine at Triberg, and certainly underpinned its continued popularity between the 1690s and about 1750. After official approval in 1697 several engaged clerical "directors" of the shrine actively promoted its reputation, giving it an importance that transcended the district around Triberg and attracted visits from princes, prelates, and abbots.[97]

From the late seventeenth century on, all shrines owed their existence to popular enthusiasm. Local officials and clergymen, rather than promoting pilgrimage, worried about the enthusiasm for new shrines. An official of the monastery of Salem appeared confused in 1701 when he asked his superiors how to deal with the "rather large *concursus* of common people" coming to see a Marian picture at Wagenhart.[98] The Clerical Council in Constance frequently discussed how to respond to new shrines, especially in the years around 1700, but never suggested that pilgrimages should be promoted.[99] Even shrines that the clergy had previously promoted were overwhelmed by popular interest. By 1710, the number of pilgrims coming to the Marian shrine in Bodman had

95 Schmalfeldt, "Sub tuum praesidium confugimus," pp. 1–302. See also Brommer (ed.), *Wallfahrten im Bistum Freiburg*, pp. 173–177.

96 Schmalfeldt, "Sub tuum praesidium confugimus," pp. 72–73, 75.

97 Schmalfeldt, "Sub tuum praesidium confugimus," esp. p. 103.

98 GLAK 61/13464, p. 196r–v.

99 EAF Ha 216, pp. 69, 74, 92, 99–100, 121, 135, 153, 175, 182, 183, 184, 185, 190–191, 193, 323–324, 344–345; EAF Ha 218, pp. 97–98, 187–188, 356, 363–364, 373.

Table 2.3. *Money offerings at the shrine at Engelwies, in the eighteenth century*

Year	Offerings (Gulden, Kreuzer, Heller)	Year	Offerings (Gulden, Kreuzer, Heller)
1714	22.5.0	1755	68.11.4
1715	21.2.6	1757	45.8.2
1722	36.16.0	1762	60.36.0
1724	83.35.0	1765	65.13.0
1725	48.0.0	1767	63.0.6
1728	77.0.2	1770	55.47.0
1730	91.43.0	1771	28.54.0
1731	31.21.6	1774	40.30.0
1733	91.43.0	1786	20.24.0
1738	54.50.0	1789	14.16.0
1754	48.4.4		

Source: Jakob Ebner, *Geschichte der Wallfahrt und des Dorfes Engelwies bei Meßkirch* (Meßkirch, 1923), p. 69.

begun to overwhelm the priests assigned to the chapel. They appealed to the patron of the shrine, the monastery of Salem, for either help or release from some of the obligations of their position.[100]

The shrine at Engelwies provides a good example of the ebb and flow of popular enthusiasm for pilgrimages and shrines and of the extent of the passion for pilgrimage in the period 1650–1750. The shrine's chronicle records a large number of miracles from the first two decades of the sixteenth century, very few between 1525 and 1650, and a new burst of miracles from the 1660s to about 1720.[101] As the offerings left at the shrine attest, after the period of miracles passed, Engelwies remained a popular destination, although the amount of alms varied considerably from year to year over the eighteenth century (see table 2.3).

Engelwies, like Birnau, had been a popular pilgrimage destination before the Reformation, and revived after the Thirty Years' War. Many more shrines followed this pattern rather than that of Endingen or Herbolzheim, which revived in the late sixteenth century. Typical was the small St. Jacobus shrine at Wolfach, in the Ortenau region.[102] The original chapel on this site was built in the early fifteenth century and destroyed by Protestants in 1540, being rebuilt in 1659–1660. The chapel

[100] GLAK 61/13465, pp. 423, 431.

[101] Brommer (ed.), *Wallfahrten im Bistum Freiburg*, pp. 222–223 and Ebner, *Engelwies*, pp. 33–45; GLAK 229/25201.

[102] Brommer (ed.), *Wallfahrten im Bistum Freiburg*, pp. 98–100.

revived as a pilgrimage destination in the 1660s, as evidenced by the founding of a "Confraternity of St. Jacobus of the Good Death," a revival that was reinforced by the discovery in 1710 of a late gothic wooden statue of St. Jacobus in a nearby well. This story, like those of many late seventeenth-century pilgrimage destinations, gave Wolfach both the status of an ancient shrine, and the power of a place where miracles had recently occurred.

New shrines had a special appeal in the period after 1650, which brings us back to the relocation of Birnau in the 1740s. The transfer of the miraculous image was clearly a problem, both for the monastery of Salem and for the local population. The city of Überlingen, for example, protested that the transfer was "an uncatholic procedure." An internal report at Salem recognized the deeper concerns of the population, commenting that many people were concerned about the *translatio* and did not see why the picture could not be left at its "ancient residence." The location *was* important, perhaps more important than the image itself. Yet the Birnauer *Gnadenbild* remained popular after its transfer. Perhaps the propaganda campaign of the Cistercians at Salem played a role in bringing pilgrims to the new shrine, as did the beauty of the church and its location.[103] Vital, however, was the flexibility of the pilgrimage tradition in the region. Pilgrims treated "Neu-Birnau" for what it was: a new shrine.

Completely new shrines posed a further problem, for they could threaten the success, or even the existence, of older sites. Episcopal authorities were sometimes called in to adjudicate conflicts between shrines. In 1697, for example, the priest at the shrine of Maria Thann, near Wangen, complained that a new pilgrimage destination at "Mintzlings" in the parish of Wohmbrechts was taking away offerings from the older shrine.[104] The Clerical Council in Constance moved to investigate this problem, but recognized the difficulty of trying to control popular devotions: "It might not be impossible that the devotions, using the usual permissible method, could in the future be confined to a particular place or day." This is hardly a confident statement and shows that church officials recognized the independence of popular pilgrimage piety.

The official Church became even more skeptical about the miracles associated with shrines and pilgrimages as the eighteenth century

[103] GLAK 98/3259, # 29. Harries, *The Bavarian Rococo Church*, pp. 222–225.

[104] EAF Ha 216, pp. 92, 100, quote p. 100. On Maria Thann, see *Zu Fuss, zu Pferd . . . Wallfahrten im Kreis Ravensburg*, p. 235.

progressed.[105] Churchmen found the "miracle discourse" which dominated the pilgrims' understanding of pilgrimage disturbing and worried that too many miracles gave the Protestants ammunition for mocking Catholic practice. Episcopal officials expressed their attitude quite succinctly when they commented in 1702 that a new shrine in the Black Forest would "bring the danger of ridicule on the Catholic religion, and will give the superstitious rabble [*leichtglaubigen pövel*] an excuse to practice devotions that the clerical authorities have not yet approved."[106]

Bishops and ecclesiastical officials put this skepticism into practice by seeking to slow the proliferation of new pilgrimages. The episcopal commission sent to investigate Triberg in 1697 sought to control the new cult. When a new, larger pilgrimage church was built at Triberg, the original tree was cut down, a small piece of it from the niche around the statue was placed over the altar, and the rest burned. Officials feared the locals would take pieces of the tree as relics.[107] This fear of popular "superstition" informed the policies of the Clerical Council in Constance when, in 1700, they ordered a tree that was becoming the focus of a new pilgrimage near Mengen be cut down and destroyed.[108] Similarly, the council ordered that a miraculous picture of Mary at Harten be moved from a roadside shrine to a quiet corner of the parish church, and declared the miracles associated with it inauthentic. The parish priest was told to prevent any further devotion to the picture, and to encourage his parishioners to "practice their devotion to the mother of God before a different picture."[109]

Church authorities viewed certain kinds of shrines, for example those which specialized in baptizing babies who had died before baptism, with special misgiving and sought to limit their use. This effort achieved little success, as the popularity of Bergatreute throughout the eighteenth century attests. This shrine was the most important destination in Southwest Germany for parents whose babies had died unbaptized.[110] A picture of a "bleeding Mary," which was first hung in the church in 1686, had the power to bring babies back to life long enough for a priest to perform the sacrament. In the two decades after 1686, one priest, Johann Michael Mietinger, performed over 2,000 such "emergency

[105] See discussion of this issue in Habermas, *Wallfahrt und Aufruhr*, esp. chs. 4 and 5. See also Ludwig Hüttl, *Marianische Wallfahrten im Süddeutsch-Österreichischen Raum. Analyse von der Reformations- bis zur Aufklärungsepoche* (Cologne and Vienna, 1985), esp. pp. 181–188.

[106] EAF A1/1424.

[107] Schmalfeldt, "Sub tuum praesidium confugimus," p. 82.

[108] EAF Ha 216, p. 184.

[109] EAF Ha 216, pp. 175, 183, 190–191, 193.

[110] *Zu Fuss, zu Pferd . . . Wallfahrten im Kreis Ravensburg*, pp. 171–175.

baptisms." The Clerical Council in Constance considered such baptisms highly questionable, commenting in 1697 that many parents considered even a slight change in color on the part of a baby enough of a "sign of life" to be called a miracle and allow baptism.[111] The council forbade any baptism, unless a doctor or witnessing cleric confirmed a "sign of life," an order the bishop reissued in 1702.[112] Yet these measures had little effect. In the 1690s similar miracles were reported in other places, for example at established shrines such as Engelwies and Wellendingen.[113] The flow of bereaved parents continued at Bergatreute as well, as the council lamented several years after its initial order.[114]

Church authorities certainly attempted to direct and supervise pilgrimage piety. Yet much of pilgrimage piety remained firmly in the hands of the population. In part the peasants controlled pilgrimage because it was communal, in the sense that pilgrims traveled to shrines in groups. Yet even when individuals went on pilgrimages, as in the case of parents who traveled to Bergatreute with a still-born child, the common people determined the relative importance and popularity of shrines.

Maria Steinbach and the multiple meaning of pilgrimage

The shrine of the *Schmerzhafte Mutter Maria* (*Mater Dolorosa*, or grieving Mary) at Steinbach in Upper Swabia was first visited by pilgrims in 1730. An elderly woman observed Mary's eyes on a statue mounted on a confessional at the side of the church move, apparently to look at the crucifix over the high altar of the parish church.[115] Her story spread to surrounding villages, and other witnesses soon confirmed that Mary's eyes moved, and that at times her face appeared to flush, as if she were crying. During the next several years, local people flocked to Steinbach to investigate the statue. Miraculous cures soon occurred, often of children, apparently a group especially favored by the *Schmerzhafte Mutter*.[116] Other miracles and benefactions followed, such as the cure of cattle and horse diseases. As at Triberg, by the time the Bishop of Constance sent a

[111] EAF Ha 216, p. 99.

[112] *Zu Fuss, zu Pferd . . . Wallfahrten im Kreis Ravensburg*, p. 171; EAF Ha 216, pp. 99–100.

[113] Engelwies: EAF A1/1421; Wellendingen: EAF Ha 216, pp. 99–100. There is evidence of such miracles in the early sixteenth century as well, at Altheim: EAF Ha 70, p. 244a (Visitation of 1620).

[114] EAF Ha 216, p. 185.

[115] HStASt. B486/Bü798, Witness # 7

[116] In general on Steinbach, see Guth, "Geschichtlicher Abriß," p. 809; *Zu Fuss, zu Pferd . . . Wallfahrten im Kreis Ravensburg*, pp. 238–241. Archival material on Steinbach: HStASt. B486/Bü793–798; EAF A1/1425; EAF Ha 225, pp. 123, 216–217; EAF Ha 226, pp. 14, 81.

commission to investigate the new shrine in the fall of 1733, the population had intensively used Steinbach for about three years.

Villagers easily integrated the shrine at Steinbach into local religious practice. The fame of the image of Mary quickly spread by word of mouth. A resident of Steinbach reported that "the reputation of the movement of the eyes" spread, that people developed "trust" in the statue, and therefore they came from near and far.[117] Other local people reported hearing about the statue and coming to Steinbach out of curiosity. Still others claimed to be skeptical, like the master cabinetmaker from Hasloch, who said "he could not under any circumstances believe that the eyes of a wooden image [*Bild*] could move . . . " yet he traveled over two hours to Steinbach to investigate.[118] Some were, however, hesitant to report what they saw, for, as one woman said later, "I did not want to say anything, [because] people would not believe me and would only laugh at me."[119] It is also apparent that many people who came to the church did not see Mary's eyes move. Enough, however, witnessed the miracle to spread its fame.

The majority of reports about Steinbach detailed the movement of Mary's eyes. This miracle provided no physical benefits to the witnesses, but was rather evidence of the sacred power manifest in Steinbach. Everyone involved with the shrine, the population, the local priests, and episcopal officials recognized its significance. If Mary's moving eyes were evidence of a sacred place, the miraculous cures attributed to Maria Steinbach provided concrete benefits to the surrounding population. In the first few years after the shrine's discovery, peasants credited Steinbach with a wide range of cures: mothers and babies were saved in childbirth, sick children were cured, children unable to talk suddenly found their voices, a priest's injured foot stopped hurting, blind children gained eyesight, and so on.[120] The frequency with which people turned to the new shrine for help indicates how quickly the shrine had become part of everyday life in the area.

Some cures were dramatic, even heart-rending episodes. The priest of Haisterkirch, Benedict Stadelhoffer, reported a story told to him by a parishioner:

> Joseph Dobler the *Schultheiß* of Ehrensberg, who is usually skeptical in such matters [*in derley sachen sonst [ein] hart glaubiger mann*], and his wife Catharina

[117] HStASt. B486/Bü798, Witness # 3. [118] HStASt. B486/Bü798, Witness # 22.

[119] HStASt. B486/Bü798, Witness # 9: *und mich nur auslachen.*

[120] EAF A1/1425. This is a large collection of reports about miracles, mostly sent in by parish priests.

Guthin, [told] how their young daughter, six years old, suffered such constant pains in both eyes that she could not look at the light. Instead she had to lie face down, and did nothing but scream from the pain day and night [*nichts als ach und wehe geschryen*]. It was enough to wring compassion from a stone [*ein stein hatte es erbarmen megen*]. All natural medicine was tried to take the child's pain away, without success. Then one evening, the father said out of pity for the child, "if only someone could take the pains from the child, I would give him 30 Gulden." [In response] a neighbor, Jacob Schmidt, advised him, "Joseph, vow a pilgrimage to Steinbach, and you will be helped." . . . Dobler, however, did not know about Steinbach, and asked "What sort of shrine is at Steinbach?" Jacob Schmidt answered "To our dear Lady, the grieving Mother." ["*Unserer liebe Frawen, der schmertzhaften Muetter*"]. He [Dobler] immediately vowed that if his child's pains were taken away, he would personally make a pilgrimage there at the next opportunity . . . and the longstanding pains disappeared from the child, and she became so healthy that she, although only four years old, made the pilgrimage with her parents, and even went half way on foot . . .[121]

Such cures did not happen every day, but they did occur in the region around Steinbach in the early 1730s.

Votive pictures from Steinbach indicate that Maria Steinbach protected the wealthy and powerful as well as commoners.[122] In 1763, Katherina Euphemia Gräfin Fugger-Boos donated a picture, crediting Mary for saving her and her traveling companions from injury when their coach fell into a ravine. Other votive pictures commemorated Maria Steinbach's intercession in favor of princes and noblemen, as well as millers and peasants.

Miracles certainly made a big impression on people from all walks of life. What is striking, however, is not so much the dramatic nature of many miracles credited to Steinbach, but rather their diversity. The Doblers' daughter was cured of a serious and painful disease; others were cured of minor fevers or an injured foot. Mary cured helpless children and young men, and also protected women in childbirth. Although Maria Steinbach paid special attention to children, she was a multi-purpose patron for the region.

The "miracles discourse" was only part of what happened at Steinbach. Pilgrims considered shrines to be places to practice devotions and most people began their visit to Steinbach by praying before the altar

[121] EAF A1/1425. This is a report from Haisterkirch.

[122] Badisches Landesmuseum Karlsruhe (ed.), *Barock in Baden-Württemberg. Vom Ende des Dreißigjährigen Krieges bis zur Französischen Revolution*, Ausstellung des Landes Baden-Württemberg unter der Schirmherrschaft von Ministerpräsident Lothar Späth (Karlsruhe, 1981). Vol. I, Katalog, pp. 675–682.

with the statue of Mary.[123] There were other kinds of devotion. One witness said he had wanted to "carry out his devotion" (*seine Andacht ablegen*) and thus attended Mass.[124] Another man testified that he went to Mass, then, after the service had ended, stayed in the church to complete his devotions, apparently meaning prayers and contemplation. The statue was even available outside Steinbach, for one peasant testified that he prayed before a picture of the *Gnadenbild* in his house.[125]

Many people at Steinbach saw Mary's eyes move while praying the Rosary. One pilgrim commented that during her prayers, "she [Mary] sometimes looked completely red, as if she had been crying."[126] That the grieving Mary wept during the prayers is not surprising, given that parts of the Rosary require the believer to contemplate the life and sufferings of Jesus. Maria Steinbach affirmed and reinforced the believers' commitment to the Rosary.

The shrine obviously became a center of the dominant cult of the Virgin. It also served to reinforce other typical devotions, especially the cult of the Eucharist, the Catholic devotion *par excellence*. Johannes Gebele reported that he went to Steinbach in 1731, "desiring to make his devotions, and during the Mass both before and after the elevation of the Host, he looked at the image of the grieving mother of God that is [located] to the right of the [high altar], and saw how this image . . . moved its eyes to look at the Eucharist . . ."[127]

Gebele was not the only pilgrim to see Mary look at the Host during the Mass, particularly at the moment of transubstantiation.[128] In the experience of the pilgrims, miracles and devotions intermingled, linking the two most popular devotions of popular Catholicism, the cult of Mary and the cult of the Eucharist.

When news of the new shrine reached Constance, episcopal officials sought ways of suppressing the shrine. In 1731, the Clerical Council discussed the case. "A reliable report has come to us that . . . a new *Wallfahrt* has been founded at Steinbach and that various superstitions have occurred there." In 1732 the council expressed distress about the reports of miracles, about the distribution of printed pictures of Maria Steinbach, and about the publication of songs about the shrine. The council then appointed a commission to investigate the miracles at

[123] Some examples: HStASt. B486/Bü797, p. 5; HStASt. B486/Bü798, Witness # 14.
[124] HStASt. B486/Bü798, Witness # 16.
[125] HStASt. B486/Bü797, pp. 7v–8r, Witness # 11.
[126] HStASt. B486/Bü798, Witness # 12.
[127] HStASt. B486/Bü798, Witness # 16.
[128] HStASt. B486/Bü798, Witness # 22. This witness, Georg Sender, saw the eyes move during Mass on several occasions, and while he prayed before the Host after Mass.

Steinbach.[129] What happened to the episcopal commission probably surprised officials in Constance. Rather than quashing the shrine, the commissioners (Franz Andreas Rettich, a member of the Clerical Council, and Elias Bruggberger, the dean of the *Landkapitel* Dietenheim and priest in Erolzheim) ended up supporting it.[130] They listened to the testimony of the faithful, read reports of parish priests in the region, and, overcoming their skepticism, gave the new shrine their support.

The minutes of the episcopal commission indicate that the commissioners and the peasants generally agreed both on the possibility of miracles and on what constituted evidence of a miracle.[131] Furthermore, if the clerics were generally skeptical of miracles, a number of peasants also came to Steinbach ready to believe the miracles were fraudulent. All parties demanded evidence of miracles, but such evidence was easy to find. The eyes on the statue moved if the witnesses saw them move, as long as there was sufficient light and their eyesight was good enough. On a few occasions the commissioners suggested that people might have been deceived by their imagination, but they readily accepted the pilgrims' denials. Miraculous cures were somewhat more complicated to certify, but here too all parties agreed on the main issues. Although people could be healed either by natural/medical means or by a miracle, the burden of proof was on the natural cure. The commissioners would ask, for example, if a cure could be attributed to a medical treatment, but always accepted the response that the cure came too long after treatment to be attributed to it. Supernatural cures were subjected to less rigorous scrutiny, and could include any cure that was not directly attributable to medical intervention. Ultimately, then, the clerical commissioners did not really come from a different world than the peasants and quite easily accepted reports of miracles.

It also seems likely that the commission, and by extension the episcopal hierarchy in general, was convinced of Mary's activity at Steinbach by the volume and vehemence of the testimony they heard. Sitting in a meeting room in Constance, the Clerical Council found it hard to believe that the eyes of a wooden statue could move. Confronted in the church in Steinbach by convinced believers who stood by their testimony under aggressive questioning, the same men changed their mind. The Steinbach commission of 1733 speaks volumes about the attitude of

[129] EAF Ha 225, pp. 123, 217; EAF Ha 226, pp. 14, 81.

[130] HStASt. B486/Bü798, p. 1r.

[131] Freitag, *Volks- und Elitenfrömmigkeit*, pp. 218–230.

the Catholic elite toward popular religion; it also reminds us of the influence of the common people on the clergy and on the elite.[132]

Steinbach demonstrates the power of the population over the nature of Catholic devotion, and, by extension, the inability and unwillingness of the clergy to control and regulate religious practice. Importantly, the regular services and devotions of Catholic life were the setting for the miraculous moving eyes at Steinbach, as they were at the many active shrines of Southwest Germany. The miracles occurred in familiar church settings, during prayer or Mass. At the same time, Steinbach confirmed and reinforced the importance of the services and devotions as well as the sacraments of the Catholic Church. In pilgrimage piety one can identify the close interplay between the everyday experience of popular Catholicism, and the development of churchliness and Catholic identity.

Communal pilgrimage

Pilgrimages to Maria Steinbach and the other shrines of Southwest Germany were not "liminal" experiences, for they did not take pilgrims out of their everyday life or "strip actors of their social personae."[133] Instead, this shrine's popularity was tied to daily experience and to the varied roles it played in peasant life. In one sense, however, Steinbach was, in its early years, unusual for pilgrimage sites. Because it was so new, most pilgrims came to Steinbach in small groups or as individuals. This shrine was apparently not the destination for communal pilgrimage processions, as were most shrines in Southwest Germany.[134]

Communal pilgrimage processions were, by the early eighteenth century, an integral part of the rhythm of rural life. The most important shrine in the southern Black Forest, the Marian shrine at Todtmoos, attracted regular processions from around the region. In the seventeenth century about thirty-five annual votive processions came to Todtmoos, some from as far away as Basel and Upper Alsace.[135] The

[132] This is a major point made by Freitag, *Volks- und Elitenfrömmigkeit.*

[133] John Eade and Michael Salnow (eds.), *Contesting the Sacred, The Anthropology of Christian Pilgrimage* (London and New York, 1991), p. 4; Turner and Turner, *Image and Pilgrimage in Christian Culture*; Hüttl, *Marianische Wallfahrten*, esp. pp. 1–16.

[134] Klaus Guth, "Geschichtlicher Abriß," p. 809 indicates that by the 1750s there were processions to Steinbach as well. In general, see Brückner, *Walldürn*; Dünninger, *Maria siegt in Franken*; Hüttl, *Marianische Wallfahrten.*

[135] Brommer (ed.), *Wallfahrten im Bistum Freiburg*, p. 158.

villagers in Niederwihl, for example, made two processional pilgrimages to Todtmoos, one on the feast of the apostles Philip and Jacob, and another on *Kreuzerfindung*. The Niederwihler referred to the shrine as "*our* glorious and miraculous Todtmoos."[136]

Shrines like Todtmoos functioned as regional religious centers, and Catholic clergy and laypeople met there periodically during the year. Processions from fifty-seven parishes came to the shrine at Birnau in the early eighteenth century.[137] The processions came from parishes around Birnau, and most were filials of the monastery of Salem, the benefactor of the shrine. According to contemporary reports, the shrine at Engelwies attracted about seventy communal pilgrimages/processions each year.[138] In the eighteenth century the inhabitants of Kreenheinstetten were particularly enthusiastic pilgrims, going to Engelwies on four Fridays and six feast days each summer.[139]

Communal pilgrimages and parish processions were often indistinguishable, contributing to the everyday character of pilgrimage piety. In Birndorf, processions and pilgrimages ranged from the lengthy journeys to the *Kalvarienberg* near Waldshut, to Todtmoos, and to Waldkirch (all several hours away), and processions during Rogation Week to the neighboring villages of Dogern and Unteralpfen, to a short procession to a miraculous picture at the nearby Steinbacher bridge, and monthly processions around the church organized by the Brotherhood of the Rosary.[140] In form, communal pilgrimages were sometimes more elaborate than processions within villages, but not always. In Birndorf some of the longer pilgrimages were optional and apparently quite plain events, while the processions within the parish on St. Martin's or Corpus Christi were ritually intricate affairs.[141] In the context of a dense processional life, communal pilgrimages to shrines were not exceptional events, but rather a religious practice embedded in the liturgical year.[142]

136 Jakob Ebner, *Geschichte der Ortschaften der Pfarrei Niederwihl (Niederwihl, Oberwihl und Rüßwihl)* (Wangen, 1956) (hereafter Ebner, *Niederwihl*), p.117.

137 GLAK 98/4242. Another document in the same file lists forty-seven processions. This latter document, although undated, may be from the seventeenth century.

138 Ebner, *Engelwies*, p. 64.

139 Ebner, *Engelwies*, p. 64. The journey was about 10km. The four Fridays represented a reduction in the number of pilgrimage processions in the original vow, which promised a procession each Friday between *Kreuzauffindung* (4 May) and *Kreuzerhöhung* (14 September).

140 Ebner, *Birndorf*, pp. 113–115.

141 Ebner, *Birndorf*, pp. 113–115.

142 Habermas, *Wallfahrt und Aufruhr*, esp. ch. 3, argues that pilgrimages became more important in the everyday life of the common people in the seventeenth and eighteenth centuries and created exceptional moments of *Gemeinschaftsgefühl* (community feeling).

CONCLUSION

Pilgrimage piety linked sacred places and the institutional Church and brought to life the tie between "*Land und Kirche*." This tie was not unique to Southwest Germany, as William Christian has demonstrated in his study of sixteenth-century Spain.[143] German shrines were, however, somewhat less local than in Spain. Shrines such as Todtmoos, Triberg, Birnau, and Steinbach became religious centers for whole clusters of parishes, rather than for one parish. German *Gnadenorte*, however, did function much like Spanish shrines. Especially after the Thirty Years' War, peasants vowed pilgrimages to shrines, miracles became a regular part of religious life, and pilgrimage piety came to define what it meant to be Catholic. Understandably, but nevertheless somewhat ironically, the population found pilgrimages more attractive as the Church stopped manipulating them. At the same time, important parts of the church establishment shared the popular enthusiasm for pilgrimage, shrines, and miracles. This attitude was especially evident among the great monasteries of the Southwest, which promoted shrines, bought relics, and resisted episcopal efforts to restrict the number of shrines.

By the end of the eighteenth century, much of the Catholic elite no longer participated in pilgrimage piety, although the parish clergy remained aware of its importance. In 1793, as the Austrian government sought to shut down chapels and shrines in its territories, Ludwig Haßler, the *Stadtpfarrer* of Rottenburg am Neckar, wrote a long letter to his ecclesiastical superior, the vicar general in Constance.[144] Haßler hoped to keep the shrine at Weggental open and his letter reveals much about both the attitude of the clergy toward shrines and the role of pilgrimage in popular Catholicism. According to the *Stadtpfarrer*, Weggental was an important shrine, and the Rottenburger, as well as the peasants from the surrounding villages, came in large numbers to the church. Haßler informed his superiors that, despite the popularity of the shrine, closing it would bring "no cause to fear violence, but it might rather lead to grumbling and discontent, also an unwillingness to pray and [to practice] other public devotions on the part of the great majority if not everyone."

Haßler proceeded to argue that the devotions practiced at shrines like Weggental were what really tied people to Christianity and the Church:

[143] Heinrich Richard Schmidt, *Konfessionalisierung im 16. Jahrhundert* (Munich, 1992), p. 2. On Spain, see Christian, *Local Religion*.

[144] HStASt. B467/769.

One may try to distinguish for the common man the essentials of Christianity [*das Wesentliche des Christentums*] as clearly as one wishes, but he still does not like to be disturbed in his longstanding external devotional practices. If this happens, then he believes (although unjustly) himself justified in throwing over all remaining devotional practices and permits himself indifference in worshipping God, diversion, and carelessness.[145]

Finally, Haßler also insisted that the devotions practiced at Weggental were an integral, in fact an indispensable part of the daily lives of his parishioners. Without the shrine, the religious and moral world of the Rottenburger would collapse:

The greatest part of the inhabitants here are busy with farming, and they work hard and diligently [*hart und scharf*] the whole week long, and so, on Sundays and feast days after parish services and the immediately following midday meal, they like to go out to the Weggentaler chapel in order to pray, which they do in about two hours . . . If . . . this church is closed, what will fill the gap? Perhaps he [the common man] will go to the inn earlier than usual, and therefore stay there longer, with the inevitable collapse of his prosperity, his health, even to the obvious disadvantage to his habits, morals, and orderliness.[146]

Haßler's letter is clearly polemical and even somewhat overwrought. Yet it also gives a sense of the embeddedness of shrines and pilgrimage piety. Josephine reformers and *Aufklärung* church leaders considered pilgrimages a marginal aspect of Catholic life. Haßler knew otherwise, for in Southwest Germany pilgrimage was central to everyday popular Catholicism.

[145] HStASt. 467/769. [146] HStASt. 467/769.

CHAPTER 3

Religious practice

Pilgrimage was just one of the many Catholic practices where popular and official Catholicism overlapped and reinforced each other. The Church and the population also agreed on the importance of most other rituals of Catholic practice: the sacraments, weekly services, regular Mass, and prayer, especially the Rosary, and the festivals of the liturgical year. The basic harmony achieved between the Church and the faithful was the result of a number of structural and institutional factors within German Catholicism, including the temporizing nature of the disciplinary aspects of Tridentine reform in Germany. Decisive, however, was the willingness of the Church to tolerate and even support popular religious practices, and the simultaneous popular appropriation of many clerical initiatives. If shrines and pilgrimage illustrate the ways in which the Catholic Church accepted popular devotions, the rapid growth of the cult of the Rosary, complete with confraternities, prayer meetings, and processions, exemplifies popular enthusiasm for clerical initiatives.[1]

THE LITURGICAL YEAR AND EVERYDAY RELIGIOUS EXPERIENCE

Early modern Catholicism was and remained a religion of ritual. Indeed, German Catholics seemed to turn with enthusiasm to rituals, as a counterpoint to the Lutheran critique of the "empty rituals" of late medieval Christianity.[2] People participated regularly in a number of

[1] Ludwig Veit and Ludwig Lenhart, *Kirche und Volksfrömmigkeit im Zeitalter des Barocks* (Freiburg, 1956), pp. 195–196. Also, Louis Châtellier, *La Religion des pauvres: les missions rurales en Europe et la formation du catholicisme moderne, XVIe–XIXe siècles* (Paris, 1993) in a more general way argues that missionaries promoted practices that appealed to the common people.

[2] Veit and Lenhart, *Kirche und Volksfrömmigkeit*, esp. pp. 1–11; Niels Rasmussen, "Liturgy and the Liturgical Arts" in John O'Malley (ed.), *Catholicism in Early Modern History* (St. Louis, 1988), esp. pp. 281–285. On rituals in late medieval Germany and in sixteenth-century Protestantism, see Susan

different, but interrelated sets of practices. Robert Scribner has argued that before the Reformation, "Most people would have experienced religion as ritual practice in at least two basic ways. One was through the rites of 'passage' marking out the stages of the individual life-cycle . . . The other was through an annual cycle of ritual constituted by the liturgical year."[3]

The rites of passage lost none of their importance in Baroque Catholicism. The rituals of the liturgical year, particularly the processions that came to mark almost all holidays, also remained essential to the experience of Catholicism through the eighteenth century. Indeed, despite the efforts of church reformers to simplify and regularize festivals, holidays, and processions, the liturgical year was at least as dense and complex in 1750 as it had been in the fifteenth century.[4]

In the two centuries after 1550 another set of rituals, regular *Gottesdienste*, particularly Sunday services, weekday masses, and prayer meetings, gained an increasingly prominent place in Catholic practice. This was a new aspect of popular Catholicism, for in late medieval religion weekly church services played a lesser role than the rites of passage and the liturgical year.[5] As regular services gained in importance, however, they did not replace the grander celebrations of the great feast days, but rather supplemented them, adding another set of rituals to the already busy calendar of Catholic practice.

These three sets of rituals, the liturgical year, weekly services, and the rites of passage, are sometimes difficult to separate out. In part they overlapped and interacted at so many points because the official sacraments of the Church were an essential part of all three systems.[6] In addition, important aspects of Catholic piety, particularly the cults of the Virgin Mary or of the Eucharist, were integral to both annual and weekly rituals. Finally, certain forms of religious expression and certain institutions played multiple roles. Processions or prayer meetings were

Karant-Nunn, *The Reformation of Ritual. An Interpretation of Early Modern Germany* (London and New York, 1997). On rituals in general, Edward Muir, *Ritual in Early Modern Europe* (Cambridge, 1997).

[3] Robert Scribner, "Ritual and Popular Religion in Catholic Germany at the Time of the Reformation" in *Popular Culture and Popular Movements in the Reformation* (London, 1987), p. 18.

[4] The number and frequency of processions probably declined after the Reformation, as has been demonstrated for the area around Mainz. Andreas Ludwig Veit, *Kirche und Kirchenreform in der Erzdiözese Mainz im Zeitalter der Glaubensspaltung und der beginnenden tridentinischen Reformation* (Freiburg, 1920), p. 71.

[5] Scribner, "Ritual and Popular Religion in Catholic Germany"; Robert W. Scribner, *The German Reformation* (Atlantic Highlands, 1986), pp. 7–11; Euan Cameron, *The European Reformation* (Oxford, 1991), pp. 9–19.

[6] An analysis of popular practice that begins with the sacraments tends to blur the differences between different sets of rituals and also overemphasizes the importance of the sacraments.

part of a great variety of rituals, and confraternities, to give one example, could fill many different roles.

The rituals of Southwest German Catholicism remained largely in the hands of the communities themselves. Town councils and village communes expected priests to baptize children and hear deathbed confessions. They organized and financed processions and church festivals, demanded that priests bless crops and fields, and requested more frequent church services. Peasants and townspeople worked to create and maintain an elaborate religious experience, seeking a greater number of religious opportunities and resisting efforts to guide or regulate devotional life. Ultimately, popular initiatives provided people with a greater choice in forms of practice. Popular involvement also meant that such devotions as processions, pilgrimage, and the Mass, which were highly communal, remained vital, even as the cult of the Rosary and other devotions with a more individual focus gained in popularity.

The rites of passage

The sacraments of the Catholic Church marked several important moments in the lives of the peasants and townspeople. Baptism, confirmation, marriage, and extreme unction were, at least in theory, experiences shared once in a lifetime by all Catholics. Popular practice was, of course, somewhat different. The sacrament of baptism had become indispensable already by the late Middle Ages, and in the sixteenth century the Catholic Church effectively inserted itself into marriage ceremonies. On the other hand, neither confirmation nor extreme unction achieved a similar status in Southwest Germany. However, in the seventeenth and eighteenth centuries Catholics viewed a deathbed confession and communion as an essential preparation for the afterlife.

There can be no doubt about the importance of baptism in popular Catholicism. It may be true, as John Bossy argues, that Tridentine reform reduced the role of baptism in creating kinship ties when it limited the number of godparents.[7] Sources from the parishes of Southwest Germany, however, emphasize not godparents but rather the absolute indispensability of the sacrament. Indeed, throughout the two

[7] On late medieval baptism, see Karant-Nunn, *The Reformation of Ritual*, pp. 43–50; John Bossy, "The Counter-Reformation and the People of Catholic Europe" *Past and Present* 47 (1970), pp. 51–70. There were conflicts over the number of godparents allowed in Schönau in the early seventeenth century: GLAK 229/94055.

centuries after 1550, villagers and townspeople insisted that priests perform baptisms in a timely fashion and lamented the dire dangers to the souls of unbaptized babies. Baptism was always the first and foremost duty of the pastor, the *Seelsorger*.

Baptism was essential for salvation, but so was a full confession of one's sins before death. In fact, these two rites of passage came to be connected, and complaints about the availability of baptism were often paired with discussions of the availability of deathbed confession and communion. Deathbed confession became more important after 1650, and, like baptism, it required a resident priest for it to take place without seriously endangering the faithful. In the 1770s, the villagers of Sisseln said that not only had two babies died without baptism, but fifteen other people had died without a last confession and communion. Villagers were also quick to criticize resident priests who either refused to visit the sick or did so reluctantly. Andreas Breth, priest in Dellmensingen, enraged his parishioners by responding slowly to such requests, by insulting the dying, and even by saying that he was glad one child had died, because it meant one less parishioner.[8]

The concern with deathbed confession and communion contrasts sharply with a lack of interest in, or even fear of, the sacrament of extreme unction. What evidence there is indicates a reluctance to take the sacrament. The priest in Schönau in 1613 said that his parishioners simply did not ask for extreme unction. In the 1670s the priest in Hochsal reported "that most [of his parishioners] shied away from extreme unction, saying that [if they took it] they would die immediately, and if they did recover they would not be allowed to put their feet on the ground again and would no longer be able to dance."[9] Such fears meant that adult Catholics avoided extreme unction and preferred to face death after confessing their sins and taking communion.

The history of the sacrament of marriage and its relationship to social practice is long and complicated.[10] The *Tametsi* decree of the Council of Trent sought to reform the sacrament of marriage, especially by putting new obstacles in the way of clandestine marriages. In practice, this reform required the publication of banns, a reform that coincided with

[8] GLAK 79/825, # 59; HStASt. B466a/106b (1692).

[9] GLAK 229/94055. Quoted from Jakob Ebner, *Geschichte der Ortschaften der Pfarrei Hochsal* (Wangen, 1958), p. 58.

[10] Joel Harrington, *Reordering Marriage and Society in Reformation Germany* (Cambridge, 1995); Steven Ozment, *When Fathers Ruled. Family Life in the Reformation* (Cambridge, 1983); Karant-Nunn, *The Reformation of Ritual*, ch. 1. Little of this work carries the study of reform of marriage past the Thirty Years' War.

the needs of parents, especially those with property to hand down. There is scattered evidence that village leaders considered it important for parish priests to announce upcoming weddings from the pulpit. On the other hand, the sacrament itself did not gain a central place in the rituals of marriage. As one priest commented, after denying that he had failed to announce some weddings, "otherwise weddings are generally laughable events."[11]

The clergy of the Catholic Church thus officiated at some of the most important rites of passage. Yet the people incorporated the sacraments of the Church selectively into their lives, giving baptism a central role, and increasingly emphasizing deathbed confession and communion. The sacrament of marriage, by contrast, was a part of popular practice without coming to dominate the event; and extreme unction had no appeal to the common people and was consciously kept at a distance. Catholic rituals and sacraments were an important part of the all-important rites of passage, as they were in all rituals of everyday life in the villages and towns.

The liturgical year

Catholic villagers and townspeople lived their religion by participating each year in a large number of feast days. These days were occasions for special church services and, quite often, processions. Almost all fieldwork and housework were forbidden on feast days, making them occasions for sociability as well as for church services. Traditionally dispersed unevenly over the calendar year, these feasts (intentionally or not) linked the liturgy of the Catholic Church with the annual rhythms of agricultural life.

Seventeenth- or eighteenth-century inhabitants of Southwest Germany would have recognized Scribner's account of the rituals of the liturgical year on the eve of the Reformation. The "ritual cycle was constituted by the great feasts which re-enacted liturgically the major mysteries of Christian belief, the Incarnation and the saving Death and Resurrection of the Lord." The heart of the liturgical year was the *Herrenjahr*, the feasts that commemorated the life of Jesus, all of which occurred between December and June. This was a set of three

[11] HStASt. B467/473 (Duty of priest to announce marriages). Quote from GLAK 98/3557. Karant-Nunn emphasizes that church ceremonies "constituted but a fraction of the wedding observance." *The Reformation of Ritual*, p. 41.

"sequences," beginning with the Christmas season (Advent to Epiphany, on January 6), followed by the feasts of Easter, highlighted by Passion Week, and ending with the five weeks after Easter, which included Pentecost, Trinity Sunday, *Kreuzwoche* (Week of the Cross), and Corpus Christi.[12]

Easter itself was the heart of the *Herrenjahr*. Peasants, townspeople, and their priests shared the conviction that the services from Good Friday to Easter Sunday were the most important of the year.[13] In 1763 the villagers of Langenschemmern and Aufhofen demanded that a priest provide not just a short service, but a full Easter celebration, complete with Mass and sermon, in their church, even though the church at Langenschemmern was a filial church.[14] The theological significance of Easter was not lost on the common people, and their sense of the solemnity of the occasion was heightened by the fact that this was one time of year when all inhabitants confessed and took communion. For most Catholics, at least until the mid-eighteenth century, the sacraments of penance and the Eucharist were closely linked to Easter and part of the rituals of the liturgical year, not expressions of individual piety.[15] The fulfillment of "Easter obligations," followed by solemn and universally attended services, was the highlight of the liturgical year.

In the eighteenth century, the increased popularity of more frequent confession and communion further enhanced the major feasts. This development was related to the clergy's efforts at promoting new devotions in keeping with the long-term goals of the Council of Trent, but also another indication of the popular drive to intensify religious life after 1650. The priest in Schlatt, in the Rhine valley, reported in 1749 that he heard confessions and gave communion at Easter and Pentecost, on the Marian holidays, and on several saints' days.[16] More frequent confession and communion, then, remained embedded in the religious

[12] This description follows Scribner, "Ritual and Popular Religion in Catholic Germany," pp. 19–20 and Muir, *Ritual in Early Modern Europe*, pp. 55–80. See also Eamon Duffy, *The Stripping of the Altars. Traditional Religion in England, 1450–1580* (New Haven, 1992), ch. 1.

[13] For the various Easter liturgies: P. Alban Dold, *Die Konstanzer Ritualientexte in ihre Entwicklung von 1482–1721* (Liturgiegeschichtliche Quellen, Heft 5/6) (Münster, 1923), pp. 133–150.

[14] GLAK 98/3848.

[15] W. David Myers, *"Poor Sinning Folk." Confession and Conscience in Counter-Reformation Germany* (Ithaca and London, 1996); Veit and Lenhart, *Kirche und Volksfrömmigkeit*, ch. 2. See also John Bossy, *Christianity in the West, 1400–1700* (London, 1985). Priests continued to complain in the late seventeenth century that their parishioners came all at once to confession the week before Easter. See GLAK 229/94055, letter of 5 August 1661.

[16] GLAK 89/107.

celebrations of the liturgical year, and did not lead directly to regular or routine practice of these sacraments.[17]

Although the most important feasts were clustered within six months, there were church festivals throughout the year. The seven feasts of the Virgin, for example, were scattered across the year.[18] Indeed, what is most striking about the liturgical year in the seventeenth and eighteenth centuries (as well as in the early sixteenth) was its density and complexity, as well as its variety from place to place. The liturgical year also changed over time, as some feasts lost importance and new ones were introduced. This dynamism was in part the consequence of the Church's promotion of new holidays and its suppression of others. More important, however, was the fact that the village and town communities regularly vowed to celebrate new holidays.

In the early eighteenth century the basic framework of the liturgical year in Birndorf, a village in Hauenstein, closely matched the pattern described by Scribner.[19] The Birndorfer celebrated the major feasts of the year as required, but over the years they had also added votive holidays to the annual cycle. Additional holidays could come at any time of the year. The villagers celebrated St. Sebastian Day (January 20) to ward off the plague and St. Agatha Day (February 5) for the prevention of fires. On the latter holiday, bread and wax were blessed.[20] The community celebrated the annual parish festival on September 20, during a lull in the liturgical year, and added the feast of St. Wendelin (October 20) to the calendar as well.

Although episcopal ordinances set the basic framework of the liturgical year, votive holidays created a different calendar in each village. This variety caused problems for priests who had to serve more than one church and required them to adapt to local traditions. In 1704, the monastery of St. Blasien agreed to send a priest to help the overworked parish priest of Bettmaringen.[21] This parish included four churches: the

[17] Thomas A. Brady uses the term "religous intensification" in reference to Germany in the period around 1500. Thomas A. Brady, Jr., *The Politics of the Reformation in Germany. Jacob Sturm (1489–1553) of Strasbourg* (New Jersey, 1997), p. 27. On more frequent confession and communion, see Veit and Lenhart, *Kirche und Volksfrömmigkeit*, pp. 109–113. Myers argues that the trend in the seventeenth and eighteenth centuries was toward frequent, regular, and routine confession, but that this kind of confession was not common before the mid-eighteenth century. Myers, "*Poor Sinning Folk.*"

[18] February 2 (Purification), March 25 (Annunciation), July 2 (Visitation), August 15 (Assumption), September 8 (Birth), November 21 (Presentation) and December 8 (Conception).

[19] Ebner, *Birndorf*, pp. 112–115.

[20] On St. Agatha Day: Dold, *Die Konstanzer Ritualientexte*, pp. 119–120.

[21] GLAK 229/7580, 229/7582, 229/7589.

mother church at Bettmaringen and filial churches in Mauchen, Oberwangen, and Wittlekofen. Each of these churches had its own calendar of feast days, creating a logistical nightmare for the priests. Services had to be held in all four churches on Christmas, Easter, Pentecost (*Pfingsten*), and the major Marian feasts, and in at least two churches on the other holidays ordered by the bishop. Services were held on some saints' days in only one church. The Bettmaringer were the only ones in the area to celebrate St. Anthony Day (January 17), St. Margaret Day (July 20), and the Purification of the Virgin (February 2) as full-fledged holidays. In Mauchen they celebrated St. Gallen (October 16) and St. Catherine (November 25), while on St. Nicholas Day (December 6) there were services only in Wittlekofen.

The great feasts of the liturgical year clearly tied the peasants and townspeople of Southwest Germany to the rituals of the international Catholic Church. Yet here, as elsewhere in Catholic Europe, local traditions and local innovation remained an integral part of Catholic devotions. One aim of Tridentine reform, as Simon Ditchfield argues, was not so much to suppress local liturgical traditions as to "universalize the particular . . . by ensuring that local devotions operated within guidelines policed" by Rome.[22] Such a program allowed, particularly in the politically and ecclesiastically fragmented parts of Germany, for considerable local variety.

In this context, popular initiative led not only to the celebration of different and varied saints' days, but also to a localization of the great feasts. Thus the Birndorfer commemorated – and in a sense relived – Christ's crucifixion by attending Good Friday services on the *Kalvarienberg* (Calvary) in Waldshut. They also turned the Jesuit-promoted St. John of Nepomuk into a local saint by erecting a statue of the saint on a nearby bridge and going on procession there rather than attending an edifying sermon in the parish church.[23]

The Mass was of course the main event on all feast days. Yet contemporary descriptions of the liturgical year, such as the one produced by the *Pfarrer* in Görwihl in the mid-eighteenth century, recognized that various semi-official practices were also integral aspects of such occasions.[24] These practices included "sacred performances," such as passion plays and reenactments of Christ's ascension to Heaven,

[22] Simon Ditchfield, *Liturgy, Sanctity and History in Tridentine Italy* (Cambridge, 1995), p. 10.

[23] Ebner, *Birndorf*, pp. 113–114. See also Ebner, *Niederwihl*, p. 118 and Ebner, *Görwihl*, pp. 118. Nepomuk was martyred by being thrown off a bridge.

[24] Ebner, *Görwihl*, pp. 115–121.

blessings and benedictions of crops and fields, and prayers for protection from the dangers of rural life.

There is limited evidence of regular performances of plays on church feasts. Josephine reformers in the 1780s and episcopal authorities in the period after 1790 certainly inveighed against what they called *Nebenvorstellungen* (side shows), abolishing for example Good Friday processions with costumed figures, *Palmesel* processions on Palm Sunday and various Ascension Day ceremonies.[25] These reformers also considered the construction of a *Krippe* (crèche) suspect, allowing them only if unaccompanied by presentations of any kind. There is no doubt that various kinds of performances did take place. On Palm Sunday, villagers (especially young men) gathered green branches to serve as palms, carried them through villages in reenactments of Christ's entrance into Jerusalem and had them blessed during the church services. In Görwihl in the middle of the eighteenth century youths guarded Christ's open grave on the nights between Good Friday and Easter, a tradition that went back to the sixteenth century, and took place in other villages as well. Palm Sunday celebrations also often included the parading of the *Palmesel*, a representation of Christ on the ass that made its way through the village or town.[26] In these cases, the people promoted or maintained practices that were accretions to the official liturgy.

Blessings and benedictions of various kinds were also an accepted and significant aspect of many feasts. These blessings were particularly important in the summer, as rural communities worried about the success of the harvest. Most significant was the blessing of the fields on Ascension Day in all villages as part of a procession conducted around the edges of the cultivated part of each parish. There were other opportunities for such blessings. The villagers of Fischbach insisted that their parish priest "give a benediction over the fields and the grapes" each time he said Mass between May and September. Bread was blessed on the feast of St. Agatha and herbs on *Mariae Himmelfahrt*, and the regulations for these ceremonies remained enshrined in the official liturgical books of the Diocese of Constance well into the eighteenth century.[27]

[25] GLAK 79/951.

[26] Ebner, *Unteralpfen*, pp. 153–154; Dold, *Die Konstanzer Ritualientexte*, pp. 126–133; Ebner, *Görwihl*, p. 117; Scribner, "Ritual and Popular Religion in Catholic Germany," pp. 23, 26. An Austrian ordinance from 1787 specifically forbade the "*auferstehungszermonie*": GLAK 79/952. An Austrian decree from 1790 forbade the "*Herumführung des Palmesels*": GLAK 79/951.

[27] EAF A1/1418; GLAK 98/3817. These benedictions were between *Kreuzerfindung* (May 3) and *Kreuzerhöhung* (September 14). Ebner, *Görwihl*, pp. 116, 120; Ebner, *Birndorf*, pp. 113, 115. See also EAF A1/742 for efforts to limit the number of these benedictions. For official rituals, see Dold, *Die Konstanzer Ritualientexte*, esp. pp. 111–169.

Blessings were part of a wider effort by the rural population to enlist divine help in overcoming everyday problems.[28] By the middle of the eighteenth century, many feast days had acquired a particular protective role. The liturgical year in the village of Hochsal, also in Hauenstein, was typical. The villagers appealed to St. Anthony (February 17) and Saints Cyriacus and Smaragdus (August 6) to protect their cattle, evidence of the importance of livestock in this pastoral region. They further turned to Saints Fabian and Sebastian for protection against the plague and St. Agatha against fire.[29] If the Hochsaler were particularly concerned about their cattle, villagers on Lake Constance or in the Rhine valley asked the saints to protect their vineyards and their grain crops.

Popular initiative linked the liturgical year to the rhythms of an agricultural world. Yet this aspect of the religious experience did not prevent people from experiencing the central feasts of the *Herrenjahr* as a commemoration of the life of Christ. Indeed, devotional and theological aspects of certain holidays could be combined with the need for protection for crops and livestock. The parish of Niederwihl provides an example of this phenomenon.[30] The parish church possessed a piece of the True Cross, which became the focus of a number of special devotions to the Cross. It is unclear whether the villagers responded to the clerical promotion of devotion to the Cross, or added these feasts on their own initiative, but by the middle of the eighteenth century they practiced an unusually large number of such devotions. The Niederwihler went on processions on both the Discovery of the True Cross (May 3) and the Elevation of the True Cross (September 14), and attended prayer meetings every Friday between those two holidays. Yet if clerical organizers of such devotions hoped that these would lead to a more inward-looking and private Christocentric religion they may have been disappointed. The Niederwihler took their relic of the Cross on procession through their fields, combining their devotion to Christ with an appeal for fertility and protection from bad weather. Even the cult of the True Cross, which scholars generally considered a typical Counter-Reformation devotion, could be easily integrated into the rural religion of these peasants.

[28] This is the same point made by William Christian, *Local Religion in Sixteenth-century Spain* (Princeton, 1981). Also see Veit and Lenhart, *Kirche und Volksfrömmigkeit*, ch. 2.

[29] Ebner, *Hochsal*, p. 60.

[30] Ebner, *Niederwihl*, pp. 114–124. On devotion to the Cross, see Châtellier, *La Religion des Pauvres*, ch. 6.

Processions

Church feasts marked important moments in the liturgical year. The population experienced feasts above all as days of processions. Indeed, after 1650 processions joined the Mass as a defining ritual of feast days. The number of processions that criss-crossed the Catholic countryside (and meandered through cities and towns) grew steadily as well. These events too were generally promoted and organized by the people themselves, who thereby continuously elaborated their religious experience.

In the early eighteenth century, eleven major processions took place each year at Ettenkirch, a village not far from Lake Constance, many to destinations as far as two hours away.[31] In addition, once a month, as well as on Palm Sunday and on All Souls' Day, there was a procession around the church. Sometimes, especially "in times of ongoing food shortage, rain, too much heat, or drought," the community demanded that the priest lead one-time votive processions. The parish priest complained about the large number of processions, saying that "in this populous area there is no parish with so many and so difficult processions as Ettenkirch, [and there is] no remuneration for the priest." The priest in Ettenkirch certainly exaggerated his difficulties, for his parish was far from unusual. Processions were just as frequent, and sometimes even more strenuous, in other parishes.[32]

When Joseph Herckhner accepted his appointment as parish priest in Fischbach, on the shores of the Lake Constance, in 1698, he learned that he was required to participate in a long list of processions.[33] The *Gemeinde* prepared a full list of processions:

1 Tuesday before Easter: the procession leaves around three in the morning in good weather, to the Marian shrine at Eriskirch.
2 Feast of St. Mark the Evangelist: procession to Manzell.
3 Discovery of the True Cross: procession to the St. George Chapel outside the village.
4 Feast of St. George: procession and service in St. George Chapel.
5 Rogation Week (*Kreuzwoche*)
Monday: to Immenstaad
Tuesday: to Manzell
Wednesday: to Bermatingen.

[31] HStASt. B467/419.
[32] For example in Birndorf, in the Black Forest. Ebner, *Birndorf*, pp. 113–115.
[33] GLAK 98/3817.

6 Ascension Day (*Christi Himmelfahrt*): at about noon "the procession goes around the fields, during which, at the usual place, the Evangelia are sung, and the benedictions are made."
7 Corpus Christi: the procession can be before or after the service, at the discretion of the *Pfarrer*.
8 Feast of martyrs John and Paul: procession to the St. George chapel, referred to as the *Hagelfeyr* ("hail festival").
9 Feast of Sts. Peter and Paul: procession to Schnetzenhausen.
10 "At the end of April, or beginning of May, at the discretion of the priest and the *Pfleger*, there is a general procession for the purposes of blessing the fields."[34]
11 "Furthermore, after the harvest has been brought in the *Pfarrer* is required, at the discretion of the commune, to do a procession of thanks for received blessings [*Empfangne Guotthathen*]"

If the new priest was a thoughtful man, he probably recognized that the processions in Fischbach varied in place and purpose in parish life. First, many processions explicitly served the needs of an agricultural world. Second, several of the processions could be considered a kind of pilgrimage (most obviously the first one), demonstrating the overlap between processional and pilgrimage piety. Third, a number of processions often linked parishes together, drawing people into a religious world beyond their locality.[35] Finally, the *Gemeinde* in Fischbach played an active role in organizing the processions.

Processions came in many shapes and sizes and it is difficult and somewhat artificial to try to divide them into neat categories. Even the variety of names people gave to processions in the seventeenth and eighteenth centuries show this diversity. The villagers of Fischbach referred to "*Creützgäng und Processionen*," possibly distinguishing between those processions in which a cross was carried and those in which it was not. On the other hand, in Niederwihl even the processions that were part of that village's special devotions to the Cross were called "*Prozessionen*," while the Dean of the Rural Chapter of Stockach referred to all processions in his district as "*Creüzgänge*." Villagers and priests also regularly referred to "*Bittgänge*," a term that refers specifically to processions of petition, although it could be used quite indiscriminately. Finally, longer processions, especially those to shrines, were called

[34] The *Pfleger* was the lay administrator of the parish, appointed by the commune.

[35] Pilgrimages had this effect as well. See also Marc R. Forster, *The Counter-Reformation in the Villages. Religion and Reform in the Bishopric of Speyer, 1560–1720* (Ithaca and London, 1992), p. 239 and above chapter 2.

"*Wallfahrten*" or "*Wallfahrtszüge*." The term *Wallfahrt* has no direct English equivalent, although it refers more to pilgrimage than procession. Modern scholars recognize the ambiguity of *Wallfahrt*, and sometimes refer to "*Wallfahrtsprozessionen*" to show the overlap of the two concepts.[36] The variety of words used to describe the occasions when people moved through their towns, villages, and fields in more or less orderly devotional formation attests to the diversity of this form of piety.

Many processions went either around the parish church, through the village, or around the boundaries of the parish. All these processions were primarily communal rites, in part because the communes organized them, and in part because they symbolically defined the physical space of the village or town. Church officials and parish priests did not oppose this aspect of processions, for it coincided with the goal of strengthening the role of the parish in rural religion.[37] Processions within the parish were an important aspect of the liturgical year; whether they were "civic rituals" that actually promoted communal unity, or whether they succeeded in persuading people that the parish should be the primary locus of religious activity, is harder to determine.[38]

The procession on Corpus Christi (*Fronleichnam*) seems to have been the most elaborate of the year, and was held in almost every town and village.[39] The procession in Rottenburg am Neckar cost over 14fl. a year, which included money for the men and boys who carried the Eucharist, the cross, and various relics, as well as for the *Stadtknecht*, who was hired to keep order. In 1642 in Görwihl children wearing wreaths (*Kränze*) led the procession, followed by the Eucharist, which was escorted by the local militia *(Schützen)*, who fired off shots after each stop of the procession. Singing was an important part of the *Fronleichnam* procession in Niederwihl in the eighteenth century, and the parish chorus took a position of honor directly in front of the sacrament. Corpus Christi

[36] GLAK 98/3817; Ebner, *Niederwihl*, pp. 117–118; EAF A1/1418, *Landkapitel* Stockach; Hans Dünninger, *Maria siegt in Franken. Die Wallfahrt nach Dettelbach als Bekenntnis* (Würzburg, 1979), esp. pp. 78–81. For people in the eighteenth century, the difference between procession and pilgrimage seems to have been the distance the participants travelled, not the purpose of the journey.

[37] Louis Châtellier, *Tradition chrétienne et renouveau catholique dans le cadre de l'ancien Diocèse de Strasbourg (1650–1770)* (Paris, 1981), ch. XII, esp. p. 451.

[38] On the role of Corpus Christi processions, see Charles Zika, "Hosts, Processions and Pilgrimages: Controlling the Sacred in Fifteenth-Century Germany" *Past and Present* 118 (1988), esp. pp. 38–48.

[39] In a 1784 survey of processions, thirty-six of thirty-eight parishes in the Rural Chapter of Breisach in the Rhine valley held *Fronleichnam* processions. Almost all of these were in, around, or through the village. EAF A1/1418.

processions stopped four times, for blessings and readings from each gospel. In Hochsal, the procession went around the church, stopping in four places: in front of the village crucifix, at the gate of the churchyard (*beim Gatter*), at the entrance of the parsonage, and in front of the church. The celebration of Corpus Christi also continued throughout the week following the feast day itself and usually included at least two other processions.[40]

Ascension Day (*Christi Himmelfahrt*) was also the occasion for a major communal procession. On this occasion the procession went "*um den Ösch*", that is around the cultivated fields of the village. The villagers of Herbolzheim, in the Rhine valley, were very attached to this ceremony. In 1743, a local official reported that the commune was protesting an attempt by the Bishop of Strasbourg to forbid this procession. The bishop had ordered the abolition of all processions that might cause conflicts with Protestant neighbors, apparently striking at one of the important meanings of this procession in confessionally fragmented regions. The Herbolzheimer participated enthusiastically in this procession. According to their pastor, they honored the Eucharist "with all possible pomp and splendor, so that the faithful participated in large numbers and always with great reverence, praying with great devotion . . . " Parish priests and village communes recognized that processions with "flying flags, crosses held high, singing and loudly recited prayers" antagonized neighboring Protestants as they passed near their villages. In the view of Catholic villagers, this was one of the reasons behind the devotions, not grounds to abolish them. In the region around Rottenburg am Neckar, where Catholics and Protestants were in close contact, processions went "around the boundaries" (*auf die Grenze*) on the feast of St. Mark, in addition to going around the fields on Ascension Day, indicating a special concern for defining boundaries.[41]

Processions on Ascension Day had a particularly strong anti-Protestant message in villages along confessional boundaries. In purely Catholic areas of the Southwest, the same processions served to define the boundaries of the parish and brought the all-powerful Eucharist into the fields. In Assmanshardt, near Biberach, the procession on this day explicitly went "around the field with a blessing of the crops of the village." The *Christi Himmelfahrt* processions also became increasingly

[40] HStASt. B466a/331, p. 3r (1765); Ebner, *Hochsal*, p. 60; Ebner, *Görwihl*, p. 119; Ebner, *Niederwihl*, p. 124; Ebner, *Birndorf*, p. 114.

[41] GLAK 79/927, quote from letters of April 20, 1743 and November 24, 1743. EAF A1/1418, *Landkapitel* Rottenburg.

elaborate, so that by the 1770s officials complained that people spent too much time in processions, that they participated on horseback, and that the firing of weapons had become too common. In the later eighteenth century, such processions were almost universal in the rural chapters of Stockach, Breisach, and Biberach, although less common in the pastoral region around St. Blasien.[42] It is, however, almost impossible to find a village that did not hold a procession that went through or around the village, once again asserting the link between place and Church.

Another group of processions went from the village church to a nearby chapel or other site for devotion. These processions were the rural equivalent of the processions that symbolically linked the churches of cities and towns together.[43] As we have seen, these processions brought the sacral landscape to life, taking parishioners out of the church and into the surrounding country. These processions also counterbalanced the longer processions, particularly the pilgrimage processions, by reinforcing parish loyalties in going to local sacred sites. The people of St. Märgen, for example, went on procession to three different chapels in their parish, while the inhabitants of Staufen processed to three chapels and the Capuchin church each year.[44] It was more common that a parish had one filial church or chapel, which was then the destination for several processions each year. In any case, processions were vital rituals and those parishes without chapels, crosses, or shrines nevertheless held processions around the fields or through the village.

Most parishes held processions on the three days of Rogation Week, known as *Kreuzwoche* or *Bittwoche*. The processions generally occurred on the Monday, Tuesday, and Wednesday before Ascension Day and often went to neighboring parish churches. If the Ascension Day processions around the arable land were manifestations of local religion, the Rogation processions brought people from several neighboring parishes together. The parishes around Bettmaringen, in the County of Bonndorf, are an example of this experience.[45] On the first day of the week, the inhabitants of Wittlekofen processed to Bettmaringen and then went together with the Bettmaringer to Mauchen for Mass. On the next day, the Mauchener, Wangener, and Wittlekofer came to Bettmaringen, and

[42] HStASt. B17/524; EAF A1/1418.

[43] Zika, "Hosts, Processions and Pilgrimages," esp. pp. 38–40. Also Natalie Davis, "The Sacred and the Body Social in Sixteenth-Century Lyon" *Past and Present* 90 (1981), esp. pp. 55–60.

[44] EAF A1/1418, *Landkapitel* Breisach.

[45] GLAK 229/7580. Other examples from Hauenstein (Ebner, *Niederwihl*, pp. 123–124) and around Fischbach (GLAK 98/3817).

on the third day "thirteen crosses" processed to the church at Wittlekofen, some with their priests and some without. Rogation Week not only added to the diversity of processional life, but also brought groups of Catholics together.

Processions easily shaded into pilgrimages, particularly in villages near important shrines. As a matter of course, shrines became the destination of processions on important feast days. The shrines then served to bring together groups of parishes for services, and functioned much as the Rogation Week processions did elsewhere. The social and communal aspects of processions, especially those to shrines, were very important. Officials of the Abbey of Salem regularly complained that their subjects went in processions to the monastery's "house shrine" of Birnau, but not in a particularly orderly fashion. Some pilgrims "wander around [the procession] without any devotion, sometimes in front of, sometimes after the cross, come to the shrine and then go home." Furthermore, the pilgrims demonstrated only a casual interest in the church services at the shrine. Typically, the pilgrims "are unwilling to wait for services there [in Birnau], so after hearing one Mass they leave, even during the service . . . "[46] Nevertheless, however they behaved during processions, villagers experienced them as an integral part of their Catholic identity.

Rogation Week processions and processions to shrines, like regional shrines and monasteries, helped to create and maintain a sense of Catholic identity that went beyond the local parish. Villagers met and participated together in services and often processed part of the way to their destination together. There is no doubt that people not only met potential spouses, but were also exposed to new devotional practices on these occasions.

Processions, like most aspects of Catholic devotional life, were organized by village communes. The large number of votive processions that filled the liturgical year were the most obvious result of communal initiative. Another indication of their popular origin is that processions could take place without the participation of a priest. Furthermore, villagers could abandon processions, even when the local priest sought to continue them. The villagers of Seefelden, for example, had by 1681 stopped participating in a series of votive processions, prompting officials to ask both the *Gemeinde* and the parish priest whether the processions should be officially abandoned.[47] Further evidence of communal

[46] GLAK 98/804, 23 October, 1704 and 9 May, 1693.

[47] GLAK 98/804, 16 August, 1681. The processions may have originated in the Thirty Years' War.

organization of processions is the fact that conflicts arose when parish priests demanded special payments to accompany them, or even refused to participate at all.[48]

Parish priests and other clergymen, including the Jesuits and Capuchins, promoted processions, as they did pilgrimages. However, the clergy's attitude toward processions, again as with pilgrimage, became increasingly skeptical over the course of the eighteenth century. Already in the 1740s the Bishop of Strasbourg moved to limit the number of processions in his diocese, but the most dramatic attack on pilgrimages occurred in the 1770s and 1780s, when the Austrian government ordered drastic reductions in the number of processions allowed in its territory. Two tendencies came together in the attack on pilgrimages. An older tradition, strong within the episcopal hierarchy, found the sporadic and undisciplined nature of processional piety hard to reconcile with the Tridentine norms of regularity and order. The edicts of the Austrian regime, of course, reflected a second set of concerns, particularly an uneasiness with the intensification of religious life that occurred in the century after the Thirty Years' War, and the sense that peasants wasted too much time and energy, and too many resources in religious activities. The fact that reformers focused their attention on reducing the number of feasts and processions is surely another indication of the importance of these rituals for popular Catholicism.[49]

Weekly and daily services

Like almost all Europeans, the people of Southwest Germany were required to attend Sunday services in their parish church. This reality gave a certain unity to religious practice across the whole region. In fact, however, services were not available in every village and hamlet of Catholic Germany, and some people had no opportunity to attend Mass every Sunday. There were also many villagers who could, if they wished, attend a number of other services in addition to those offered on Sundays and feast days. As with other aspects of Catholic practice, the number of weekly (and daily) services grew in most places in the

48 See for example HStASt. B467/546 (Hirrlingen) and HStASt. B467/500 (Hailtingen). Even Austrian reformers in the 1780s sought the cooperation of communal authorities when they tried to reduce the number of processions to other parishes. See EAF A1/1418, *Landkapitel* Waldshut, parish of Niederalpfen.

49 On reforms see Eva Kimminich, *Religiöse Volksbräuche im Räderwerk der Obrigkeiten. Ein Beitrag zu Auswirkung aufklärerischer Reformprogramme am Oberrhein und in Vorarlberg* (Frankfurt, 1989).

seventeenth and eighteenth centuries, leading not to uniformity but to greater diversity.

Christopher Klingenberg, priest in Roggenbeuren, in the Linzgau, performed two masses a week in the 1620s.[50] He read the required anniversary masses and, like most of his colleagues, offered no catechism classes. His parishioners considered Klingenberg satisfactory in his job performance and decent in lifestyle, calling him "neither a gambler nor extravagant." In 1666, Johan Bluemenegg, the parish priest in Breitenau (in the Breisgau), read Mass and gave a sermon on Sundays and holidays.[51] This priest was well trained and diligent and also provided catechism classes, although, as he admitted, only once every six or seven weeks or so. The weekly services offered by Klingenberg and Bluemenegg are quite representative of the whole period from 1580 to about 1700. By about 1600 there were few priests who failed to provide weekly masses, and most gave sermons as well, but other services, such as catechism classes or prayer meetings, were much rarer.

The number of services expanded after 1650. In 1699, the priest in Fischbach was required to read two masses a week and give a sermon each Sunday. Furthermore, he had to lead Rosary prayers, hold evening services on Saturday and participate in monthly processions as well. The priest in Heitersheim in the Rhine valley in the 1730s had somewhat fewer obligations, but still read a Mass, gave a sermon, taught catechism, and led two prayer meetings each week. *Pfarrer* Fesser, priest in Altdorf near Weingarten, added to his own busy schedule by organizing prayer meetings on Saturdays, in addition to Mass, sermons, Vespers, and the praying of the Rosary on Sunday afternoons.[52]

Schönau was probably a typical rural village with a resident priest in the mid-eighteenth century. Weekly Mass and a Sunday sermon were services "according to ancient tradition"[53] and were required of all residents, while Vespers, prayer meetings, and catechism classes were more recent innovations offered to those who sought a more intense religious life. Villagers who lived without resident priests also demanded weekly masses, but, as in the villages around Bettmaringen, where one priest served several churches, they often had to get by with fewer.[54] In Mauchen, for example, there was a Sunday Mass only every other week, although if there was no Mass on Sunday the parishioners were

[50] EAF Ha 70, pp. 234r–235r (Visitation of 1620).
[51] EAF Ha 63, pp. 591–592 (Visitation of 1666).
[52] GLAK 98/3817; GLAK 89/106; HStASt. B466a/14 (1741).
[53] GLAK 229/94041. [54] GLAK 229/7580.

compensated with two weekday masses. When village communes appealed for a resident priest, they consistently pointed to the need for regular Sunday services and more frequent masses.[55]

For the people of Southwest Germany, the Mass remained the single most important religious ceremony. Occurring regularly, it was the central ritual of almost all important feast days and became an important part of processional and pilgrimage piety. It was easily the most highly visible sacrament of the Church. Furthermore, the Mass was obviously a vital part of the cult of the Eucharist, which became one of the defining features of Catholic identity.[56] All descriptions of church services in the villages and towns, whether in visitation reports or in documents produced by rural communes themselves, begin with a discussion of the number of masses the clergy provided in the parishes.[57]

Behind the demand for regular masses were several important elements of popular Catholicism. There was an ongoing sense of the spiritual benefits of witnessing the elevation of the Host for the individual and a related belief in the value of the Mass for the unity and salvation of the community.[58] There was no great shift in these attitudes in the centuries after 1550. The Council of Trent attacked a number of late medieval practices, especially the practice of selling new masses or the asking of alms for the performance of masses, which had developed from the popular sense that witnessing the Mass led to directly to salvation. These criticisms of popular practice could have reduced the role of the Mass, but the Council, the new orders, and the Catholic clergy rejected the more symbolic Eucharistic theology of the Protestants and continued to emphasize the mystery and power of transubstantiation and the Eucharist. Thus popular traditions and clerical promotion came together to strengthen the centrality of the Eucharist in Catholic practice. In the countryside of Southwest Germany, these trends

[55] See chapter 5 for an extensive discussion of petitions for more priests.

[56] Veit and Lenhart, *Kirche und Volksfrömmigkeit*, esp. ch. 3; Richard van Dülmen, *Kultur und Alltag in der frühen Neuzeit*, Vol. III *Religion, Magie, Aufklärung, 16.–18. Jahrhundert* (Munich, 1994), esp. p. 71.

[57] Visitations from before the Thirty Years' War tend to discuss the presence or absence of church services. After the war they were assumed to take place. See for example EAF Ha 70, pp. 233r–265r (*Landkapitel* Linzgau, 1620) and EAF Ha 62, pp. 341r–345r (*Landkapitel* Villingen, 1608) and pp. 362r-371v (*Landkapitel* Waldshut, 1608). EAF Ha 63, pp. 583–752 (*Landkapitel* Breisach, 1666) contains many details on church services. For reports from communes, see GLAK 98/3817 (Fischbach), GLAK 229/94041 (Schönau), and GLAK 229/7580 (Bettmaringen and vicinity).

[58] John Bossy, *Christianity in the West*, ch. 4, esp. pp. 72–75; John Bossy, "The Mass as a Social Institution, 1200–1700" *Past and Present* 100 (1983), pp. 29–61; Duffy, *The Stripping of the Altars*, ch. 3; Veit and Lenhart, *Kirche und Volksfrömmigkeit*, pp. 99–102; Rev. H. J. Schroeder, *Canons and Decrees of the Council of Trent* (London, 1941), pp. 144–152.

caused an ongoing demand for regular and indeed frequent masses.[59]

Priests complained about their parishioners' behavior during the Mass, as they had for centuries. In the late sixteenth century, officials of the monastery of Salem forbade their subjects from coming in and out of the church or from standing around gossiping in the churchyard during the reading of the Mass. A century later, *Pfarrer* Hauneld, priest in Schönau, complained to his immediate superior, the Abbot of St. Blasien, that his parishioners loitered and drank in front of the church during services.[60] Such complaints were standard features of the grievances of discontented clergymen and they reflect not a popular rejection of the Mass, but the unwillingness of some to treat the whole church service with the kind of reverence the clergy wanted.

One of the religious goals of communes from the late seventeenth century on was to expand the number of masses available in local churches and to require the resident priest to officiate at a certain number each week. Petitions for new parishes and/or resident priests regularly asked for more masses soon after explaining the need for a priest to do baptisms and hear the confessions of the sick and dying. The inhabitants of the small Austrian town of Elzach wanted their three priests to celebrate at least one Mass a day in the parish church, as well as several endowed masses a week in a nearby chapel. The priest in Aach complained that "those in the village" (*die im Dorf*) were trying to obligate him to hold Sunday and feast day masses, which he claimed was an innovation. In the mid-eighteenth century the villagers of Schlatt complained that the Franciscan friars who served their parish rushed through Sunday Mass in order to get back to their monastery, thereby undermining the value of the ritual for the village.[61] The inhabitants of isolated farms and hamlets, especially in the wilds of the Black Forest, often complained about irregular and insufficient church services.[62] The Mass was essential; peasants attended it in large numbers and considered regular masses part of what their priest should provide.[63]

59 See the complaints of the commune of Hailtingen against the parish priest who neglected certain masses: HStASt. B467/500.

60 GLAK 98/804; GLAK 229/94046. Compare the example of Speyer: Forster, *The Counter-Reformation in the Villages*, p. 115.

61 Elzach: GLAK 229/24473 (16 January, 1693). There were still problems in 1777 (GLAK 79/825, # 54). Aach: GLAK 229/42, p. 57r (1674). Schlatt: GLAK 79/825, # 26.

62 Niederwinden: GLAK 79/825, # 92. The inhabitants of Buchenbach had the same problem: GLAK 79/825, # 97.

63 It was illegal and caused great scandal for someone to intentionally not attend Mass. See HStASt. B467/546 for the example of the *Schultheiss* of Hirrlingen who was involved in a dispute with the parish priest and "had no hesitation" about missing Mass.

Sermons became an integral part of Sunday and feast day services by the late sixteenth century. Priests always complained about the attention span of their audiences, but pastors risked the wrath of their parishioners if they decided to forgo a sermon. *Pfarrer* Struber of Schönau was already unpopular in his parish, but he made things even worse when he decided to skip his sermon on Good Friday 1661. Struber reported that on that day attendance was poor due to bad weather and that he had decided to hear confessions instead of preaching, arguing that "it is more useful and of greater merit to do something for the salvation of your fellow man than to preach with poor results to these Endymions."[64] Struber, although a local man by birth who perhaps should have known better, considered the sermon nothing more than a chance to edify and educate his parishioners, while confession was of direct benefit to the individual. For the people of Schönau, however, the sermon had become part of the ritual. A Sunday service, and particularly the service on a major holiday, was not complete without a sermon. In the eighteenth century the Schönauer explicitly linked the Mass and the sermon, stating that the second duty of their *Pfarrer* (after baptizing babies) was "as tradition prescribes to read Mass and also to preach each Sunday and feast day."[65]

Catechism classes also gradually became part of the regular services in most rural parishes. These services gained popular acceptance more slowly than did sermons, no doubt because they required active participation on the part of both the priests and the population. Before 1620 there is little evidence of regular classes in the countryside and considerable indication of popular resistance to catechism.[66] After the Thirty Years' War the Church abandoned the effort to catechize the population as a whole and turned its attention to children. The classes came to be known as *Kinderlehr*, were held every Sunday after services, and were widely accepted. Catechism classes were quite universal in the district around Breisach in 1666, although they were not held weekly in every parish. The parishes of Schönau and Fischbach both listed "*Christliche oder kinderlehr*" as one of the obligations of the parish priest and expected him to ring the bells to announce the classes at noon each Sunday. The *Gemeinde* of Dettingen pleaded for a resident priest because the village's

[64] GLAK 229/94055, 5 August, 1661: ". . . *als mit schlächten frücht Endymionibus zuepredigen.*" Endymion is the subject of a Greek legend of seduction and sexuality.

[65] GLAK 229/94041.

[66] See the visitation reports, for example EAF Ha 70, pp. 233r–265r (*Landkapitel* Linzgau, 1620) and EAF Ha 63, pp. 1139–1152 (*Landkapitel* Freiburg, 1585).

children were "poorly educated" without regular catechism lessons.[67] Popular opposition to catechism classes had faded, but the Church's expectations of what the classes might accomplish diminished as well.

Another important element in the intensification of popular Catholicism after 1650 was the growth of the cult of the Rosary. After 1650, the people of Southwest Germany responded to the clerical promotion of this cult by incorporating the vocal and mental prayers of the Rosary into processions, into the celebration of Marian and Eucharistic holidays, and into regular weekly services. Devotion to the Rosary also led to the spread of prayer meetings to rural parishes, an innovation that brought a new form of religious practice to the countryside.

The Rosary allowed, indeed required, parishioners to participate actively in services. By incorporating the prayers into existing services, priests may have considered the Rosary a way to keep the attention of their audience. Although they became an integral part of most Marian holidays, Rosary prayers could be incorporated into almost any service. In Birndorf the faithful prayed two rosaries during the St. Sebastian Day services and on the feast of St. George. In eighteenth-century Görwihl the Rosary became part of the blessing of salt and water on Epiphany in January.[68]

Indeed, by the middle of the eighteenth century the Rosary not only supplemented the existing liturgy, but also began to replace certain traditional services. In Fischbach in 1698, the parish priest had the option of performing Vesper services or leading Rosary prayers on the afternoon of high feast days. In the 1730s the priest in Heitersheim had the same choice on Sundays, although he was still expected to hold Vespers on feast days. Furthermore, Rosary prayers eventually replaced Vesper services on Saturday evenings and on the eve of major feasts.[69] The Rosary demanded more active participation by the faithful than attendance at Vespers, an important change in the character of religious practice.

The cult of the Rosary came to play a role in almost all church services and was part of the general expansion of religious services in Catholic villages. Monthly prayer meetings, often organized by confraternities of the Rosary, and weekly prayers during Lent, further

[67] EAF Ha 63, pp. 583–752. GLAK 229/94041 (Schönau) and GLAK 98/3817 (Fischbach). Announcing the classes with the bells may indicate their importance, as bells also announced Mass. See Veit and Lenhart, *Kirche und Volksfrömmigkeit*, pp. 133–134; GLAK 229/18138, p. 42r.

[68] Ebner, *Birndorf*, p. 113; Ebner, *Görwihl*, p. 115.

[69] GLAK 98/3817; GLAK 89/106; Ebner, *Niederwihl*, pp. 124–125; Ebner, *Birndorf*, p. 115; GLAK 98/3817 (Fischbach); HStASt. B466a/14.

supplemented the Sunday afternoon prayers, and contributed to the ubiquity of the Rosary. Pilgrims prayed the Rosary at shrines, considering it a primary way to perform their devotion (*Andacht*) at the end of a pilgrimage. In less populated places, there were benches where people who could not get to a church could pray on Sunday afternoon, presumably in small groups.[70]

Although elements within the clergy promoted the cult of the Rosary, most evidence indicates that, at least after 1650, the population supported this initiative. Indeed, opposition to individual prayers and to prayer meetings sometimes came from parish priests, who considered these services a new imposition on their time. In 1763 *Pfarrer* Joseph Wild of Hirrlingen argued that he had no obligation to lead monthly prayer meetings in his church, even if his predecessors had done so.[71] An episcopal commission rejected Wild's argument and ordered him to lead the meetings without demanding an additional fee. By this period, Rosary meetings were popular among the religiously active and village communes considered participation in them one of the basic duties of a parish priest.[72]

The Rosary was the dominant new devotional form in the countryside, but it was not the only one. In the 1770s and 1780s stations of the cross were built into some churches, evidence of another set of devotions.[73] Devotion to the Cross was important in some villages, as in Niederwihl, where the parish church possessed a fragment of the True Cross. During Rogation Week the villagers of Mettenberg held processions to crosses built on the three roads out of the village, a possible indication of special attention to the Cross.[74] Jesuit missionaries operating in the countryside often encouraged devotion to the Cross, and missionaries were sporadically active in Southwest Germany.[75]

[70] Evidence of *Bettstunde*: HStASt. B467/546; GLAK 98/804. On *Andacht*, see above, chapter 2, section on Steinbach. On Lent, see Ebner, *Görwihl*. p. 116; Ebner, *Birndorf*, p. 113; Ebner, *Niederwihl*, p. 122; GLAK 79/825: "*in welchen dz Volck an Sontägen nachmittags einen Rosenkranz zu bethen pflegt . . .*"

[71] HStASt. B467/546.

[72] Popular initiative can be found in the promotion of other kinds of prayers too, as in the endowment of a special Mass and prayer at Amtzell in 1750. HStASt. B467/90.

[73] GLAK 98/4033 (Sulmingen); HStASt. B61/1098 (Grünenbach); HStASt. B481/77 (Ringschnaidt); HStASt. B481/78 (Rottum); HStASt. B17/360 (Liptingen). HStASt. B61/1098 also states that there were already stations in the church in Urlau. See Châtellier, *La Religion des Pauvres*, pp. 166–168. Châtellier points out that stations were a kind of pilgrimage. Depending on the prayers, stations could be part of the cult of the Rosary.

[74] EAF A1/1418 (*Landkapitel* Biberach).

[75] On missions in general, see Châtellier, *La Religion des pauvres*, esp. ch. 6. Evidence of missions in GLAK 98/3975, HStASt. B17/498, GLAK 118/178, and GLAK 119/424.

Some of the devotions that characterized Catholic practice in other parts of Catholic Germany appear to have had relatively little resonance in the Southwest. As we have seen, the cult of the Eucharist resonated strongly. The Host was a focus of pilgrimage piety, taken on processions, and set out for worship in churches, and, of course, it represented the centerpiece of the Mass. Yet devotion to the Sacred Heart, the *Herz-Jesu-Verehrung*, which spread rapidly in Austria in the eighteenth century, was unimportant in the Southwest. There were very few Sacred Heart confraternities, especially compared with the large number of new Marian congregations.[76]

The numbers and kinds of confraternities can provide some evidence about the nature of religious practice. Most significantly, they confirm that, although the population was open to new devotions, the cult of Mary dominated religious life in the villages. The lists compiled by the Austrian authorities in the 1780s show that a majority of confraternities were Marian (see table 3.1 later).[77] Of the 164 confraternities, 73 were dedicated to the Rosary and another 19 were directly devoted to Mary. However, almost every devotional innovation of the seventeenth and eighteenth centuries was also represented by a confraternity, an indication of the popular willingness to try new practices. The cults of St. Ann, St. John of Nepomuk, the Christocentric devotions to the Passion, or the cult of the Good Death, could all be found in the Southwest, and they all contributed to the growing variety of Catholic practice. Yet none of these devotions achieved anything like the popular support of the Rosary.

The vitality and the churchliness of popular Catholicism could be found not only in the highly visible processions and pilgrimages, but also in the growing number of regular daily and weekly devotions. Dedicated believers found more opportunities to attend services, pray, view the Eucharist, or take communion, opportunities they had often organized themselves. By the middle of the eighteenth century, frequent and regular services had achieved an important place in rural religion, supplementing and elaborating on the vibrant but irregular rituals of the liturgical year and the once-in-a-lifetime rites of passage.

Popular Catholicism was and remained highly ritualized. The people

[76] *Bruderschaft des Rosenkranzes und herzen Jesu*, Munderlingen: HStASt. B17/361. Other confraternities of the *Herz Jesu* in Heitersheim, Riegel, St. Mergen, and in the Ursuline convent in Freiburg: GLAK 79/837. On Austria, see Anna Coreth, *Liebe ohne Mass. Geschichte der Herz-Jesu-Verehrung in Österreich im 18. Jahrhundert* (Salterrae, 1994).

[77] HStASt. B17/360, B17/361.

not only played a major role in determining which rituals survived and prospered, but also participated actively in the official liturgy of the Church. This essential churchliness did not preclude tension, especially in the context of both popular initiatives and clerical reforms. In general, though, a basic clerical toleration of popular religion and the popular willingness to embrace the official liturgy dominated religious life in the villages and towns.

An analysis of the rites of passage, the liturgical year, and day-to-day church services reveals other tensions in Baroque Catholicism. Traditionally, Catholics experienced the liturgy of the Church sporadically and irregularly as it followed the rhythms of the liturgical year. In the sixteenth century, after the collapse of both pilgrimage and processional piety, and in a setting with a very uneven parochial structure, the population probably participated even more sporadically in the official (and even the unofficial or semi-official) liturgy.[78] The irregular aspect of the Catholic liturgy lived on in the liturgical year and in processional and pilgrimage piety. Indeed, after 1650, these aspects of ritual life were further developed and elaborated, at the initiative of both the clergy and the population.

The frequent but irregular services of the liturgical year existed in creative tension with the more regular services offered in each parish church or local chapel. Many church reformers sought to increase the importance of weekly services (the *Wochenlauf*), in an effort to increase the presence of religion in the day-to-day life of the population. Thus church ordinances demanded that priests begin Sunday services at the same time each week. Even more ambitiously, the Church tried to link different days of the week to particular saints or particular Catholic practices, making, for example, Wednesday St. Joseph Day and Thursday Eucharist Day.[79] The population supported increasing the number of weekly services and was not opposed to regularizing the times of services. The attempt to institute regular devotions for each day of the week does not appear to have had much popular support, but the cult of the Rosary and other new devotions did have the effect of encouraging more regular devotions.

One of the aims of Tridentine reform was to bring local liturgies more in line with Roman traditions. In Southwest Germany, however, there is little evidence of "Romanization." The Rituals of the Diocese of

[78] Veit and Lenhart argue that this was a problem caused by the penetration of Protestant ideas into Catholic practice. Veit and Lenhart, *Kirche und Volksfrömmigkeit*, ch. 1.

[79] See Veit and Lenhart, *Kirche und Volksfrömmigkeit*, pp. 141–142.

Constance, that is, the official manuals of the liturgy, continued to recognize and approve local and regional practices well into the eighteenth century, only accepting the *Rituale Romanorum* of 1614 as a normative in 1766.[80] This broad tendency was clearly reflected in liturgical practice in the parishes, which remained highly local and variable through the eighteenth century

Catholic practice in Southwest Germany remained embedded in the "official corporate worship of the Church."[81] Yet the trend toward more daily and weekly services and devotions tended to reinforce another development within Catholicism: a more individual and private devotional life. Catholicism in the Baroque became a religion of *both* "meditative devotion and demonstrative processions."[82] Weekly Mass, processions, group pilgrimages, and the holidays of the liturgical year reminded Catholics that they were part of a wider collectivity, which most of them probably identified as the local parish. At the same time, however, new devotional practices, such as the Rosary, and the availability and accessibility of popular devotional literature allowed and encouraged people to practice their religion alone and in private. When corporate practices, such as processions, pilgrimages, and feast days, came under official attack after about 1750, these more private and personal devotions assumed a new and dominant role in popular religion.

THE RISE OF INDIVIDUAL DEVOTION

A casual visitor to a small town or village in Southwest Germany in the middle of the eighteenth century would surely have commented on the vibrant communal religion practiced by the inhabitants. If she stayed longer than a few weeks she would probably have witnessed several large church services, a procession or two, and perhaps the departure or arrival of a large communal pilgrimage. Yet if the visitor had a discerning eye for religious practice, she might have also noticed some villagers and peasants quietly praying in the corner of the church, at a roadside shrine or crucifix, or in their own home.

80 Werner Groß, "Liturgische Bücher" in Elmar Kuhn, Eva Maser, Rudolf Reinhardt and Petra Sachs (eds.), *Die Bischöfe von Konstanz*, Vol. I *Geschichte* (Friedrichshafen, 1988), pp. 145–148. Groß states that Constance was unusual in its willingness to accept local liturgical traditions. Dold, *Die Konstanzer Ritualientexte* gives a similar impression.

81 Niels Rasmussen, "Liturgy and the Liturgical Arts", in John O'Malley (ed.), *Catholicism in Early Modern Europe. A Guide to Research* (St Louis, 1988), p. 281.

82 Van Dülmen, *Kultur und Alltag in der frühen Neuzeit*, p. 72.

Private devotion, practiced particularly by women alone or in small groups, was the future of western Catholicism.[83] This kind of religious practice had always been a part of Christianity, but in the eighteenth century individual devotion spread from the monasteries and from particular urban milieus to the wider population. Although the majority of German Catholics continued to practice and understand their religious life as communal and collective, a significant minority also came to practice devotions, to do their *Andacht*, as individual believers.

A clear distinction between group and individual devotion is hard to maintain. Historians have been aware of the mix of communal and individual devotion, especially after 1650. Michael Pammer describes Baroque Catholicism as "a time of the confessional, a period of exhibiting and praying to the Eucharist . . . a time of pilgrimages and processions, of Marian congregations and Rosary and other confraternities, of wayside crosses, crucifixes, chapels, and popular religious books."[84] Louis Châtellier emphasizes that three sets of collective practices, confraternities, processions, and pilgrimages, characterized Catholic practice in seventeenth- and eighteenth-century Alsace, yet he also points to the growth of individual religiosity in the eighteenth century.[85]

Processions and pilgrimages, along with the main ceremonies of the liturgical year, were primarily communal events. Yet we have seen how pilgrimage piety was open to individual devotion, even in the context of communal pilgrimage processions. Certain devotional practices, especially the prayers of the Rosary, provided the opportunity for individuals to incorporate a more personal religious experience into the weekly services or even the great feasts of the liturgical year. An analysis of individual devotional practices cannot, then, be easily detached from the discussion of the communal religion.

Perhaps surprisingly, confraternities played a major role in promoting individual devotion. There are a number of reasons for this. Confraternities existed at two important intersections. First, confraternities were, both in their form and in their function, a meeting place for clerical promotion and popular initiative. Second, *Bruderschaften*,

[83] Jonathan Sperber, *Popular Catholicism in Nineteenth-Century Germany* (Princeton, 1984), esp. ch. 2; David Blackbourn, *Marpingen, Apparitions of the Virgin Mary in Nineteenth-Century Germany* (New York, 1994), pp. 30–31; Margaret Lavinia Anderson, "The Limits of Secularization: on the Problem of the Catholic Revival in Nineteenth-Century Germany" *Historical Journal* 38 (1995), pp. 647–670; Hugh McLeod, *Religion and the People of Western Europe, 1789–1989* (Oxford, 1997).

[84] Michael Pammer, *Glaubensabfall und wahre Andacht. Barock Religiösität, Reformkatholizismus, und Laizismus in Oberösterreich, 1700–1820* (Munich, 1994), pp. 6–7.

[85] Châtellier, *Tradition chrétienne et renouveau catholique*, esp. p. 451.

precisely because they were so adaptable, could reinforce both communal and individual devotions. The trend for confraternities, as elsewhere in Catholic Europe, was "an evolution of devotion toward individual prayer and a direct dialogue between the believer and God."[86]

One can also find the individual religious experience by examining the ways in which the people of Southwest Germany understood the concept of devotion (*Andacht*). Devotion came to mean a wide variety of practices, again illuminating the diverse nature of popular Catholicism. Here too the trend appears to have been in the direction of more personal, heart-felt, internalized religion. Finally, somewhat more speculatively, the growing importance of personal or individual devotion may be related to the feminization of everyday Catholicism, which appears to have set in after about 1750. This feminization was an active process, not only the result of men beginning to withdraw from religious life.[87] It would not be surprising to find that women participated disproportionately in those aspects of Catholicism, such as private prayer or voluntary church services, which were less directly controlled by male-dominated communal institutions. It is important to emphasize, however, that neither men nor women abandoned traditional communal Catholicism before the end of the eighteenth century, even as some of them expanded their religious practice through the cultivation of a more introspective piety.

Confraternities

Confraternities played a major role in urban religion in the late Middle Ages, but only came to the Catholic countryside in large numbers after 1650. By the middle of the eighteenth century, they had become an important part of rural religion. Confraternities proved to be highly flexible institutions. They could be used by religious orders or parish priests to promote new devotions or to channel existing practices, but they could also be founded by groups of laypeople or by village communes. Some had only male members, but most admitted "sisters" as well as "brothers." Confraternities also filled different roles. Some followed the model of late medieval fraternal organizations and served

86 Marie-Hélène Froeschlé-Chopard, *Espace et Sacré en Provence (XVIe–XXe siècle)* (Paris, 1994), p. 559.

87 See Rudolf Schlögl, *Glaube und Religion in der Säkularisierung. Die katholische Stadt – Köln, Aachen, Münster – 1700–1840* (Munich, 1995), pp. 331–332. Note that even in cities full-fledged feminization only occurs after about 1800. Compare Timothy Tackett, *Religion, Revolution, and Regional Culture in Eighteenth-Century France: The Ecclesiastical Oath of 1791* (Princeton, 1986), p. 248 and Jean Delumeau (ed.), *La Religion de ma mère. Les femmes et la transmission de la foi* (Paris, 1992).

to provide prayers for the souls of dead members.[88] Some, for example the St. Sebastian confraternities, organized their members to seek the intercession and protection of a powerful patron. Many were essentially devotional, offering indulgences to encourage particular devotional practices, such as praying the Rosary or frequent confession and communion. Many, if not the majority of confraternities fell somewhere in between, having devotional, protective, and intercessionary functions. The result was a "colorful variety" of confraternities, even as the Church struggled to regulate and regularize these associations.[89]

Confraternities achieved an important place in Southwest Germany as part of a new system of religious practices, not as a revival of late medieval practices.[90] Communal by their very nature, confraternities certainly brought people together to practice their Catholicism. At the same time, they also promoted individual devotion. Devotional confraternities generally required attendance at Mass and processions, but they also emphasized regular individual prayer, as well as frequent confession and communion. Rural confraternities were also public, open, and inclusive, extending membership to all residents of a parish and even allowing non-members to participate in the devotions they organized.[91] Broad membership, perhaps paradoxically, reduced the social coercion possible in smaller fraternities, for example those organized by guilds in cities and towns, where only the religiously committed members of the community were active participants.

Devotional confraternities predominated in the eighteenth century. The surveys performed by Austrian officials in the 1770s and 1780s show that about 40 percent of all confraternities were dedicated to the Rosary (see table 3.1). The surveys also indicate that a wide variety of confraternities could be found in the Austrian lands. Newer-style "Counter-Reformation" confraternities were strongly represented. All of these, including those dedicated to the Holy Family, St. John of Nepomuk, the Passion, the Cross, and the Sacred Heart, were essentially devotional. It is more difficult to determine the nature of the Marian or St. Sebastian

[88] Late medieval confraternities: see A.N. Galpern, *The Religions of the People in 16th-Century Champagne* (Cambridge, MA, 1976); Duffy, *The Stripping of the Altars*, pp. 142–154; Ludwig Remling, *Bruderschaften in Franken. Kirchen- und Sozialgeschichtliche Untersuchung zum spätmittelalterlichen und frühneuzeitlichen Bruderschaftswesen* (Würzburg, 1986).

[89] Remling, *Bruderschaften in Franken*, p. 35.

[90] Here following Thomas Paul Becker, *Konfessionalisierung in Kurköln. Untersuchungen zur Durchsetzung der katholischen Reform in den Dekanaten Ahrgau und Bonn anhand von Visitationsprotokollen 1583–1761* (Bonn, 1989), pp. 182–183.

[91] See the example of the St. George *Bruderschaft* in Bermatingen: GLAK 98/3218.

Table 3.1. *Confraternities in Austrian lands in the eighteenth century*

Name/Type	1781	1784/1785
Total	113	164
Rosary	44 (=38%)	70 (=42%)
Rosary/Scapular	2	2
Scapular	4	2
Marian	17	19
Eucharist	2	6
Christ		
Passion	1	7
Sacred Heart	3	1
Cross	1	1
Other	2	1
Trinity	1	1
Holy Ghost	1	0
Holy Family/St. Joseph	5	3
Saints		
General	13	23
St. Sebastian	11	10
St. Anna	2	4
St. John Nepomuk	3	2
St. Francis Xavier	0	1
Good Death	0	3
Occupational groups	1	4
Other	0	4

Sources: 1781: GLAK 79/837; 1785/86: HStASt. B17/360, B17/361.

confraternities, although the latter generally organized ceremonies seeking St. Sebastian's intercession against disease.[92]

One gains an even greater sense of the variety and importance of brotherhoods by examining the resources of these institutions. Many had considerable capital invested and regular incomes sufficient to pay for ornaments, the hiring of priests for services, and even contributions to major repairs of churches.[93] The wealthiest confraternities listed in the survey of 1784/1785 were in towns. The Confraternity of the Rosary

[92] Confraternities were sometimes dedicated to both St. Sebastian and St. Roche, the latter a specialist against the plague. See Beuggen, HStASt. B17/360, and Leutkirch: Herman Schmid, "Die Statuten des Landkapitels Linzgau von 1699 als historisch-statistisch-topographische Quelle" *FDA* 111 (1991), p. 209.

[93] HStASt. B17/360, B17/361.

and Scapular in Bräunlingen and the Rosary Confraternity in Waldshut both had endowments of over 5,000fl. and incomes around 200fl. a year. Rural confraternities could also be well funded, like those in Herznach and Frick, with incomes of 186fl. and 117fl. respectively. Some were quite poor, such as the Confraternity of the Rosary in Pfärrich, which had no income and no endowment, except for 12fl. worth of church ornaments. However, by the 1780s most confraternities had sufficient resources to support devotional activities and to contribute to the decoration of churches and chapels.

A similar picture emerges if we examine a somewhat earlier period. There were eighteen confraternities in the thirty parishes the Rural Chapter of Stockach in 1708.[94] Confraternities were certainly not universal. Half of the parishes had no confraternity, and the St. Sebastian *Bruderschaften* in Bondorf and Mindersdorf, the Confraternity of the Cross in Liptingen, and the Marian Confraternity in Sipplingen were reported to be almost moribund. On the other hand, the other fourteen confraternities were "flourishing." Interestingly, people in the parishes did not always respond to the clerical promotion of new confraternities. According to episcopal visitors, some "new-style" confraternities (such as that of the Cross) were in decline, while the St. Sebastian confraternities in Mühlingen and Winterspüren, probably of a more traditional type, were "genuinely flourishing." On the other hand, four Rosary confraternities, as well as a confraternity dedicated to St. Joseph and another to the Holy Family, were also doing well, a sign that the inhabitants were willing to patronize those confraternities promoted by the Tridentine Church.

Confraternities of the Rosary were the most common kind of *Bruderschaften* in the countryside in the eighteenth century. These confraternities were almost all founded after 1650, much later than was the case in Catalonia, where by 1635 the cult of the Rosary was almost universal, and later than in southeastern France as well.[95] The late arrival of the Rosary is certainly an indication of the weakness of Tridentine reforms, but it does not necessarily mean a lack of popular interest in this devotion. In fact, after 1650 both the parish clergy and the wider population supported these confraternities.

Confraternities of the Rosary enjoyed the support and promotion of

[94] EAF A1/725.

[95] On Catalonia: Henry Kamen, *The Phoenix and the Flame. Catalonia and the Counter Reformation* (New Haven, 1993), pp. 148–150. On France: Froeschlé-Chopard, *Espace et Sacré en Provence*, Part III, ch. 1.

both the Dominicans and the Jesuits and were sometimes founded with the direct participation of the orders. The *Rosenkranz Bruderschaft* in Reinstetten, for example, was founded by a Dominican in 1682. Indeed, Rosary confraternities were affiliated with the Dominican-managed archconfraternity, which allowed each branch to benefit from the indulgences and privileges granted the central body.[96] On the other hand, the archconfraternity did not exercise oversight over village confraternities, nor did the Dominicans prevent new foundations. The Rosary confraternity in Herten, for example, was probably founded by the commune, which managed its property without consulting the parish priest. Of course, parish priests could organize new confraternities, as did Fridolin Senn in Görwihl in 1669 and Jakob Schlichtig in Niederwihl in 1753.[97]

The rapid spread of confraternities of the Rosary was only part of a more general spread of confraternities after 1650. Visitation reports give some indication of this process, although episcopal visitors showed little interest in confraternities before the Thirty Years' War. Thus there are no references to confraternities in the extensive 1620 visitation report on the Rural Chapter of Linzgau. In 1651 the visitors identified twelve confraternities and in 1699 twenty-three confraternities in the twenty to twenty-five parishes in the Linzgau.[98] Some of the growth reflected the popularity of the Rosary. There are ten Rosary confraternities listed in 1699, only three in 1651. There were, however, other kinds of new confraternities as well. A Holy Family Confraternity was founded in Linz (1682), a confraternity dedicated to Mary of Mount Carmel in Weildorf, and a confraternity dedicated to Mary, St. Sebastian, and St. Roche in Leutkirch.

Limited evidence about the foundation of new confraternities confirms that their number expanded dramatically between 1650 and about 1770 (see table 3.2). Indeed, foundations clustered in the periods 1660–1710 and 1730–1770, overlapping to some extent with the peak periods of pilgrimage piety. It is also striking that few confraternities were founded

96 HStASt. B481/76 (Reinstetten). In the visitation of the *Landkapitel* Linzgau in 1699, all Rosary confraternities were listed as part of the archconfraternity. Schmid, "Die Statuten des Landkapitels Linzgau von 1699," pp. 203–211. The confraternity in the episcopal residence town of Meersburg was closely affiliated with the Dominican house in Constance. See also Ebner, *Görwihl*, pp. 122–131.

97 HStASt. B17/361; Ebner, *Niederwihl*, p. 126; Ebner, *Görwihl*, p. 122.

98 EAF Ha 70, pp. 233r–265r, 442r–462r; Schmid, "Die Statuten des Landkapitels Linzgau von 1699," pp. 203–211. The 1651 report is clearly not complete, failing to list the Confraternity of the Immaculate Conception founded in Bermatingen in 1518. This confraternity may well have been inactive in 1651, in the immediate aftermath of the Thirty Years' War.

Table 3.2. *New confraternities, Southwest Germany*

Date	*Parish*	*Confraternity*	*Source*
Pre-Reformation			
1460	Waldsee	St. Sebastian	HStASt. B17/360
1463	Vöhringen	St. Anna	HStASt. B17/361
1504	Laufenburg	St. Sebastian	HStASt. B17/360
1510	Meersburg	St. Anna	Schmid, "Die Statuten"
1518	Siggingen	St. Sebastian	Schmid, "Die Statuten"
1518	Horb	St. Sebastian	HStASt. B17/360
1518	Bermatingen	Immac. Conception	Schmid, "Die Statuten"
Post-Trent			
1584	Laufenburg	Corpus Christi	HStASt. B17/360
1607	Laufenburg	RK	HStASt. B17/361
1611	Meersburg	Immac. Conception	Schmid, "Die Statuten"
1634	Rheinfelden	RK	HStASt. B17/361
Post-Thirty Years' War			
1657	Meersburg	RK	Schmid, "Die Statuten"
1657	Birndorf	RK	Ebner, *Birndorf*, p. 111
1663	Hornussen	RK	HStASt. B17/361
1665	Mettau	RK	HStASt. B17/361
1666	Rißtissen	Scapular	HStASt. B467/748
1669	Unteralpfen	Sorrowing Mary	Ebner, *Hochsal*, pp. 65–66
1670	Berg	St. Sebastian	HStASt. B17/361
1670	Görwihl	RK	Ebner, *Görwihl*, p. 121
1670s/1680s	Hochsal	RK	Ebner, *Hochsal*, p. 66
1670s/1680s	Dogern	RK	Ebner, *Hochsal*, p. 66
1679	Essendorf	RK	HStASt. B467/407
before 1682	Rheinfelden	St. Sebastian	HStASt. B17/361
1682	Essendorf	St. Joseph	HStASt. B467/407
1682	Reinstetten	RK	HStASt. B481/76
1682	Balgheim	Trinity	HStASt. B467/124
1682	Linz	Holy Family	Schmid, "Die Statuten"
1685	Hoßkirch	Scapular	HStASt. B467/568
1686	Waldkirch	St. Joseph	Ebner, *Hochsal*, p. 66
1688	Wurmlingen	St. Sebastian	HStASt. B466a/Bü421
1698	Glottertal	RK	HStASt. B17/360
Eighteenth century			
before 1700	Wyhlen	RK	HStASt. B17/361
1702	Wölfinswihl	RK	HStASt. B17/361
1703	Reinstetten	St. Anna (Renov.)	HStASt. B481/76
1707	Horb	RK (Renov.)	HStASt. B17/360
1709	Bermatingen	St. George	GLAK 98/3218
1720	Altheim	RK	HStASt. B17/361
1733	Ehingen	RK	HStASt. B17/361

Table 3.2. *(Cont.)*

Date	*Parish*	*Confraternity*	*Source*
1733	Luttingen	RK (Renov.?)	Ebner, *Luttingen*, p. 20
1736	Eicken	RK	HStASt. B17/360
1738	Stetten	RK	HStASt. B17/361
1738/1739	Blumenfeld	St. John Nepom.	GLAK 229/10186
1739	Binsdorf	Good Death	HStASt. B17/361
1742	Waldkirch	RK (Renov.)	HStASt. B17/360
1755	Niederwihl	RK	Ebner, *Niederwihl*, p. 126
1760	Sigmaringenst.	Freyw. Verbund.	HStASt. B17/361
1761	Essendorf	Passion/Sorrow. Mary	HStASt. B467/407
1764	Kappel	Schutz Engel	HStASt. B17/360
1766	Villingen	Eucharist	GLAK 79/837
1766	Rottenburg	St. John Nepom.	HStASt. B38/1648
1769	Scherzingen	RK	HStASt. B17/361
1769	Amtzell	Holy Family/ Good Death	HStASt. B467/90
1770s	Haitersheim	Sacred Heart	GLAK 79/837

Notes: Dates are the best available. It is sometimes unclear whether the founding date is that of an application for episcopal approval, of the first available documents, or of the actual date of episcopal confirmation.
RK = *Rosenkranz* (i.e. Rosary)
Renov. = "Renovation" (renewal) of an existing confraternity

in the immediate post-Trent period, or that those founded in this period left few traces in post-1650 documents. Confraternities could only survive with popular support, which, at least in the countryside, was not forthcoming in the decades around 1600.

Popular enthusiasm for confraternities meant that several could survive in one place. Indeed, the success of one *Bruderschaft* could lead to the foundation of a second brotherhood. A Rosary Confraternity came into being between 1666 and 1679 in Essendorf, followed shortly by the foundation of a St. Joseph Confraternity in 1682.[99] In Reinstetten a Rosary Confraternity founded in 1682 seems to have created a new enthusiasm for confraternities, leading the villagers to resuscitate an older St. Anna Confraternity in 1702.[100] By the middle of the eighteenth century, it was the latter *Bruderschaft* that dominated village devotional life, while the *Rosenkranz* Confraternity was in decline. Despite the broad importance of the Rosary confraternities, the population supported a

[99] HStASt. B467/407. [100] HStASt. B481/76.

variety of confraternities, just as they favored variety in all aspects of their religious life.

Confraternities not only varied in their dedications, they also performed diverse devotional roles. The town of Waldsee provides a particularly good example of this variety. In the eighteenth century this small town had six confraternities.[101] One of them, the St. Anton *Bruderschaft*, was for the monks in the Franciscan house. The St. Sebastian *Bruderschaft* was the oldest (founded 1460) and the richest (annual income of over 1200fl. in 1784/1785) brotherhood. This confraternity supported a benefice for a priest who was responsible for providing masses for the deceased members. Austrian officials described a second confraternity, the St. Jacob *Bruderschaft*, as "more of a secular brotherhood [*Verbrüderung*]," probably meaning it provided masses for the deceased and helped widows and destitute brothers. The same officials also reported that there was a fairly new *Verbrüderung* organized by some inhabitants "among themselves" which paid out two *Gulden* for each deceased member, to cover the expenses of a funeral and masses for their souls. This same brotherhood also paid for the candles used at weekly prayer meetings held at a chapel outside the village dedicated to the local saint Beth.[102] There was a Rosary Confraternity in Waldsee, which paid for seventy-six masses each year as well as for monthly sermons. The endowment and donations collected by this confraternity also funded the decoration of an altar in the parish church where the biggest expense was for the clothing for a statue of Mary. Finally, there was a Confraternity of the Passion in the cemetery church of the town. This was possibly a penitential confraternity or a confraternity that assisted at funerals.[103]

The various confraternities in Waldsee give a vivid picture of the diversity of confraternities in the eighteenth century. They also reveal several important aspects of local religious life. All the confraternities, except that of the Rosary, provided masses for the dead and probably had procured indulgences for members. The people of Waldsee were deeply involved with the world of the dead and poured considerable resources into saving the souls of their relatives and neighbors. This engagement with the dead was not a remnant of medieval practices but

[101] Sources are HStASt. B61/2328, B17/360, B17/361.

[102] The *Guten Beth* was canonized in 1767 and her shrine was in nearby Reute. See chapter 2.

[103] There is also reference to a Holy Family Confraternity in Waldsee, but no specifics about its function or resources: HStASt. B61/2328.

rather paralleled the development and expansion of the cult of the dead in Italy in the period after about 1600.[104]

Several of the confraternities that paid for masses for the dead also organized prayer meetings and could be described as partly devotional. Most importantly, the Rosary Confraternity was normally a devotional confraternity, providing additional masses and sermons. In addition, although not described directly in the sources, the *Rosenkranz Bruderschaft* surely organized prayer meetings and processions. There was, then, coexistence, often within the same confraternity, between purely devotional practices and those activities designed to help the souls of the dead. It is difficult to distinguish neatly between functions that were clearly communal and those that encouraged personal piety. Prayer meetings and church services could obviously fulfill both individual and communal functions.

Endowed masses for the dead might reflect each member's concern for his or her individual soul, a concern for deceased family members, or a concern for souls in purgatory more generally. Such a mix of concerns motivated Johan Schreiber, who wrote a will in 1719.[105] Schreiber endowed a perpetual Mass at the altar of the Marian Confraternity in Bermatingen for himself and his family. He then did the same with the St. George *Bruderschaft* in the same church. Finally, he endowed a Mass in the parish church exclusively for himself. Schreiber obviously had sufficient resources with which to help his own soul and those of his family. By turning to two different confraternities and the parish church, he also appears to have identified with several different religious communities.

Even a Confraternity of the Rosary had a number of functions, some of which were not really devotional. The regulations of the Rosary Confraternity in Görwihl reflect the complex role of such organizations.[106] The "Ordinance and Statutes" of the confraternity had a series of rules. Members were expected to pray three full rosaries while contemplating the life of Christ each week. This rather demanding devotional practice was made somewhat easier by allowing participants to break up their prayers into shorter segments. The rules explicitly state that members can pray outside the church, at home, or in the fields.

[104] Michael Carroll, *Veiled Threats. The Logic of Popular Catholicism in Italy* (Baltimore and London, 1996), esp. chs. 4 and 5.

[105] GLAK 98/3218. This will led to a long dispute over how many masses the priest in Bermatingen was actually required to perform.

[106] Ebner, *Görwihl*, pp. 122–131. Date is 1670.

Second, the confraternity organized processions monthly and on the four major Marian feasts, and members were required to participate, if at all possible. The third rule specified how members were to improve their daily behavior:

> Because the *Bruderschaft* was founded above all for the purpose of rooting out sins and vices, so that the costly blood and great merits of Jesus Christ should not be lost on any persons, public evils like swearing, cursing, gambling, excessive drinking, scolding, slandering, quarreling, and the like should, with the help of the secular authority, be avoided and punished [*abgestraft*].[107]

The brothers and sisters were to assist each other by admonishing those who transgressed and to steel themselves against such behavior by confessing and taking communion several times each year.

These regulations were clearly devotional, aimed at helping individuals become better Christians and better people. The confraternity had, however, other purposes as well. Members were to pray on the days after the major feasts of the liturgical year for the souls of both the living and the dead. Sisters and brothers earned indulgences for praying at the altars of the church and for participating in services on the *Bruderschaftsfest*, which fell on the first Sunday in October, the anniversary of the Battle of Lepanto (1571).[108] Finally, any member who performed his weekly Rosary prayers tapped into the benefits earned by the good works of all the members of the Archconfraternity of the Rosary across the world. The Confraternity of the Rosary organized several kinds of religious practices. The prayers, meditations, and processions, as well as frequent confession and communion, reinforced the devotions to Mary and Christ. The confraternity also provided benefits for the deceased members, reflecting considerable popular concern for the dead. This essentially communal aspect of the confraternities of the Rosary serves to remind us that the shift to "intimate devotion" was far from complete before 1800.[109]

Other confraternities in Southwest Germany, especially those founded after 1650, had a similar mix of functions, no doubt because the Rosary confraternities provided both the clergy and the laity with a model of effective and acceptable fraternal organizations. The St. George *Bruderschaft* founded in 1709 in Bermatingen had many of the

[107] Translated from Ebner, *Görwihl*, p. 123, which is probably not a direct quote from the original sources but appears to be a somewhat sanitized version of the original.

[108] This victory was attributed to the intercession of the Virgin.

[109] See Froeschlé-Chopard, *Espace et Sacré en Provence*, esp. pp. 458–459.

same regulations as the Rosary Confraternity in Görwihl.[110] Members prayed the Ave Maria a certain number of times daily, weekly, and monthly, and they participated in services and processions, especially on the Feast of St. George, for which they earned indulgences. The confraternity also funded masses for dead members. Why then did the people and the parish priest of Bermatingen not found a Rosary Confraternity?

The Bermatinger chose to dedicate their new confraternity to St. George rather than to the Rosary because they already had a close relationship with St. George. A statue of the saint that stood on an altar in the parish church had attracted pilgrims since at least the Thirty Years' War. In 1709 the Bermatinger credited St. George with protecting them from a cattle disease which struck the surrounding villages. The parish priest then decided to found a confraternity to organize local devotion to St. George and perhaps to encourage certain practices, such as frequent confession and communion. Such practices could be best encouraged in a confraternity dedicated to a saint with local ties. Once again, the Church adapted to local conditions. Put differently, the devotional preferences of the population led official religion in particular directions.[111]

The St. George *Bruderschaft* in Bermatingen was not unusual. In 1688 the inhabitants of Wurmlingen asked their official parish priest, the abbot of the monastery of Kreuzlingen, to help them obtain approval for a new St. Sebastian Confraternity.[112] As in other communities, the members of this confraternity were enjoined to pray regularly, to avoid cursing and the like, to confess and take communion five times a year, and to attend quite a number of designated services. This confraternity was also deeply committed to helping the souls of the dead. Members earned many indulgences for their own benefit, but were also encouraged to accompany the Eucharist when it was being carried to the sick and dying. In addition, they were rewarded for joining funeral processions and required to pray for the souls in purgatory whenever they passed a cemetery.

This coexistence of individual devotional practices and concern for the souls of the dead can also be found in the confraternities dedicated to St. John of Nepomuk, a saint whose cult was promoted by both the Tridentine clergy and the Austrian monarchy. In 1738/1739 the local officials in Blumenfeld requested permission from higher authorities (in

[110] GLAK 98/3218. [111] Compare discussion of this issue in Carroll, *Veiled Threats*.
[112] HStASt. B466a/421.

this case the house of the Teutonic Knights in Mainau) to institute a *Bruderschaft* dedicated to this saint.[113] The parishioners complained that there was no confraternity in the parish, "nor anything else [providing] comforting indulgences for the souls." The people considered the confraternity primarily as a way of acquiring indulgences, but it also organized a number of church services. The confraternity seems to have encouraged personal devotion as well, for soon after its founding officials suggested moving the statue of St. John from a side altar to the main altar of the parish church because of the large number of people "doing their devotions" in front of it.[114]

In addition, confraternities funded the decoration of churches, thereby indirectly affecting devotional practices.[115] Confraternities paid for the decoration of statues, pictures, and altars affiliated directly with the brotherhood. They also owned utensils used in services, including chalices and the like, as well as flags and other decorations used in processions. Austrian officials condescendingly described the property of the St. Anna *Bruderschaft* in Tannau:

> Silver: two crowns, but only brass and silver plated, one scepter, also brass and silver plated, two old poor rosaries, without any silver at all.
> Ornaments and clothes: one somewhat old red velvet garment, with a bit of gold trim. Another garment, old and very bad.
> Linen: two old cuffs. Otherwise nothing.[116]

Confraternities clearly supported certain kinds of devotions by paying for ornaments used for the Mass, rosaries for prayer meetings, and especially flags and placards for processions.

During the mid-eighteenth century several Rosary confraternities liquidated large endowments to pay for major rebuilding of parish churches. In 1742 the parish church in Reinstetten was rebuilt with such funds and in 1775 the same occurred in Heimbach.[117] This development may indicate a decline in the activities of these confraternities, but it is more likely a sign of the complete integration of the confraternity in parish life. Most parishioners were members of the confraternity; they saw no essential difference between the brotherhood

[113] GLAK 229/10186.
[114] Another St. John of Nepomuk Confraternity was founded in 1766. It seems to have promoted a similar mix of practices: HStASt. B38/1648.
[115] This issue is the subject of Froeschlé-Chopard, *Espace et Sacré en Provence*.
[116] HStASt. B17/360. See the example of the St. Sebastian *Bruderschaft* in Waldsee: HStASt. B61/2327. The garments were probably for dressing a statue of the saint.
[117] Reinstetten: HStASt. B481/76. Heimbach: GLAK 79/836.

and the parish, and thus used the confraternities' resources to pay for construction.[118] Interestingly, this use of confraternity assets for pastoral purposes was exactly what Josephine reformers proposed in the 1770s and 1780s. Although it is hard to say how often such a thing occurred, it indicates a popular flexibility about the use of resources that had been collected for religious purposes, the importance and influence of confraternities, and the primacy of the parish.

Confraternities are another obvious example of the interplay of clerical promotion and popular initiative. The religious orders, especially the Dominicans, Jesuits, and Capuchins, were all active in Southwest Germany. The Dominicans had a special relationship with the confraternities of the Rosary and the Jesuits managed Marian sodalities in the towns. The latter all-male congregations continued to prosper in the eighteenth century in towns such as Rottenburg, where (according to Jesuit records) membership grew from 1,000 in 1712 to 5,400 in 1769. The Capuchins read masses for confraternities in some places and were even members of village confraternities, as in Unteralpfen in the eighteenth century. The Carmelites were also active, helping to found Scapular confraternities in Rißtissen (1666/1667) and in Hoßkirch (1685).[119]

Parish priests often took the initiative in founding and organizing confraternities, for example writing the requests for episcopal confirmation. These initiatives were, however, often the result of priests responding to pressure from their parishioners so that villagers and townspeople were really behind new confraternities. The population accepted that clergymen supervised confraternities, indeed they needed priests to read masses and expected and demanded that priests participate in other services. Often local clergy and local people worked together for the foundation of confraternities. "The *Pfarrer* from Hoßkirch, the churchwardens [*heiligen Pfleger*], and also all the parishioners all strongly request . . . consent to found a Blessed Scapular *Bruderschaft* there." The villagers in Wurmlingen took the initiative in founding the St. Sebastian *Bruderschaft* in 1688, as, apparently, did the inhabitants of Blumenfeld in the 1730s, when they petitioned for a St. John of Nepomuk Confraternity. Even more common was probably the kind of indirect initiative

[118] Châtellier makes much the same point about confraternities in Alsace.

[119] Bernhard Duhr, *Geschichte der Jesuiten in den Ländern deutsche Zunge von 16. bis 18 Jahrhundert* (4 vols., Freiburg im Breisgau, 1907–1921), Vol. IV Part I, p. 288; Ebner, *Unteralpfen*, pp. 123–124; HStASt. B467/748, B467/568.

taken by the inhabitants of Bermatingen, who practiced devotions to St. George, prompting the *Pfarrer* to found a confraternity in the saint's honor.[120]

Laypeople often controlled the funds of confraternities, even when the orders or local priests had control of religious services and membership. In 1666 episcopal visitors complained that the lay superintendents (*procuratores*) of the Rosary Confraternity in Tunsel controlled the endowment and considered themselves unremovable. In the 1780s Austrian officials received an accounting of the financial condition of the Confraternity of the Rosary in Herten directly from village officials, in the absence of the *Pfarrer*.[121] Indeed, Austrian officials expected local authorities to exercise such oversight, reprimanding the mayor and town council of Neuenburg for not regularly inspecting the accounts of the local Rosary Confraternity.

Confraternities became more important as the eighteenth century progressed. As was the case in Alsace, most villages had at least one such brotherhood by the 1750s.[122] Furthermore, the new rural confraternities were not just for *Brüder*, for they admitted men and women. The statutes of the St. George *Bruderschaft* in Bermatingen state: "All and any Catholic Christian, of both sexes, cleric and lay, high and low estate, rich and poor, big and small, members of another confraternity or not, can be admitted after they have read the statutes, or heard them read."[123] This inclusiveness was different from the tradition of both guild fraternities and the Jesuit-inspired Marian sodalities in the towns, which admitted only men and were organized around professional and educational groups. Such confraternities continued to operate in towns, but rural confraternities had wide membership that could include most adult inhabitants.[124] It would not be stretching the evidence too far to suggest that rural confraternities, indeed Catholic practice as experienced through confraternities, gave popular religion an increasingly democratic flavor in the eighteenth century.[125]

[120] HStASt. B467/568, B466a/421; GLAK 229/10186, 98/3218.

[121] HStASt. B17/360.

[122] Châtellier, *Tradition chrétienne et renouveau catholique*, pp. 439–460.

[123] GLAK 98/3218.

[124] Membership of the Rosary Confraternity in Görwihl between 1670 and 1683 consisted of 232 women and 161 men. Ebner, *Görwihl*, p. 126. In Birndorf, 64 percent of the members between 1697 and 1740 were female: Ebner, *Birndorf*, p. 111.

[125] This point is made by Louis Châtellier, *La Religion des Pauvres*, esp. Part III.

Personal and private devotion

Religious devotion practiced in the context of confraternities became gradually more personal and individual. This trend was, however, ambiguous, since confraternities also became important sources of indulgences and masses for the dead in the period after 1650. Concern for the fate of the souls of the dead had of course both personal and communal aspects, as did most aspects of popular religiosity. There are also other indications that personal and individual elements of popular Catholicism acquired a more prominent place in the eighteenth century.

We have seen how pilgrims practiced a variety of devotions (*Andacht*) at shrines such as Maria Steinbach. The term *Andacht* itself was ambiguous enough to encompass group and individual practices, for example masses attended by large crowds and private prayers before the *Gnadenbild*. Yet individual and even private devotion was very much on the mind of the pilgrims when they spoke of *Andacht*. Their religious practice at the shrine reflected this interest. Thus pilgrimage, transformed into highly communal practice after 1650, began to acquire individual aspects again in the eighteenth century.

Pilgrims at Steinbach not only practiced individual devotions at the shrine, but those who witnessed miracles reacted in very personal, heart-felt ways. When asked to explain their feelings upon witnessing the miraculous moving eyes, peasants discussed their fear, joy, and motivation to greater devotion. The testimony of a 58-year-old woman is perhaps most telling. This witness's first reaction to the miracle was very personal: she was "terrified . . . fear caused her to sweat profusely, and it seemed to her as if the whole church was completely filled with fire. [She could not move] and she thought, I am such a sinful person, I will live more piously in the future, I will confess more often and pray more."[126]

This witness recovered from shock and fear by attending Mass, where she was comforted by the presence of others. She also went to confession, where she hesitated to speak of her experience. She reported that the local priest thought she was struggling to confess a "concealed sin . . . and said that she should confess it, whatever it is." She then told about the miracle and the priest calmed her fears, explaining that "this [the miraculous moving eyes] was a great act of grace, and God will let us

[126] HStASt. B486/798, Witness no. 9.

know if he does not want the blessed Virgin to be honored in this picture and a pilgrimage to develop."

This story suggests the personal and individual nature of one pilgrim's experience at Steinbach. It also shows that confession had an important place in this personal religiosity and served as a way both to examine one's sins and to find answers to psychological distress. Such a personal experience was not exceptional at Steinbach, but more often pilgrims arrived in groups and witnessed the miracles in the company of many other people. Individual devotion did not destroy the essentially communal nature of popular Catholicism.

Changes in the practice of the sacrament of confession may also have occurred in this period. However, if there was a trend toward frequent, routine, private, and secret confession in Southwest Germany, it was at best tentative.[127] W. David Myers argues convincingly that the Tridentine Church promoted confession as a persuasive and effective way of changing believers' lives, not as a disciplinary tool.[128] Yet he also recognizes that traditional confessional practice, that is a routine annual confession at Easter, remained the norm in German villages through the eighteenth century. Furthermore, the confessional box, the symbol of private, individual confession, remained rare in Southwest Germany before 1800, especially outside the towns. Here again, there was coexistence of a variety of ways of practicing this sacrament.

Growing literacy and the availability of a wider range of devotional literature aimed at a popular audience also gave impetus to the trend toward more individual piety. Southwest Germany was not isolated from the Europe-wide trend toward greater literacy and wider reading.[129] Furthermore, the Catholic elite, whether in the orders, in the church hierarchy, or in the state bureaucracy, recognized the need for a Catholic literature. In the century after 1650, this literature, in the form of sermon collections, devotional pamphlets, and catechetical works, was widely available and aimed at a popular as well as an educated audience.[130]

The impact of devotional literature on popular religiosity has, however, yet to be studied. Sixteenth-century miracle books, for example,

[127] This is the thesis of John Bossy. See *Christianity in the West* and "The Counter-Reformation and the People of Catholic Europe."

[128] Myers, "*Poor Sinning Folk.*"

[129] Peter Burke, *Popular Culture in Early Modern Europe* (New York, 1978), pp. 250–259; van Dülmen, *Kultur und Alltag in der Frühen Neuzeit*, Part IV.

[130] Dieter Breuer, *Oberdeutsche Literatur 1560–1650. Deutsche Literaturgeschichte und Territorialgeschichte in frühabsolutistischer Zeit* (Munich, 1979), esp. ch. 3.

often promoted group pilgrimage and communal religious practices.[131] In the century after 1650 miracle stories from pilgrimage sites and sermon collections made up the bulk of "popular" devotional literature. The Jesuits also continued to write and produce religious plays for the laity. In the later seventeenth century they oriented these toward a somewhat wider audience, no longer producing them exclusively for a highly educated middle-class audience. The topics and themes of this literature included the Holy Family, the lives of saints, especially the newer ones, stories of miracles, and horror stories about the devil.[132] Several important questions about devotional literature remain difficult to answer. We do not yet know enough about the reception of written materials in the countryside or about the ways in which the clergy and orders served as intermediaries, for example as preachers.[133] Second, devotional literature did not in and of itself encourage or facilitate more individual devotion. In fact, it seems likely that some devotional works encouraged pilgrimages and processions and reinforced the importance of the Mass and the liturgy of the Church in general. Like all other new developments, the wider spread of devotional literature served primarily to bring more variety and diversity to popular Catholicism.

Rudolf Schlögl has argued that there was a link between an increasingly individual and intensive religiosity and the feminization of Catholicism.[134] Schlögl, in his investigation of the Catholic cities of Cologne, Aachen, and Münster, finds that women remained more loyal to the Catholic Church in the eighteenth century than men, continuing, for example, to endow masses after men no longer did so. Such a shift only occurred in these Catholic cities in the later eighteenth century; there is little evidence of the same trend in the Catholic countryside.

The central role of the clergy and the village communes certainly meant that women had a limited role in the institutions that dominated

[131] On Catholic literature in this period, see: Breuer, *Oberdeutsche Literatur 1560–1650*; Jean-Marie Valentin (ed.), *Gegenreformation und Literatur. Beiträge zur interdisziplinären Erforschung der katholischen Reformbewegung* (Amsterdam, 1976); Heribert Smolinsky, "Volksfrömmigkeit und religiöse Literatur im Zeitalter der Konfessionalisierung" in Hansgeorg Molitor and Heribert Smolinsky (eds.), *Volksfrömmigkeit in der frühen Neuzeit* (Münster, 1994); Dieter Breuer (ed.), *Frömmigkeit in der frühen Neuzeit. Studien zu religiösen Literatur des 17. Jahrhunderts in Deutschland* (Amsterdam, 1984); Wolfgang Brückner, Peter Blickle, and Dieter Breuer (eds.), *Literatur und Volk im 17. Jahrhundert. Probleme populärer Kultur in Deutschland* (Wiesbaden, 1985); Soergel, *Wondrous in His Saints.*

[132] R. Po-chia Hsia, *Social Discipline in the Reformation: Central Europe, 1550–1750* (London and New York, 1989), pp. 90–104.

[133] For a discussion of some of these issues, see Roger Chartier, *The Cultural Origins of the French Revolution* (Durham, NC and London, 1991), esp. ch. 5.

[134] Schlögl, *Glaube und Religion in der Säkularisierung*, pp. 250–252. More generally, see Delumeau (ed.), *La Religion de ma mère.*

religious life. Yet if we return to Steinbach, we find that women played a vital role in the less formal, yet central, aspects of popular religion. The first witnesses of the moving eyes at Steinbach were women, and most of the healing miracles benefitted women or children. Furthermore, despite the effort of episcopal investigators to find male testimony to miracles, the vast majority of witnesses were women. As Rebekka Habermas points out, the Church allowed women almost equal participation in the "world of miracles." Women, especially those of childbearing age, sought the intercession of Mary and the saints more often than men did.[135] Women in Upper Swabia certainly turned to Maria Steinbach in such circumstances, as did women across Southwest Germany.

Confraternities also provided women with an opportunity to organize their own religious practice. As we have seen, rural confraternities almost always had male and female members. As one would expect, all official positions in these institutions were held by men. Nevertheless, devotions such as the Rosary allowed individuals considerable freedom and the regulations of the confraternities permitted prayers to take place at almost any time or place. If the Church itself, as well the formal liturgy of the Mass and the organization of processions, remained a male preserve, shrines, prayer meetings, roadside crucifixes, and other religious places and practices were dominated by women. Thus there were male and female spheres within popular Catholicism, although women and men all participated actively in most important religious practices.

Women even asserted themselves within the parish church itself. In the 1720s a group of women from the village of Blumenfeld got into a dispute with their *Pfarrer* over the placement of seats in the church.[136] After the priest placed his mother and his housekeeper in especially good locations, several women protested by standing in the central aisle of the church throughout a service. The dispute revolved around the priest's authority to decide seating arrangements and soon involved local communal officials, but it also underscores the importance women attached to church services and a clear lack of passive obedience to authority.

The fact that women could be, and were, active in religious life in Southwest Germany is not, of course, evidence of the feminization of Catholicism. In fact, feminization, in the sense of a withdrawal of many

135 Rebekka Habermas, *Wallfahrt und Aufruhr. Zur Geschichte des Wunderglaubens in der frühen Neuzeit* (Frankfurt, 1991).

136 GLAK 93/252.

men from active participation in services or devotions so that only women and children continued to attend church, did not occur before 1800. It is just as hard to find evidence for secularization, in the sense of a general decline in participation in the official cult, in the eighteenth century.

Richard van Dülmen postulates that in the seventeenth and eighteenth centuries, "as a result of social pressure and long-term indoctrination there was a process of internalization, the development of a Christian consciousness, a [growing] consciousness of sin and the wish to 'live cleanly'."[137] There was a trend toward the internalization of religion in the Catholic Southwest, but could a "Christian consciousness" really be the consequence of indoctrination? Perhaps Louis Châtellier is closer to the mark when he argues that, after the middle of the eighteenth century, "the religion of the poor became that of all Catholics." This "*religion des pauvres*" was not imposed from above, nor can it be characterized as communal as opposed to the individualized religion of the Catholic elite, for it too had an important place for an active laity, for prayer, and for personal religion. What eighteenth-century Catholics wanted was not so much a self-reflective religion as one that allowed them a personal relationship with God, Christ, and Mary. "More than receiving preaching and catechism, the people needed to bear witness," something they did within the sacramental and ritual framework of the Church.[138]

[137] Van Dülmen, *Kultur und Alltag in der frühen Neuzeit*, p. 137.
[138] Châtellier, *La Religion des pauvres*, ch. 12, p. 278.

CHAPTER 4

Clericalism in the villages

CLERICALISM AND COMMUNALISM

On April 16, 1764 the neighboring communes of Langenschemmern and Aufhofen in Upper Swabia wrote a long letter to the Bishop of Constance.[1] The community leaders protested an episcopal ordinance that forbade church services in Langenschemmern on Easter Sunday and on a number of other high feast days of the Catholic calendar. The decree ordered that the villagers attend these services in the church in the neighboring village of Schemmerberg. But these peasants wanted to hear Mass and receive communion in their own village church on the most important day of the Christian calendar.

The residents of Langenschemmern and Aufhofen, like many other peasants in Southwest Germany, lived in a so-called filial parish. By the mid-eighteenth century there was a priest living in Langenschemmern, but he was only a chaplain (*Kaplan*), and the legally recognized parish priest resided in Schemmerberg, about fifteen kilometers away. This priest and the patron of the parish, the Cistercian monastery of Salem, asserted the ancient rights of the "mother church." The monastery's incorporation of the parish of Schemmerberg justified its right to collect the tithe in the filial villages and permitted the parish priest to collect all fees and offerings made by the faithful. Fees and offerings were, by tradition, given at Easter and three high feasts (Christmas, Pentecost, Corpus Christi).[2] The villagers from Langenschemmern and Aufhofen reluctantly paid these fees; they were not, however, willing to go to the services in Schemmerberg.

[1] GLAK 98/3848.

[2] On the liturgical year, see Robert W. Scribner, "Ritual and Popular Religion in Catholic Germany at the Time of the Reformation" in *Popular Culture and Popular Movements in the Reformation* (London, 1987); Charles Phythian-Adams, *Local History and Folklore: A New Framework* (London, 1975), pp. 21–25; Eamon Duffy, *The Stripping of the Altars: Traditional Religion in England, 1400–1580* (New Haven, 1992), esp. ch. 1; Ludwig Veit and Ludwig Lenhart, *Kirche und Volksfrömmigkeit im Zeitalter des Barocks* (Freiburg, 1956).

The villagers gave a number of reasons for wanting services in their own church. Some of these reflected the practical problems and dangers of rural life in the eighteenth century. The peasants did not want to leave their villages empty, for fear of robbers, vagabonds, and fire. They also claimed that there were many old and sick people who could not make the walk to Schemmerberg. Finally, they pointed out that the church there was too small to hold all the parishioners, and that those coming from far away did not get seats. The church in Schemmerberg was so full, especially at Easter, that many people had to stand outside and could neither hear the sermon nor see the priest and the altar.[3]

Important religious matters were at issue here. Certainly practical problems concerned the villagers, as did the insult to their honor when they had to stand in the back of the church, or even outside, while the Schemmerberger occupied the well-placed seats.[4] Because they did have a resident vicar, the people of Langenschemmern did not complain about the lack of a priest to do emergency baptisms or hear the confessions of the dying, a major concern in many filial churches. However, their request highlights a number of other significant religious concerns. The inhabitants of Langenschemmern and Aufhofen wanted their own priest to give them the full range of services, with full ceremony, in the village church on Easter. The villagers considered both the "silent Mass" held early on Easter morning and the sermon by the *Kaplan* insufficient. They rejected the argument of the priest in Schemmerberg who said that the villagers had a better opportunity to show their devotion in the filial than in the mother church: "[The early mass and sermon] are more pleasing to God, and better for their souls, than going to one mass [in the afternoon] and spending the whole morning with nothing to do except idle loitering [*miessigang*], especially the single men."[5]

The people of Langenschemmern wanted their church elevated to the status of a real parish, which would mean full services on all holidays in their community, complete with a sermon, communion, and the elevation of the Host, and they wanted to witness all of this from inside the church. They also demanded that "their priest" perform this Mass, not the priest from Schemmerberg. The villagers' spiritual needs

[3] Marc R. Forster, *The Counter-Reformation in the Villages. Religion and Reform in the Bishopric of Speyer, 1560–1720* (Ithaca and London, 1992), esp. pp. 36–38.

[4] The problem of seats was probably most important to the leaders of the Langenschemmern *Gemeinde*, who were the elite of that village and surely had seats in their own church. The poorer peasants probably did not have seats in either church.

[5] GLAK 98/3848.

certainly required a priest, but their religion was also strongly local and communal.

This incident illustrates two interlocking aspects of Catholicism in Southwest Germany. The first of these was a kind of clericalism, reflected above all in the laity's demand that resident priests perform and sanctify Catholic rituals.[6] The second attribute was the continuing communal control of parishes. Clericalism and communalism evolved together and remained central characteristics of Southwest German Catholicism through the eighteenth century. Their interplay prevented the clergy from controlling Catholic life. Most significantly, although the people honored the special role of the priest and even expected his leadership – precisely as Tridentine reformers hoped – communities did not allow the priest to control the village parish.[7]

Clericalism and communalism were closely intertwined, and they even reinforced each other. The desire for more, and more active, priests led communes to press for the creation of new parishes and benefices. The ecclesiastical hierarchy was, mostly for financial reasons, generally reluctant to support such projects, and communities had to make monetary contributions as well as expend political capital to achieve their goals. Communes did not take this initiative without consciously retaining influence over the behavior of the clergymen hired in the new positions. Furthermore, the central importance of the priest in the religious life of communities caused the parishioners, and especially their leaders, to carefully monitor the professional performance of their pastors. Those priests who failed to carry out their duties were quickly criticized. If they continued to neglect their office, parishioners brought pressure to bear for their removal.

Clericalism and communalism were not new in the early modern period. The Church had always sought to "clericalize" Christianity, although with mixed success. In the fifteenth century, for example, the church leaders sought to control access to the sacred and to "professionalize" the clergy. The laity, however, often bypassed the parish priest, turning to mendicants for the sacraments and to lay confraternities for devotion.[8] Communes played a major role in the religious life of

[6] I have taken the concept of clericalism from Timothy Tackett, *Religion, Revolution, and Regional Culture in Eighteenth-Century France: The Ecclesiastical Oath of 1791* (Princeton, 1986). I realize that there are problems with using the term, especially since it evokes the nineteenth-century use of clericalism, which was often pejorative.

[7] John Bossy, "The Counter-Reformation and the People of Catholic Europe," *Past and Present* 47 (1970), pp. 51–70.

[8] Robert W. Scribner, *The German Reformation* (Atlantic Highlands, 1986), pp. 12–13.

fifteenth-century Germany, and rural Catholicism in southern Germany and Switzerland was to a great extent communalized by 1500.[9] This was probably the logical outcome of the simultaneous creation of the parochial structure in the European countryside in the Middle Ages, and the elaboration of communal institutions, especially in the German-speaking lands. There is considerable debate about the extent to which peasant communes lost their autonomy to more efficient state structures in the early modern period. It is an indication, however, of the strength of communes that they remained influential in organizing local religious life through the eighteenth century.

It is admittedly artificial, but practically necessary, to separate the analysis of clericalism (the subject of this chapter) and communalism (the subject of chapter 5). Furthermore, as the example of Langenschemmern shows, it is particularly important to avoid conceiving of the development of clericalism as a top-down process, that is as the imposition of an elite or clerical model on a passive or resistant population. Caution is also important in considering the role of communes. These institutions could organize popular resistance to innovation, but at other times they could push for important religious reforms. By seeking to strengthen the parish, for example, Catholic reformers helped to reinforce communalism in ways that peasants and townspeople often found appealing. Clericalism and communalism had clerical and lay, elite and popular origins, neither was static, and together they were the central organizing features of Catholicism in Southwest Germany.

By promoting an ideal that put the parish priest at the center of local religious life, the Council of Trent gave important impetus to clericalism. This vision actually coincided in important ways with the ecclesio-political views of German peasants and townspeople. The people accepted that priests were indispensable for religious practice. Town councils and rural communes had, at least since the later fifteenth century, consistently sought to make the priest the servant of the community. Church policies from the late sixteenth century on reinforced this perspective by focusing reforms on the personal lifestyle and

[9] Peter Blickle, *Communal Reformation: The Quest for Salvation in Sixteenth-Century Germany* (New Jersey, 1992); Rosi Fuhrmann, "Die Kirche im Dorf. Kommunale Initiativen zur Organisation von Seelsorge vor der Reformation" in Peter Blickle (ed.), *Zugänge zur bäuerlichen Reformation. Bauer und Reformation* (Zürich, 1987); Franziska Conrad, *Reformation in der bäuerlichen Gesellschaft: Zur Rezeption reformatorischer Theologie im Elsaß* (Stuttgart, 1984); Heide Wunder, *Die bäuerliche Gemeinde in Deutschland* (Göttingen, 1986); Peter Blickle, *Deutsche Untertanen: ein Widerspruch* (Munich, 1981); Robert W. Scribner, "Communalism: Universal Category or Ideological Construct? A Debate in the Historiography of Early Modern Germany and Switzerland" *Historical Journal* 37, 1 (1994), pp. 199–207, esp. pp. 204–205.

professional performance of the parish clergy. The population and the Tridentine reformers highly valued the role of the pastor.

The concern of both reformers and the population for pastoral services (*Seelsorge*) tended to clash with the institutional structure of the German Church, which was organized around the benefice, understood as a kind of property. Monasteries, convents, military orders, collegiate chapters, and even some priests never really accepted that the primary aim of the benefice system should be to pay for pastoral services for the common people. Much of the history of the clergy in the early modern period can be seen as the slow triumph of a pastoral ideal supported by church reformers and the people over the traditional benefice system which benefitted monasteries and ecclesiastical chapters.

The pastoral ideal helped to create the clericalism that developed in Southwest Germany after 1650. Timothy Tackett has argued that clericalism was also important in France in the eighteenth century. In Tackett's definition, clericalism "involved a relatively greater internalization of sacerdotal functions in one's view of the nature and workings of religion" and was strong in those parts of France, especially in the west, which resisted the revolutionary reorganization of the Church in the 1790s.[10] Tackett argues that the development of clericalism (which he calls clericalization) was in part a consequence of Tridentine reform:

> Perhaps, in practical terms, the ultimate measure of success of the push toward clericalization under the Old Regime was not the extent to which the clergy was able to crush popular religion – which was all but impossible in the short run – but rather the extent to which the clergy was able to impose its influence while still maintaining a viable and flexible *modus vivendi* with the popular expressions of religious sentiment.[11]

It appears that much of Catholic Germany experienced a similar process of clericalization. Here too there were "cultural and structural features" which made the people receptive to a clericalized religion. As in some regions of France, one can identify a "certain degree of tolerance and accommodation" on the part of the ecclesiastical hierarchy. Furthermore, the same "clustering of variables which converged to help foster particularly strong clerical . . . orientations" in western France can be found in Southwest Germany as well. These variables included a large clerical establishment, local and rural recruitment of the parish clergy, and "a missionary tradition sympathetic to certain aspects of popular religion."[12]

[10] Tackett, *Religion, Revolution, and Regional Culture*, p. 249.
[11] Tackett, *Religion, Revolution, and Regional Culture*, p. 235.
[12] Tackett, *Religion, Revolution, and Regional Culture*, pp. 248–249.

Both the triumph of the pastoral ideal and the growth of clericalism must be understood in the context of developments in popular religion. Priests became indispensable for all important Catholic religious practices, and the population not only accepted the important role of a priest, but insisted on his participation. Most importantly, of course, the priest had to administer the sacraments, several of which were vital to popular religion. But, by the eighteenth century, people also expected a priest to be present at the rituals of the liturgical year, pilgrimages, processions, and even prayer meetings. As priests became more essential to religious life, the people of the villages and towns of Southwest Germany also accepted that "public rituals must be legitimated by the clergy," in order to be truly Catholic. Clericalism thus became an essential aspect of the people's confessional identity.[13]

CLERICALISM AND ANTI-CLERICALISM

The population of Southwest Germany actively sought to expand the number of priests living and working in rural parishes. Primarily they did this by seeking the creation of new parishes for villages without a parish church and by trying to organize and finance new benefices for additional resident clergy. Village communes and town councils supplemented these projects by working to revive moribund benefices and by trying to require that all clergymen, regardless of the kind of benefice they held, perform pastoral services.

If the desire for more priests is evidence of a kind of clericalism, it is also evidence of the absence (or weakness) of anti-clerical attitudes. Of course there were tensions between priests and their parishioners, ranging from the disputes about the place of the priest and his family in the community to constant bickering over tithes. Financial conflicts did not, however, define the relationship between parish priests and the population. Instead, monasteries, ecclesiastical chapters, and military orders were the primary target of economic discontent with the clergy, since many parishes were incorporated by these institutions, which then collected the tithe. As a result, parish priests received the bulk of their income from more distant institutions, rather than directly from their parishioners. In fact, it could happen that parish priests and villagers worked together to force monasteries to pay priests a larger portion of the tithe.

[13] Michael Carroll, *Veiled Threats. The Logic of Popular Catholicism in Italy* (Baltimore and London, 1996), p. 11.

Peasants could draw on the older, and very rich, anti-clerical tradition in criticizing the wealth and political power of the Catholic Church. In 1711 a certain Barbara Schick stood in the fields and screamed at *Pfarrer* Frick of Achstetten that his servants were taking too large a tithe from her flax harvest.[14] Perhaps even more common was the kind of complaint made by the villagers of Donzdorf against their pastor:

> Everyone knows that he is good at sleeping well, eating, drinking, and taking walks. In one word, he is a great lover of fancy foods [*delicatenspeissen*] and drink and he is more concerned with them than he is with serving his large parish, the generous income of which he spares no trouble bringing in, without being able to show how he has earned a single *Heller*.[15]

Even this complaint, however, implies that the *Pfarrer*'s love of money and luxury was a personal failing, not a characteristic of the clergy as a whole.

Another kind of anti-clericalism, in which peasants expressed hostility toward overly zealous priests, was dominant in whole regions of France. This attitude is difficult to find in Southwest Germany, even in the eighteenth century as priests became wealthier and better educated.[16] Peasants of course resented priests who were too closely linked to repressive lords, but this problem was apparently not widespread. In general, peasants appear to have separated the religious function of the priest from his sometime role as petty bureaucrat, property manager, and tithe collector.[17]

Villagers and townspeople not only tolerated the presence of priests; they wanted more priests in the villages. Indeed, this search for new priests is the clearest indication of the steady clericalization of rural Catholicism. Communities actively organized and supported the creation of permanent benefices or, if this was not possible, arranged for and funded temporary clergymen, mostly mendicant friars from nearby towns. The reasoning behind these measures was fairly standard. In 1651, for example, the residents of Waldmössingen asked the bishop for a priest of their own, or if this was not possible, for an Augustinian to

[14] HStASt. B467/4.

[15] HStASt. B466a/113. This was in 1743.

[16] For France see Philip T. Hoffman, *Church and Community in the Diocese of Lyon, 1500–1789* (New Haven, 1984); Tackett, *Religion, Revolution, and Regional Culture.*

[17] Monasteries, which generally collected tithes themselves, remained a focus of popular resentment. Peasants in the southern Black Forest fought the monastery of St. Blasien tooth and nail, but rarely does one find anti-clerical rhetoric in their conflicts with the monastery. David M. Luebke, *His Majesty's Rebels. Communities, Factions, and Rural Revolt in the Black Forest, 1725–1745* (Ithaca and London, 1997).

come from the town of Oberndorf on a weekly basis. The one-and-a-half-hour journey to Oberndorf was too long for the villagers to undertake every week, and as a result many had not received communion in years. Many children were growing up having never been to Mass or catechism class. The villagers were willing to contribute in several ways to the project: "With the donations and alms of generous and good-hearted people, and with our own sweat and blood we have completed the building of a church." Permission to bring a priest to this church would, the peasants informed the bishop, honor God, and "lead us weak mortal people to salvation."[18]

The request of the Waldmössinger, while couched in the grim language of the immediate aftermath of the Thirty Years' War, was echoed time and again in the seventeenth and eighteenth centuries by other peasants. In 1777 the *Gemeinde* of Schlatt protested to the Austrian regime in Freiburg that they were poorly served by the Franciscans hired by their lords, the Knights of Malta (the *Johanniter*).[19] The commune argued that the villagers paid enough tithe to support a resident priest, who would surely do a better job. The mendicants endangered the souls of the faithful because they could not always come to Schlatt in time for emergency baptisms or to give the sacraments to the dying. The villagers also considered the services that the Franciscans offered insufficient:

> The mendicant priests assigned to this parish read two masses a week, including Sunday and holidays. These services consist of a sermon, although not always, or sometimes a catechism lesson instead, and then the mass itself, all of which happens in quick succession, so that they [the Franciscans] can get home as soon as possible.[20]

Testimony before a mixed episcopal and Austrian commission that met in October 1775 to discuss the possibility of installing a resident priest in the village of Seebronn illuminates various aspects of clericalism.[21] This commission was the result of a campaign by the commune of Seebronn that began in the late seventeenth century. Seebronn had been served for several centuries by priests from the town of Rottenburg, over an hour's walk away. The Seebronner claimed that their village had been a full parish in the early sixteenth century, and thus they were only asking for the restoration of an existing parish. In 1694, apparently with the support of the officials of the Austrian County of

18 HStASt. B466a/402.
19 GLAK 79/825, # 26; see also GLAK 89/107.
20 GLAK 79/825, # 26.
21 HStASt. B466a/356.

Hohenberg, the commune produced a proposal for a resident priest. This endeavor failed due to an inability to find the funds to pay for a parsonage and a salary sufficient for a resident clergyman.

By the 1770s the *Gemeinde* had the support of both episcopal and Austrian officials. The commune's letter of request and the testimony of communal representatives at the commission's hearing emphasized that in the absence of a resident priest people had died without the sacraments. According to testimony, which was disputed by the *Pfarrer* in Rottenburg, several men and horses had to make the trip to Rottenburg to fetch a priest in bad weather. Sometimes this journey was made in vain, since, as the Seebronner graciously conceded, the Rottenburg clergymen were burdened with many duties in the town. The priest in Hailtingen, another neighboring parish, sometimes came to Seebronn in an emergency, but he was apparently sickly and often not available. Altogether, four people had died without the sacraments in the previous six years.

The villagers' representatives also stressed that they needed a resident priest because Seebronn was surrounded by Lutheran villages. This argument had several features. In the first place, a priest was needed to counteract the threat that Lutheran neighbors posed to religion and morality in the village. The villagers pointed to the case of Hans Jakob Schäfer as evidence of this danger. About forty years earlier Schäfer had developed friendships in a nearby Lutheran village, and had then committed adultery with his step-daughter, left his wife and moved away from Seebronn, married a Lutheran woman and converted to Lutheranism. The *Gemeinde* argued that "this case would most likely [*ganz vermutlich*] have been prevented if a pastor [*Seelsorger*] had been in Seebronn. [A pastor] would have stopped him from associating with the Lutherans."

A resident priest would also prevent a reoccurrence of the Schäfer disaster by teaching morals to the youth of the village. Apparently there was a school in Seebronn, but outside priests who conducted services in the village could not come to teach religion and morals as they did several times a week in their home parish. The villagers' concern for public morality was no doubt real, but one also senses that their desire for a resident priest was closely linked to their sense of Catholic identity. The presence of a priest marked the village as Catholic, but the absence of a priest allowed people like Schäfer to cross confessional boundaries with impunity.

The villagers of Seebronn asserted their confessional identity in other ways as well. They pointed out that the Eucharist was set out on the altar in the village church and worshipped there on a regular basis. Baptisms and funerals, as well as the other sacraments, were all performed in Seebronn, evidence that it was a full-fledged parish rather than a filial church. Although this legal point was important, the villagers' concern was with the sacraments as religious practices. Their petition spoke about the indispensability of a resident priest for both rites of passage (baptism, deathbed confession) and regular devotions, such as praying before the Eucharist.

The Seebronner, like other villagers seeking a new parish, collided with the complex and rigid benefice system of the region. The tithe in Seebronn was divided between six different parties, and episcopal officials hoped to persuade all of them to contribute to a parsonage and salary for a resident priest. The largest tithe-holder (*Zehntherr*) was the University of Freiburg, which, like most major ecclesiastical institutions, had no interest in releasing resources for pastoral services. Professor Wild, representing the university, attempted to undermine the argument for a resident priest, pointing out (in the tone of the Enlightenment) that teachers were as important as priests for public morality. Wild claimed that the university had not found a collapse of morals in Seebronn: "In fact," he said, "we have learned quite the opposite, that they [the Seebronner] are well educated in Christianity." Perhaps more importantly for the commissioners, the university (again, like monasteries, military orders, and other ecclesiastical institutions) possessed a well-organized archive that could produce documents to support its case. Professor Wild quite aggressively suggested that other funds, especially the so-called *Jesuiten Fonds*, which consisted of the resources taken by the Austrian government from the abolished Society of Jesus, be used for the creation of a parish in Seebronn.[22] "The property from the Rottenburg area is used by the University in Freiburg for just as useful and valuable a purpose for the State and the Church, [it is] also a work that is just as pleasing to God, as the placing of a resident priest in Seebronn will ever be."

The fact that five other institutions also held pieces of the tithe further weakened the plan to revive the parish of Seebronn. Some of those holding the smaller portions, such as the monastery of Kreuzlingen and the commune of Seebronn itself, offered to contribute. Other tithe-holders, such as the preacher at the collegiate chapter and the *Spital*

[22] When it abolished the society in Austria in 1773, the Austrian government designated the Jesuit resources specifically for the improvement of pastoral services.

(poorhouse) in Rottenburg, claimed they were too poor to contribute even if they wanted to. The consequence was that prohibitively complex negotiations were needed to find resources. In this, the Seebronn case was not unusual. Everywhere in Southwest Germany the complexity of the legal status and financial resources of rural parishes, together with the recalcitrance of larger ecclesiastical institutions, made every effort to install more *Seelsorger* extremely difficult.

The kind of clericalism that was so apparent in Waldmössingen, Schlatt, and Seebronn was not new for the population or for the Church. Yet after 1650 and especially after 1700, it had grown strong enough to weaken the benefice system. If the pastoral ideology of the Council of Trent was an important factor in undermining the resistance of ecclesiastical institutions, popular demand for more pastors drove the process. Village communes demonstrated their commitment to finding more priests by allocating more of their own resources to the local parish. In 1737, for example, the commune of Molpertshausen agreed to contribute stones and other building material to repair its church, and in 1763 the same commune arranged for full services in this church on major feasts, in part by donating a field to the parish for the upkeep of a resident priest. In other places villagers had fewer resources, but offered to contribute work teams for building or made regular contributions of wood from communal forests.[23]

Parish priests themselves pressed for the placement of more clergy in the countryside, sometimes directly and sometimes as spokespersons or letter writers for rural communities. Priests became more active in the eighteenth century, when population growth often left them overworked. In the 1780s, as the Austrian government openly strove to improve pastoral services, priests publicly asked for assistants. The parish priests in Elzach and Obersäckingen both sent statistics showing the rising number of baptisms in their parishes as evidence of their growing workload.[24] Both priests wanted larger incomes so they could hire an assistant and thus fulfill their pastoral duties more effectively.

Demands for more priests came then from below, from the people and the clergy in the parishes. These requests kept the Clerical Council

[23] HStASt. B486/1273. Also see GLAK 61/13465, pp. 458–460 and 567–575 for an example of the complicated negotiations for the building of a new church in Mainwangen in 1707.

[24] Obersäckingen (1781): GLAK 79/837. Elzach (1786): GLAK 229/24467. The request from the *Pfarrer* in Elzach was especially sophisticated, pointing to the higher number of baptisms than funerals, concluding that the number of parishioners was growing dramatically. The priest in Obersäckingen asked Austrian officials to keep his request secret, for fear of retribution from the Abbess of St. Fridolin in Säckingen, patron of his parish.

(*Geistliche Rat*) of the Bishops of Constance busy in the first decades of the eighteenth century.[25] The council faced a variety of initiatives. One way to expand the number of clergy was to hire assistant priests, primissaries (*Frühmesser*), and chaplains. In 1708, for example, the Teutonic Knights reported that the parishioners of the filial church in Dettingen wanted the priest in Dingelsdorf to hire a "permanent assistant."[26] Beginning in 1709, the inhabitants and a local nobleman in Laupheim attempted to force the monastery of Ochsenhausen to hire and pay a primissary in their parish. Although the council supported this endeavor, Ochsenhausen tenaciously resisted, prompting episcopal officials to threaten legal action in 1714. In both these cases the additional priest was eventually installed.[27]

The villagers of Unteressendorf and a number of surrounding villages struggled for decades to organize the funds for a chaplain in their parish. In 1720, the four communes that made up the large parish of Unteressendorf submitted a first request for a chaplain to the episcopal curia in Constance. The villagers claimed that a resident chaplain had lived in the village before the Thirty Years' War, a claim confirmed by documents held by the University of Freiburg, the patron of the parish.[28] Otherwise, the villagers presented the usual arguments for another resident priest. The parish was large and as a result the *Pfarrer* was overworked. He could not hear all the confessions, could not provide as many masses as the villagers desired, and when he had to travel to the outlying villages of the parish, he came late to church. As in Seebronn, the university resisted new financial obligations for years, even under pressure from the Count of Waldsee, the secular lord of the area. But the village did not give up. After thirty years of negotiations and various proposals, a second priest did come to the parish.

The Clerical Council in Constance also received a number of proposals for the creation of new parishes in this period, discussing three such projects in one three-year period, at Möhringen (1710), Ingerkingen (1711), and Dettingen (1712).[29] In general, episcopal officials responded positively to these schemes. It is significant that in all cases monasteries resisted new parishes, while communes, with modest support from episcopal officials, applied pressure for change. The peasants could be

[25] EAF Ha 216, Ha 217, Ha 218. [26] EAF Ha 217, pp. 301, 303.

[27] EAF Ha 217, pp. 46–47, 70–71, 105–106, 184–185, 213. Ha 218, pp. 362–363, 382–383, 501–502, 522–524. Other examples of revival of secondary benefices: *Caplanei* in Hummertsried (HStASt. B486/438); *Frühmesserei* in Nusplingen (HStASt. B467/684).

[28] HStASt. B467/407, B467/408.

[29] EAF Ha 218, pp. 52–55, 227–228, 235–236, 250, 291–293, 398–399.

most imaginative about the arrangements for new parishes, a sign that they wanted results. The residents of Immenriedt proposed that the property of the parish priest in Kißlegg, where the mother church was located, be freed from a number of taxes and dues. This would increase his income by 100 *Gulden*, allowing him to hire an assistant to conduct services in Immenriedt. The villagers were rewarded for their initiative.[30]

There are other indications of the growing importance of clergy for the population. In the century after the Thirty Years' War, pastoral work absorbed many holders of *beneficia simplicia*, who theoretically were not required to provide such services. Austrian officials recognized that in practice the distinction between pastors and other priests was not always clear. Officials in Freiburg reported in the 1780s that "there are chaplains and *Frühmesser* who are not only responsible for reading endowed masses, or who voluntarily help parish priests, but who are also obliged to do pastoral duties, and sometimes must exercise all parish duties in filial churches and for the parishioners who belong to them."[31] Church services, including all the essential sacraments, were often provided in an *ad hoc* fashion. The church of Oberried, a filial of the parish church of Kirchzarten, was sometimes served by the parish priest (coming from the mother church), sometimes by a vicar who also lived in Kirchzarten, and sometimes by a vicar who came from the nearby city of Freiburg. Finally, the villagers reported that "in an emergency and sometimes upon request, the Benedictine monks from the Monastery of Oberried jump in, out of charity, to help with hearing confessions or with visiting the sick."[32] Such a haphazard system did not sit well with people who considered such services absolutely essential.

The case of Oberried shows that monks and mendicants played a significant pastoral role by the mid-eighteenth century, something that in the 1770s and 1780s surprised Austrian officials intent on abolishing monasteries. Much of the monk/priests' work was unofficial, as villagers called on Capuchins, Augustinians, Franciscans, and Dominicans from nearby towns when they needed a priest. The regular clergy performed especially important services in the many towns and small cities of the regions, where parish priests were few and overburdened.[33] When

[30] EAF Ha 218, pp. 335–336, 418–419, 426–27.

[31] GLAK 79/837.

[32] GLAK 79/825. The date was 1777.

[33] GLAK 118/186. Richard Goldthwaite, *Wealth and the Demand for Art in Italy, 1300–1600* (Baltimore and London, 1993), p. 133, points out that there were far fewer parishes in German cities than in Italian cities.

questioned in the 1780s about the usefulness of monasteries, magistrates almost uniformly applauded the regulars. The Capuchins received the most praise, especially for their work in the mountainous regions near Waldshut, Staufen, and Tettnang. One town council argued that "they are not just useful, but necessary."[34] The parish structure, which despite the efforts of the people changed only slowly, required that the Capuchins and other orders filled the needs of a clericalized religion. There is a certain irony in the idea that clericalism, a fundamental goal of Catholic reformers, depended on the diversity and variety of the Catholic Church in Germany, considering that localism and diversity ran counter to the spirit of the organizational reforms of Trent.

Popular clericalism was fairly flexible. People in towns welcomed the assistance monks and friars gave to overworked parish priests. Villagers also called on the Capuchins and other friars to perform important services and recognized their qualifications to sanctify church rituals. A resident priest was, however, essential to rural Catholicism and visiting priests could not permanently substitute for a real parish priest. In Southwest Germany regular priests often found themselves in the role of non-resident priests. The Franciscans did not satisfy the inhabitants of Schlatt, not because they were unqualified to perform the necessary services, or even primarily because they were poor pastors, but because they did not live in the village.

Whether bishops, church reformers, or the common people liked it or not, many monks served as parish priests. The monastery of St. Blasien provides an instructive example of this problematic issue. This Benedictine abbey sent a large number of monks to perform pastoral services in its incorporated parishes and in the parishes under its patronage. This situation led to regular conflicts with the Bishops of Constance, who sought to examine and discipline such priests, as well as collect a variety of fees.[35]

Yet the Benedictine monks who served rural parishes were as effective pastors as were the secular priests, especially when they resided in the parishes they served. Indeed, St. Blasien, like the monastery of Weingarten in Upper Swabia, moved earlier and more effectively to discipline its dependents than did the bishops. A late sixteenth-century decree from St. Blasien admonishes all its priests, in good Tridentine fashion, not only to fulfill their pastoral duties, but also to behave properly. Priests were to reside in their parishes, to avoid conflicts with parishioners, to

[34] HStASt. B17/426.

[35] See above, chapter 1, for a discussion of these issues.

stay out of the inn, and to always wear a habit in public.[36] Monk/priests in rural parishes lived under the watchful eye of both their parishioners and their monastic superiors, who were closer and more attentive than episcopal authorities in Constance.

The inhabitants of the Black Forest villages served by Benedictine priests demonstrated little interest in the ecclesiastical status or training of their priests. When they complained about their pastors, they used exactly the same terms their neighbors used to complain about secular priests. The villagers of Schönau had strong communal traditions and a combative relationship with the priests sent them by the abbey. In the 1570s several conflicts over tithes and fishing rights led to verbal and even physical confrontations between the priest and several men in the village. When new conflicts arose in 1613, the dispute revolved around the pastoral services provided by the priest, including the number of sermons he gave, the quality of his catechism lessons, and the number of godfathers allowed at baptisms. Further conflicts erupted in the 1620s and in the 1660s. In the latter period, the commune of Schönau once again attacked the pastoral work done by the priest, Father Giselbertus Strankhaar.[37] Conflicts in Schönau were never exclusively about the professional performance of the priest, but the quality of pastoral services took a central place in the disputes in the seventeenth century. For the peasants, the fact that the priests were monks was never an issue as it was for episcopal officials.

There is, then, little evidence that parishioners treated resident monk/priests any differently than secular priests, or that they operated any differently in villages.[38] If the monks did not reside in their parishes, however, they had the same problems that plagued other non-resident priests. In the 1780s St. Blasien had to explain to Austrian officials why quite a number of churches in its jurisdiction were served by monk/priests walking or riding out from the abbey.[39] The abbot argued that it was impractical and counterproductive to send priests to isolated and impoverished villages. "Clergymen sent to such places would not last long without suffering a collapse, without becoming completely helpless, or without becoming themselves completely uncivilized." He also specifically asked that the village of Menzenschwand continue to be served

[36] GLAK 99/342.

[37] GLAK 229/94055. The villagers, following local tradition, wanted two godfathers. The priest, following episcopal decrees, refused to allow more than one. See below, chapter 5, for more on this dispute.

[38] Episcopal officials claimed otherwise in 1712. See GLAK 99/364.

[39] GLAK 79/850.

by a priest coming from St. Blasien, an hour and a half away, because the place was perched between two mountains and was so unhealthy, "that the majority of the inhabitants become imbeciles."[40]

St. Blasien was fighting a losing battle. The monastery continued to view incorporated parishes as benefices and thus sources of income. Abbots and monks accepted that they had to provide certain pastoral services in exchange for these resources, but they had not internalized the clericalism that informed both popular Catholicism and the activities of the Josephine reformers, who sought to reorganize the parish structure and create new parishes. By the 1770s and 1780s Austrian officials and communal leaders agreed priests could not be effective pastors if they did not reside in their parishes

Popular clericalism in the seventeenth and eighteenth centuries stressed the indispensability of the priest in the village. This attitude was the logical outcome of the importance of the everyday devotions and rituals of Catholicism, most (if not all) of which required the participation of a consecrated cleric. Clericalism did not mean that people expressed or practiced unquestioned loyalty to the Catholic clergy, as the regular conflicts between priests and their parishioners attest. At the same time, however, the improved professional performance of the parish priests and the rising quality of their education probably enhanced their standing in the villages.

THE PROFESSIONALIZATION OF THE PARISH CLERGY

Parish priests, in Southwest Germany as elsewhere in the Catholic world, inhabited the intersection of a number of different worlds. Literate and increasingly educated, they often lived among uneducated and primarily illiterate people. Members of a legally distinct order, they were none-the-less an integral part of the daily life of villages and small towns. Although they internalized, at least to some degree, a special code of personal behavior and claimed an identity as part of the international Catholic Church, most priests still lived near their hometown, maintained close relations with their families, and never completely abandoned the culture of their childhood. In one sense, however, by the seventeenth and eighteenth centuries the place of the priest became somewhat less ambiguous than it had been traditionally. Although priests still held benefices and continued to manage property, in

[40] GLAK 79/850: *ohne selbst gleichsam zu verwilden* and *daß ein grosser theil der Innwohner blödsinnig wird.*

the post-Tridentine period they considered themselves primarily pastors, not holders of benefices. The decrees of the Council did succeed in remaking the clergy, or, at the very least, dramatically shifted the priorities of the secular clergy. In Southwest Germany, the parish clergy's commitment to *Seelsorge* coincided with and reinforced the clericalism of the population. Parish priests were not only pressured to fulfill the pastoral role their parishioners expected of them; they fulfilled it because they understood it to be their duty.

There were two particularly important aspects of the changing character of the clergy. First, by the second half of the seventeenth century the behavior of parish priests more often than not approached the ideal of the Catholic pastor. Even in the most isolated villages, parish priests were (as a rule) celibate, sober, and generally above moral reproach, while also trying to avoid entanglements in local conflicts. Priests also gradually detached themselves from village and town society, developing at the same time ties with other priests, and living more and more within a kind of clerical culture. After 1650 the growing material ease of parish priests also helped this process along. All these changes were of course interrelated, as the pressures of maintaining a clerical lifestyle set priests apart from their neighbors while simultaneously drawing them to each other. A developing clerical culture could and sometimes did lead to conflicts with parishioners, who were constantly on guard against clerical "arrogance." Yet the willingness of most parish priests to fulfill their all-important pastoral duties prevented a real rift between the clergy and the Catholic population before the end of the eighteenth century.[41]

Clerical celibacy

Concubinage was widespread in the Bishopric of Constance in the 1570s and 1580s. It is, however, impossible to determine the percentage of priests living in long-term relationships with women. In the Rural Chapter of Engen episcopal visitors found (among sixteen *Pfarrer*), four concubines in 1576, twelve in 1581, and three in 1590. In the area around Biberach in 1588, at least five of sixteen parish priests had their children, and presumably the children's mothers, living with them. In fact, episcopal visitors found concubinage in all parts of the Bishopric of

[41] Compare the discussions of these issues for several regions of France: Timothy Tackett, *Priest and Parish in Eighteenth Century France. A Social and Political Study of the Curés of the Diocese of Dauphiné, 1750–1791* (Princeton, 1977) and Hoffman, *Church and Community in the Diocese of Lyon.*

Constance in this period, in the Breisgau, in Upper Swabia, in the area of Lake Constance, and in Switzerland. If concubinage was not universal, it was common and not considered unusual.[42] It is remarkable, then, that by about 1610, and certainly by the 1620s, open, public concubinage was gone.

Clerical concubinage was eliminated across Catholic Germany in this period, perhaps somewhat later in the Southwest than in Bavaria, but somewhat earlier than in Switzerland.[43] As we have seen, concubinage attracted the attention of Austrian (and other secular) authorities and was a focus of church reforms in the period 1580–1620.[44] Reformers in this period were in fact so obsessed with concubinage that even the most isolated parish priest had to send his concubine away. When the Teutonic Knights pushed *Pfarrer* Reüderlin of Blumenfeld to retire in 1619, he was one of the last priests in Southwest Germany who openly lived with a concubine and her children.[45]

Clerical celibacy became one of the clearest and most public markers of the Catholic clergy. Just as there is no evidence, outside of educated circles, of criticism of concubinage in the sixteenth century, there is no indication that the wider population objected to clerical celibacy in the seventeenth and eighteenth centuries.[46] In fact, after 1650, complaints about priests almost never mention sexual issues or celibacy in any context. Priests were apparently not considered dangerous sexual predators, but their celibacy, while accepted, did not accord them a special status either. The presence of celibate clergymen was one aspect of a locality's identity as Catholic, as opposed to a Protestant village with a married pastor. Yet as we have seen, requests for resident priests emphasized their indispensability as pastors, and not their personal presence or behavior.

Whatever the population thought of celibacy, by about 1600 the clergy certainly considered it part of its identity. Parish priests,

[42] Jörn Sieglerschmidt, "Der niedere Klerus um 1600. Eine vergleichende Untersuchung am Beispiel des Landdekanats Engen" in Kuhn et al. (eds.), *Die Bischöfe von Konstanz* Vol. I, *Geschichte* (Friedrichshafen, 1988), p. 118; EAF Ha 63, pp. 13–14; Moritz Gmelin, "Aus Visitationsprotokollen der Diözese Konstanz von 1571–1586. Ein Beitrag zur Geschichte des Klerus" *ZGO* 25 (1873), pp. 129–204.

[43] Johan Georg Mayer, *Das Konzil von Trent und die Gegenreformation in der Schweiz* (Stans, 1901), pp. 32–33.

[44] See chapter 1.

[45] GLAK 229/10173. A priest in the parish of Minseln, also under the control of the Teutonic Knights, had a concubine in 1623. See GLAK 86/90.

[46] For further discussion of popular attitudes toward concubinage, see Forster, *The Counter-Reformation in the Villages*, pp. 22–28, 204–205. Attitudes in the Southwest were similar to those in Speyer. See Sieglerschmidt, "Der niedere Klerus um 1600," p. 118.

moreover, saw themselves as something more than just members of the clerical estate. They were also pastors, which distinguished them from monks, nuns, chapter canons, university professors, and other clergymen. The high value placed on pastoral service by the Council of Trent, by the Jesuits and other new orders, and by the Catholic laity enhanced the self-confidence of the parish priests, who had traditionally taken second place to the rich and powerful regular clergy of Southwest Germany. Improved education, higher incomes and better living conditions, more stable careers, and a growing number of positions for pastors further improved the status and confidence of the parish priests.

Salem and the secular clergy

The changing status of the parish clergy is well illustrated by the relationship between the Cistercian Abbey of Salem and the priests who served in the monastery's parishes. There had always been tension in this relationship, although abbots and monks had never displayed much interest in conditions in the parishes themselves. Like St. Blasien, Salem always considered its parishes sources of income and sought to limit the amount of money it expended for pastoral work.[47] Tensions appear to have increased in the eighteenth century, probably due to the Cistercians' suspicion that the secular priests were the bishop's men. This mistrust was not unfounded, since after 1735 the parish clergy was increasingly trained at the episcopal seminary in Meersburg. Furthermore, there are indications that in the eighteenth century personal and professional bonds between parish priests strengthened, at the expense of their ties to the monastery.

Because monks from Salem itself did not serve as parish priests, as did the Benedictine monks from St. Blasien, Salem had less direct control of the priests than did some monasteries. Priest/monks from Salem only served in parishes during and directly after the Thirty Years' War. Otherwise, Cistercians had no direct role in the villages, although they did serve as confessors at the shrines of Birnau and Bodman, and at Salem itself.[48] The abbey did consider the parish priests subordinates, as even the legal status of the parish priest demonstrated. Most priests served parishes that were incorporated into the monastery and were

[47] Marc R. Forster, "Kirchenreform, katholische Konfessionalisierung und Dorfreligion um Kloster Salem, 1650–1750," *RJfKG* 16 (1997), pp. 93–110.

[48] GLAK 98/666.

thus not true parish priests (*Parochi*, *Pfarrer*), but rather vicars (*Pfarrvicarii*), serving in the place of the "real" pastor, the Abbot of Salem.

Salem also demanded obedience from "its" priests, if only to limit financial demands on the monastery. Monastic officials tried to encourage loyalty through a system of appointments and promotion that rewarded long service in the monastery's parishes.[49] After 1650, political stability allowed Salem to perfect this system, appointing young priests to poorly paid chaplaincies and promoting them later to well-paying parishes. Some of the *Protokolle* of the discussions of these appointments among the leadership of the monastery have survived for the eighteenth century.[50] The monks discussed the qualifications of the candidates and referred to letters of recommendation. They gave particular preference to priests who had served in Salem benefices, and to those priests who were natives of Salem villages. Thus in 1755, the monks voted to appoint Constantin Flach, the *Pfarrer* in the poor parish of Mimmenhausen, to the well-endowed parish of Ostrach. Flach, like all the candidates for Ostrach, was credited with being "zealous in doctrine and devotion," but had the additional qualification of being a native of Salem itself. At the same time, the monks promoted an assistant priest (*Helfer* or *cooperator*) to the post in Mimmenhausen. A slightly different set of considerations came into play in 1758 when Salem filled the "entry-level" position of chaplain in Äpfingen. In this case, the monks chose Innocentius Endres over four other applicants. In choosing Endres, the monks pointed to his recommendation by the *Gemeinde* in Äpfingen, his experience in pastoral work, and his wealthy brother, who had agreed to support the destitute sisters of the previous (and now deceased) chaplain. Salem made appointments, then, with a variety of considerations in mind.

Despite this careful and organized program, parish priests did not behave as clients of the monastery. In fact, a growing sense of corporate loyalty brought the secular clergy of the region around Salem (the Linzgau) together, despite the variety of parish patrons they worked for and despite the political fragmentation of the region. In the eighteenth century, most priests had a common educational background and socialized regularly at the meetings of the rural chapter (*Landkapitel*). Furthermore, as the episcopal administration became more active in the countryside, sending commissions to investigate disputes and enforcing

[49] This method was also employed by the military orders, especially the Knights of St. John in the villages around Heitersheim. See GLAK Abt. 89.

[50] GLAK 98/696, 98/3377.

episcopal jurisdiction more aggressively, secular priests may have felt less beholden to either parish patrons or secular lords.[51]

Evidence from priests' death inventories shows that the social status, financial resources, and educational level of the parish clergy rose quite dramatically in the century after 1650. Two examples illustrate the general pattern. In 1684 Johan Baptist Kramer, priest in Bermatingen, left a modest inheritance, which included a library of fifty-eight books, but little cash.[52] By contrast, in 1751 Franz Ersing, *Pfarrer* in the Salem parish of Urnau, left an estate valued at over 1,600fl. and a library that contained more than 170 titles.[53] Priests like Ersing certainly had no reason to feel inferior to the wealthy and educated Cistercians at Salem.

Ersing's 1751 will also provides evidence of the social and professional world of a parish priest. The *Pfarrer* had clearly maintained his ties to his family, who lived in the towns of Biberach and Ravensburg, and he left considerable sums of money to his siblings, nieces, and nephews. Furthermore, he was enmeshed in a social world made up of his fellow priests, and it was to these priests that Ersing left the management of his pious donations. Similarly, Johannes Haff, priest in Bermatingen, had five neighboring priests witness his will in 1730.[54]

The tone of relations between priests and the monastery reflected the growing self-confidence of the secular clergy. There were more clashes between priests and the monastery in the eighteenth century. Herr Carl Ruez, *Pfarrer* in Mimmenhausen, seems to have sought conflict with Salem in order to assert his rights and authority. In 1771, against both ancient tradition and the express order of Salem officials in the area, he refused to allow the villagers to ring the church bells to announce mowing of the common meadow. Asked to explain himself, Ruez was unrepentant: "In his answer, the *Herr Pfarrer* let it be known that there is no lordship that is so hard on the clergy as Salmansweil [Salem] . . ."[55] Some priests behaved, from the perspective of the monastery, even worse. In 1768, *Pfarrer* Flach in Mainwangen incited Salem's subjects in that village to resist new taxes and duties. A Salem official in the area reported that communal officials were considering a law suit against the monastery, "and the rumor is going around in Mainwangen that the *Herr* [*Pfarrer*] had advised them to do so."[56] Of course there were ongoing conflicts between the *Pfarrer* and the monastery over the priests'

[51] There is clear evidence of a more active episcopal administration, both in the records in EAF, esp. the *Protokolle des Geistlichen Rats*, and in HStASt. B466a and B467.

[52] GLAK 98/3212. [53] GLAK 98/3666. [54] GLAK 98/3213.

[55] GLAK 98/3449, pp. 6r, 12r. [56] GLAK 98/3397.

income, over taxes and dues they should pay, and over the repairs of parsonages. As far as many priests were concerned, Salem was no different than any other territorial lord. In the midst of one dispute with Salem a priest was reported to say, "He is even more ashamed of this [the dispute with Salem], since a clerical authority [*geistliche obrigkeit*] is doing it. He could take it better from a secular lord, [but] this is really scandalous [*ärgerlich*]. He was once happy to be a priest, but now he would rather be, begging your pardon, a swineherd."[57]

Toward a professional parish clergy

The experience of the Salem priests highlights several important characteristics of the new-style priests who served in the seventeenth and eighteenth centuries. It is certainly possible to speak of a professionalization of the clergy. Parish priests lived and worked in careers that provided increasingly stable positions, improved material conditions, and better and more consistent professional training. Almost all parish priests benefitted from these developments, which led in turn to a greater sense of the importance of the pastoral work they performed.

After about 1700 priests served longer in one parish than they had either in the decades after 1650 or in the period 1580–1620. The absence of major military campaigns in the eighteenth century, especially compared with the ravages of the Thirty Years' War, had a great deal to do with the stability of clerical careers. Population growth, which set in after 1700, led to increasing revenues from tithes. Monasteries and other tithe-holders of course profited immensely from this conjuncture. But then they had to share these profits with the parish priests, who could point to the importance of the pastoral services they provided and to popular pressure for more priests in their negotiations for more pay. Well-remunerated priests did not need to seek a better parish and stayed longer in their parishes.[58]

The average age of parish priests in the parishes of the *Landkapitel* of Stockach rose steadily between 1665 and 1708. In 1665 most priests were in their early thirties, with an average age of 30.5 years.[59] By 1708, the average age had risen to 53.4 years. Only one of the twenty-five priests whose ages are listed was in his thirties, while seven were over sixty.

57 GLAK 98/3449, p. 4v.

58 EAF A1/725 (Visitations of 1665, 1685, 1702, 1706, 1708). Compare Forster, *The Counter-Reformation in the Villages*, pp. 194–199 and Tackett, *Priest and Parish*, ch. 4.

59 In calculating this average I left out the two oldest priests, aged fifty and seventy.

Since priests were most often appointed to parishes in their early thirties, a priest in his fifties had served a parish for twenty or more years. When the members of the Rural Chapter of Stockach gathered for a meeting in the second decade of the eighteenth century, eleven of the twenty-nine priests had been in their parishes for more than twenty-three years, and twenty-one of the twenty-nine had been in place over ten years. It appears that a whole generation of parish priests took parishes in the 1670s and 1680s and remained in place for thirty or more years.

The *Landkapitel* Linzgau was just as stable as Stockach.[60] In 1741, five of twenty-six priests had served over twenty years in their parishes, a further ten had been in place over fifteen years. There had been a generational change in the Linzgau in the early 1720s, probably at the time when the generation of priests who dominated in Stockach in 1708 died or retired. The turnover of priests was very small in any given year, once again pointing to a stable group of *Pfarrer* serving long careers.

The longevity of priests in individual parishes implies not only stability, but also more consistent pastoral services. Individual parishes found their priests staying longer. The town of Endingen had ten different priests between 1570 and 1620.[61] The same number of pastors served in the 130 years after 1650. The parish of Fischbach was clearly a less attractive post than Endingen, where many priests stayed until they died. Priests served two to five years in Fischbach and then resigned to take a better parish. Yet in the eighteenth century, several priests remained much longer, including Johan Joseph Herckner, who held the parish from 1698 to 1722, and Christian Pfister, who served in Fischbach from 1723 until his death in 1758.[62]

A career as a country priest became more attractive after 1650. Indeed, clerical incomes seem to have improved already in the decades around 1600. As we have seen, Austrian officials began to study ways to improve parish incomes as early as 1570. In the 1620s in the *Landkapitel* of Engen, priests earned an average of 240fl. a year, giving them a similar income to the highest local officials, and certainly making them far better off than their peasant parishioners.[63]

Gains made in the first decades of the seventeenth century did not survive the 1630s and the disaster of the Thirty Years' War. After 1650, however, the incomes of parish priests steadily improved, despite the unwillingness of monasteries and military orders to support pastoral work. Monasteries such as Salem managed their property well, and, as

[60] GLAK 98/687. [61] GLAK 229/2530. [62] GLAK 98/3819.
[63] Sieglerschmidt, "Der niedere Klerus um 1600," pp. 120–121.

we have seen, priests were increasingly well paid there. Clerical incomes rose in other places as well. Priests in Austrian territories apparently received good incomes, earning over 300fl. a year, and often in the 400–500fl. range, in almost all parishes surveyed in 1777.[64] Priests serving the military orders were somewhat poorer. The priests dependent on the Commandary of the Teutonic Knights in Beuggen received their income almost exclusively in kind, which meant it changed little over time. The *Pfarrer* in Möhlin, for example, received 24 *Viertel* of spelt (*Dinkel*), 10 *Viertel* of oats, 10 *Saum* of wine, and a tiny amount of money each year throughout the eighteenth century.[65] These priests only improved their style of life to the extent that they were able to sell surplus grain and wine and profit from rising prices.

None-the-less, most parish priests lived a comfortable life. Johan Jacob de la Cour, who served the parish of Owingen for twenty-four years at the turn of the eighteenth century, left extensive debts at his death in 1721, mostly back taxes owed to the bishop.[66] Because of his financial problems, de la Cour lived modestly, yet he also had to maintain appearances. The *Pfarrer* owned silver worth over 40fl., linens, some furniture and a small library. He had considerable grain and wine reserves as well. Taken together, de la Cour's death inventory gives a picture of a financially strapped country priest struggling to keep up a proper priestly lifestyle.

Johan Franz Schneider, who died in 1724 as priest in Bermatingen, a Salem parish, was probably unusually wealthy.[67] He had fairly large amounts of grain and wine stored in his house (although less than de la Cour hoarded) and owned at least three head of cattle. Schneider was wealthy enough to have lent out about 4,000fl., including large loans to the monastery of Salem and to the city of Riedlingen. It is also a sign of his wealth that the *Pfarrer* had many small debts in the village, to the apothecary, a doctor, the local butcher, a shepherd and so on. Indeed, the *Pfarrhaus* in Bermatingen played an important economic role in the community, as a source of loans and as a locus of consumption.

Parish priests had, of course, always spent money in villages, although those priests who worked their own fields were generally subsistence and not commercial farmers. After 1650, however, few priests still farmed

64 GLAK 79/425. This is about a doubling of the 240fl. a year reported for the early 1620s. It compares favorably with priests' incomes in Alsace, where Louis Châtellier writes of "*au fond, un clergé de pays riche.*" Châtellier, *Tradition chrétienne et renouveau catholique dans le cadre de l'ancien Diocèse de Strasbourg (1650–1770)* (Paris, 1981), pp. 379–386.

65 GLAK 86/80, 86/145.

66 GLAK 98/3513, 98/3514.

67 The death inventory of this priest is in GLAK 98/3193.

and most became either rentiers or gentlemen farmers.[68] Christopher Legler, who died as *Pfarrer* in Bermatingen in 1635, was a little of each.[69] He hired at least three maids, not just to keep house but also to take care of his cattle and perhaps a kitchen garden. At his death Legler owed money to a *Rebbauman*, that is someone who took care of his vineyard, as well as to several local peasants for transporting grain and wine. Although Legler obviously lived in part from tithes collected in kind and from food produced on the property of his benefice, he also had to buy food and other supplies, as evidenced by debts to the butcher and the innkeeper. In the middle of the eighteenth century, the *Pfarrer* in Weildorf was almost a rural entrepreneur.[70] He rented out his fields, sold all the tithe he received, and bought food and other necessities with cash. The priest in Görwihl built a whole new parsonage between 1723 and 1726, partly, according to one report, because he needed room to store produce from the tithe which he planned to collect and sell himself, rather than auctioning it off to local farmers.[71] Priests engaged in such activities were very much part of the economic world of the village; they were, however, landlords and entrepreneurs, not peasant-priests as many had been in the sixteenth century.

Parsonages came to reflect the status of priests. The parsonage built in the 1720s in Görwihl was, according to the parish chronicle, built in the style of a large farmer's house which provided roomy living quarters for the *Pfarrer* on the second floor, with space for livestock and tools on the ground floor.[72] The parsonage inhabited by Schneider in Bermatingen was comfortably furnished and equipped, with silverware, linens, and cooking utensils. The house itself was spacious, with six *Kammern* in addition to the kitchen, including rooms for two live-in servants, the housekeeper and the maid. There were ten paintings and a mirror on the walls as well, although the assessors labeled six of the paintings "poor."[73] This house was not unlike the parsonage built in the village of Sulmingen in 1765, for which plans and drawings survive.[74] This too had six rooms on two floors and provided living space for the *Pfarrer* and two maids. The parsonage was fronted by formal gardens and a large crest

[68] There were still priests who worked in the fields. Ebner asserts that Johan Baptist Brutschin, *Pfarrer* in Niederwihl from 1712 to 1736, "managed" (*bewirtschaftete*) the parish property himself, although he probably did not plow the fields himself. Ebner, *Niederwihl*, pp. 26–27.

[69] GLAK 98/3203. [70] GLAK 98/679. [71] Ebner, *Görwihl*, p. 67.

[72] Ebner, *Görwihl*, p. 67.

[73] Paintings also appear in the inventory of Franz Ersing, *Pfarrer* in Urnau. He had nine paintings, including several of some value.

[74] GLAK 98/4031.

over the front door demonstrated the status of the priest. In the eighteenth century, most rural priests clearly lived like comfortable middle-class town dwellers, not like their peasant parishioners. Priests like Johan Martin Finck, who in 1709 was living in a peasant-like house in Leipferdingen, were the exception. Finck recognized that he was being treated poorly, complained bitterly about sharing a run-down building with the cows and other livestock, and demanded an improvement in his quarters.[75]

The size of libraries in Catholic parsonages provides further evidence of improvement in the educational level and material resources of priests. The library of *Pfarrer* de la Cour, which consisted of ten books, was exceptionally modest for an eighteenth-century clergyman.[76] The 170-book library of *Pfarrer* Ersing, employed by Salem in Urnau, was also exceptional, although the collection of Hans Jakob Eisenmann, *Pfarrer* of St. Peter in Endingen, who died in 1795, almost matched it.[77] Libraries, of course, reflected the fact that priests were as a rule educated at urban secondary schools, often those run by the Jesuits, then at university and seminary.

Advances in clerical education are well documented. The founding of an episcopal seminary in Meersburg in 1735 symbolizes the ultimate success of this project, although the seminary came late and never dominated the training of parish priests.[78] To the distress of episcopal officials, training for parish priests in Southwest Germany remained decentralized and somewhat haphazard through the eighteenth century, as priests studied at a variety of secondary schools and universities. What was important from the perspective of priests themselves, parish patrons, and local communities, however, was that country priests not only maintained and used substantial libraries, but were also specifically trained as pastors.

Educated and experienced priests were candidates for open benefices, especially the better paying ones. In 1763, there were three well-qualified finalists for the position of parish priest in the Austrian town of Binsdorf.[79] Jacob Luib had studied theology and canon law at university and had seventeen years' experience as chaplain in Binsdorf. The town

[75] GLAK 93/252.

[76] GLAK 98/3514. The books were valued at 5fl., 45kr. They included a bible, a breviary, two collections of sermons, and a number of other devotional works.

[77] On Ersing, see above. Eisenmann, see GLAK 229/25051. He had 129 books. See Peter Schmidt, "Die Priesterausbildung" in *Die Bischöfe von Konstanz*, Vol. I, pp. 135–142.

[78] See below, chapter 6, for a more extensive discussion of this issue.

[79] HStASt. B38/573.

council further praised Luib's talent as a musician and his willingness to teach "the fundamentals of the Latin language" to the school children. The other two candidates, Johan Baptist Deuffel (or Teuffel, an unfortunate name for a priest) and Dominicus Aman had of course studied at university and, like Luib, had experience as pastors, eight and five years' respectively. A panel of priests examined all three candidates and asked them (in Latin) to respond to a number of theoretical situations they might face as pastor. Luib, Deuffel, and Aman all gave detailed answers that reflected both pastoral experience and a detailed knowledge of canon law. They had no difficulty satisfying the examiners.[80] The candidates also presented impressive recommendations from a variety of clergymen and from representatives of the parishioners they had served. The town council of Binsdorf recommended Luib, who was well known in the village, and the Austrian authorities appointed him. The surplus of well-trained, highly educated, and well-qualified priests was a key feature of eighteenth-century Catholicism in this part of Germany.

The letters of recommendation sent to Binsdorf show the personal and professional ties among priests. Deuffel had recommendations from the priest under whom he had served as chaplain, from priests in the two rural chapters where he had been posted, and from Joseph Pachmayer SJ, professor at the *Gymnasium* in Rottweil. Luib received recommendations from the outgoing priest in Binsdorf, who had been his superior for the previous seventeen years, and from the prioress of the Dominican convent in Binsdorf. Aman also earned recommendations from his superior, as well as from several other priests. The candidates were not isolated in their parishes, but were part of a network of priests who knew and associated with each other.

All three priests are also examples of an important eighteenth-century phenomenon, that of priests serving long apprenticeships as vicars, chaplains, or assistant priests. As we have seen, pressure from communities led to the creation of more benefices for such subordinate priests. This situation contributed to the creation of a separate clerical culture, especially since priests often lived together in large parsonages. Conflicts over money, status, authority, and the distribution of work were of course not unusual, but it is significant that in the eighteenth century priests did not in fact work alone.[81]

[80] The examination board consisted of the rector of the parish in Rottenburg (the closest Catholic city), a Jesuit professor of moral theology, and a Carmelite father.

[81] In his extensive 1759 will, Joseph Antonius Ignatius Herderer, *Pfarrer* in Deißlingen, left his vicar a similar amount of money as he did his nieces and nephews. There were extensive conflicts between the elderly *Pfarrer* in Geislingen and his vicar in 1727: HStASt. B466a/163.

The rural priests of Southwest Germany were also members of rural chapters (*Landkapitel*), which became important for clerical sociability.[82] The rural chapters were for the most part founded in the fifteenth century as priestly brotherhoods, which aimed to provide proper burials, masses for dead members, and social occasions. After losing importance in the early sixteenth century, the chapters initially regained significance as administrative districts, serving in particular as the basic geographical unit for the episcopal visitations undertaken in the late sixteenth century.[83] After 1650 the corporate character of the *Landkapitel* reemerged, although the chapters also continued to play a role in administration.

The rural chapters clearly modeled themselves after the more prestigious ecclesiastical chapters, demonstrating the continued prestige of the collegiate ideal, even among the pastors of the countryside. By the second half of the seventeenth century, however, parish priests could look to other kinds of *Stifter* as models. In the late sixteenth century, for example, the clergy of the imperial city of Überlingen had reorganized itself into a chapter, with regulations aimed at strengthening clerical discipline in the city and improving pastoral services.[84] By contrast, when rural chapters began to publish their statutes in the 1670s and 1680s, however, the emphasis was on the corporate and devotional aspects of these institutions.

The statutes of the *Landkapitel* of Ebingen contain extensive regulations for the admission of new members, including a description of the liturgy used in the ceremony of induction. The statutes then go on to describe the officers (dean, *Camerarius*, deputies, secretary) and the fee schedule for the members. This was not a voluntary organization and all priests in the district were expected to pay an annual fee and attend meetings. The most important clauses of the statutes describe the benefits that accrued to members, especially a proper priestly funeral and masses and prayers for the deceased.[85]

This corporate aspect of the rural chapters coexisted with the administrative aspect emphasized by episcopal officials. Priests attended the

82 Peter Thaddäus Lang, "Die Statuten des *Landkapitels* Ebingen aus dem Jahre 1755" *FDA* 113 (1993), pp. 177–199; Hermann Schmid, "Die Statuten des Landkapitels Linzgau als historisch-statistisch-topographische Quelle" *FDA* 111 (1991), pp. 187–211. Compare discussion of rural chapters in Speyer: Forster, *The Counter-Reformation in the Villages*, pp. 198–199.

83 Episcopal officials used the term "rural chapter" rather than "deanery" (*Dekanat*) as the administrative category between the diocese and the parish, although the dean (*Dekan*, *Decanus*) remained the title given to the head of the chapter.

84 Wilfried Enderle, *Konfessionsbildung und Ratsregiment in der katholischen Reichsstadt Überlingen (1500–1618)* (Stuttgart, 1990), pp. 382–384.

85 Lang, "Die Statuten des *Landkapitels* Ebingen," pp. 184–187, 192–199.

meetings of the chapters, held in the home parish of the dean or in the biggest town of the district, in order to socialize with men of similar background and education, to hear the latest episcopal ordinances, and to discuss common problems.[86] For the members, then, the administrative role of the chapters probably enhanced their value. The masses and prayers for the dead were by no means secondary. The existence of a number of clerical confraternities, in the countryside as well as in the cities, further supplemented the devotional aspects of clerical culture. The St. Nicolaus *Bruderschaft*, located in the village of Grünenbach, was revived in 1736 in order to provide prayers and masses for deceased clergymen throughout Upper Swabia.[87]

Parish priests were part of a clerical culture that overlapped with both the world of their parishioners and the world of the regular clergy. By the eighteenth century priests were as well educated as most monks and, although less erudite than the Jesuits, they often felt superior to the mendicant orders. Priests were not isolated, often worked in pairs, and met each other regularly at the rural chapters. Yet their religious culture was not markedly different from that of their more educated parishioners, and even in the villages they did not stand out as representatives of another world. Pilgrimages and processions, confraternities and the liturgy, masses and prayers for the dead were at the heart of their Catholicism as well.

There was considerable variety even within clerical culture. Many parish priests in the area around Rottweil, for example, had a close relationship with the Jesuit house in that town. In the 1720s and 1730s several priests left considerable sums of money in their wills to the Jesuits, including *Pfarrer* Rebholz of Schörzingen, who left 12,000fl.[88] The Jesuits cultivated ties with the local parish clergy, inviting priests to services and dinner on the feasts of the Jesuit saints Ignatius and Xavier. The Jesuit chronicle from Rottweil emphasizes the respect the fathers had for neighboring priests, listing by name the priests who gave sermons on the these important feasts. Jesuit influence was strong around Rottweil, but the Capuchins had considerable influence in a number of other regions.[89] A parish priest had some choice of confessors, and his selection indicates whom he found both congenial and worthy of personal respect. In the *Landkapitel* of Waldshut, about half of

[86] Compare Tackett, *Priest and Parish*, p. 85. [87] EAF A1/362.

[88] Dankwart Schmid (ed.), *Die Hauschronik der Jesuiten von Rottweil 1652–1773. Historiae Synopsis Domesticae Societatis Jesu Rottweil* (Rottweil, 1989), pp. 79, 109–113, 151, 153.

[89] Stockach: EAF A1/725; Waldshut: EAF Ha 78, pp. 249v, 283r–288v.

the priests confessed to Capuchin fathers, five or six times a year in the early seventeenth century, and several times a month by the early eighteenth century.[90] The Franciscans in Saulgau were similarly influential in their area, hearing the confessions of quite a number of neighboring pastors.[91]

Jesuit or Capuchin houses were centers of clerical culture in some regions, but certainly not all. Priests often confessed to a neighbor, travelling once a week or once every other week to a nearby church to confess. Often priests confessed to each other, perhaps not an effective method of finding hidden sins, but surely a practice that created personal bonds between priests. In addition to the formal relationship between confessor and penitent, priests had, of course, personal friendships with neighboring priests. Such personal friendship between clergymen played a part in the tragic death of *Pfarrer* Johan Ignatius Vogel of Wurmlingen.[92] Vogel died after several falls from a horse, accidents that witnesses attributed to the *Pfarrer*'s overindulgence in wine while visiting an old friend, the dean of the monastery of Ohingen, a couple of hours' ride from his parsonage.

The development of a parish clergy with its own code of professional behavior, clear career paths and opportunities, and a distinct social and cultural world, was slowed down by two important factors. First, parish priests never escaped from the world of their families. Second, the benefice system forced them to court powerful patrons, manage property, and serve as local administrators. These duties and concerns often came into conflict with the pastoral emphasis that was at the heart of a parish priest's work.

Priests who served in Southwest Germany were local men. Generally they came from the towns and cities of the region and served in the countryside near their hometown. Of the twenty-eight priests in the *Landkapitel* of Stockach in 1708, nine were natives of the city of Constance; others came from the towns of Feldkirch, Bregenz, Überlingen, Radolfzell, and Meersburg, all located on or near Lake Constance.[93] Only one priest grew up far from the region, coming from Lucerne in Switzerland. Priests in the Rural Chapter of Waldshut in 1695 almost all came from the towns of the district itself, or from the adjacent part of Switzerland.[94]

90 EAF Ha 62. pp. 362r–369v, EAF Ha 78, pp. 283r–285r; EAF A1/738.

91 EAF Ha 62, p. 324 (Visitation of 1608). The Franciscans in Freiburg played a similar role in the 1660s: EAF Ha 63, pp. 583–637, 713–722.

92 HStASt. B466a/420. 93 EAF A1/725. 94 EAF Ha 78, pp 343r–345v.

The examples from the region around Salem show that parish priests kept their ties to their families when they took a rural parish. Priests left large portions of their inheritances to siblings, nieces, and nephews, even when, like *Pfarrer* Herderer of Deislingen, they also left large bequests to their parishes and to other religious endowments.[95] Herderer even combined his interest in promoting Catholic devotion with his concern for his family by giving 3,000fl. for the completion of a *Kalvarienberg* (a life-size representation of the crucifixion) and stations of the cross outside a chapel in his hometown of Rottweil. This project was dear to his heart because it had been planned, but never brought to completion, by his father. Family loyalties understandably prevented priests from identifying completely with their clerical profession, although to the extent that they did not serve in their hometown, direct conflicts between familial and clerical obligations did not arise.

Priests lived on the proceeds of the benefices they held, or on a portion of the benefice if the parish was incorporated into a monastery, chapter, or military order. The benefice system often required priests to closely manage parish property, to buy and sell grain and wine, and to attend to other economic matters that had nothing to do with their duties as pastors. This problem was, of course, far from new and had troubled parish priests, as well as monasteries and other ecclesiastical institutions, for centuries.[96] Priests seem to have found managing a benefice more problematic after 1650. Although *Pfarrer* Spick in Mainwangen complained bitterly about the economic problems of his post in the immediate aftermath of the Thirty Years' War, he was a very worldly administrator.[97] Spick spent his own money on repairs to the parsonage, explaining to the parish patron, the monastery of Salem, exactly what windows, doors, shelves, and cabinets had been built and how the danger of fire had necessitated the construction of a new stove. Because of the poor condition of the parsonage, Spick wanted to store grain in the church, which contributed to conflicts with the *Vogt* (a local official), who had stored his harvest there for years. Spick exacerbated this dispute when he took the lease of the parish property away from the *Vogt*'s brother, who, he said, was ruining the land. Spick was a careful and active manager of his benefice, but a parish priest's business dealings could easily cause conflicts with his parishioners. In 1754, the *Pfarrer*

95 HStASt. B466a/105.

96 See esp. Francis Rapp, *Réformes et Réformation à Strasbourg. Eglise et société dans le Diocèse de Strasbourg (1450–1525)* (Paris, 1974).

97 GLAK 98/3397.

in Ettenkirch had become a wine merchant, selling within the village and apparently serving as a middleman for smaller producers. His parishioners were not impressed, complaining that he enjoyed rather too much of his own product and had been too drunk on one occasion to perform a proper deathbed confession.[98]

Episcopal officials expressed concern in the 1740s that clergymen, especially parish priests, managed their benefices poorly, lived beyond their means, and were squandering the resources of the Church.[99] Officials made an example of Franz Leopold Beck, whom they removed from the parish of Dormettingen for running up extensive debts, which they feared would encumber the benefice for decades. In 1727 problems arose in Geislingen between the aged parish priest, Franz Breiwisch, and his vicar.[100] The vicar, Adam Holzapfel, claimed that various members of the priest's family lived in the parsonage and were using up the resources of the benefice, while also behaving in an unseemly fashion. Indeed, Breiwisch continued to pile up debts before resigning the parish several years later.

Parish priests had to administer their benefices as well as the sacraments. Although clerical incomes rose in the eighteenth century, priests had to work hard to find the money to maintain a proper lifestyle. In 1777, the priest in Elzach wrote: "If one balances the income and expenses, it is apparent that each *Pfarrer* in Elzach must manage his household carefully and be sparing in his own expenses, if he is to live honorably and does not wish to run into debt."[101] Economic issues and the nature of the benefice system, as well as personal and family ties, continued to pull priests in many directions. In this context, the professionalization of the parish clergy was a tendency, but never a completed process.

CONCLUSION

The clericalism of peasants and townspeople in Southwest Germany, especially their need for priests to perform services and sanctify devotions, came through clearly in their protests against priests. It can also be found in statements about popular priests. When village communes recommended priests for new positions, they focused their attention on the same issues – baptisms, confessions of the sick, sermons, teaching, and regular services – that caused problems with priests:

[98] HStASt. B61/930. [99] HStASt. B466a/114. [100] HStASt. B466a/163.
[101] GLAK 79/825, no. 4.

> We, the *Schultheis*, *Bürgermeister*, council members, representatives of the village of Äpfingen declare in our name and the name of the whole commune, in what way the honorable and learned Herr Carl Schwickhardt was in all his acts and behavior diligent and sober throughout the time he served here as chaplain. His conduct, especially his particular eloquence from the pulpit, his tireless diligence in catechism, his caring, sensitive, and fearless visiting and communicating of the sick, and his diligent hearing of confessions, not only earned him the love and esteem of those under his pastoral care, but also earned him the praise of many in the surrounding area.[102]

Clericalism meant that the population had accepted and internalized the view that priests were indispensable for religious practice. It thus meant that priests were powerful and important. As we have seen, however, priests were not dealing with submissive and obedient parishioners. Indeed they had to earn the trust of their flock, and if they failed to do so, they found life in the village quite unpleasant. The tension between the importance and even the power of the parish priest and the self-assurance of rural communes and town councils was an enduring aspect of local Catholicism.

[102] GLAK 98/696. This recommendation went to the monastery of Salem in 1761. See below, chapter 5, for complaints about priests.

CHAPTER 5

The communal church in German Catholicism

The people of Southwest Germany considered priests essential for the proper functioning of local Catholicism. They did not, however, concede control of local religion to either the official Church or to parish priests. Rural communes and town councils continued to play a strong role in local Catholicism. The "communal church," which dominated religious life in the century before the Reformation, did not disappear in the sixteenth century, but rather continued to be an organizing force in the following two centuries.

Popular initiative was behind much of Catholic practice, and the people most often expressed themselves through the institutions of the commune. Communes managed parish finances, oversaw the performance of the clergy, and influenced the appointment and removal of priests. They organized and promoted devotions, particularly pilgrimages, processions, confraternities, and prayer meetings. Communes also funded and supported the construction of churches and chapels and the placement of stations of the cross, new altars, and other decorations in existing churches.[1]

The continuities between the communal church of the pre-Reformation era, as described by Peter Blickle and others, and the communal church of post-Tridentine Catholicism are striking, but not as surprising as they first appear.[2] The communal church around 1500 developed out

[1] W.M. Jacob argues much the same for England. See *Lay People and Religion in the Early Eighteenth Century* (Cambridge, 1996).

[2] On the communal church: Peter Blickle, *The Revolution of 1525. The German Peasants' War in New Perspective* (Baltimore, 1981); Peter Blickle, *Communal Reformation: The Quest for Salvation in Sixteenth-Century Germany* (New Jersey, 1992); Peter Blickle (ed.), *Zugänge zur bäuerlichen Reformation* (Zurich, 1987); Franziska Conrad, *Reformation in der bäuerlichen Gesellschaft: Zur Rezeption reformatorischer Theologie im Elsaß* (Stuttgart, 1984); Robert W. Scribner, "Communalism: Universal Category or Ideological Construct? A Debate in the Historiography of Early Modern Germany and Switzerland" *Historical Journal* 37, 1 (1994), pp. 199–207; Rosi Fuhrmann, *Kirche und Dorf: Religiöse Bedürfnisse und kirchliche Stiftung auf dem Lande vor der Reformation* (Stuttgart, 1995); Marc R. Forster, *The Counter-Reformation in the Villages. Religion and Reform in the Bishopric of Speyer, 1560–1720* (Ithaca

of the basic localism in religious life and reflected the strong role communes took in administering village life more generally. Throughout the early modern period communalism remained an organizing principle with strong roots in German villages and towns. In their religious role, communes contributed a strong element of reciprocity to lay–clergy relations. Peasants (and townspeople) demanded that priests, in exchange for payment of the tithe, perform a range of essential duties and that they live as members of the community.

The role of the commune evolved from its heyday in the early sixteenth century. After about 1580, church reforms placed the parish at the center of religious practice and, by emphasizing the parish community, probably strengthened the communal church.[3] The theoretical importance of the parish (which was nothing new for the Catholic Church) was reinforced in practice by episcopal visitations, which always required the participation of parishioners, a role usually filled by representatives of the *Gemeinde*. After 1650, both secular and episcopal officials increasingly expected and even demanded that communes submit accounts and report on the administration of parishes as well as comment on the professional performance of the clergy. Consultation with communes reflected, as we have seen, the elite and the popular obsession with pastoral work.

Communalism is a useful term for conceptualizing the ecclesio-political organization of local Catholicism, particularly because it counterbalances the tendency to overemphasize the hierarchical structure of the Catholic Church. At the same time, as Robert Scribner has emphasized, communalism should not be considered a universal or fundamental aspect of German history. Early modern Germans used the noun *Gemeinde* and the adjective *gemein* in many different ways.[4]

and London, 1992), esp. ch. 1. On communes and communalism more generally, Heide Wunder, *Die bäuerliche Gemeinde in Deutschland* (Göttingen, 1986) and Robert W. Scribner, "Communities and the Nature of Power" in Robert W. Scribner (ed.), *Germany: A New Social and Economic History*, Vol. I *1450–1600*, pp. 29–326.

[3] John Bossy, "The Counter-Reformation and the People of Catholic Europe" *Past and Present* 47 (1970), pp. 51–70 and Thomas W. Robisheaux, "The World of the Village" in Thomas A. Brady, Jr., Heiko A. Oberman, and James D. Tracy (eds.), *Handbook of European History 1400–1600. Late Middle Ages, Renaissance, and Reformation*, Vol. I *Structures and Assertions* (Leiden, 1994), p. 103.

[4] Scribner, "Communalism: Universal Category or Ideological Construct?", pp. 199–207, esp. 204–205; Heinrich Richard Schmidt, "Die Christianisierung des Sozialverhaltens als permanente Reformation. Aus der Praxis reformierte Sittengerichte in der Schweiz während der frühen Neuzeit" in Peter Blickle and Johannes Kunische (eds.), *Kommunalisierung und Christianisierung. Voraussetzungen und Folgen der Reformation. 1400–1600*, *Zeitschrift für historische Forschung*, Beiheft 9 (Berlin, 1980), pp. 113–163; Scribner, "Communities and the Nature of Power" in *Germany: A New Social and Economic History*, pp. 291–325.

Gemeinde, for example, often designated the public property and rights of a village, and thus resonated with a sense of commonality and collective rights and powers. In other contexts, however, the commune consisted of a small group of property-holding inhabitants with political power. The tension between the universalist, even democratic, meaning inherent in the communal discourse, and the control of much of communal life by certain elements in the villages and towns was very much a part of the communal church.[5]

Not surprisingly, then, it is often difficult to determine who is really speaking in the many documents produced in the name of "the whole commune [*die ganze Gemeinde*]." The authors were clearly the elected and/or appointed representatives of the commune. At the same time, these men usually claimed to represent all residents of the village and, in religious matters, often sought to speak for all parishioners (*Pfarrkinder*), a much larger group than the enfranchised population of a village or town. A healthy skepticism about claims to speak for the wider community is essential, especially since conflicts and divisions within towns and villages were endemic, and often appear in the sources.

There was, nevertheless, a broad consensus about the relationship between the Church and the communes in the Catholic countryside. Conflicts certainly erupted within communities over who was allowed to exploit the material resources of the parishes, over who controlled confraternities and other organizations, over issues of precedence and prestige, for example in the assignment of seats in churches, and over the appointment of priests, especially when candidates had family ties in the community. Such conflicts did not, however, call into question the basic premises of the communal church, that is that the parish, the local church, and the local clergy should be managed and controlled as much as possible by the *Gemeinde*.

THE COMMUNAL CHURCH

The administration of the parish

Not every village in Southwest Germany had its own church, let alone its own parish. Some parishes contained many villages, hamlets, and isolated settlements, many, if not all, of which had some sort of communal institutions. Yet villagers considered a church and a resident priest

[5] See the discussion in Randolph C. Head, *Early Modern Democracy in the Grisons. Social Order and Political Language in a Swiss Mountain Canton, 1470–1620* (Cambridge, 1995), esp. ch. 1.

one of the markers of a true village, an essential part of any human settlement. Membership in a local religious community, the *Pfarrgemeinde*, was part of and reinforced a broader sense of communal identity, and thus parish affairs were always very much a concern of village communes and town councils.[6] The ongoing efforts of communes to organize new benefices and fund the building of churches are clear evidence of the importance of the priests and churches for communes.

People did not clearly distinguish the *Gemeinde* as social and political structure from the religious community, the *Pfarrgemeinde*.[7] Catholic practice remained highly communal, as reflected in the importance of the Eucharist and the popularity of group pilgrimages and communal processions. While it is true, as Scribner argues, that "the sense of belonging to the religious community was . . . heavily qualified by the principles of exclusion inherent in the notion of the commune," it is also true that a sense of sacramental community, asserted weekly at the Mass, also remained part of village life.

There were also many concrete, practical links between the commune and the local Catholic Church. The most obvious of these was that communes had an indispensable role in the administration of the parish. Communes appointed, for example, both the churchwardens, the *Kirchenpfleger*, and the sacristan, the *Messmer*.[8] Communal officials, or administrators appointed by communes, managed parish affairs on a day-to-day basis, with regular input from parish priests, and occasional interference from parish patrons and state authorities.

The commune always participated in the management of parish property. In Schönau in 1613, for example, the village council prepared the annual accounts (*Rechnungen*) without consulting with the priest. In 1624 the same village council asserted its right to draft these accounts, which clearly symbolized control of this property, without informing either the priest or the patron of the parish, the monastery of St. Blasien.[9] Even when the Austrian government forced the Schönauer to make concessions, as happened in 1624, the priest was allowed only to witness the submission of the accounts, not to participate in their preparation.

[6] Karl Siegfried Bader, *Dorfgenossenschaft und Dorfgemeinde* (Cologne, 1962), pp. 182–213, esp. p. 213. See also Bernd Moeller, *Imperial Cities and the Reformation. Three Essays* (1st edn. 1962; Durham, 1982), pp. 41–115 on the sense of "sacral community."

[7] Bader, *Dorfgenossenschaft und Dorfgemeinde*, p. 211. Scribner, "Communities and the Nature of Power" in *Germany: A New Social and Economic History*, pp. 308–309.

[8] On sacristan: GLAK 118/175. [9] GLAK 229/94055.

The control that communes exerted over parish finances of course depended on the degree to which parish patrons and local lords effectively interfered in such matters. The Cistercians at Salem, for example, kept detailed records of parish property, especially in the twelve parishes incorporated into the monastery.[10] The monastery of St. Blasien, by contrast, reported in the 1780s that "in Schönau, Todtnau, and Niederwihl, church property, the settlement of parish accounts, and the management [of the property] are not in the monastery's jurisdiction, rather it is all handled by the peasants."[11] Even strong lords depended on communal officials to collect rents and tithes, and they did not necessarily trust parish priests to be any more effective or honest in financial matters than local laypeople.

When Austrian officials attempted to survey all church property in the 1780s, they naively sent forms to parish priests and ecclesiastical institutions.[12] The reports that came in, however, were generally filed by communal officials, the *Kirchenpfleger*. Town councils, such as that of Villingen, kept tight control of the parishes, allowing, according to one priest, their priests no say whatsoever. The *Kirchenpfleger* in Breunlingen managed the large endowments of that town's parish church, a filial church, and a chapel. The situation in villages was the same. Priests, such as the chaplain in Riegel, even complained that communal officials not only controlled parish finances, but also misled Austrian officials by failing to list resources that should have been given to the clergy.

Overseeing the finances of the parish gave communal officials, especially the *Kirchenpfleger*, some power over the priest. Most clergymen in parishes received a part of their income from parish property. In the village of Fischbach, admittedly an unusual case, the parish priest received his *whole* salary directly from the *Gemeinde*, in the form of four cash payments, as well as grain and wine rents from the parish property, and other fees.[13] Even more important for most priests was the small tithe, which in most places communal officials collected and then gave to the priest.[14] This situation caused, of course, endemic conflict between priests and their parishioners.

In the early eighteenth century the commune of Blumenfeld, a village belonging to the Teutonic Knights, handled much of the administration

[10] GLAK 98/2314. [11] GLAK 79/837 (23 July, 1781).

[12] These forms were called *Fassionen*, and are in GLAK 79/837 and in HStASt. B17/512.

[13] GLAK 98/3817; Agreement from 1698.

[14] In 1674 the priest in Aach complained that he had no idea about what was happening with church finances or the tithe. GLAK 229/42.

of the parish.[15] It sometimes required the mediation of the Knights to resolve disputes between the parish priest and the commune. The priest in this period, Bernard Ziegler, did not always receive the full support of the Knights. The commune retained, for example, the right to decide whether the priest or the sacristan should receive the small fee given for bringing the sacrament to the sick and dying. The Knights were only concerned that the fee be paid, and left its distribution to communal officials in the village.

Communal officials always possessed keys to the church sacristy, baptistery, and offerings chest. Indeed, throughout the seventeenth century parish priests struggled to secure a key for themselves so that they would not have to seek out communal officials to enter the church.[16] Priests usually did obtain keys to the church, but often not to offerings boxes. In Owingen the monastery of Salem supported the mayor of the village when he refused to give a copy of the key to an offerings box to the priest.[17] The possession and control of keys was, of course, highly symbolic, a symbolism which was not lost on the parties involved.

Church bells were also important symbols for villagers, as well as an omnipresent part of daily life. Bells rang to announce church services of all kinds, but also to call people to work on communal projects or to attend communal meetings, as well as to warn against threats such as fire or approaching armies. Communal officials generally considered bells, more than any other part of the church, communal property. Not only did they keep a careful eye on the condition of the bells, but they also regularly claimed their right to decide when they were to be rung.[18]

By claiming control of bells and keys, communal officials asserted that the parish church belonged to the community. Communal officials had legal support for this view, since communes were often responsible for the upkeep of at least part of the church. This fact meant that most proposals to rebuild and decorate parish churches came from communes, even when, as in the case of incorporated parishes, outside institutions were required to pay for such work. As with much else in parish life, villagers, through the communes, closely supervised changes to the local churches and chapels. The villagers in Schönau, for

[15] GLAK 229/10182. [16] GLAK 229/94055, Schönau.

[17] GLAK 61/13463, p. 309r. This *Opferstock* also held money from an endowment given to maintain a roadside cross and picture.

[18] Repair of bells: GLAK 93/248 (Mindersdorf, 1683). Conflicts over ringing bells: GLAK 229/106232 (Schönau, 1679) and GLAK 98/3449, p. 3r (Mimmenhausen, 1769). Compare Jacob, *Lay People and Religion*, p. 13.

example, hung pictures and installed chairs in their church without consulting the parish priest.[19]

Chairs and pews became a big issue after 1650, as peasants built them into rural churches for the first time. Conflicts over seating took place at several levels: priests squabbled with communal officials over who should determine seating arrangements, and the villagers feuded with each other over the best seats in church, with the priest often taking sides.[20] In Blumenfeld in 1726, *Pfarrer* Johan Thomas Metzger tried to bring, as he called it, "order" (*Ordnung*) to the new seating installed in his church.[21] He placed his mother, his housekeeper (*Haushälterin*), the chaplain's maid, and the wife of a local official (the *Obervogt*) in the front row. Although Metzger thought this arrangement came close to matching the way the women had previously stood during services, regularizing the seating caused an uproar. Several women did not like the fact that the priest's mother sat in the front row and protested by standing in the main aisle through a whole Sunday service. Communal officials then intervened, perhaps in support of their wives, arguing that the new seating violated tradition, and complained to their superiors that the priest planned to take away "private chairs" and divide them among all parishioners. *Pfarrer* Metzger may in fact have wanted to go a step beyond arranging a good seat for his mother by supporting the majority of his parishioners against a village elite. Village leaders asserted that Metzger was innovating, and that he was motivated by "ambition."

Disputes between villagers over seating often turned ugly. In 1717, parishioners from outlying villages in the large parish of Altdorf complained that communal officials in Altdorf were trying to reserve several rows of seats for themselves and their families.[22] Traditionally, these seats had been reserved for parishioners who had traveled into town for weddings and funerals. The abbot of the nearby Abbey of Weingarten informed episcopal officials that, in contrast to what was normal in most parishes in the region, "communal officials [*Gemeindts Leüthen*] want to give themselves a higher profile [*grössere Figur*] than they ever had before." Ultimately, this dispute had to be adjudicated in the bishop's

[19] GLAK 229/94055. See chapter 2 for more on building, rebuilding, and decorating churches and chapels.

[20] Scribner, "Communities and the Nature of Power" in *Germany: A New Social and Economic History*, pp. 308–309.

[21] GLAK 93/252.

[22] HStASt. B467/47. The parish of Altdorf/Weingarten had over 7,000 parishioners in the early eighteenth century.

court, where a compromise was reached, assigning each party some of the choice seats near the pulpit.

The late eighteenth-century dispute over seats in the parish church of Amtzell was partly about the growing role of women in Catholic life, as several women tried to sit on the "men's side" of the church.[23] It was also a dispute over who controlled the use of pews. In this case, the conflict was arbitrated, and eventually resolved, by negotiations between a local lord, the Freiherr von Reichlin, state officials, and communal officials. Neither the parish priest nor the episcopal authority was mentioned, and all parties considered the pews pieces of property, to be disposed of as secular officials, the commune, and the pews' owners saw fit.

Gemeinden participated constantly in the administration of parishes, in the villages as well as in cities. This involvement was unremarkable to contemporaries, except perhaps when communes explicitly refused to allow parish priests to participate in parish matters. Communal administration of parishes certainly underpinned the communal church.

Communal supervision of the clergy

Although the communes rarely had direct control over the appointment, disciplining, and removal of the local clergy, they nevertheless worked hard to influence these matters. *Gemeinden* did not passively wait for priests to be appointed, but instead brought indirect pressure on monasteries, chapters, and government officials who had the right to appoint priests. Communes also kept a close eye on the professional performance of the clergy and did not hesitate to seek the removal of priests who did not meet their expectations.

The town council of the small Austrian town of Binsdorf held the right to nominate the community's parish priest, who was then proposed (officially "presented") by the emperor to the Bishop of Constance.[24] All evidence indicates that Austrian officials respected the choices of the council. In 1587, at a time when the Habsburg government aggressively sought to eradicate concubinage among parish priests, officials in Innsbruck approved the council's nomination of Jacob Armbruster, who was known to have a concubine. In 1589 the council and commune further consolidated their hold over the priest by permanently adding the income of a chapel, over which they had patronage, to the resources of the parish.[25]

[23] HStASt. B61/432. [24] HStASt. B37a/134. [25] HStASt. B37a/135.

By the eighteenth century, the mayor, council, and commune of Binsdorf had lost some control over the appointment of the parish priest. In 1762 the Binsdorfer nominated three candidates for the vacant parish and sent their names to Austrian officials. A government commission then interviewed the three finalists, one of whom the Austrians then presented to the bishop. However, officials did not want to antagonize the town. The candidate recommended first and most strongly by the *Gemeinde* received the post. According to Austrian officials he did no better than the others in the examination but was appointed because he had good recommendations "from his whole flock where he will be the shepherd . . ."[26]

Binsdorf was an exceptional but not isolated case and there were other parishes where the commune had the right to appoint priests. Although the monastery of Salem was the official patron of the parish of Fischbach, the commune had the *jus nominandi*, that is the right to nominate a priest when the parish came vacant.[27] Between 1580 and 1777, the *Gemeinde* nominated twenty-two priests and Salem presented each one to the bishop for investiture. The strength of the communal church in Fischbach is partly a reflection of Salem's indifference to pastoral services in its parishes. The commune did not miss its chance to control the pastor, requiring that all new priests swear an extensive oath which specified all the duties of the *Pfarrer*.

The Binsdorfer and Fischbacher had a juridical right to nominate a priest, which gave them a special role in appointments. Other communes were sometimes less successful in getting their candidates appointed. In 1588 the commune in Deilingen also recommended a priest who had a concubine, but Austrian officials appointed someone else. More often, however, the intercession of the commune helped a candidate. In 1593 Jacob Dietpold became *Pfarrer* in Durbheim after a strong recommendation by the commune.[28] In this case, officials regretted having rejected Dietpold's application several years earlier, since the villagers liked Dietpold and treated the other priest whom the authorities had appointed very badly.

Towns and villages often had more control over appointments to chaplaincies than they did over parishes. Thus as the number and importance of such positions grew after 1650, communes gained more influence over the clergy who served them. Indeed, as early as 1573 the council of the small town of Aach im Hegau claimed the right to present

[26] HStASt. B38/573: *besonder von dem ganzen Schaff-Stall. dene er als hirth vorgestanden.*

[27] GLAK 98/3817; GLAK 98/3819.

[28] HStASt. B37a/147; HStASt. B37a/156.

priests for two chaplaincies, both of which had been vacant for a long time.[29] Church officials accepted this claim and chaplains served in Aach between the 1590s and the Thirty Years' War. In the late seventeenth century the town council continued to present priests for these benefices.

The town council of Burkheim, an Austrian town in the Kaiserstuhl, had somewhat more authority over the clergy than the *Rat* in Aach. In 1737 the Burkheimer claimed that they had always filled the chaplaincy without consulting higher authorities.[30] They pointed to the original endowment of 1624 to support this claim and further asserted that they had appointed chaplains earlier in 1737, as well as in 1709, 1707, and 1676. An episcopal decree from 1739 limited these powers by requiring Austrian approval of new chaplains, but the town council remained very active in supervising the local clergy.[31]

Village communes also exerted pressure on parish patrons after the finalists for a position became known. In 1755 the commune and many residents of Ingerkingen petitioned against the appointment of one Herr Belling to their parish.[32] Belling had served as assistant priest in the parish and was, according to the villagers,

> nothing but a trouble-maker, who interferes entirely too often in secular matters, so that when the peasants have business with one another, he reports the parties to the authorities and supports one side or the other. [Furthermore], he goes around at night and listens at windows to hear what is going on. He even complained to the *Oberpfleger* [a Salem official] that the priest in [the neighboring village of] Schemmerberg kept poor order in his parish, although [this priest] receives the highest praise from everyone [else].

This case was complicated by the fact that Belling had been born in Ingerkingen and had friends as well as many enemies in the village. The Abbot of Salem, patron of the parish, had the final say and appointed a different priest: "[T]he said vicar [Belling] is little trusted by many, or even the majority of the parishioners in Ingerkingen, and, because of having enemies and other personal matters, he would probably cause them to stay away [from church]."

The heightened concern of episcopal officials for the quality of pastoral services in the villages, together with the fragmented ecclesio-political structure of Southwest Germany, gave communes and town councils many opportunities to express their views about their pastors.

[29] GLAK 229/42; GLAK 229/43.

[30] GLAK 229/16208, pp. 10r–v, 36r–37r, 39r.

[31] The town council came into conflict with several parish priests in the late sixteenth century as well. See GLAK 229/16206.

[32] GLAK 98/3841.

When, in 1738, episcopal officials conducted a visitation of the parishes of the Knights of Malta (the *Johanniter*) in the Rhine valley south of Freiburg, they questioned communal officials closely about the job done by the priests hired by the Knights.[33] The Knights were not pleased with this investigation, insisting that the bishop's officials only ask about pastoral matters. In most villages the visitors spoke to communal representatives alone, that is without the *Pfarrer* being present. While the villagers expressed few major concerns, they openly and enthusiastically used the opportunity to comment on problems in the parishes, from the need for church repairs to the failures of some priests to provide complete services. Episcopal officials began their survey believing that the Knights failed to support proper pastoral care and therefore gave credence to communal complaints. The adept use of the opportunity provided by visitations was just one method by which communes exerted influence over the clergy to improve the quality of pastoral care.

Communes often used well-placed and well-constructed letters to get rid of unwanted priests. In the 1580s and 1590s peasants knew they had to accuse unsatisfactory priests of concubinage in order to have them removed, even when other concerns were really more important to the people. In 1584 the commune of Weilen unter den Rennen petitioned the Austrian government for the removal of their priest, Jacob Krafftenfels.[34] The letter listed ten complaints emphasizing his difficult and combative behavior, especially in conflicts over the tithe, and his unwillingness to obey communal regulations regarding the use of meadows. Almost only in passing, in point number seven of the petition, does the letter mention Krafftenfels's concubine and nine children. The letter concludes with an appeal to get rid of this priest and "give us a competent and peaceful priest . . ." Leaving nothing to chance, the commune also denounced Krafftenfels to the episcopal court, angering Austrian officials, who wanted to limit episcopal authority in Austrian parishes. In the end, their concerted effort succeeded and Krafftenfels was removed.

By the late seventeenth century, concubinage was no longer widespread; consequently when communal leaders sought to remove a priest, they now emphasized his professional failings. There was even a change in the language used about the relationship between priests and parishioners. A 1655 comment by the town council of Aach is illuminating. The council told their priest that they "wanted to be obedient

[33] GLAK 89/106. [34] HStASt. B37a/272.

parishioners," but wished that he would treat them with more "*milde*," that is more gently.[35] By the later part of the century, trust had replaced obedience as the desired characteristic of the priest/parishioner relationship. The priest in Tafertsweiler, according to his parishioners in 1692, did not begin Sunday services at a regular time, neglected catechism lessons, and did not hold a series of votive masses against bad weather at five in the morning as required. Such failings led to a "loss of trust," a favorite reason for removing a priest in the eighteenth century.[36]

The commune of Mindersdorf knew exactly how to pressure their lords (and patrons of the parish), the Teutonic Knights.[37] When the commune came into conflict with their parish priest in 1689, they began by petitioning the Knights to remove the priest, emphasizing that villagers had demonstrated a lack of trust by travelling to other villages to take communion. Communal officials then bolstered their position by complaining about the priest's debts and by making vague accusations about the *Pfarrer*'s relationship with his housekeeper. Finally, they put further pressure on the Knights by writing to episcopal officials, including the vicar general in Constance, and requesting the appointment of an episcopal commission to investigate conditions in Mindersdorf. Officials of the Knights were incensed to hear that the commune had gone as far as appointing deputies to testify to this commission without consulting higher authorities. Despite their shock at the independent behavior of their subjects, the Knights buckled under and removed the offending priest from Mindersdorf.

Communes certainly knew how to pull the right strings with higher authorities and how to manipulate the jurisdictional jungle of Southwest Germany. Communes found such strategies less effective in some areas, particularly in the more tightly governed Austrian territories. Furthermore, at times communes no doubt worked to remove priests, not because they were ineffective, incompetent, or corrupt, but because they had powerful enemies in the parish. A certain sophistication about the workings of power, however, does not mean that communal officials were not genuinely concerned with the performance of the clergy. The ability and dedication of the priest were central to the success of

35 GLAK 229/42.

36 GLAK 61/13463, pp. 320r–23r. There was a similar case in Hailtingen in 1750: HStASt. B467/500. On "loss of trust" see GLAK 93/248 (Mindersdorf, 1747); HStASt. B38/574 (Binsdorf, 1783); HStASt. B486/661 (Kirchdorf, 1654).

37 GLAK 93/248.

clericalized Catholicism. Rural communes, whether they had considerable independent authority or a limited role within strong state structures, saw it as part of their job to make sure local clergymen did their duty.

Organizing devotional life

Communes went beyond overseeing the behavior and effectiveness of priests and organized much of the religious life of the parish themselves. Some of this function resulted directly from the communal role in the creation of new benefices. The *Gemeinde* of Nusplingen made sure that the holder of the new chaplaincy knew exactly what his duties were.[38] He was expected to assist the parish priest, especially with confession and Sunday services; to read Mass on Tuesdays for the community and extra masses during Lent; and to read two additional masses a week for the souls of the benefactors of the chaplaincy.

Communes hired priests to perform religious functions, often without consulting ecclesiastical officials. Thus the commune of Böhringen brought in an Augustinian monk to conduct services in the village church. Both the commune and the monk were surprised and shocked when the *Pfarrer* in Gössingen, the official parish priest of this filial church, complained. The villagers were even more stunned to hear the priest argue "that the honorable *Gemeinde* of Böhringen had no power to order a priest [to perform services]."[39] Indeed, the Böhringer asserted this right by withholding the tithe from the priest in Gössingen because he did not hold services in their church.

Communes organized many of the popular initiatives that were so important to Baroque Catholicism. The role taken by communes is not surprising, since communal practices remained so central to Catholic practice. Communes had the clout to make sure that priests participated in processions and pilgrimages. Priests sometimes resisted new obligations. In 1750 the vicar general in Constance resolved such a conflict in Hailtingen in the following way:

> The parish priest must accompany the bi-annual communal procession to the chapel in Weiler, although this [procession] began and has taken place up to now as a freely held devotion of the community. Devotion and yearning [for salvation?] are as dependent on the [priest's] presence and eagerness as on that of his flock. [The priest] will receive the usual 40 Kreuzer . . .[40]

[38] HStASt. B467/684. [39] HStASt. B467/473 (1719).
[40] HStASt. B467/500. See also HStASt. B467/546.

The breadth of the communal involvement in local religion is illustrated by the negotiations between the *Gemeinde* of Hirrlingen and Joseph Wild, the parish priest in 1768.[41] A dispute had developed over several years involving the fees Wild received for funerals and marriages, his participation in processions and prayer meetings, and the tone the *Pfarrer* took with his parishioners. In negotiations brokered by an episcopal commission, the commune aggressively took the position that fees should be as small as possible and that the priest should perform all church services without additional payment.[42] Communal representatives also complained that Wild insulted people from the pulpit and struck disobedient youths. The implication that the all-important "trust" between priest and parishioners was in danger earned Wild a reprimand from episcopal officials. The final agreement was of course a compromise, but strongly limited the fees the priest could receive, and required him to perform many services without remuneration. Episcopal officials clearly agreed with the communal view that extra fees were undesirable; they nowhere denied the right of the commune to concern itself with the organization of local religious life.

Communes like the one in Hirrlingen were enmeshed in almost all aspects of local religious life. Communes founded many new confraternities, sometimes in response to clerical initiatives, sometimes not. *Gemeinden* demanded that priests perform traditional blessings and benedictions, even when the Church considered such practices suspect.[43] Even more than priests, communes had to respond to popular pressure for a denser devotional life. In Molpertshausen the commune found a way to pay for more services on major holidays, giving the parish priest the use of a piece of parish property in exchange for saying these masses.[44] In the late eighteenth century, communes organized and funded the erection of stations of the cross in parish churches.[45] Communes and town councils clearly participated actively in religious life, particularly as watchdogs over the clergy, but as organizers and innovators as well. The communalism of local religion linked the Church to popular religion and contributed importantly to the vitality of Catholicism in the century after 1650.

41 HStASt. B467/546.

42 This position closely resembles the *wohlfeile Kirche* described by Peter Blickle for the period around 1500. Blickle, *Communal Reformation*, pp. 33–40.

43 See above, chapter 3.

44 HStASt. B486/1273 (1770).

45 HStASt. B61/1098; HStASt. B481/77; HStASt. B481/78.

THE PRIEST IN THE VILLAGE

The interplay of communalism and clericalism could make life very difficult for parish priests. In practice, priests found they had to reconcile several visions of how a pastor should behave among his parishioners. The official Church wanted priests to fulfill all pastoral duties while acting as a model of morality and piety, engaging the hearts and minds of their parishioners, and simultaneously avoiding personal ties in the community and remaining aloof from local conflicts. As if this model did not contain enough internal contradictions, villagers and townspeople had a rather different idea of the place of the priest. The population expected priests to be members of the community, and to obey its social and economic regulations, while reliably fulfilling the responsibilities of their "jobs." Parish priests trained in seminaries and universities knew the clerical model, yet as local men they also understood and often accepted the popular communal view.

These different visions caused tension in the priest–parishioner relationship. Everyone agreed, however, on the centrality of pastoral services, and thus these built-in tensions did not dominate local religious life. Indeed, the consensus around the importance of pastoral services meant that there was no inherent popular/elite or church/people dissonance and no structural reason why Catholicism should not operate smoothly. Yet despite the basic peacefulness of religious life in the towns and villages of Southwest Germany, there were always conflicts between priests and parishioners. The details of these conflicts provide an important window on the life of clergymen living among the population and on the nature of popular clericalism and communalism.

Seefelden, 1620s

From the perspective of the population, the old and dispersed parish of Seefelden, on the shores of Lake Constance, was very poorly organized.[46] In 1629, the parish had 1,288 parishioners living in twenty-three different places (*Ortschaften*), including the three large villages of Nußdorf, Mimmenhausen, and Oberuhldingen. Almost all parishioners had to walk a considerable distance to get to the parish church, as only twenty-four people lived in Seefelden itself. Furthermore, although

[46] Hermann Schmid, "Aus der älteren Geschichte der Pfarrei Seefelden. Ein Überblick unter besonderer Berücksichtigung des Pfarrurbars von 1629" *FDA* 111 (1991), pp. 171–185. See also GLAK 98/758.

there were eight churches in the parish, in the 1620s there were only two resident priests, and in the 1650s only one.[47]

The shortage of priests around Seefelden brought two responses from the villagers. First, they complained to their lord, the monastery of Salem, and to the bishop about their *Pfarrer*, whom the villagers accused of being either incompetent or unwilling to perform all their duties. Second, the larger communes demanded the creation of their own parishes. In the 1620s the communes of Mimmenhausen, Nußdorf, and Oberuhldingen all submitted complaints about *Pfarrer* Jodocus Birbaumer.[48] The villagers recognized that the parish of Seefelden was too large for one priest, but their complaints focused on Birbaumer's failure to fulfill his duties. He was reluctant, they claimed, to hear confessions, refused to travel to the outlying villages of the parish to baptize children, did not read all the masses required of him, and would not accompany processions to the nearby shrine at Birnau. Part of the problem came from the fact that the villagers considered the *Pfarrer* a servant of the parish, whereas Birbaumer saw himself as a church official charged with implementing the decrees of the bishop. Thus the villagers complained that he did not appear to lead the Forty Hours devotion until four in the afternoon, when the local tradition was to hold this devotion at two.[49] Birbaumer responded that he came at four because this was the time designated in episcopal ordinances. The *Pfarrer* refused to accommodate his parishioners in other ways. He apparently would not hear confessions after Wednesday of Easter week, did not always announce marriages from the pulpit, and when he had to miss services due to illness, did not inform parish officials far enough in advance for them to hire a substitute.

The tone of Birbaumer's answer to these charges is dismissive, even condescending. He responded to the charge that he did not announce weddings by saying "weddings are, vulgarly put, laughable matters." His letter is liberally sprinkled with Latin, asserting his affinity with the educated monks at Salem and canons in Constance, and his distance from his parishioners. He concludes his letters with three points:

1 It is amazing that in eleven years the parishioners have never complained etc. and furthermore,

[47] EAF Ha 70, pp. 257v–258v, 460r–460v.

[48] GLAK 98/3557. This is a long letter addressed to the Cathedral Chapter in Constance (patron of the parish) against the *Pfarrer* and the response of the *Pfarrer*. Also EAF Ha 70, pp. 257v–258v.

[49] The Forty Hours devotion may in fact have been quite new in this region. Ludwig Veit and Ludwig Lenhart, *Kirche und Volksfrömmigkeit im Zeitalter des Barocks* (Freiburg, 1956), pp. 207–208.

2 it is amazing, if not a miracle, that our ancestors, predecessors, and authorities have not said about what the pastor ought to offer and furthermore

3 it is very amazing that the visitors, who are always very diligent and wise, in the same way, have never heard, never found out anything, have never held an investigation about such things, and never reported anything or corrected anything.[50]

Birbaumer and his parishioners had different ideas about the place of the priest. At the same time, the vehemence of the villagers' protests indicates the importance of the priest, especially for baptisms, burials, and the Mass. Indeed, the biggest complaint about Birbaumer was that he was physically unable to perform services correctly:

For example, first of all, his hands and feet are in such miserable and bad condition, as has been seen in various places, [that] he has allowed the holy sacrament to fall to the ground as he is elevating it or when his parishioners want to communicate.

Secondly, due to lameness of his limbs, he cannot lift the Host during the elevation high enough that the attending *Pfarrkinder* can see and worship it. And since he cannot bend or stoop down, the communicants have to receive the sacrament standing, the sacristan has to lift the *Paten* and the *corporal* for him, and put away and carry the monstrance, and also lead and drag him in and out of the church and to the altar.[51]

The *Pfarrer* vehemently denied that he had ever dropped the Host on the ground ("*nunquam, nunquam*"). However, the attitude of his parishioners, as callous as it now appears, indicates how important the priest was, and provides us with a glimpse of the popular mentality. The Elevation of the Host and Communion were rituals that an ordained priest should perform the same way each time. Furthermore, the dignity and solemnity of the occasion depended on the personal appearance and behavior of the priest. The villagers probably did not expect Birbaumer to be above human weakness, yet their complaints were a catalogue of his failings. It was vital that he be capable of performing his duties; during the Mass he should rise to a greater role, be something more than one of their neighbors. Standing in front of the altar, leaning on the sacristan and unable to raise the Host properly at the central moment of the Mass, the partly crippled *Pfarrer* did not fit his parishioners' image of a priest.

[50] GLAK 98/3557. [51] GLAK 98/3557.

Schönau, 1661

In 1661 the *Vogt* (a kind of mayor) and council of the Black Forest village of Schönau criticized their priest, Father Giselbertus Strankhaar.[52] The priest's biggest problem appears to have been a personal lifestyle that clearly bothered the villagers. Strankhaar was a worldly priest, who admitted leaving his parish on one occasion to go to Basel, but not, he said, out of curiosity or for pleasure, but in order to make some important purchases. The *Pfarrer* believed that the Schönauer disliked him because he had "free access to the *Waldvogt* [the most important Austrian official in the area] . . . [and] because they fear my relatives [who also lived in the village]."

The villagers, however, highlighted another aspect of Stankhaar's domestic arrangements. According to their report, the priest was raising several young dogs and a wolf in the parsonage. The peasants feared that the wolf would injure the village children, and even expressed deeper fears:

> Everyone knows the true nature of a wolf and the father should keep it under control so that it does not hurt anyone . . . [and] it is not a good idea to raise a wolf in our valley . . . and even less advisable that he enter the church. A serious accident [*unglück*] could easily result from this wolf.

Strankhaar responded aggressively to these attacks, calling the Schönauer lazy, neglectful, superstitious, and *Idioten*. He did not deny that he kept a wolf and dogs, but maintained that they remained locked in the yard of the parsonage and had not harmed anyone. "[I] must in passing comment, that it is nicer [*melius*] to live with dogs and wolves, and that one receives more loyalty from them than from my ungrateful parishioners."

The Schönauer linked their displeasure over Strankhaar's personal life with an attack on his pastoral work. According to his parishioners, the *Pfarrer* did not teach the youth to pray the Our Father or the Hail Mary, had failed to preach on a Palm Sunday and a Good Friday, did not support the parish confraternity, and refused on several occasions to hear confessions. Importantly, the village council lamented that "Father Giselbertus has never after the sermon prayed an Our Father or an Ave Maria or the 'Offneschult' or the 'gemein bet', and instead

[52] GLAK 229/94055. Father Giselbertus was probably a Benedictine from St. Blasien. The parish was incorporated into the monastery, which also had extensive juridical rights, many serfs, and considerable estates in the area. See David M. Luebke, *His Majesty's Rebels. Communities, Factions, and Rural Revolt in the Black Forest, 1725–1745* (Ithaca and London, 1997).

after the sermon often raises issues that bring more discord than unity."

The dispute over teaching children basic prayers was a consequence of expectations of the people and the extensive demands the benefice system put on parish priests. The village council asked Strankhaar to teach the prayers from the pulpit, as part of the church services. The *Pfarrer* asserted that teaching prayers was not one of his duties. He stated, however, that "when [he] observed that they are ignorant and inexperienced in all one should know as a Christian," he had done his best in his sermons to teach his flock about the sacraments, the ten commandments, the seven deadly sins, "the seven opposing virtues," as well as various other subjects he considered essential. Frustrated by the failure of this effort, Strankhaar told the *Vogt* that the Schönauer were raising their children badly and that they needed a teacher for the village. In fact, as both the *Pfarrer* and the commune recognized, the size of the parish was the biggest problem. Children from outlying villages and hamlets could not come to catechism classes, some parishioners could not attend church services at all, and Strankhaar had to travel very far to visit the sick and conduct emergency baptisms.[53]

The dispute between Strankhaar and the Schönauer came down to a clash over clerical authority. The priest was quite forceful, attempting, for example, to enforce episcopal regulations that sought to regulate the traditional Palm Sunday celebrations.[54] During Lent Strankhaar sent the sacristan to tell people to come to confession, asserting his control over the sacrament. Strankhaar even admitted that he sometimes "carped" about his parishioners' failings in his sermons. The villagers did not accept this and accused the priest of shirking his proper duties. In their view, the parish priest was certainly indispensable, but he should accommodate his parishioners, not the other way around.

Dellmensingen, 1692

Andre Breth, *Pfarrer* in Dellmensingen, was often ill.[55] According to his parishioners, the consequence of his poor health was that he often neglected pastoral services and that he was short-tempered, especially with children:

[53] The parish had over 1,100 parishioners at this time, living in thirty-two different places.

[54] The priest demanded that a new *Palmesel* be constructed, with proper feet and a wagon. Compare several discussions of Palm Sunday celebrations: Ebner, *Unteralpfen*, pp. 153–154; Scribner, "Ritual and Popular Religion in Catholic Germany at the Time of the Reformation" in *Popular Culture and Popular Movements in the Reformation* (London, 1987), pp. 24–26.

[55] HStASt. B466a/106b.

[When children come for catechism lessons, the *Pfarrer*] often sends them home again with scornful words, as for example, he asks them if they can say an Our Father, or [he asks] how many gods are there, and if one child answers, he does not know, he [the *Pfarrer*] tells him, in no uncertain terms [*gibt Er Ihme zu verstehen*], go home, I cannot teach it to you, have your father teach you, he is a ruffian [*Strolch*] like you . . .

Breth managed to insult his flock even while neglecting his duties. During Lent 1692 he only preached three times, and even then "when he climbed into the pulpit, he usually used the time more for insults than for proper admonitions." The Dellmensinger were quite offended when he gave them permission to confess to other priests, stating that, as far as he was concerned, they could confess wherever they wanted.

As elsewhere, emotions ran highest over the issues of baptism and deathbed confessions. Breth was reluctant to visit the sick, sometimes arrived late, and could be most insensitive. He was quoted as saying that the death of one child was a good thing, as it meant fewer people under his pastoral care. The *Pfarrer* apparently had a great fear of death and hated funerals, refusing to go closer to graves than a distance of ten paces. When giving the sacrament to the sick, he stood as far as possible from the communicant and trembled so much that witnesses feared he would drop the Host.

In addition to failing in his duties to individual parishioners, Breth did not perform services to the wider community. Perhaps because of illness, the *Pfarrer* usually rode a horse when leaving the village:

When a procession, short or long, takes place, it is hard for most people to keep up with him [since he is] riding. As a result, he does not participate in pilgrimages [*Wallfahrten*] and lets his flock go along with whatever neighboring cross they want, which causes the Dellmensinger to be ridiculed, and otherwise spoken to insultingly.

The case of *Pfarrer* Breth was no doubt more complicated than the complaints of his parishioners indicate. Like the Seefeldener in the 1620s, the Dellmensinger had no sympathy for the priest's physical and psychological problems, although they did indicate that they would be satisfied if he hired an assistant. There were also long-standing tithe disputes between the priest and the *Gemeinde*, which no doubt contributed to the tensions in the parish. Breth was a far from an ideal priest, whether measured by the standards of the official Church or by those of the population.

Bermatingen, 1701

Franz Schneider, *Pfarrer* in Bermatingen, had powerful enemies in his parish. The *Ammann* (*Amtmann* or headman) and the commune wrote an extensive attack on their pastor, stating "that they have neither love nor trust for him."[56] The concept of trust (*Vertrauen*) between priests and parishioners became important in the eighteenth century. According to village leaders, Schneider lost trust by neglecting important pastoral duties while also seeking to collect new fees and tithes. The commune listed three sets of charges.

The first accusation stated that Schneider was "attempting a whole range of innovations [*allerhand newerung suecht*]." He wanted to collect half of the offerings given to the Marian Confraternity in the village, contrary to tradition and the statutes of the confraternity. He also tried to collect the offerings made at Mass, although traditionally the priest, along with the poor, had only received a fixed fee. Schneider also pressed poorly founded claims to part of the wine tithe.

Communal leaders asserted that Schneider had done nothing to earn more money and fees and compared the energy with which he pursued new sources of income with his lackadaisical approach to pastoral services: "By contrast [he] is neglectful in church services [*Gottesdienst*], in that he rarely preaches, and even then never at the right time, and never during the early mass on Sundays and holidays. [He] very seldom sits to hear confessions, as other pastors [*Pfarr verweser*] have done."

The second charge against Schneider was that he spent too much time away from Bermatingen. His parishioners accused him of attending every parish festival (*Kirchweih*) in the region, often staying away for three, four, or five days. He often traveled with the other priest in the village, the primissary, "whom he is similarly leading astray." Because the parish festivals were held on feast days, he only held early Mass on those days, neglecting not only high Mass but prayer meetings as well. In his absence, several children had died without baptism. When asked to baptize a child one evening after returning from such a festival, Schneider swore at the parents and made them cool their heels for a long time in front of the church.

The third complaint against the *Pfarrer* focused on his attitude toward processions. According to the *Gemeinde*, previous pastors had always

[56] GLAK 98/3217.

accompanied processions and communal pilgrimages, celebrating a Mass at the destination. Schneider refused to do this, holding Mass in Bermatingen instead. When the parish superintendent, the *Dorfpfleger*, tried to remind him of his duty, Schneider stated "he would do what he wants when he wants, and the *Gemeinde* can complain wherever they want."

Schneider responded to these attacks in a long Latin letter. The priest considered *Amtmann* Dilger the ringleader of his opponents. Schneider said that Dilger treated him with disrespect in public, stole money from the parish, and inappropriately controlled the confraternity. The *Pfarrer* did not deny his unwillingness to go on processions and quoted Dilger's assertion of communal authority over the priest:

> Yes, *Herr Pfarrer*, I certainly hope you go against the commune, and when we want something you will have to do it, and when we want you to go with the Cross [ie. go on procession], you will go with us, but without payment, since it would be an insult and a disgrace if you asked for such a thing.

Schneider sought to personalize the conflict in Bermatingen, perhaps hoping to avoid the enmity of the whole village. The Abbey of Salem, lord of the village, found him more contentious and difficult than other priests in its villages and sided with the commune. Schneider, like Breth in Dellmensingen, was exceptional, particularly in refusing to participate in processions. We cannot know of course the extent to which he really neglected pastoral services. It is clear, however, that the villagers of Bermatingen considered such services essential and that they knew that they could effectively attack an unpopular priest by accusing him of being a poor pastor. Bermatingen is an obvious example of the coexistence and interplay of clericalism and communalism.

CONCLUSION

Beginning in the 1760s and reaching a peak in the 1780s, a thorough reform of Catholic institutions was undertaken by the Austrian government in its territories. Motivated by Enlightenment principles of rationalization and the promotion of economic productivity, "Josephine" reformers enacted a series of decrees, most of which encountered widespread opposition. Peasants and townspeople both resisted the closing of shrines, convents, and monasteries as well as the dissolution of confraternities, and ignored the abolition of church holidays, processions, and pilgrimages.[57]

One aspect of the reforms, however, received popular support: the efforts to reorganize the parish structure and create a number of new parishes. Here reforms played right into the communal and clericalized structures of popular Catholicism. Austrian officials asked priests, local officials, and communes to indicate villages that deserved new parishes or chapels, thereby intimating that communities with over 700 inhabitants and/or requiring more than an hour's walk to the nearest church would receive funding.[58] Communes, especially, responded energetically to this opportunity, providing the requested data, and often writing extensive petitions for new parishes. In this area at least, popular Catholicism and *Aufklärung*-Catholicism coincided.

The coexistence of clericalism and communalism suggests that there was no clear division between official and popular Catholicism in Southwest Germany. Catholicism became more dependent on the presence and performance of the parish priest, yet this clericalization occurred, at least in part, because of popular pressure. Communes maintained an important role, but the village elites who controlled them were both representatives of the village community and agents of higher authorities. Clericalism and communalism were fundamental aspects of the dynamic between popular and official religion that created the successful Catholicism of Southwest Germany.

[57] Thomas Paul Becker, *Konfessionalisierung in Kurköln: Untersuchungen zur Durchsetzung der katholischen Reform in den Dekanaten Ahrgau und Bonn anhand von Visitationsprotokollen 1583–1761* (Bonn, 1989), esp. pp. 311–315; Eva Kimminich, *Religiöse Volksbräuche im Räderwerk der Obrigkeiten. Ein Beitrag zur Auswirkung aufklärerischer Reformprogramme am Oberrhein und in Vorarlberg* (Frankfurt am Main, 1989); Leonard Swidler, *Aufklärung Catholicism, 1780–1850. Liturgical and other Reforms in the Catholic Aufklärung* (Missoula, 1978).

[58] HStASt. B61/213; GLAK 79/822.

CHAPTER 6

Reformers and intermediaries, 1650–1750

Throughout the early modern period, the Catholic elite, both clerics and laypeople, initiated and promoted important changes in Southwest German Catholicism. For the purpose of analysis, this elite can be divided into three groups: the Tridentine reformers, the confessionalizers, and the new orders, primarily the Jesuits and Capuchins. There was, of course, considerable overlap between these groups, but each had a somewhat different set of aims and they clashed quite frequently after 1650 as before. The splits within the reform-minded elements of the Catholic elite were further exacerbated by the presence of important elements within the Church – especially in the monasteries, convents, and military orders – that remained highly skeptical of all reform.

As we saw in chapter 1, Tridentine reform was the central program of the Church in Southwest Germany during the period 1580–1620. In this period, church officials, supported (and sometimes pushed) by Catholic secular authorities, engaged in all the standard activities of Tridentine reformers. The Bishops of Constance and neighboring bishops issued reform decrees, held diocesan synods, conducted extensive visitations of rural parishes, punished priests with concubines, and attempted to found and finance an episcopal seminary.[1] Yet these activities had to be abandoned during the Thirty Years' War and were not resumed with the same vigor after the war ended. It is nevertheless important to examine the continued efforts of Tridentine reformers in the century after 1650. Reformers found that most gains of the decades around 1600 had disappeared in the war, and they were forced to start the process of reform over again.[2]

[1] Elmar L. Kuhn, Eva Moser, Rudolf Reinhardt, and Petra Sachs (eds.), *Die Bischöfe von Konstanz*, Vol. I *Geschichte*, (Friederichshafen, 1988); Anton Schindling and Walter Ziegler (eds.), *Die Territorien des Reichs im Zeitalter der Reformation und Konfessionalisierung. Land und Konfession*, Vol. V *Der Südwesten* (Münster, 1993); Herrmann Tüchle, *Von der Reformation bis zur Säkularisation. Geschichte der katholischen Kirche im Raum des späteren Bistums Rottenburg-Stuttgart* (Ostfildern, 1981).

[2] Marc R. Forster, "With and Without Confessionalization. Varieties of Early Modern German Catholicism" *Journal of Early Modern History* 1, 4 (1997), pp. 315–343.

Confessionalizers were also active in Southwest Germany. Indeed they were often the same people who supported Tridentine reform. In fact, confessionalization in Catholic Germany is not always easy to distinguish conceptually from Catholic reform or the Counter-Reformation. Confessionalization usefully denotes the program, driven primarily by state officials, to create and enforce religious unity and to encourage Catholic identity with the aim of strengthening loyalty to the confessional state. In its most aggressive form, as practiced for example in Bavaria, confessionalization included a strong disciplinary component, including the use of fines and imprisonment to enforce church attendance and punish non-Catholics. This program certainly informed the policy of some rulers in Southwest Germany in the sixty or so years after 1560, especially the Austrian regime in Upper and Outer Austria (*Oberösterreich*, *Vorderösterreich*). Most obviously, Austrian officials made a concerted effort first to punish Protestants and then to banish the most recalcitrant non-Catholics from their territories.[3] Like Tridentine reformers, confessionalizers had to return to square one after 1650, albeit in an atmosphere much less charged with confessional disputes.

Both processes, Tridentine reform and confessionalization, continued to operate from within a hierarchical model. Reformers of both stripes focused on improving the effectiveness of institutions and their agents and emphasized jurisdictional issues. They believed strongly that the effective application of disciplinary measures would encourage their subjects to become "better Catholics." Most reformers had only a passing interest in religious practice *per se*, and when they did investigate popular Catholicism, they focused their attention on what they considered "abuses," an ever-changing category of practices that the lay and clerical elite did not find proper or fitting for devout believers. This relative lack of elite interest in religious practice diminished its ability to create or shape a popular Catholic identity, since it was precisely Catholic rites and practices that attracted the loyalty of the population.

The religious orders, particularly the Jesuits and Capuchins, were a new element in the late seventeenth century. The orders involved themselves much more actively with religious practice than did church reformers within the church hierarchy or in the administration of the Catholic states. In their roles as preachers, teachers, and pastors, by promoting certain shrines and confraternities, and by mingling regularly with the common people of the villages and towns, the Jesuits and Capuchins exerted considerable influence over Catholic culture.

[3] Dieter Stievermann, "Österreichische Vorlande" in Schindling and Ziegler (eds.), *Die Territorien des Reichs*, pp. 269–275. Examples from Rottenburg am Neckar in TLA, Ferdinandea 178(1), 1578.

Although the Jesuits, in particular, self-consciously maintained their distance from local religion and always considered themselves "reformers from above," their place in daily religious life often resembled that of religious intermediaries such as the parish priests.

An important characteristic of the Catholicism of this part of Germany was the fact that the gap between elite and popular religion was not wide. As we have seen, all elements of the population participated in processions and pilgrimage, the festivals of the liturgical year, and weekly services. Although one can identify differences in emphasis, for example an earlier urban and elite interest in private devotion, Southwest German Catholicism cannot be neatly divided into elite and popular types. An important reason for this was the work of intermediaries, particularly the parish priests. A second reason for the relative absence of elite/popular conflict was the clericalism of the people, which meant that they respected the work and ideas of the clergy.

In analyzing the elite contribution to Catholic culture, one has to move beyond the strong inclination in historical writing to overestimate the role of church reformers. A close examination of developments after 1650 highlights the fact that the same limits that hindered Tridentine reform in the period leading up to the Thirty Years' War remained in place. By following Tridentine reform up to the middle of the eighteenth century, we can develop a better understanding of the contributions of all social groups involved in the development of Catholic identity.[4]

REFORM AND CONFESSIONALIZATION

Tridentine reform after 1650

The reforming zeal set in motion by the Council of Trent and taken up by new orders such as the Jesuits continued to inspire church reform after 1650. The reform decrees of the Council provided a blueprint for institutional reform and informed the policies of popes, bishops, and church officials well into the eighteenth century. Tridentine reformers also played an important role in increasing the emphasis on pastoral work, thus expanding the role of the parish priests in local religion. After 1650, however, Tridentine reformers in the episcopal administration could not recreate the strict program of regulation based on synods and

[4] Scholarship on the Counter-Reformation and Tridentine reform in Germany tends to focus on the so-called "Confessional Age," that is, the period from 1550 to 1650. The volumes in the series published by Anton Schindling and Walter Ziegler are classic examples of this periodization: *Die Territorien des Reichs im Zeitalter der Reformation.*

visitations that had developed before 1620, nor could they implement a unified way of educating the clergy. As a result, Tridentine reform continued after 1650, but was no longer as central as it had been earlier in the century.

Nevertheless, the 1712 report of Johan Franz Schenk von Stauffenberg, Bishop of Constance, to the pope (the *Status Liminorum*) demonstrates how important the Council of Trent remained for the Church hierarchy.[5] The bishop was primarily concerned with gaining the support of the Papal Curia in his campaign to assert episcopal jurisdiction against secular lords, to reduce the privileges of exempt monasteries and military orders, and to limit the power of the papal nuncio in Lucerne over the Swiss parts of his diocese. Von Stauffenberg also complained extensively about his poverty, noting that he did not even have the resources to proceed legally against wealthy monasteries.[6]

The *Status Liminorum* is, then, full of issues of canon law, particularly as it concerns episcopal authority. The writers of the report, keenly aware that the decrees of the Council of Trent reinforced the powers of the bishops, referred to them constantly. The report points, for example, to Session 24 of the Council of Trent, in an effort to make monks conduct marriages according to diocesan law, and to Session 25, chapter 3 when arguing that no new monasteries should be founded without episcopal permission.[7] At another point the report criticizes monasteries for publishing books without episcopal permission, a violation of another Tridentine decree.[8] Many of the references indicate, of course, how weak the authority of the bishop was compared with the Tridentine ideal. However, the report also demonstrates how the attitudes and concerns of leading clergymen in the diocese continued to be deeply influenced by the Council.[9]

The 1712 report also paints the picture of a bishop particularly concerned with the quality of pastoral care (*cura animarum*, *Seelsorge*) in the diocese. The report returns again and again to the need to reduce the privileges of monasteries, military orders, and secular lords in order to improve the *cura animarum*. The report refers to the decree of Session 25,

[5] Copy of this report in GLAK 99/364 (*Relatio concernens modernum Statum Episcopatus Constantiensis . . . nomine Joannis Francisci Episcopi . . . in Visitatione Sacrorum Liminum suo ordine . . .*). Von Stauffenberg was Bishop of Constance from 1704 to 1740.

[6] GLAK 99/364, pp. 6–7.

[7] GLAK 99/364, pp. 15, 17; Rev. H.J. Schroeder (ed.), *Canons and Decrees of the Council of Trent* (London, 1941).

[8] GLAK 99/364, p. 22; Schroeder, *Canons and Decrees of the Council of Trent*, pp. 17–20.

[9] References to Trent occur regularly in episcopal decrees and ordinances in the period 1650–1750. See for example, GLAK 82/594, an ordinance concerning clerical behavior from 1719.

chapter 11, which gives the bishop the right to visit and examine those regulars who provide pastoral care in incorporated parishes.[10] The bishop criticizes monasteries for hindering or preventing communities from going on pilgrimage or instituting pilgrimages.[11] Finally, the report concludes with an extensive discussion of the difficulties faced by people who lived too far from their parish church to receive regular pastoral care. The bishop proposes that the mendicants, "who exist in truth in very large numbers throughout this diocese," be given the job of providing services in isolated areas. Here we find von Stauffenberg neatly combining his critique of the regular clergy, and particularly of the mendicants whose numbers he considered excessive, with his concern for pastoral care.[12]

By the second half of the seventeenth century, most discussions of pastoral care shared a common set of assumptions and a common discourse. Rural communities, town councils, episcopal officials, and parish priests more or less agreed on the central attributes of a good pastor. Requests from villagers for the installation of a resident priest always insisted that the priest provide regular masses and sermons, that he be available for baptisms, deathbed confessions, and communion, and that he teach catechism classes in the village.[13] Episcopal ordinances emphasized the same list of pastoral services, but stressed the importance of the pastor's sobriety and dignity rather more than the population as a whole.[14] The development of a fairly unified discourse on pastoral care was clearly an achievement of Tridentine reform, although part of its success can be attributed to the fact that it was linked to popular traditions that considered the priest the servant of the parish.[15]

In contrast to this achievement, Tridentine reformers in Southwest Germany had little success in creating new institutions after 1650. This was especially true in the Bishopric of Constance, despite the fact that a whole range of Tridentine-inspired institutions were proposed or even

[10] GLAK 99/364, p. 15; Schroeder, *Canons and Decrees of the Council of Trent*, pp. 224–225.

[11] GLAK 99/364, p. 16.

[12] GLAK 99/364, pp. 25–26. This attitude presages some of the central arguments of "Enlightenment" (*Aufklärung*) church leaders later in the century.

[13] See above, chapters 4 and 5.

[14] GLAK 82/594.

[15] Peter Blickle, *The Revolution of 1525. The German Peasants' War in New Perspective* (Baltimore, 1981); Peter Blickle, *Communal Reformation: The Quest for Salvation in Sixteenth-Century Germany* (New Jersey, 1992); Rosi Fuhrmann, *Kirche und Dorf: Religiöse Bedürfnisse und kirchliche Stiftung auf dem Lande vor der Reformation* (Stuttgart, 1995); Marc R. Forster, *The Counter-Reformation in the Villages. Religion and Reform in the Bishopric of Speyer, 1560–1720* (Ithaca and London, 1992), ch. 1.

initiated before the Thirty Years' War. Regular episcopal visitations, diocesan synods, a seminary, reform of liturgical books, and the organization of a stronger episcopal administration were all on the agenda of late sixteenth-century reformers. After 1650, however, the only truly effective Tridentine institution within the episcopal administration was the Clerical Council (*Geistliche Rat*).[16]

Founded in 1594, the Clerical Council continued to play a leading role in church reform through the eighteenth century.[17] As it had in the decades around 1600, the council advised the bishops, helped organize diocesan visitations, promoted the reform of the clergy, and analyzed reports about suspicious religious practices. The members of the *Geistliche Rat* included some of the most influential members of the church hierarchy. In the mid-eighteenth century, the vicar general, the highest official of the diocese served as president, and three canons of the Cathedral Chapter served as councilors, along with seven other clergymen, most of whom held important and lucrative benefices in ecclesiastical chapters in the city of Constance.[18] Most Bishops of Constance did not attend meetings of the council, a sign of their lack of interest in the spiritual administration of the diocese. Nevertheless, the makeup of the council gave it enough power and influence to promote Tridentine reform.

The minutes (*Protokolle*) of the Clerical Council from the early eighteenth century indicate the range of the council's activities.[19] In 1711, for instance, the council examined a proposal by the Count of Montfort to found a new chapel in the village of Henighofen, one of a large number of projects for new churches and benefices in this period.[20] The council also investigated the behavior of the clergy, often disciplining individuals and sometimes examining whole groups of clerics. Thus, in 1706–1707 the councilors turned their attention to thirty or so hermits in the diocese, who, they believed, needed more supervision.[21] In this case, the *Rat* proposed that the deans of the rural chapters (the local administrators of the diocese) should be polled about the numbers, behavior, qualifications, and affiliations of the hermits.[22] The *Geistliche Rat* also

[16] In this sense, Constance was not much different from other dioceses in the south and west. Church institutions in Bavaria, Austria, and the Franconian bishoprics were more developed.

[17] Georg Weiland, "Die geistliche Zentralverwaltung des Bistums" in Kuhn et al. (eds.), *Die Bischöfe von Konstanz*, Vol. I *Geschichte*, pp. 69–72.

[18] Weiland, "Die geistliche Zentralverwaltung des Bistums," p. 74.

[19] EAF Ha 216, 217, 218 (Minutes from 1694 to 1714).

[20] EAF Ha 218, pp. 214–217.

[21] EAF Ha 216, p. 396; Ha 217, pp. 20, 39, 104–105, 230–231.

[22] EAF Ha 217, pp. 230–231.

issued very general ordinances dealing with the religious and moral behavior of the population, ordinances that can be characterized as efforts at social discipline. On November 23, 1707 the council discussed the following report:

> It is reported that carnal sins have been increasing in a dangerous way throughout Swabia . . . Furthermore we have also noticed that the frightful cursing and swearing has gone past a tolerable level [*über die massen im schwang gehe*]. Similarly, Sundays and feast days are everywhere poorly respected.[23]

The council concluded that the bishop should be informed of these developments, that the relevant previous ordinances should be reissued, and that secular authorities should be encouraged to punish these violations more aggressively.

It was also the job of the Clerical Council to organize episcopal commissions to investigate problems at the local level. The council used commissions more and more frequently in the eighteenth century, a clear indication of a growing "episcopal self-confidence" and an activist mentality in the church hierarchy.[24] The commissions ranged in importance from those sent to investigate miracles at major new shrines such as Triberg (1690s) and Steinbach (1733), to those conducting brief investigations of local disputes.[25] Several examples give the flavor of this activity. In 1712 an episcopal commission was appointed to investigate a dispute in Achstetten, where a female parishioner accused the parish priest of striking her in the face.[26] In 1713 a councilor was sent to investigate the relocation of the parish church in the village of Wasenweiler.[27]

The Clerical Council kept the decrees of the Council of Trent clearly in mind. In the early eighteenth century the councilors regularly considered plans for an episcopal seminary, as they had in the late sixteenth century.[28] They encouraged and supported episcopal visitations, sending lists of special concerns to the officials charged with investigating rural parishes, generally the deans of the rural chapters.[29] The council constantly sought to defend and strengthen episcopal authority and jurisdiction, a campaign that achieved some success in the eighteenth century. In a variety of ways, then, the *Geistliche Rat* can be

23 EAF Ha 217, p. 113.
24 Rudolf Reinhardt, "Die frühe Neuzeit" in Kuhn et al. (eds.), *Die Bischöfe von Konstanz*, Vol. I *Geschichte*, p. 41.
25 On Triberg and Steinbach see above, chapter 2.
26 HStASt. B467/4.
27 EAF Ha 218, pp. 406–407.
28 See above, chapter 1. Also EAF Ha 217, pp. 344–346.
29 EAF Ha 217, pp. 123–124.

correctly considered the most important force for Tridentine reform in the Bishopric of Constance and in Southwest Germany in general.[30]

The ability of Tridentine reformers, in the Clerical Council and elsewhere, to influence religious life at the local level was hindered by the general failure to establish other "reforming" institutions. After 1650, no diocesan synods met in the Bishopric of Constance, episcopal visitations lost many of their reformist elements, and the education of the clergy continued in a haphazard manner. The result was that the Clerical Council generally had few permanent institutions through which to operate, and found itself forced to use *ad hoc* measures such as commissions.

Episcopal visitations had been one of the favorite tools of earlier church reformers. In the decades around 1600, reformers conducted a number of detailed visitations of rural parishes, which then led to a generally successful campaign against clerical absenteeism, pluralism, and concubinage.[31] Regular visitations of rural parishes also took place after 1650, including some detailed ones in the immediate aftermath of the Thirty Years' War. As elsewhere in Germany, however, the late seventeenth- and eighteenth-century visitations lacked a reforming character.[32] Surviving visitation reports are generally laconic lists of parishes, priests, incomes, and property.[33] The deans of the rural chapters, rather than reforming officials from the episcopal administration, now conducted most visitations, and they gradually assumed the character of ritualized inspections. Generally the visitors exhibited little interest in popular religious practice, focusing on the qualifications and performance of the parish priests.

In fact, the visitors dug less deeply into conditions in the parishes than they had in the decades around 1600. The report on the visitation of the Rural Chapter of Waldshut in 1710 contains a one-page report on each parish.[34] The priest presented his qualifications and reported where and how often he went to confession and a scribe recorded his age and native town. The visitors then examined the priest's library, the church itself, and the inventory of church ornaments. The visitors asked local lay

[30] I am agreeing with the assessment of Georg Weiland in "Die geistliche Zentralverwaltung des Bistums," p. 70.

[31] See above, chapter 1. On visitations in the Bishopric of Constance: Peter Thaddäus Lang, "Die Visitationen" in Kuhn et al. (eds.), *Die Bischöfe von Konstanz*, Vol. I *Geschichte*, pp. 103–109.

[32] Compare Speyer: Forster, *The Counter-Reformation in the Villages*, chs. 6 and 7.

[33] This discussion based on EAF A1/725 (*Landkapitel* Stockach, 1665, 1685, 1702, 1708), EAF A1/738 (*Landkapitel* Waldshut, 1710), EAF A1/729 (*Landkapitel* Stühlingen 1702, 1704, 1706).

[34] EAF A1/738.

leaders to comment on the lifestyle and performance of the priest and, finally, they asked the priest if he had any complaints about his parishioners. Unfortunately, the inspectors apparently did not push these potentially interesting lines of inquiry. In the reports, the villagers almost universally praise the "vigilance" of their priests, while the priests have very few comments on the religious lives of the population. The Waldshut report is not dramatically different from others from this period. Visitations functioned as a routine inspection of the parishes, and certainly allowed parishioners to complain about unsatisfactory pastors, but neither the visitors nor the priests saw them as tools of religious reform or social discipline.

Ongoing jurisdictional disputes and the usual practical problems further reduced the role and effectiveness of the visitations.[35] The Bishops of Constance oversaw an enormous diocese, but did not possess the resources to administer it. Furthermore, the great abbeys, military orders, and secular lords remained reluctant to allow episcopal visitors to inspect the parishes under their control. This issue of jurisdiction, which went right to the heart of monastic claims of exemption from episcopal authority, was perhaps more bitterly contested in the century after 1650 than it had been before the war. The result was that episcopal visitors never entered large portions of the Catholic Southwest. As Peter Thaddäus Lang comments, "such an incomplete visitation system was hard to use as a method of imposing reforms demanded by the Council of Trent."[36]

Tridentine reformers understood that the parish clergy was the most important force for the development of reformed religious life in the villages and towns. If regulatory institutions such as visitations did not effectively control the professional performance of the clergy, perhaps the educational system could be counted on to provide the kinds of priests who would bring Tridentine Catholicism to the villages. In important ways this was the case. The educational level of the parish clergy (and, in fact, of the regular clergy as well) rose steadily from the late sixteenth century on. A consequence of this improved education was that, by the second half of the seventeenth century, the behavior and pastoral work of the parish clergy approached the ideal set by the Council of Trent.[37]

After the failure of efforts to establish and fund an episcopal seminary in the Bishopric of Constance in the late sixteenth century, a more

[35] Lang, "Die Visitationen," pp. 108–109. [36] Lang, "Die Visitationen," p. 109.

[37] See above, chapter 4. Priests' performance also improved because of pressure from village communes and town councils.

fragmented system for educating the clergy developed.[38] The Jesuits trained the majority of the priests who served in Southwest Germany at their secondary schools in Freiburg, Constance, Rottenburg, Feldkirch, and Rottweil, and then at the universities they dominated, particularly in Freiburg and Dillingen. Priests were trained in other places as well, some in the parsonage of the local priest, and others at schools run by the monasteries and military orders. The result was an increasingly well-educated clergy, but far from a uniform group of Tridentine-minded parish priests.

The founding of the episcopal seminary at Meersburg in 1735 brought a measure of unity to the education of priests. The *Seminarium clericorum* was generally a requirement for ordination and provided a year of pastoral training for young men who had already completed their theoretical studies at a university.[39] This seminary gave bishops more control over the quality of the parish clergy, and reflected the central concern with pastoral work that informed church reform in Southwest Germany.

Tridentine reform in Southwest Germany remained alive after 1650, but in a modest way. The church hierarchy could, for example, take some credit for stressing pastoral care within the Church. At the same time, the Catholic people were also responsible for this development, for they demanded that priests devote themselves more consistently to the care of their parishioners. These demands then often dovetailed with the priests' own understanding of their role in the parishes. Similarly, church institutions remained too weak to serve as effective tools for remaking Catholicism in this part of Germany, even when there were clergymen, such as some on the Clerical Council, who were inclined to pursue a more vigorous program.

Confessionalization after 1650

Since confessionalization depended on active and well-organized state structures, its development in Southwest Germany, with its weak and fragmented states, was necessarily limited. The Habsburg state was

[38] On the earlier efforts to found an episcopal seminary, see above, chapter 1. Peter Schmidt, "Die Priesterausbildung" in *Die Bischöfe von Konstanz*, Vol. I *Geschichte*, pp. 135–142; Georg Föllinger, "Zur Priesterausbildung in den Bistümern Köln, Paderborn und Kontanz nach dem Tridentinum" in Walter Brandmüller, Herbert Immenkotter, and Erwin Iserloh (eds.), *Ecclesia Militans. Studien zur Konzilien- und Reformationsgeschichte. Remigius Bäumer zur 70. Geburtstag gewidmet*, Vol. I *Zur Konziliengeschichte* (Paderborn, Munich, Vienna, and Zurich, 1988), pp. 367–397.

[39] Schmidt, "Die Priesterausbildung," pp. 138–139.

really the only territory that had the organization for such a program, but even there the fragmented nature of the *Vorderösterreich* territories was an obstacle to effective policies.[40] Moreover, Austrian authorities had no reason to be concerned with the Protestant threat after 1650. The sense of danger – sometimes outright panic – that was so much a part of the language of the Catholic authorities in the decades before 1620 disappeared after 1650.[41] When Austrian officials discovered a small group of "heretics" (either Anabaptists or Lutherans) in the remote Bärenthal in the early eighteenth century, they organized a Jesuit mission to the valley and worked to provide funds for a resident priest, hoping to "convert" the locals. Only later did they suggest banishing the most stubborn souls, apparently at the suggestion of the Jesuits.[42] As the Protestant threat faded, confessionalization lost much of its urgency for Austrian and other Catholic officials.

Outside of Outer Austria a policy of confessionalization, such as that practiced in large and "enclosed" Catholic states such as Bavaria or the Franconian Prince-Bishopric of Würzburg, was almost impossible.[43] In most cases, Catholic princes were abbots and abbesses, commanders of the military orders (the Teutonic Knights and the Knights of St. John), and various counts and imperial knights. Few had the resources to construct the bureaucracy needed to regulate the religious lives of their subjects, and few considered such a program necessary or useful. In the late seventeenth century even the Austrian authorities turned away from disciplinary measures and toward more sophisticated propaganda measures. The Austrians especially played up the special links between the Habsburg family and the Church. *Pietas Austriaca* became a kind of patriotic Catholic piety emphasizing the cults of the Cross, the Eucharist, and the Virgin Mary. This cult certainly served the purposes of the Habsburg state, but it did so by presenting the monarch as a model of proper piety and by supporting certain rites and cults. While such a policy smacks of cultural hegemony, it is a far cry from the forced conversion of Bohemia undertaken by the Habsburgs in the 1620s.[44]

[40] Rudolf Reinhardt, *Die Beziehungen von Hochstift und Diözese Konstanz zu Habsburg-Österreich in der Neuzeit: Zugleich ein Beitrag zur archivalischen Erforschung des Problems "Kirche und Staat." Beiträge zur Geschichte der Reichskirche in der Neuzeit*, Vol. II (Wiesbaden, 1966), p. 10.

[41] Sense of panic: TLA Ferd. 178(1); Tüchle, *Von der Reformation bis zur Säkularisation*, pp. 148–149.

[42] HStASt. B37a/133.

[43] "Enclosed states" consisted of contiguous territories. They contained few, if any, outlying districts surrounded by other principalities.

[44] Anna Coreth, *Pietas Austriaca* (Munich, 1959; 2nd edn, 1982). Popular Catholicism in Austria clearly influenced the official cult of the Habsburg court as well.

Other Catholic princes also attempted to create special links to the Church. The massive building program undertaken by all the abbeys of the Southwest in the eighteenth century was part of this effort.[45] The Cistercian Abbey of Salem was particularly active in the pursuit of such a policy.[46] The abbots and monks clearly considered the construction and decoration of churches and chapels an integral part of a policy of strengthening their rule over their subject population.[47] But was this confessionalization? The abbey, as secular lord and as an important religious institution, was in a position to combine secular and spiritual authority to impose religious uniformity. Furthermore, Salem was engaged in state building, including the strengthening of judicial institutions and the improvement of the efficiency of financial administration. Despite such "statist" tendencies, Salem's religious policy emphasized propaganda, not discipline. The monastery promoted the shrines at Birnau and Bodman and appealed to the long history of the monastery to promote loyalty and obedience. It is not clear if these measures persuaded peasants to pay their taxes and tithes willingly, but they did contribute to enthusiastic participation in pilgrimage piety and to the strength of Catholic identity more generally.

Other monasteries, military orders, and even smaller secular lords promoted churchliness and considered the Catholic Church an important institution for maintaining social peace and promoting morality.[48] On the other hand, the clergy and the religious institutions of Southwest Germany remained quite independent of state authorities, preventing the close cooperation of Church and state that characterized confessionalization in Bavaria and elsewhere. When the Habsburgs began in the middle of the eighteenth century to pursue policies designed to undermine the power and authority of the Catholic Church, it had become clear that the Church had become a hindrance to state-building.

[45] See above, chapter 2, "The sacral landscape."

[46] Erika Dillman and Hans-Jürgen Schulz, *Salem. Geschichte und Gegenwart* (Salem, 1989); Erika Dillman, *Stephan I. Fundamente des Barock. Salem an der Wende zum 18. Jahrhundert* (Tettnang, 1988); Erika Dillman, *Anselm II. Glanz und Ende eine Epoche. Eine Studie über den letzten großen Abt der Reichsabtei Salem* (Salem, 1987).

[47] Hans Martin Maurer, "Die Ausbildung der Territorialgewalt oberschwäbischer Klöster von 14. bis 17. Jahrhundert" *Blätter für deutsche Landesgeschichte* 109 (1973), esp. pp. 184–188.

[48] Wolfgang von Hippel, "Klosterherrschaft und Klosterwirtschaft in Oberschwaben am Ende des alten Reiches. Das Beispiel Schussenried" in Heinrich R. Schmidt, André Holenstein, and Andreas Würgler (eds.), *Gemeinde, Reformation und Widerstand. Festschrift für Peter Blickle zum 60. Geburtstag* (Tübingen, 1998), pp. 457–474.

The Jesuits and Capuchins

In a series of studies, Louis Châtellier has argued that the Jesuits played a central role in the creation of modern Catholicism and in the development of Catholic identity.[49] Châtellier argues that the Jesuits conducted a two-pronged program that was especially important in Northern and Central Europe. First, beginning in the middle of the sixteenth century, the Jesuits focused their attention on the literate, urban population. Central to this program were the Marian sodalities. These were organized along social and occupational lines and excluded women, with the conscious aim of disciplining religious practice and creating a male Catholic elite.[50] The Jesuits encouraged clergymen, leading townspeople, and aristocrats to confess and communicate more frequently, to participate in processions and confraternities, and, for the most committed, to follow the course of the Jesuit Spiritual Exercises.

The second part of the Jesuit program began later, around the middle of the seventeenth century. Châtellier describes the ways in which the Jesuits moved their proselytizing from the cities and towns into the countryside and how they developed what he calls a "religion of the poor." The defining practice of this program was the rural mission, in which the Jesuits (as well as a number of other missionary orders) traveled through the countryside, organizing what were in effect revival meetings. The fathers gave sermons and put on religious plays, held processions, heard confessions, said Mass, and gave communion. The missionaries encouraged a visually and emotionally charged Catholicism, together with a theological perspective that was increasingly aimed at and supportive of the peasants and the poor.

Châtellier further argues that the Jesuits implemented these programs across Europe, but that they emphasized different things in different places, and different things to different people. The effort to create a lay Catholic elite was strongest in the center of Europe, in the towns and cities of Belgium, eastern France, and western Germany. The religion of the poor was promoted in western France, Italy, Bavaria, and Poland. The scope of Châtellier's works is too great to make easy conclusions about all of Catholic Europe. His detailed study of Alsace, however,

[49] Louis Châtellier, *Tradition chrétienne et renouveau catholique dans le cadre de l'ancien Diocèse de Strasbourg (1650–1770)* (Paris, 1981); *Europe of the Devout. The Catholic Reformation and the Formation of a New Society* (Cambridge, 1989); *La Religion des pauvres: les missions rurales en Europe et la formation du catholicisme moderne, XVIe–XIXe siècles* (Paris, 1993).

[50] See also Forster, *The Counter-Reformation in the Villages*, pp. 66–74, 124–126, 135–142, 216–225; R. Po-chia Hsia, *Religion and Society in Münster: 1535–1618* (New Haven, 1984), esp. ch. 3.

shows both programs at work, although the Jesuit missions to the countryside, especially in the first half of the eighteenth century, had the most lasting effect on Alsatian Catholicism.[51]

Southwest Germany experienced both aspects of the program described by Châtellier. From their houses in Freiburg, Constance, Rottweil, and Rottenburg am Neckar the Jesuits exercised a powerful influence over the secular clergy, had an important role in urban religiosity, and sent missions to evangelize the countryside.[52] This influence gave the Society of Jesus a significant role in the creation of Catholic identity. There were, however, constraints on the Jesuits that prevented them from dominating local or regional religious life.

The Capuchins were the second widely influential new order in Southwest Germany, as they were across all of Catholic Germany. These reformed Franciscan friars became a much larger and more widely spread presence than the Jesuits, especially after 1650. There were about six hundred friars living in thirty-nine Capuchin houses in (and on the edges) of the Bishopric of Constance in the eighteenth century.[53] Capuchin houses were smaller than Jesuit ones and the friars did not run large educational establishments, as did the Society of Jesus. Instead, the Capuchins were active as free-lance pastors, serving as preachers, confessors at shrines, and temporary parish priests. There have been few studies of the Capuchins, in part because they left few written documents and it is therefore easy to underestimate the barefoot fathers.[54]

Despite their influence, neither the Capuchins nor the Jesuits could take the initiative in religious practice away from the people. The Jesuits were hampered by the small number of their order's houses in Southwest Germany. The Capuchins had much less interest in controlling or regulating popular Catholicism and, by extension, cannot be considered forces for elite religious reform. Instead, the friars supported popular practices, especially processions and pilgrimages, even undermining at times efforts by other elements in the Church to clean up and regulate such practice. It is not surprising that in 1806 Catholic officials in the

[51] Châtellier, *Tradition chrétienne et renouveau catholique*.

[52] The basic history of the German Jesuits remains Bernhard Duhr, *Geschichte der Jesuiten in den Ländern deutsche Zunge von 16. bis 18 Jahrhundert* (4 vols., Freiburg in Breisgau, 1907–1921). After 1650, there were between sixty and seventy-five Jesuits living and working in these four houses.

[53] P. Beda Mayer, "Vorderösterreichische Kapuzinerprovinz" in *Der Franziskusorden. Die Kapuziner und Kapuzinerinnen in der Schweiz* [*Helvetia Sacra*, Section V, Vol. II, Part I], (Berne, 1974), pp. 774–790. These thirty-nine houses do not include houses in the Swiss parts of the diocese.

[54] This study does not rectify this shortcoming. My information on the Capuchins is limited and often indirect.

newly formed Kingdom of Württemberg proposed the abolition of several Capuchin houses, claiming that the friars were responsible for the "bigotry and superstition" of popular Catholicism.[55]

The Jesuits came later to Southwest Germany than they did to Bavaria, Franconia, or the Rhineland. The college in Constance was founded in 1604, the house in Freiburg in 1620.[56] Earlier efforts to found colleges, promoted primarily by the Habsburgs, failed, although the colleges in Alsace, at Molsheim (founded 1582, refounded 1592) and at Ensisheim (founded 1614/1615), had some influence in the region. The colleges in Rottenburg and Rottweil came even later, at the end of Thirty Years' War, and the college at Rottweil had to be abandoned between 1672 and 1692.[57]

Jesuit activity in this part of Germany emphasized the education of the clergy and a lay Catholic elite, that is the first aspect of the Jesuit program described by Châtellier. The Jesuit *Gymnasien* were popular and well attended, training many generations of middle-class and aristocratic Catholic men. In Freiburg the Jesuits also taught in the faculties of philosophy and theology at the university, eagerly taking on the role of making Freiburg a counterweight to the Protestant universities in Tübingen, Strasbourg, and Basel.[58] The Jesuits in all these colleges served as preachers in the cities' main churches and organized Marian sodalities for their students and the local clergy. In Freiburg the Jesuits founded four sodalities in the 1620s, one for *Gymnasium* students, one for university students, one for "young" (presumably unmarried) artisans, and one for married citizens. These all-male organizations were part of the goal of creating devotional structures aimed at specific social groups.[59] Operating either directly through visiting preachers or missionaries, or indirectly through priests educated in Jesuit schools, the

[55] Hermann Schmid, "Bettel und Herrenklöster im Hochstift Konstanz" in Kuhn et al. (eds.), *Die Bischöfe von Konstanz*, Vol. I *Geschichte*, p. 233.

[56] Theodor Kurrus, "Die Jesuiten in Freiburg und in den Vorlanden" in Hans Maier and Volker Press (eds.), *Vorderösterreich in der frühen Neuzeit* (Sigmaringen, 1989), p. 192; Duhr, *Geschichte der Jesuiten*, Vol. II Part I, pp. 259–263, 268–269. For a detailed discussion of the founding of the Jesuit college in Constance, see Wolfgang Zimmermann, *Rekatholisierung, Konfessionalisierung und Ratsregiment. Der Prozeß des politischen und religiösen Wandels in der österreichischen Stadt Konstanz 1548–1637* (Sigmaringen, 1994), pp. 133–154.

[57] Rottenburg: Duhr, *Geschichte der Jesuiten*, Vol. II Part I, pp. 277–278; Vol. III, pp. 143–145. Rottweil: Duhr, *Geschichte der Jesuiten*, Vol. III, pp. 145–150; Dankwart Schmid (ed.), *Die Hauschronik der Jesuiten von Rottweil 1652–1773. Synopsis Historiae Domesticae Societatis Jesu Rottweil* (Rottweil, 1989).

[58] Kurrus, "Die Jesuiten in Freiburg und in den Vorlanden"; Duhr, *Geschichte der Jesuiten*, Vol. III, pp. 268–269.

[59] Duhr, *Geschichte der Jesuiten*, Vol. III, pp. 269.

Jesuits promoted the founding of Marian *Bürgercongregationen* in smaller towns as well. Sodalities were founded in Altdorf, Horb, Rottenburg, Rheinfelden, and Villingen.[60]

The Jesuits remained influential in these cities and towns until the abolition of the order in 1773. It is a sign of both the wealth and the political support the Jesuits could muster that in Freiburg in the 1720s the Jesuit house was completely rebuilt and major construction was undertaken in the Jesuit church. Even as late as 1769 the Jesuits started a major renovation of the Freiburg *Gymnasium*.[61] The Jesuits in Rottweil came into conflict with the town council early in the eighteenth century, yet by mid-century had a large following. They claimed in 1754 that "the influx [of people] into the [Jesuit] church is always enormous, more than it has ever been in human memory; in particular the church is completely full [*ringsum ganz gefüllt*] for Sunday sermons; the holy confessionals are surrounded on all sides by those eager to confess. In no other year has there been such a demand . . ."[62]

The Jesuits also gave a great deal of attention to their relationship with the rest of the clergy, particularly the parish priests. The Jesuit house in Rottweil received more support from the rural clergy than from town officials. We have seen that priests left considerable sums of money to the Jesuits and that the Jesuits invited neighboring priests to give sermons in their church on the feasts of St. Ignatius and St. Xavier.[63] The Jesuits also organized retreats for parish priests, in which the clergymen went through the intense experience of Loyola's "Spiritual Exercises". In the mid-eighteenth century, Jesuits from Constance traveled to the countryside to hold three-day Exercises for groups of twenty to forty priests.[64]

The spiritual retreats held for country priests were part of the Jesuit program to evangelize the countryside. This project was, by inclination as well as necessity, more sporadic than the effort to motivate and educate the urban population. Although they were less of a presence than in Bavaria and Franconia, Jesuit missionaries were not unknown in the villages of Southwest Germany between 1700 and 1750, the period Châtellier calls the "golden age of missions."[65] A full-blown mission passed through the villages around Schemmerberg in 1724.[66] Although a

[60] Villingen: GLAK 79/837. Other towns: HStASt. B17/360; HStASt. B17/361.
[61] Duhr, *Geschichte der Jesuiten*, Vol. IV Part I, p. 296.
[62] Schmid (ed.), *Die Hauschronik der Jesuiten von Rottweil 1652–1773*, pp. 65–71, 173.
[63] See above, chapter 4. [64] Duhr, *Geschichte der Jesuiten*, Vol. IV Part I, p. 304.
[65] Châtellier, *La Religion des pauvres*, p. 120; Duhr, *Geschichte der Jesuiten*, Vol. IV Part II, pp. 206–216.
[66] GLAK 98/3975.

brief conflict with the secular officials of the monastery of Salem slowed the progress of this mission, the fathers reported a successful stay in Schemmerberg before moving on to the town of Messkirch.

Jesuit missionaries came to some areas on a regular basis. In 1731 Austrian officials admonished local officials around Stockach to support the activities of Carolus Malliardo, who had missionized in this area on two other occasions in the previous nine years.[67] Malliardo reported a variety of obstacles, stating that although he always received official permission from the bishop to conduct his missions, some towns and territories did not accept his papers. Even Austrian officials in Innsbruck, who ostensibly favored his work, told local authorities to support the missionaries only as long as their activities did not interfere with their subjects' work in the fields.

Joseph Rueff SJ, "Missionary Superior of Swabia," made a special effort to defend his planned mission in the Rhine valley in 1773. In a letter to the Austrian *Landvogt* (a kind of district governor) in Offenburg, Rueff explained that he needed the support of secular officials for his mission to succeed. In particular, he needed help in disciplining the "overly free youth."

> The mission has nothing else as its aim than the honor of God and the perpetual salvation of souls. As means to this end, it employs a clear and emphatic presentation of basic truths which will awaken hearts to the contemplation and consideration of God's commandments, the general duties of a Christian and the particular [duties] of one's *Stand* [estate] and official position. [The mission will also] motivate people to repent the mistakes and negligence they discover and motivate them to a more confident decision to energetically mend their ways in the future.[68]

With the society under attack in Austria at this time, Rueff was somewhat defensive. He insisted that the missions did not take people away from agricultural work, did not lead to a lack of discipline, and did not undermine loyalty to secular authorities.

By the 1760s and 1770s Jesuit missionaries faced considerable opposition. In 1767 town officials turned away a Jesuit mission from Villingen, stating "we already have preachers."[69] Jesuits reported that many priests in Austrian territories found their missionary work "bothersome [*unangenehm*]," perhaps believing that the missions undermined the centrality of the parish and the parish priest in religious life. Many *Pfarrer* ostentatiously stayed away from the events the Jesuits organized, a sign

[67] GLAK 118/178. [68] GLAK 119/424.

[69] HStASt. B17/498. On criticism of missions, see Châtellier, *La Religion des pauvres*, pp. 114–118.

of the declining influence of the order. The Austrian *Oberamt* of Burgau argued that the sermons and theatrical performances were particularly bad.

In the case of some people more bad than good comes from these [missions], and there is [even] more reason now for a decision to reject them than there was in the days of the late *Landvogt* Remschwags, who each time refused to allow the mission to be held and called them superfluous, due to the various costs and the waste of time.[70]

Yet at the same time the *Obervogt* admitted that the Jesuits attracted large crowds of enthusiastic country people and that they had great influence over the "devotion and dedication to prayer of the people."

These missions were probably little different from the missions to the Bavarian countryside held in this period, or the mission/visitation held in the Bishopric of Speyer in 1683.[71] In addition to preaching and promoting new devotions, the Jesuits left behind crosses and other visual signs of their visit. In the 1770s, missionaries in Austrian territories reported visiting about twenty towns and villages, spending about a week in each place.[72] A detailed description of a mission from the same period sets out a week-long cycle of sermons, catechism lessons, and devotional exercises. The plan of this mission, like the ones Châtellier describes, demonstrates both attempts to guide and reform popular religion and a willingness to appeal to the practices that were central to popular practice.[73] Thus the morning sermons served to reinforce popular understanding of and devotion to the sacraments, the Virgin Mary, and the Mass. Afternoon catechism lessons were more disciplinary in nature, admonishing people to avoid blasphemy and scandal, while encouraging them to obey their superiors, to act more charitably toward their neighbors, and to be more attentive to their children's religious education.

Châtellier argues that at the heart of this missionary project was an effort to bring God and Christ more to the center of popular religious practice.[74] Aspects of this endeavor can be seen in the Southwest German missions described above. The Jesuits gave sermons and organized meditations on religious issues that were not vital to the rituals of

[70] HStASt. B17/498.

[71] Bavaria: Châtellier, *La Religion des pauvres*, p. 108. Speyer: Forster, *The Counter-Reformation in the Villages*, pp. 220–221. The political fragmentation of Southwest Germany made organizing and obtaining permission for missions there more complicated than it was in Bavaria.

[72] HStASt. B17/498. [73] Châtellier, *La Religion des pauvres*, Part II.

[74] Châtellier says that the missionaries succeeded in changing "*l'idée même de religion.*" *La Religion des pauvres*, p. 126.

popular Catholicism, for example the Passion of Christ, the compassion and goodness of God, the Last Judgment, and the mortal sins. Yet it was the Marian and Eucharistic devotions that were given pride of place in the missions, as a strategy to capture the interest and fervor of the people. Although people participated enthusiastically in missions and even embraced some of the new practices and devotions the Jesuits promoted, the missions did not function primarily to reorient religious practice. Instead, the missions expanded the number of devotions available to people, rather than focusing devotional life on what the Jesuits and the clerical elite considered central.

The Jesuit missionaries were popular and they contributed to diversity and variety of Catholic practice, but they did not impose their religious vision on the population. Their long-term influence was especially limited by the sporadic nature of their work. According to their parish priests, the inhabitants of Görwihl and the surrounding area of the southern Black Forest enthusiastically participated in a Jesuit mission in 1759.[75] Although the *Pfarrer* in Görwihl complained about the cost and effort involved in the two-week-long mission, he praised the zealousness of the two missionaries and the positive effect of the mission on the people. The 1759 mission was, however, the only mission to this region in the eighteenth century. The Jesuits left little behind when they departed, except perhaps the memory of a moment of intense, but short-lived, religious fervor. Was the experience of a mission very different from that of a procession or pilgrimage organized and led by the commune and the local priest?

The Capuchins are a hazier presence in the villages and towns than the Jesuits, yet they were clearly an important part of Catholic life. The number of Capuchins living in Southwest Germany grew steadily between 1650 and the 1770s, an indication of their expanding role.[76] Whether they were leading processions and pilgrimages, hearing confessions and giving communion, or supervising the administration of shrines, the Capuchins provided a reservoir of priests and lay brothers who could step in and support the intensive religious life of the Catholic population.

Villagers knew the Capuchins as temporary priests and as helpers for parish priests during Easter or at other busy times of the year. The friars initially carved out this position during and immediately after the Thirty

[75] Ebner, *Görwihl*, p. 14; Ebner, *Niederwihl*, p. 126.

[76] Number of Capuchins in the Outer Austrian Capuchin Province: 330 in 1668, 349 in 1678, 556 in 1726, 641 in 1775. Mayer, "Vorderösterreichische Kapuzinerprovinz," p. 781.

Years' War. In the 1640s the town council of Aach delivered a barrel of wine to the Capuchin house in Engen, as payment for the masses the friars read in the town church in the absence of a resident priest.[77] The Capuchin house in Meersburg, founded in the early 1650s, immediately became a major source of priests for the surrounding parishes.[78]

In the eighteenth century the Capuchins became regular visitors to parishes, where they helped parish priests deal with the flood of communicants during Lent, and especially during Easter Week itself. During Easter Week Capuchins from Laufenburg traveled through the southern Black Forest helping priests. They arrived in Görwihl on Palm Sunday, remaining there to hear confessions and give communion until Wednesday. From Görwihl they traveled on to Niederwihl, hearing confessions Wednesday afternoon and Thursday morning. From there at least one friar went to Hochsal to give the Good Friday sermon in the parish church there.[79] In this region, and no doubt in other areas in the vicinity of Capuchin houses, the friars were an active presence during the most important period of the liturgical year.

The Capuchins also heard confessions at Christmas time, at least in Görwihl, and were hired to accompany processions.[80] On the feast of the Apostles Philip and Jacob (May 1), a Capuchin friar sometimes read Mass in the parish church in Niederwihl, for those inhabitants who had not gone with the parish priest on pilgrimage to Todtmoos.[81] The Capuchins, like the Jesuits, promoted devotions to the saints and martyrs of their order and advertised the indulgences and special dispensations they had acquired in the countryside.[82] By frequently serving as confessors of parish priests, the Capuchins were undoubtedly able to influence the nature of devotional life in the countryside.[83]

However, parish priests did not always appreciate the efforts of the Capuchins. Priests sometimes feared that the friars might undermine their authority, especially when handling confessions. A second area of dispute revolved around financial issues, as when the Capuchins received fees for performing sacraments and other services that might have otherwise gone to the parish priest. In 1719, a combination of these

[77] GLAK 229/42.

[78] Hermann Schmid, "Bettel und Herrenklöster im Hochstift" in Kuhn et al. (eds.), *Die Bischöfe von Konstanz*, Vol. I *Geschichte*, p. 232.

[79] Ebner, *Görwihl*, p. 116; Ebner, *Niederwihl*, p. 116.

[80] Ebner, *Görwihl*, p. 121.

[81] Ebner, *Niederwihl*, p. 117.

[82] Ebner, *Niederwihl*, p. 116 (Feast of *Kapuzinermärtyrer* Fidelis at the houses in Laufenburg and Waldshut); p. 119 (Feast of the "Portuncula Indulgence" also in Laufenburg and Waldshut).

[83] See above, chapter 4.

issues caused the *Pfarrer* in Gösslingen, Moritz Letzgus, to refuse to allow the Capuchins to perform services in the filial church of Böhringen.[84] Letzgus's refusal led, in turn, to vehement protests from the inhabitants of Böhringen and from Austrian officials, who said that the Capuchins were needed because the priest did such a very poor job serving his parishioners.

In the towns, the Capuchins rarely appeared in local records until they were about to be sent away by the Austrian authorities. The town fathers of Breisach reported to their superiors in 1783 that the friars (along with the Augustinians) were "indispensable" for pastoral work, especially since the priests who held the four "prebend" benefices in the town did not fulfill their assigned duties.[85] Other town councils expressed the same view, emphasizing that the Capuchins helped overworked parish priests provide necessary pastoral services. The *Oberamt* in Tettnang went even further in praising the Capuchins, commenting that during epidemics the friars were both active and in demand. Together with the Augustinians and other Franciscan friars, the Capuchins had an important place in local religion, making possible the intensive devotional life favored by the population.

The Jesuits and Capuchins did not dominate Catholicism in Southwest Germany, yet they did contribute to local religious life. The orders' influence was felt when they introduced new devotions in towns and villages, and when priests they had taught took positions in the parishes. Yet this influence was not the same thing as domination. The Jesuits had a limited physical presence, which prevented them from instituting an ambitious program of reform and reorientation of popular Catholicism. The Capuchins were found in more towns and villages, but their activities focused on promoting and supporting existing aspects of popular religion, rather than sanitizing or reframing popular practice. One can certainly locate important traces of Jesuit and Capuchin influence in Southwest German Catholicism, but the orders were only a part of the whole story.

INTERMEDIARIES

The Jesuits and Capuchins functioned, in fact, more as intermediaries between the people and the official Church, than as "agents of the Counter-Reformation."[86] Parish priests also found themselves caught

[84] HStASt. B467/473. [85] HStASt. B17/426.

[86] This term comes from Philip Hoffman, *Church and Community in the Diocese of Lyon, 1500–1789* (New Haven, 1984).

between the demands of their parishioners and the rules and regulations of the Church. Resident parish priests, in particular, faced daily pressure to maintain a proper clerical lifestyle, provide the services the people wanted, and, at the same time, maintain good relations with their neighbors. Whether or not they wanted to be, *Pfarrer* were intermediaries.

Many priests may not have experienced the pressures from their superiors and their parishioners as obviously contradictory. In the seventeenth and eighteenth centuries, priests were more often trained to educate and accommodate their parishioners than to discipline and regulate their religious lives. Furthermore, bishops (and the secular authorities) rarely endeavored to change local religious life, and thus priests were under little pressure from above to challenge local practices. Rural communes and town councils were, by contrast, consistently engaged in local religion, and it behooved priests to cooperate with them. When episcopal officials took an active role in the eighteenth century, they did so primarily to enforce episcopal jurisdiction against secular authorities. Thus priests could expect support from episcopal visitors or the Clerical Council in jurisdictional disputes in the parishes, but not necessarily in disputes over religious practice or the pastoral responsibilities of the priest.

The parish priest played several roles in the parish, some of which were inherently contradictory. As tax collector, landlord, and representative of the state, he could easily find himself at loggerheads with his parishioners. As pastor, he had (and usually felt) a duty to serve the spiritual needs of the community. As village or town resident, a priest had to get along with his neighbors. Finally, villagers and townspeople considered the priest a servant of the parish, a role most priests found they had to fill as well.

Southwest Germany was not a great place for priests who wanted to rule their parishes with an iron hand. Strong communal structures and self-assured villagers could, and did, engage authoritarian priests in long drawn-out disputes. The communalism of rural Catholicism meant that priests, whatever their pretensions, did not have undisputed power over their parishes. Most priests learned quickly that they had certain powers and considerable influence, but they also learned the limits of their parishioners' clericalism.

Between 1650 and 1750, then, those clergymen who were in constant contact with the Catholic population gave precedence to their role as pastors, that is as spiritual intermediaries for the community. This role was congenial for most parish priests because it was assuming a growing status within the Church and because it was the role they had been trained to fulfill. The position of pastor was also respected and honored within the parishes. Most *Pfarrer* realized that they would be both more comfortable and more effective as pastors than as representatives of the Church or the state. As they increasingly internalized the pastoral ideal, parish priests became by necessity intermediaries between the population and higher authorities. When the rural clergy resisted Josephine reforms in the 1770s and 1780s, they did so as much to support their parishioners as to champion the ecclesiastical hierarchy's defense of the "liberties of the Church."

Monasteries also played an intermediary role between the wider Church and the Catholic population. Monasteries had a more indirect role than parish priests but we have seen that in many parts of Southwest Germany their influence was very pervasive. Monasteries appointed priests to incorporated parishes, or, in the case of the Benedictines, sent monks to serve as parish priests. Monks promoted and patronized shrines, sometimes serving as confessors and directors of the larger shrines, such as Birnau or Todtmoos. Of course monasteries were also wealthy and powerful landowners and usually secular lords holding legal jurisdiction and other powers.

Monasteries, along with the commanderies of the military orders, provided a layer of ecclesiastical institutions closer to the people than were the bishops, but not as enmeshed in village life as were parish priests. When one considers that these institutions were also both ecclesiastical and secular powers, one can see the ambiguity in their relationship to religious life. This ambiguity was also found in the monastic relationship to Tridentine reform. In fact, in the century after 1650, monasteries felt less obligation to obey Tridentine decrees or demonstrate their commitment to reform from above.

Despite their skepticism about Trent, monasteries did not really neglect rural parishes, at least after 1650. In fact, at times they demonstrated a sincere concern for the quality of parochial care in the countryside. In 1661, the Abbot of St. Blasien reported that, due to a shortage of priests, he had been forced to hire young, inexperienced priests, many of whom were Swiss.[87] The Swiss priests were unaware of local traditions and often came into conflict with their parishioners. According to the abbot, once these priests received their investiture, they began to extort money from their parishioners, "which the patrons and the parishioners

[87] GLAK 99/349.

must unhappily suffer through." The abbot asked the bishop to avoid giving parishes to Swiss priests, and offered to support the education of local men. In 1669 this effort began to bear fruit, and the abbot reported that two young men who had been educated at the monastery were ready to begin hands-on training in the parishes.[88]

The archive of the Abbey of St. Blasien demonstrates that the Benedictines administered their parishes carefully. Beginning in the 1650s, officials kept careful records of all priests appointed to parishes and the circumstances of their leaving the parish (death, transfer to a new position, dismissal). Often monastic officials added comments on priests' educational background and they sometimes made notes about their pastoral work.[89] As with the rest of the monastic archive, these notes were meant to support St. Blasien's rights and privileges, but they also indicate how concern for administrative efficiency forced bureaucrats to deal with local issues and concerns.

St. Blasien, like Salem, considered the priests it appointed both monastic employees and part of the monastic community.[90] In the early eighteenth century, St. Blasien issued regulations for secular priests it appointed.[91] The priests were reminded that they were serving as "vicars" for the true parish priest, who was the abbot. Any disrespect or lack of obedience toward the monastery would not be tolerated. Priests were expected to exhibit "next to good Latin, exemplary lifestyle and behavior, [and] zeal in church services and pastoral work." Furthermore, a priest should protect St. Blasien's rights in the parish. Monastic officials also conducted regular visitations of villages. Finally, new priests were also informed that, when a St. Blasien priest died, the rest of the priests would be informed and they should perform a special Mass for the soul of their deceased colleague. Taken together, the regulations reflect an effort to integrate the priests into a monastic community, but also uncompromising protection of monastic rights. We cannot be sure that parish priests wanted to be clients of St. Blasien, or of the extent to which they developed other loyalties, for instance to a community of neighboring priests. The development of such professional ties was probably more difficult in the mountainous region around St. Blasien than it was for the priests around Salem on the shore of Lake Constance.

There was certainly tension between monasteries and the secular clergy, but there was apparently little friction between monasteries and

[88] GLAK 99/349. [89] GLAK 99/342; GLAK 99/348.
[90] See above, chapter 4 for the relationship between Salem and the secular clergy.
[91] GLAK 99/348.

the population over religious matters. When a monastery took steps to shape rural religion, its policies rarely caused conflict. In the early eighteenth century, for example, Abbot Stephan I of Salem sponsored a program of rebuilding chapels. Between 1708 and 1718, Salem built the Maria Victoria Chapel at Stephansfeld, and rebuilt chapels in Oberuhldingen and Gebhardsweiler.[92] The abbot's building program was, of course, motivated by a desire to represent Salem's power and piety in architecture. But the construction of chapels also reflected the monastery's commitment to local religious traditions against the episcopal *Amtskirche* represented by the parishes. The population of course welcomed more chapels, for it meant more places to worship and more priests to administer services. In this case we see Salem reinforcing the clericalization of rural Catholicism, while providing alternatives to the parish church as a place of worship.

The relationship between monasteries and popular religion was not characterized by conflict and tension. Particularly after 1650, there was generally a good relationship between the people and monastic institutions and there is little evidence of endemic or systematic dispute about proper religious practice between abbots, abbesses, monks, and nuns, and the mass of peasants and townspeople. Modern Catholicism was created by a variety of different groups. Parish priests certainly played an essential intermediary role in the creation of religious belief and practice, but monasteries, which were so important in the ecclesiastical structure of Southwest Germany, also had an impact on religious developments.

Certainly Wolfgang Seibrich is correct to emphasize how monasteries defended traditional institutions against the institutional centralization set in motion by the Council of Trent. Seibrich also points out that the older orders prevented the full acceptance of a discourse of pastoral care and anti-Protestantism within Catholicism, especially before and during the Thirty Years' War. Whether or not we agree with Seibrich that the dominance of such ideas would have represented "a shift in emphasis with momentous consequences [*einer folgenschweren Akzentverschiebung*]", monasteries remained institutional representations of a Catholicism that antedated Trent.[93]

[92] Dillman, *Stephan I*, p. 47. GLAK 98/3590.

[93] Wolfgang Seibrich, *Gegenreformation als Restauration. Die restaurativen Bemühungen der alten Orden im deutschen Reich von 1580 bis 1648* (Münster, 1991), esp. pp. 1–8; Marc R. Forster, "The Elite and Popular Foundations of German Catholicism in the Age of Confessionalism: The Reichskirche" *Central European History*, 26 (1994), pp. 311–325.

Monasteries were, again to use Seibrich's terminology, more "popular" (*volkskirchlich*) than "institutional" (*amtskirchlich*), at least in certain ways.[94] Yet abbots and monks could be as bureaucratic and rationalistic as any bishop could. Their political, financial, and religious interests were, however, local and regional and they did not identify themselves easily even with their orders, let alone with the international Church. Each monastery favored defending and extending its particular privileges and exemptions, even if this undermined the wider Church. The cultural world of the *Reichsklöster* clashed at many levels with the world of international Catholicism.

All the monasteries of Southwest Germany contributed to Catholic culture by resisting centralization and supporting particularism. The monastic contribution was neither acculturating nor confessionalizing. Instead, as promoters of local shrines, as patrons of rural parishes, as homes for sons of local families, as centers of religious devotion, and as ancient sacred places, monasteries added to the diversity and localism of Southwest German Catholicism.

POPULAR CATHOLICISM, LOCAL RELIGION AND REGIONAL PATTERNS

It is easier to locate and describe the different ways in which the clerical elite, the state, the religious orders, and the population promoted trends in Catholic practice than it is to analyze the interplay of these different forces. Why did the population participate in the creation of Catholic identity by defending some traditional practices, while promoting changes in others? What caused peasants and townspeople to favor or support some religious practices and reject others? How much initiative did the elite in fact keep in religious matters, and in what areas? Many of these questions can only be answered tentatively.

Popular support for the elaboration of pilgrimages, processions, especially votive processions, benedictions of various kinds, and the festivals of the liturgical year, demonstrates a predilection for those aspects of Catholicism that served an agricultural society.[95] Social and economic crises also contributed to the creation of new devotions. Most obviously, many new shrines were established during or immediately

[94] Seibrich, *Gegenreformation als Restauration*, esp. pp. 1–8; von Hippel, "Klosterherrschaft und Klosterwirtschaft in Oberschwaben," p. 468.

[95] This is an obvious point, made by many scholars, perhaps best of all by William Christian, *Local Religion in Sixteenth-Century Spain* (Princeton, 1981).

after the Thirty Years' War, or were created in the eighteenth century but referred back to miracles purported to have occurred during the disasters of the 1630s and 1640s. Votive masses, processions, or other devotions appeared as the result of local or regional crop failures, animal diseases, or outbreaks of plague.

However, a straightforward link between social and economic crisis and the development of new religious devotions is overly simplistic. New ideas constantly reached the parishes of Southwest Germany. The cult of the Rosary provides a good example. Initially promoted by the religious orders, this devotion also spread from parish to parish without the direct participation of the clergy. People prayed the Rosary at shrines, providing an example to people from neighboring villages, or, in the case of more important shrines, for people from a wider region. Nor should we forget that the cult of the Rosary, like most of the major devotions within German Catholicism, could develop in different institutional settings. Most people prayed the Rosary at meetings organized by confraternities. The confraternities were in turn embedded in a clericalized and communalized religion. Confraternities were often created by village communes, but with the participation of the parish priests, who were in turn indispensable for the services the confraternities organized. A similar analysis can be made for the way pilgrimages, processions, and even the festivals of the liturgical year developed. The structures and institutions of this part of Germany played a central role in the way new religious ideas were received and implemented.

A second approach to this problem is to consider the religious discourses within which Baroque Catholicism developed. The concepts and language important to Tridentine reformers, for example, contributed significantly to religious life, even at the local level. I have highlighted how everyone came to share a similar concept of pastoral care (*Seelsorge*) by about 1700. Yet *Seelsorge* was also a vital aspect of an older communal discourse about the parish and the role of the clergy, which emphasized the parish priest as the servant of the communal church. Here, then, what we might call a "Tridentine" discourse and a "communal" discourse converged. Baroque Catholicism was open to various discourses, including ideas about personal and individual devotion, which came to the parishes first in sermons and then, with growing literacy, through the influx of devotional literature in the eighteenth century. In the end, though, a kind of traditionalist discourse dominated religion in the countryside. Peasants certainly gave preference to the devotions associated with the local sacred landscape, or to practices they considered time-honored. Catholicism in Southwest Germany was by no means a coherent system, but rather a hodgepodge of different influences that coalesced in a general pattern of religious practice.

Although it is important to acknowledge the fluidity and flexibility of Catholicism, one can nevertheless identify certain fundamental characteristics of popular religion. The population actively participated in its own religious life, thus bringing more variety and diversity into the daily practice of Catholicism. Tridentine reformers and confessionalizers, primarily in the episcopal and state bureaucracies, were rather less active, but they too promoted new and different devotions, while seeking to impose order and rationality on popular religion. They could not realize the latter goal in Southwest Germany, where institutional and political particularism held sway and where the people defended their own religious life. Finally, the Jesuits, the Capuchins, and the other orders pursued their own agendas, many of which tapped into popular religious practices and contributed to the diversity of the region.

Southwest German Catholicism had its own peculiarities. Studying the ideal of parish life presented at the Council of Trent, or indeed the experience of French, Spanish, or even Bavarian Catholics, teaches us relatively little about Catholicism in this part of Germany.[96] The diversity of the region was so profound that one might argue that each town and village had it own kind of local religion.[97] It is therefore important to locate and identify patterns of religious practice and institutions within this larger region. If one examines the mixtures of the factors discussed above, it is possible to divide Southwest Germany as a whole into *Landschaften* or districts with similar kinds of Catholicism and similar religious styles.

Three broad factors – political structures, monastic institutions, and the sacral landscape (particularly the most important shrines) – are fairly easy to identify as factors in creating different religious styles in the regions of Southwest Germany.[98] Other influences, for example the

[96] Here I refer especially to the general works on Catholicism such as Jean Delumeau, *Catholicism between Luther and Voltaire: A New View of the Counter-Reformation* (London, 1977) and John Bossy, *Christianity in the West, 1400–1700* (London, 1985). R. Po-chia Hsia, *The World of Catholic Renewal. 1540–1770* (Cambridge, 1998) is more sensitive to the national and regional diversity within Catholic Europe.

[97] Christian, *Local Religion in Sixteenth-Century Spain*. To some degree this is Ebner's point of view in his books on parishes in Hauenstein.

[98] Many scholars emphasize the importance of political structures, for example Anton Schindling and Walter Ziegler (eds.), *Die Territorien des Reichs*. Historians of Southwest Germany also recognize the importance of monasteries. See esp. Franz Quarthal (ed.), *Die Benediktinerklöster in Baden-Württemberg* (Augsburg, 1975). On sacral landscape, see above, chapter 2 and *Zu Fuss, zu Pferd . . . Wallfahrten im Kreis Ravensburg* (Biberach, 1990).

strength of the communal church, the importance of the Jesuits, Capuchins, and other orders, the impact of larger towns on rural religion, and (most difficult to assess) traditions of popular religion, also played a role. Of course it is impossible to take all factors into account, and there is the danger of overplaying the differences between the different *Landschaften*. The diversity of Catholicism in this part of Germany was nevertheless real.

The lands governed by the Habsburgs formed one group of regions. Here the Austrian authorities worked continuously to improve the efficiency and effectiveness of the bureaucracy.[99] While this state-building suffered numerous setbacks, townspeople and villagers in *Vorderösterreich* faced an increasingly active government. The Austrian *Regierung*, regional authorities, and local officials all dealt with religious issues on a regular basis. Because of close relations with Tyrol and Austria proper, Outer Austria was also more open to wider developments in Catholicism and to the religious policies of the emperors in Vienna. More concretely, Austrian authorities interfered in the appointment of priests and in the regulation of popular religion, especially processions and pilgrimages, even before the extensive reforms of the 1770s and 1780s.

Outer Austria was not a uniform territory, especially in religious style. The villages in the Breisgau and Ortenau, in the Rhine valley (Region I, see map 4), for example, were embedded in a dense sacral landscape, with many churches and chapels. There were no dominant shrines in this region, but many smaller sacred sites. Cities, especially Freiburg, served as religious centers. The parish clergy in this area had often studied at the university in Freiburg and frequently went to the city to confess at the Jesuit church or one of the mendicant churches there. Finally, Catholics in this area had many Protestant neighbors, which in the late seventeenth century heightened the sense of Catholic identity.[100]

The religiosity of the Austrian territories in the mountains between Freiburg and Villingen (Region II) developed somewhat differently. Austrian rule was less direct in this area, since noble families and monasteries controlled local government. Monasteries such as Waldkirch, St. Peter im Schwarzwald, and St. Märgen had a large role in

[99] See articles in Hans Maier and Volker Press (eds.), *Vorderösterreich in der frühen Neuzeit* (Sigmaringen, 1989) and Dieter Stievermann, "Österreichische Vorlande" in Schindling and Ziegler (eds.), *Die Territorien des Reichs*, Vol. V *Der Südwesten*, pp. 256–277.

[100] Compare how the existence of Protestant neighbors affected Catholic confessionalism in Speyer: Forster, *The Counter-Reformation in the Villages*. For the long-term consequences, see Helmut Walser Smith, "Religion and Conflict: Protestants, Catholics, and Anti-Semitism in the State of Baden in the Era of Wilhelm II" *Central European History* 27,3 (1994), pp. 288–314.

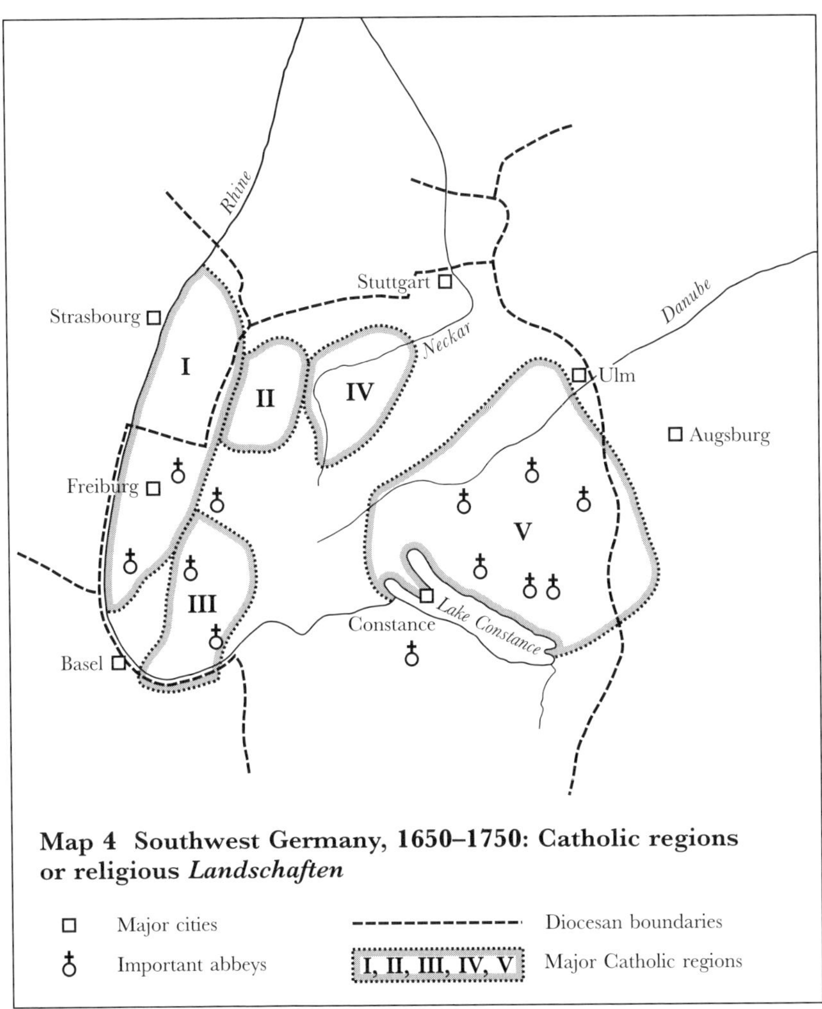

Map 4 Southwest Germany, 1650–1750: Catholic regions or religious *Landschaften*

rural religion, appointing many priests. These mountain valleys had very few parishes and, especially in the eighteenth century, a limited number of sacred sites. Pilgrimage piety came to be dominated by the shrine at Triberg, which drew communal processions from quite far away.

The region around St. Blasien in the southern Black Forest, which included the County of Hauenstein (Region III), was even less directly governed by Austria.[101] Abbeys, especially St. Blasien, but also St. Fridolin in Säckingen, and St. Trudpert, appointed almost all the parish priests, often using monks to serve the parishes. There were few parishes in this mountainous region as well, and the communes took a strong role in their administration and in the organization of processions, pilgrimage, and church festivals. The shrine at Todtmoos was extremely popular, although less so among the Austrian villages in the Rhine valley and northern Switzerland.[102]

The Austrian County of Hohenberg, around Rottenburg am Neckar (Region IV), was firmly ruled by Austrian authorities. The fact that this area was surrounded by Protestant Württemberg had a major impact on local religiosity, as did the presence from the mid-seventeenth century of a very active Jesuit college in Rottenburg.[103] There were no important monasteries in this area, no dominant shrine, and a modest number of churches. Indeed, the religious style of this group of villages and towns may have been more anti-Protestant than anywhere else in the Southwest.

The heart of the Catholic Southwest was Upper Swabia (Region V). This was a politically fragmented region, which included Austrian territories, a number of middle-sized secular lordships, and many ecclesiastical principalities.[104] The landscape itself was dominated by rich and powerful abbeys, such as Salem, Ochsenhausen, Weingarten, Zwiefalten, Schussenried, and Rot an der Rot, convents such as Wald, Baindt, Gutenzell, and Heiligkreuztal, and the commanderies of the Teutonic Knights in Althausen and Mainau. The sacral landscape was very dense, as was the parish network, especially compared with the mountainous regions to the west. This was a land of roadside crosses and Baroque churches, processions and shrines, relics and local saints.

Stretching from Lake Constance to the mountains of the Schwäbisch Alb, from Ulm to Constance, and from Vorarlberg to the boundaries of Württemberg, Upper Swabia was itself a diverse region. Each large monastery governed a group of villages, hired and fired the

101 David M. Luebke, *His Majesty's Rebels. Communities, Factions, and Rural Revolt in the Black Forest, 1725–1745* (Ithaca and London, 1997). Note that the *Grafschaft Bonndorf*, subject like much of Hauenstein to St. Blasien, was not under Austrian authority at all.

102 The Austrian villages on the left bank of the Rhine, now in Switzerland, formed a mini-*Landschaft* of their own. They were known as the Frickthal, Möhlinbach, and Rheinthal. See GLAK 79/837.

103 The Jesuits also administered the shrine at Weggental, just outside Rottenburg: HStASt. B466a/324.

104 Secular territories included those of the Counts of Heiligenberg, the Fugger counts, the Counts of Waldburg, and the Counts of Königsegg.

parish clergy, and sought to direct local Catholicism. Most monasteries had a kind of "house shrine," many of which were centers of popular cults in the eighteenth century. Salem promoted Birnau, Schussenried Steinhausen, and Rot Steinbach. These shrines drew pilgrims primarily from the villages governed by the monastery, creating close religious ties between villages.[105] Peasants also shared a religious culture through processions, which went from village to village, particularly during Rogation Week. Similarly, people gathered at the annual feasts of church patron saints, an excuse for a large party that frequently distressed church officials and some priests. The parish clergy was part of this world, partly because monasteries favored hiring local men, partly because abbots promoted the parish clergy through the parishes affiliated with each individual monastery, and partly because the priests often studied at monastery schools. The result of these various links was a kind of localized Catholic culture centered on the monasteries.

Upper Swabia was, then, a kind of microcosm of Southwest Germany more generally. Catholicism here exhibited certain general characteristics – an intense interest in pilgrimages, a dense sacral landscape, and many influential monasteries – but one is always impressed with the diversity and variety of the region as well. Furthermore, as the Bishops of Constance lived in this part of the Southwest, the episcopal administration became especially active here in the eighteenth century. Episcopal activity reinforced the already strong sense of regional pride, which the clerical elite at least linked to the German Church (the *Reichskirche*) and the imperial constitution.

A sense of Catholic identity in the century after 1650 meant *Kirchlichkeit*, a loyalty to the Catholic Church. What did the Catholic Church mean to the people of Southwest Germany? For the Jesuits and perhaps a few members of the episcopal hierarchy, the Church was the international Church. But for most of the church leadership, the Catholic Church was the German Church or the imperial Church.[106] Many prominent Catholics might even have been more specific, emphasizing their commitment to the institutions peculiar to their particular corner of Germany. As for most of the common people, "the Church" meant the church or chapel where they worshipped. They would have referred to their parish, the local area they inhabited, and perhaps the diocese in

[105] Monasteries had an interest in limiting their subjects' social ties solely to monastic villages so as not to undermine serfdom.

[106] Forster, "The Elite and Popular Foundations of German Catholicism."

which they lived, as a distant representation of the wider Church as an institution.[107] More likely, however, most people would have spoken of the religious practices that made them Catholic, for their identity had been formed around the rituals, devotions, and cults in which they participated through the years and over the course of their lives in their own villages and towns.

[107] Peasant leaders were perfectly cognizant of the jurisdictional setting in which they lived. They were adept at playing off episcopal and secular authorities and appealed directly to the bishop when they were dissatisfied with local priests or monasteries.

Conclusion

The creation of Catholic identity in Southwest Germany was closely intertwined with the development and nature of Baroque Catholicism. Since the 1970s, historians have had much to say about "confessionalization," emphasizing the role of the state and church institutions in imposing religious conformity. Other studies, like this one, point to the appeal of Catholic practices and argue that the wider population played a central role in developing their own identity as Catholics. All historians point to the vitality and popularity of Baroque Catholicism and the churchliness of the people as evidence of the strength of popular Catholic confessionalism.

A clearer understanding of what Baroque Catholicism was and how it developed should improve our understanding of long-term developments in German Catholicism. The chronology of popular Catholicism in Germany indicates several periods of religious revival, beginning with the intensification of religious life in the fifteenth and early sixteenth centuries.[1] The religious enthusiasm of Baroque Catholicism between 1650 and 1750 was the next stage of Catholic regeneration. Historians have also identified a revival of popular Catholicism from about 1850 until the First World War.[2] These periods of Catholic resurgence were interrupted by crises, the first caused by the Protestant Reformation and the second by the Enlightenment, the French Revolution, and secularization.

[1] Euan Cameron, *The European Reformation* (Oxford, 1991), esp. ch. 1; Bernd Moeller, "Piety in Germany around 1500" in Steven Ozment (ed.) *The Reformation in Medieval Perspective* (Chicago, 1971), pp. 50–75; John Bossy, *Christianity in the West* (Oxford, 1985), esp. Part I; Eamon Duffy, *The Stripping of the Altars. Traditional Religion in England 1400–1580* (New Haven, 1992); Robert W. Scribner, "Elements of Popular Belief" in Thomas A. Brady Jr., Heiko Oberman, and James D. Tracy (eds.), *Handbook of European History 1400–1600. Late Middle Ages, Renaissance, and Reformation*, Vol. I, (Leiden, 1994), pp. 238–242.

[2] Margaret Lavinia Anderson, "The Limits of Secularization: On the Problem of the Catholic Revival in Nineteenth-Century Germany" *Historical Journal* 38 (1995), pp. 647–670; Jonathan Sperber, *Popular Catholicism in Nineteenth-Century Germany* (Princeton, 1984); David Blackbourn, *Marpingen. Apparitions of the Virgin Mary in Nineteenth-Century Germany* (New York, 1994).

There were some obvious continuities across these periods of revival. Pilgrimage piety was a defining aspect of late medieval Christianity, Baroque Catholicism, and late nineteenth-century Catholicism, and the Catholic population demonstrated consistent commitment to the sacraments and liturgy of the Church in all three periods. Such continuities are important and no doubt reflect important structural aspects of popular Catholic practice. Perhaps more profoundly, such structures also reflect the dynamism of popular religion. Pilgrimage, for example, evolved from one period to the next, with individual pilgrims dominating the late Middle Ages, communal pilgrimages the Baroque, and the mass pilgrimage the nineteenth century. German Catholicism regularly experienced what Wolfgang Brückner calls "renewal as selective tradition."[3]

Communalism and clericalism were also not innovations of the early modern period, nor did they disappear at the end of the eighteenth century. The interplay of these two aspects of rural and small-town Catholicism demonstrates the continuous dynamic between religious change imposed from above and the role of the laypeople of all classes in the development of religious practice and belief. This study shows the important role the common believer played in Baroque Catholicism. The people had been just as active in the less strongly governed Germany of the late Middle Ages. In the *Kaiserreich*, Bismarck's *Kulturkampf* gave German Catholicism both a "critical, independent stance towards state authority" and allowed ultramontanism to develop "populist and ultimately even democratic elements."[4]

The Catholic Church tolerated a kind of populism in Germany and never strongly opposed democratic developments as it did in France or Italy. Catholicism also supported and flourished in the communal context. The *gemeinde Kirche*, the communal church of the pre-Reformation era, so clearly identified by the studies of Peter Blickle and Rosi Fuhrmann, remained an essential characteristic of post-Tridentine Catholicism, particularly in the Southwest and in Switzerland. Catholic reformers had a problematic relationship with communal power, as they sought to impose more effective hierarchical administrative and disciplinary structures, while simultaneously promoting the centrality of

[3] Wolfgang Brückner, "Zum Wandel der religiösen Kultur im 18. Jahrhundert. Einkreisungsversuche des 'Barockfrommen' zwischen Mittelalter und Massenmissionierung" in Ernst Hinrichs und Günter Wiegelmann (eds.), *Sozialer und kultureller Wandel in der ländlichen Welt des 18. Jahrhunderts* (Wolfenbüttel, 1982), pp. 67–70.

[4] Quotes from Anderson, "The Limits of Secularization," p. 666.

the parish and parochial services. In a region such as the Southwest, with strong communal traditions, a weak episcopal administration, and few strong state structures, the communal church dominated.

Ties between Church and community remained vital in the nineteenth century as well. As Margaret Anderson has argued, "in Catholicism, when the community is strong, then religious life is vigorous."[5] The reverse appears to have been true as well: a vigorous religious life helped maintain strong communal ties. Localism and particularism did not decline in the Southwest as they did in industrializing parts of Germany, and the "home towns" (and villages) of the region were the breeding grounds for the Catholic revival after 1850.[6] Some historians have also argued that South German Catholics, at least outside Bavaria, while just as religiously devout as Westphalians or Franconians, were politically more liberal and democratic than their northern Catholic counterparts.[7] Surely the survival of the communal church through the early modern period made it more possible for nineteenth-century peasants and townspeople to combine democratic politics and Catholic devotion.

Peter Blickle has sought the origins of a German democratic political tradition in the communalism of late medieval Southern Germany and Switzerland.[8] Yet Blickle also links communalism and Protestant theology, seeing the defeat of the people in the Peasants' War as a defeat for the communal church as well.[9] Whatever the fate of the communal church in the Protestant state churches of the early modern era, it survived in Catholic Southwest Germany. It may appear ironic to some (particularly scholars of France) that the Catholicism of the Baroque left room for forceful and effective communal and popular activity, and that it even functioned as a training ground for democracy.[10]

Now that the "confessional-national story," which placed the Reformation, Protestantism, and the rise of Prussia at the center of German

[5] Anderson, "The Limits of Secularization," p. 668.

[6] On "locality and commune" see David Blackbourn, *Class, Religion and Local Politics in Wilhelmine Germany. The Centre Party in Württemberg before 1914* (New Haven, 1980), ch. 2, esp. pp. 71–73 and Irmtraud Götz von Olenhusen, *Klerus und abweichendes Verhalten. Zur Sozialgeschichte katholischer Priester im 19. Jahrhundert: Die Erzdiözese Freiburg* (Göttingen, 1994). See also Mack Walker, *German Home Towns: Community, State, and General Estate, 1648–1871* (Ithaca, 1971).

[7] Sperber, *Popular Catholicism in Nineteenth-Century Germany*, pp. 290–292.

[8] Peter Blickle, *Obedient Germans?: A Rebuttal. A New View of German History* (Charlottesville, 1997).

[9] Peter Blickle, *Communal Reformation: The Quest for Salvation in Sixteenth-Century Germany* (New Jersey, 1992) and *The Revolution of 1525. The German Peasants' War in New Perspective* (Baltimore, 1981).

[10] Louis Châtellier has argued much the same for important elements in eighteenth-century Catholicism across Europe: *La Religion des pauvres: les missions rurales en Europe et la formation du catholicisme moderne, XVIe–XIXe siècles* (Paris, 1993).

history, is losing its grip, historians are studying developments in Catholic Germany with the aim of both illustrating the variety and regionalism of modern Germany and discovering alternative "stories."[11] At one level, this study is a part of that project. Ultimately, though, my aim is more modest. A better understanding of the origins of Catholic identity and the realities and nuances of Baroque Catholicism means that we understand the lives and motivations, hopes and fears, beliefs and values of the people of the villages and towns of Southwest Germany on their own terms. Such an understanding should always be the historian's primary objective.

[11] Thomas A. Brady Jr., *The Politics of the Reformation in Germany. Jacob Sturm (1489–1553) of Strasbourg* (New Jersey, 1997), pp. 1–5.

Bibliography

PRIMARY SOURCES

ARCHIVES

Badisches Generallandesarchiv Karlsruhe (GLAK)

Abteilung 61 Protokolle
Abteilung 65 Handschriften
Abteilung 79 Akten Breisgau Generalia
Abteilung 81 Akten Ensisheim
Abteilung 82 Akten Konstanz Generalia
Abteilung 82a Akten Konstanz
Abteilung 86 Akten Beuggen
Abteilung 89 Akten Heitersheim
Abteilung 93 Akten Mainau
Abteilung 98 Akten Salem
Abteilung 99 Akten St. Blasien
Abteilung 107 Akten Stift Waldkirch
Abteilung 109 Akten Bonndorf
Abteilung 118 Akten Nellenburg
Abteilung 119 Akten Ortenau
Abteilung 122 Akten Triberg
Abteilung 89 Akten Kenzingen, Stadt
Abteilung 229 Specialakten der kleineren Ämter und Städte und der Landgemeinden.

Erzbischöfliches Archiv Freiburg (EAF)

Handschriften (Ha)
Visitationen (Ha 62, 63, 70, 78)
Protokolle des Geistlichen Rats (Ha 207, 216, 217, 218)
Abteilung A1 Bistum Konstanz, Generalia

Hauptstaatsarchiv Stuttgart (HStASt.)

Abteilung B17 Vorderösterreichische Regierung

Abteilung B19 Hohenberg
Abteilung B37a Hohenberg
Abteilung B38 Hohenberg
Abteilung B61 Landvogtei Schwaben
Abteilung B466a Bistum Konstanz (Regierung Meersburg)
Abteilung B467 Bistum Konstanz (Ordinariat)
Abteilung B481 Kloster Ochsenhausen
Abteilung B486 Prämonstratenserkloster Rot an der Rot
Abteilung B505 Kloster-Reichstift Schußenried

Tiroler Landesarchiv Innsbruck (TLA)

Hofregistratur, Ferdinandea
Hofregistratur, Leopoldina

PUBLISHED SOURCES

Dold, P. Alban, *Die Konstanzer Ritualientexte in ihre Entwicklung von 1482–1721* (Liturgiegeschichtliche Quellen, Part V/VI), Münster: Aschendorff, 1923.

Gmelin, Moritz, "Aus Visitationsprotokollen der Diözese Konstanz von 1571–1586. Ein Beitrag zur Geschichte des Klerus" *Zeitschrift für die Geschichte des Oberrheins* 25 (1873), pp. 129–204.

Keller, Erwin, "Bischöflich-konstanzische Erlasse und Hirtenbriefe. Ein Beitrag zur Seelsorgsgeschichte im Bistum Konstanz" *Freiburger Diözesan Archiv* 102 (1982), pp. 16–59.

Kraus, Johan, "Aus den Visitationsakten des ehemaligen Kapitels Trochtelfingen 1574–1709" *Freiburger Diözesan Archiv* 73 (1953), pp. 145–181.

Lang, Peter Thaddäus, "Die Statuten des Landkapitels Ebingen aus dem Jahre 1755" *Freiburger Diözesan Archiv* 113 (1993), pp. 177–199.

Schmid, Dankwart (ed.), *Die Hauschronik der Jesuiten von Rottweil 1652–1773. Synopsis Historiae Domesticae Societatis Jesu Rottweil*, Rottweil: Stadtarchiv Rottweil, 1989.

Schmid, Hermann, "Aus der älteren Geschichte der Pfarrei Seefelden. Ein Überblick unter besonderer Berücksichtigung des Pfarrurbars von 1629" *Freiburger Diözesan Archiv* 111 (1991), pp. 171–185.

"Die Statuten des Landkapitels Linzgau von 1699 als historisch-statistisch-topographische Quelle" *Freiburger Diözesan Archiv* 111 (1991), pp. 187–211.

Schroeder, Rev. H.J. *Canons and Decrees of the Council of Trent*, London: B. Herder, 1941.

SECONDARY WORKS

Anderson, Margaret Lavinia, "The Limits of Secularization: On the Problem of the Catholic Revival in Nineteenth-Century Germany" *Historical Journal* 38 (1995), pp. 647–670.

Bader, Karl Siegfried, *Dorfgenossenschaft und Dorfgemeinde*, Part II *Studien zur Rechtsgeschichte des mittelalterlichen Dorfes*, Cologne: Bohlau Verlag, 1962.

Badisches Landesmuseum Karlsruhe (ed.), *Barock in Baden-Württemberg. Vom Ende des Dreißigjährigen Krieges bis zur Französischen Revolution*, Ausstellung des Landes Baden-Württemberg unter der Schirmherrschaft von Ministerpräsident Lothar Späth, Vol. I, Katalog; Vol. II, Aufsätze. Karlsruhe: G. Braun, 1981.

Baier, Hermann, "Die Stellung der Abtei Salem in Staat und Kirche" *Freiburger Diözesan Archiv* 35 (1934).

Becker, Thomas Paul, *Konfessionalisierung in Kurköln. Untersuchungen zu Durchsetzung der katholischen Reform in den Dekanaten Ahrgau und Bonn anhand von Visitationsprotokollen 1583–1761*, Bonn: Edition Röhrscheid, 1989.

Blackbourn, David, *Class, Religion and Local Politics in Wilhelmine Germany. The Centre Party in Württemberg before 1914*, New Haven: Yale University Press, 1980.

Marpingen, Apparitions of the Virgin Mary in Nineteenth-Century Germany, New York: Knopf, 1994.

Blickle, Peter, *Communal Reformation: The Quest for Salvation in Sixteenth-Century Germany*, New Jersey: Humanities Press, 1992.

Deutsche Untertanen: ein Widerspruch, Munich: C.H. Beck, 1981. English: *Obedient Germans?: A Rebuttal. A New View of German History*, Charlottesville: University of Virginia Press, 1997.

The Revolution of 1525. The German Peasants' War in New Perspective, Baltimore: The Johns Hopkins University Press, 1981.

Blickle, Peter (ed.), *Zugänge zur bäuerlichen Reformation*, Zurich: Chronos, 1987.

Bossy, John, *Christianity in the West, 1400–1700*, London: Oxford University Press, 1985.

"The Counter-Reformation and the People of Catholic Europe" *Past and Present* 47 (1970), pp. 51–70.

"The Mass as a Social Institution, 1200–1700" *Past and Present* 100 (1983), pp. 29–61.

Brady Jr., Thomas A., *The Politics of the Reformation in Germany. Jacob Sturm (1489–1553) of Strasbourg*, New Jersey: Humanities Press, 1997.

Breuer, Dieter (ed.), *Frömmigkeit in der frühen Neuzeit. Studien zu religiösen Literatur des 17. Jahrhunderts in Deutschland*, Amsterdam: Rodopi, 1984.

Oberdeutsche Literatur 1560–1650. Deutsche Literaturgeschichte und Territorialgeschichte in frühabsolutistischer Zeit, Munich: C.H. Beck'sche Verlagsbuchhandlung, 1979.

Brommer, Hermann (ed.), *Wallfahrten im Bistum Freiburg*, Munich and Zurich: Verlag Schnell und Steiner, 1990.

Brückner, Wolfgang, *Die Verehrung des Heiligen Blutes in Walldürn*, Aschaffenburg: Paul Pattloch-Verlag, 1958.

"Zum Wandel der religiösen Kultur im 18. Jahrhundert. Einkreisungsversuche des 'Barockfrommen' zwischen Mittelalter und Massenmissionierung" in Ernst Hinrichs und Günter Wiegelmann (eds.), *Sozialer und kultureller Wandel in der ländlichen Welt des 18. Jahrhunderts*, Wolfenbüttel: Herzog August Bibliothek, 1982, pp. 65–83.

Brückner, Wolfgang, Blickle, Peter, and Breuer, Dieter (eds.), *Literatur und Volk im 17. Jahrhundert. Probleme populärer Kultur in Deutschland*, Wiesbaden: Otto Harrassowitz, 1985.

Bücking, Jürgen, *Frühabsolutismus und Kirchenreform in Tirol (1565–1665). Ein Beitrag zum Ringen zwischen "Staat" und "Kirche" in der frühen Neuzeit*, Wiesbaden: Franz Steiner Verlag, 1972.

Bühler, Beat, "Hochstift und Diözese Konstanz im Jahre 1587" *Freiburger Diözesan Archiv* 107 (1987), pp. 35–44.

Burke, Peter, *Popular Culture in Early Modern Europe*, New York: Harper & Row, 1978.

Burkhardt, Martin, Dobras, Wolfgang, and Zimmermann, Wolfgang (eds.), *Konstanz in der frühen Neuzeit. Reformation, Verlust der Reichsfreiheit, Österreichische Zeit*, Vol. III *Geschichte der Stadt Konstanz*, Constance: Verlag Stadler, 1991.

Cameron, Euan, *The European Reformation*, Oxford University Press, 1991.

Carroll, Michael, *Veiled Threats. The Logic of Popular Catholicism in Italy*, Baltimore and London: The Johns Hopkins University Press, 1996.

Chartier, Roger, *The Cultural Origins of the French Revolution*, Durham and London: Duke University Press, 1991.

Châtellier, Louis, *Europe of the Devout. The Catholic Reformation and the Formation of a New Society*, Cambridge University Press, 1989.

La Religion des pauvres: les missions rurales en Europe et la formation du catholicisme moderne, XVIe–XIXe siècles, Paris: Aubier, Histoires, 1993.

Tradition chrétienne et renouveau catholique dans le cadre de l'ancien Diocèse de Strasbourg (1650–1770), Paris: Ophrys, 1981.

Christian, William, *Local Religion in Sixteenth-Century Spain*, Princeton University Press, 1981.

Conrad, Franziska, *Reformation in der bäuerlichen Gesellschaft: Zur Rezeption reformatorischer Theologie im Elsaß*, Stuttgart: Franz Steiner Verlag Wiesbaden, 1984.

Coreth, Anna, *Liebe ohne Mass. Geschichte der Herz-Jesu-Verehrung in Österreich im 18. Jahrhundert*, Salterrae: Maria Roggendorf, 1994.

Pietas Austriaca: österreichische Frömmigkeit im Barock, Munich: Oldenbourg, 1982

Croix, Alain, *La Bretagne au 16e et 17e siècles. La vie – la mort – la foi*, Paris: Maloine SA, 1981.

Davis, Natalie, "The Sacred and the Body Social in Sixteenth-Century Lyon" *Past and Present* 90 (1981), pp. 40–69.

Delumeau, Jean, *Catholicism between Luther and Voltaire: A New View of the Counter-Reformation*, London: Burns & Oates, 1977.

Delumeau, Jean (ed.), *La Religion de ma mère. Les femmes et la transmission de la foi*, Paris: Cerf, 1992.

Dillman, Erika, *Anselm II. Glanz und Ende eine Epoche. Eine Studie über den letzten großen Abt der Reichsabtei Salem*, Salem: Margräfliche Museen Druck und Verlag, 1987.

Stephan I. Fundamente des Barock. Salem an der Wende zum 18. Jahrhundert, Tettnang: Druck und Verlag Senn, 1988.

Dillman, Erika and Schulz, Hans-Jürgen, *Salem. Geschichte und Gegenwart*, Salem: Margräfliche Museen Druck und Verlag, 1989.

Ditchfield, Simon, *Liturgy, Sanctity and History in Tridentine Italy*, Cambridge University Press, 1995.

Duffy, Eamon, *The Stripping of the Altars. Traditional Religion in England, 1450–1580*, New Haven: Yale University Press, 1992.

Duhr, Bernhard, *Geschichte der Jesuiten in den Ländern deutsche Zunge von 16. bis 18 Jahrhundert*, 4 vols., Freiburg im Breisgau: Herdersche Verlagshandlung, 1907–1921.

van Dülmen, Richard, *Kultur und Alltag in der frühen Neuzeit*, Vol. III *Religion, Magie, Aufklärung, 16–18 Jahrhundert*, Munich: Beck, 1994.

Dünninger, Hans, *Maria siegt in Franken. Die Wallfahrt nach Dettelbach als Bekenntnis*, Würzburg: Echter Verlag, 1979.

DuPlessis, Robert S., *Transitions to Capitalism in Early Modern Europe*, Cambridge University Press, 1993.

Dupront, Alphonse, "Pilgrimage and Sacred Places" in Jacques Revel and Lynn Hunt (eds.), *Histories. French Constructions of the Past*, New York: New Press, 1995.

Eade, John and Salnow, Michael (eds.), *Contesting the Sacred, The Anthropology of Christian Pilgrimage*, London and New York: Routledge, 1991.

Ebner, Jakob, *Aus der Geschichte der Ortschaften der Pfarrei Birndorf (bei Waldshut am Hochrhein)*, Karlsruhe: Verlag Leo Wetzel, 1938.

Aus der Geschichte des Hauersteiner Dorfes Unteralpfen, 2nd edn., Karlsruhe: Verlag Leo Wetzel, n.d.

Geschichte der Ortschaften der Pfarrei Hochsal, Wangen: Sclbstverlag des Verfassers, 1958.

Geschichte der Ortschaften der Pfarrei Luttingen am Hochrhein (Luttingen, Hauenstein, Grunholz und Stadenhausen), Unteralpfen: Selbstverlag des Verfassers, 1956.

Geschichte der Ortschaften der Pfarrei Niederwihl (Niederwihl, Oberwihl und Rüßwihl), Wangen: Selbstverlag des Verfassers, 1956.

Geschichte der Pfarrei Görwihl im Hotzenwald, Wangen: Selbstverlag des Verfassers, 1953.

Geschichte der Wallfahrt und des Dorfes Engelwies bei Meßkirch, Meßkirch, 1923.

Enderle, Wilfried, "Die katholischen Reichsstädte im Zeitalter der Reformation und Konfessionsbildung" *Zeitschrift der Savigny-Stiftung für Rechtsgeschichte, Kanonistische Abteilung* 106 (1989), pp. 228–269.

Konfessionsbildung und Ratsregiment in der katholischen Reichsstadt Überlingen (500–1618), Stuttgart: Kohlhammer, 1990.

Evans, R.J.W., "Kings and the Queen of the Arts" *The New York Review of Books*, 43, 9 (May 23, 1996), pp. 21–24.

Föllinger, Georg, "Zur Priesterausbildung in den Bistümern Köln, Paderborn und Konstanz nach dem Tridentinum," in Walter Brandmüller, Herbert Immenkotter, and Erwin Iserloh (eds.), *Ecclesia Militans. Studien zur Konzilien- und Reformationsgeschichte. Remigius Bäumer zum 70. Geburtstag gewidmet*,

Vol. I *Zur Konziliengeschichte*, Paderborn, Munich, Vienna, and Zurich: Fernand Schöningh, 1988, pp. 367–397.

Forster, Marc R., "Kirchenreform, katholische Konfessionalisierung und Dorfreligion um Kloster Salem, 1650–1750" *Rottenburger Jahrbuch für Kirchengeschichte* 16 (1997), pp. 93–110.

The Counter-Reformation in the Villages. Religion and Reform in the Bishopric of Speyer, 1560–1720, Ithaca and London: Cornell University Press, 1992.

"The Elite and Popular Foundations of German Catholicism in the Age of Confessionalism: The Reichskirche" *Central European History* 26 (1994), pp. 311–325.

"With and Without Confessionalization: Varieties of Early Modern German Catholicism" *Journal of Early Modern History* 1,4 (1998), pp. 315–343.

François, Etienne, *Die unsichtbare Grenze. Protestanten und Katholiken in Augsburg, 1648–1806*, Sigmaringen: Thorbecke, 1991.

Freitag, Werner, "Konfessionelle Kulturen und innere Staatsbildung" *Westfälische Forschungen* 42 (1992), pp. 75–191.

Volks- und Elitenfrömmigkeit in der frühen Neuzeit. Marienwallfahrten im Fürstbistum Münster, Paderborn: Ferdinand Schöningh, 1991.

Froeschlé-Chopard, Marie-Hélène, *Espace et Sacré en Provence (XVIe–XXe siècle)*, Paris: Cerf, 1994.

Fuhrmann, Rosi, "Die Kirche im Dorf. Kommunale Initiativen zur Organisation von Seelsorge vor der Reformation" in Peter Blickle (ed.), *Zugänge zur bäuerlichen Reformation. Bauer und Reformation*, Zurich: Chronos, 1987, pp. 147–186.

Kirche und Dorf: Religiöse Bedürfnisse und kirchliche Stiftung auf dem Lande vor der Reformation, Stuttgart: Gustav Fischer Verlag, 1995.

Galpern, A.N., *The Religions of the People in 16th-Century Champagne*, Cambridge, MA: Harvard University Press, 1976.

Gentilcore, David, *From Bishop to Witch. The System of the Sacred in Early Modern Terra d'Otranto*, Manchester and New York: Manchester University Press, 1992.

Goldthwaite, Richard, *Wealth and the Demand for Art in Italy, 1300–1600*, Baltimore and London: The Johns Hopkins University Press, 1993.

Götz von Olenhusen, Irmtraud, *Klerus und abweichendes Verhalten. Zur Sozialgeschichte katholischer Priester im 19. Jahrhundert: Die Erzdiözese Freiburg*, Göttingen: Vandenhoeck und Ruprecht, 1994.

Guth, Klaus, "Geschichtlicher Abriß der marianischen Wallfahrtsbewegungen im deutschsprachigen Raum" in Wolfgang Beinert and Heinrich Petri (eds.), *Handbuch der Marienkunde*, Regensburg: Verlag Friederich Pustet, 1984.

Habermas, Rebekka, *Wallfahrt und Aufruhr: Zur Geschichte des Wunderglaubens in der frühen Neuzeit*, Frankfurt: Campus Verlag, 1991.

Harries, Karsten, *The Bavarian Rococo Church. Between Faith and Asceticism*, New Haven: Yale University Press, 1983.

Harrington, Joel, *Reordering Marriage and Society in Reformation Germany*, Cambridge University Press, 1995.

Haumann, Heiko and Schadek, Hans (eds.), *Geschichte der Stadt Freiburg im Breisgau*, Vol. II, *Vom Bauernkrieg bis zum Ende der habsburgischen Herrschaft; Im Auftrag der Stadt Freiburg i.Br.*, Stuttgart: Konrad Theiss Verlag, 1994.

Head, Randolph C., *Early Modern Democracy in the Grisons. Social Order and Political Language in a Swiss Mountain Canton, 1470–1620*, Cambridge University Press, 1995.

Heidegger, Heinrich and Ott, Hugo (eds.), *St. Blasien. Festschrift aus Anlaß des 200 jährigen Bestehens der Kloster- und Pfarrkirche*, Zurich and Munich: Verlag Schnell und Steiner, 1983.

Hersche, Peter, "Intendierte Rückständigkeit: Zur Charakteristik des geistlichen Staates im alten Reich" in Georg Schmidt (ed.), *Stände und Gesellschaft im alten Reich*, Stuttgart: Franz Steiner Verlag Wiesbaden, 1989, pp. 133–149.

Himmelein, Volker, Merten, Klaus, Setzler, Wilfried, and Anstett, Peter (eds.), *Barock in Baden-Württemberg*, Stuttgart: Konrad Theiss Verlag, 1981.

von Hippel, Wolfgang, "Klosterherrschaft und Klosterwirtschaft in Oberschwaben am Ende des alten Reiches. Das Beispiel Schussenried" in Heinrich R. Schmidt, André Holenstein, and Andreas Würgler (eds.), *Gemeinde, Reformation und Widerstand. Festschrift für Peter Blickle zum 60. Geburtstag*, Tübingen: bibliotheca academica Verlag, 1998, pp. 457–474.

Hitchcock, Henry-Russell, *German Rococo. The Zimmermann Brothers*, London: Allen Lane, 1968.

Rococo Architecture in Southern Germany, London: Phaidon, 1968.

Hoffman, Philip T., *Church and Community in the Diocese of Lyon, 1500–1789*, New Haven: Yale University Press, 1984.

Hsia, R. Po-chia, *Religion and Society in Münster: 1535–1618*, New Haven: Yale University Press, 1984.

Social Discipline in the Reformation: Central Europe, 1550–1750, London and New York: Routledge, 1989.

The World of Catholic Renewal. 1540–1770, Cambridge University Press, 1998.

Hüttl, Ludwig, *Marianische Wallfahrten im Süddeutsch-Österreichischen Raum. Analysen von der Reformations- bis zur Aufklärungsepoche*, Cologne and Vienna: Böhlau Verlag, 1985.

Jacob, W.M., *Lay People and Religion in the Early Eighteenth Century*, Cambridge University Press, 1996.

Kamen, Henry, *The Phoenix and the Flame: Catalonia and the Counter Reformation*, New Haven: Yale University Press, 1993.

Karant-Nunn, Susan, *The Reformation of Ritual. An Interpretation of Early Modern Germany*, London and New York: Routledge, 1997.

Kaufmann, Thomas DaCosta, *Court, Cloister, and City. The Art and Culture of Central Europe. 1450–1800*, University of Chicago Press, 1995.

Kimminich, Eva, *Religiöse Volksbräuche im Räderwerk der Obrigkeiten. Ein Beitrag zur Auswirkung aufklärerischer Reformprogramme am Oberrhein und in Vorarlberg*, Frankfurt am Main: P. Lang, 1989.

Die Kommission für Geschichtliche Landeskunde in Baden-Württemberg (ed.), *Historischer Atlas von Baden-Württemberg*, Stuttgart: Die Kommission, 1972–.

Kraus, Johan, "Aus den Visitationsakten des ehemaligen Kapitels Trochtelfingen 1574–1709" *Freiburger Diözesan Archiv* 73 (1953), pp. 145–181.

Kuhn, Elmar, Moses, Eva, Reinhardt, Rudolf, and Sachs, Petra (eds.), *Die Bischöfe von Konstanz*, Vol. I *Geschichte*, Friederichshafen: Verlag Robert Gessler, 1988.

Kuhn-Rehfus, Maren, *Das Zisterzienserinnenkloster Wald*, *Germania Sacra*, n.s. 30, Berlin and New York: Walter de Gruyter, 1992.

Kurzkataloge der volkstümlichen Kult- und Andachtsstätten der Erzdiözese Freiburg und der Diözesen Limburg, Mainz, Rottenburg-Stuttgart und Speyer, Würzburg: Richard Mayt, 1982.

Lang, Peter Thaddäus, "Die Erforschung der frühneuzeitlichen Kirchenvisitationen. Neuere Veröffentlichungen in Deutschland" *Rottenburger Jahrbuch für Kirchengeschichte* 16 (1997), pp. 185–193.

Lottin, Alain, *Lille, Citadelle de la Contre-Réforme (1598–1668)*, Lille: Westhoeck, 1984.

Luebke, David M., *His Majesty's Rebels. Communities, Factions, and Rural Revolt in the Black Forest, 1725–1745*, Ithaca and London: Cornell University Press, 1997.

Luria, Keith, *Territories of Grace. Cultural Change in the Seventeenth Century Diocese of Grenoble*, Berkeley: University of California Press, 1991.

McLeod, Hugh, *Religion and the People of Western Europe, 1789–1989*, Oxford University Press, 1997.

Maier, Hans and Press, Volker (eds.), *Vorderösterreich in der frühen Neuzeit*, Sigmaringen: Thorbecke, 1989.

Maier, Konstantin, "Die Konstanzer Diözesansynoden im Mittelalter und in der Neuzeit" *Rottenburger Jahrbuch für Kirchengeschichte* 5 (1986), pp. 53–89.

Maurer, Hans Martin, "Die Ausbildung der Territorialgewalt oberschwäbischer Klöster von 14. bis 17. Jahrhundert" *Blätter für deutsche Landesgeschichte* 109 (1973), pp. 155–195.

Mayer, Johan Georg, *Das Konzil von Trent und die Gegenreformation in der Schweiz*, Stans: Hans und Matt, 1901.

Mayer, P. Beda, "Vorderösterreichische Kapuzinerprovinz" in *Der Franziskusorden. Die Kapuziner und Kapuzinerinnen in der Schweiz* [*Helvetia Sacra*, Section V, Vol. II, Part I], Bern: Franke Verlag, 1974, pp. 774–790.

Metz, Friedrich (ed.), *Vorderösterreich. Eine geschichtliche Landeskunde*, 2nd rev. edn., Freiburg: Rombach, 1967.

Moeller, Bernd, *Imperial Cities and the Reformation. Three Essays*, Durham: Labyrinth Press, 1982.

"Piety in Germany around 1500" in Steven Ozment (ed.), *The Reformation in Medieval Perspective*, Chicago: Quadrangle Books, 1971, pp. 50–75.

Mühleisen, Hans-Otto, *Das Vermächtnis der Abtei. 900 Jahre St. Peter auf dem Schwarzwald*, Karlsruhe: Badenia Verlag, 1993.

Muir, Edward, *Ritual in Early Modern Europe*, Cambridge University Press, 1997.

Müller, Wolfgang, "Die Kirchlichen Verhältnisse" in *Vorderösterreich. Eine geschichtliche Landeskunde*, Freiburg, 1967.

Myers, W. David, *"Poor, Sinning Folk." Confession and Conscience in Counter-*

Reformation Germany, Ithaca and London: Cornell University Press, 1996.

Nalle, Sara T., *God in La Mancha: Religious Reform and the People of Cuenca, 1500–1650*, Baltimore: The Johns Hopkins University Press, 1992.

Ogilvie, Sheilagh (ed.), *Germany. A New Social and Economic History*, Vol. II *1630–1800*, London: Arnold, 1996.

O'Malley, John (ed.), *Catholicism in Early Modern Europe. A Guide to Research*, St. Louis: Center for Reformation Research, 1988.

Ott, Hugo, "Die Benediktinerabtei St. Blasien in den Reformbestrebungen seit 1567, besonders unter Abt Kaspar II. (1571–1596)" *Freiburger Diözesan Archiv* 84 (1964), pp. 142–197.

Ozment, Steven, *When Fathers Ruled. Family Life in the Reformation*, Cambridge, MA: Harvard University Press, 1983.

Pammer, Michael, *Glaubensabfall und wahre Andacht. Barock Religiösität, Reformkatholizismus, und Laizismus in Oberösterreich, 1700–1820*, Munich: Oldenbourg, 1994.

Phythian-Adams, Charles, *Local History and Folklore: A New Framework*, London: Bedford Square Press, 1975.

Quarthal, Franz (ed.), *Die Benediktinerklöster in Baden-Württemberg.* [*Germania Benedictina*, Vol. V, Baden-Württemberg], Augsburg: Kommissionsverlag Winfried Werk, 1975.

Rapp, Francis, *Réformes et Réformation à Strasbourg. Eglise et société dans le Diocèse de Strasbourg (1450–1525)*, Paris: Ophrys, 1974.

Rasmussen, Niels, "Liturgy and the Liturgical Arts" in John O'Malley (ed.), *Catholicism in Early Modern Ceremony. A Guide to Research*, St. Louis, 1988.

Reinhard, Wolfgang, "Gegenreformation als Modernisierung? Prolegomena zu einer Theorie des konfessionellen Zeitalters" *Archiv für Reformationsgeschichte* 68 (1977), pp. 226–52.

Reinhard, Wolfgang and Schilling, Heinz (eds.), *Die katholische Konfessionalisierung*, Heidelberg: Gütersloher Verlagshaus, 1995.

Reinhardt, Rudolf, *Die Beziehungen von Hochstift und Diözese Konstanz zu Habsburg-Österreich in der Neuzeit: Zugleich ein Beitrag zur archivalischen Erforschung des Problems "Kirche und Staat." Beiträge zur Geschichte der Reichskirche in der Neuzeit*, vol. II, Wiesbaden: Franz Steiner Verlag, 1966.

Restauration, Visitation, Inspiration. Die Reformbestrebungen in der Benediktinerabtei Weingarten von 1567 bis 1627, Stuttgart: Kohlhammer, 1960.

Remling, Ludwig, *Bruderschaften in Franken. Kirchen- und Sozialgeschichtliche Untersuchung zum spätmittelalterlichen und frühneuzeitlichen Bruderschaftswesen*, Würzburg: Fernand Schöningh, 1986.

Robisheaux, Thomas W., "The World of the Village" in Thomas A. Brady, Jr., Heiko A. Oberman, and James D. Tracy (eds.), *Handbook of European History 1400–1600. Late Middle Ages, Renaissance, and Reformation*, Vol. I *Structures and Assertions*, Leiden: E. J. Brill, 1994, pp. 79–104.

Rothkrug, Lionel, "German Holiness and Western Sanctity in Medieval and Modern History" *Historical Reflections/Réflexions Historiques* 15 (1988), pp. 161–249.

"Holy Shrines, Religious Dissonance, and Satan in the Origins of the German Reformation" *Historical Reflections/Réflexions Historiques* 14 (1987), pp. 143–286.

"Popular Religion and Holy Shrines. Their Influence on the Origins of the German Reformation and their Role in German Cultural Development" in James Obelkevich (ed.), *Religion and the People, 800–1700*, Chapel Hill: University of North Carolina Press, 1979.

Sabean, David, *Power in the Blood. Popular Culture and Village Discourse in Early Modern Germany*, Cambridge University Press, 1984.

Property, Production, and Family in Neckarhausen, 1700–1870, Cambridge University Press, 1990.

Schilling, Heinz, "Confessionalization in the Empire: Religious and Societal Change in Germany between 1555 and 1620," in Heinz Schilling, *Religion, Political Culture and the Emergence of Early Modern Society. Essays in German and Dutch History*, Leiden: E.J. Brill, 1992, pp. 205–245.

Schindling, Anton and Ziegler, Walter (eds.), *Die Territorien des Reichs im Zeitalter der Reformation und Konfessionalisierung. Land und Konfession*, Vol. I *Der Südosten*, Münster: Aschendorff, 1989.

Die Territorien des Reichs im Zeitalter der Reformation und Konfessionalisierung. Land und Konfession, Vol. V *Der Südwesten*, Münster: Aschendorff, 1993.

Schlögl, Rudolf, *Glaube und Religion in der Säkularisierung. Die katholische Stadt - Köln, Aachen, Münster - 1700–1840*, Munich: Oldenbourg, 1995.

Schmalfeldt, Kristiane, "Sub tuum praesidium confugimus. Unser Liebe Frau in der Tanne zu Triberg" *Freiburger Diözesan Archiv* 108 (1988), pp. 1–302.

Schmidt, Heinrich Richard, "Die Christianisierung des Sozialverhaltens als permanente Reformation. Aus der Praxis reformierte Sittengerichte in der Schweiz während der frühen Neuzeit" in Peter Blickle and Johannes Kunische (eds.), *Kommunalisierung und Christianisierung. Voraussetzungen und Folgen der Reformation. 1400–1600, Zeitschrift für historische Forschung*, Supplementary Volume IX, Berlin: Duncker und Humblot, 1980, pp. 113–163.

Konfessionalisierung im 16. Jahrhundert, Munich: Oldenbourg, 1992.

"Sozialdisziplinierung? Ein Plädoyer für das Ende des Etatismus in der Konfessionalisierungsforschung" *Historische Zeitschrift* 265 (1997), pp. 639–682.

Scribner, Robert W., "Communalism: Universal Category or Ideological Construct? A Debate in the Historiography of Early Modern Germany and Switzerland" *Historical Journal* 37, 1 (1994), pp. 199–207.

"Elements of Popular Belief" in Thomas A. Brady Jr., Heiko Oberman, and James D. Tracy (eds.), *Handbook of European History 1400–1600. Late Middle Ages, Renaissance, and Reformation*, Vol. I *Structures and Assertions*, Leiden: E. J. Brill, 1994, pp. 231–262.

"Ritual and Popular Religion in Catholic Germany at the Time of the Reformation" in Robert W. Scribner, *Popular Culture and Popular Movements in the Reformation*, London: Hambledon Press, 1987.

The German Reformation, Atlantic Highlands: Humanities Press, 1986.

Scribner, Robert W. (ed.), *Germany. A New Social and Economic History*, Vol. I, *1450–1650*, London: Arnold, 1996.

Seibrich, Wolfgang, *Gegenreformation als Restauration. Die restaurativen Bemühungen der alten Orden im deutschen Reich von 1580 bis 1648*, Münster: Aschendorff, 1991.

Smith, Helmut Walser, "Religion and Conflict: Protestants, Catholics, and Anti-Semitism in the State of Baden in the Era of Wilhelm II" *Central European History* 27,3 (1994), pp. 288–314.

Smolinsky, Heribert, "Volksfrömmigkeit und religiöse Literatur im Zeitalter der Konfessionalisierung" in Hansgeorg Molitor and Heribert Smolinsky (eds.), *Volksfrömmigkeit in der frühen Neuzeit*, Münster: Aschendorff, 1994.

Soergel, Philip, *Wondrous in His Saints. Counter-Reformation Propaganda in Bavaria*, Berkeley: University of California Press, 1993.

Sperber, Jonathan, *Popular Catholicism in Nineteenth-Century Germany*, Princeton University Press, 1984.

Swidler, Leonard, *Aufklärung Catholicism, 1780–1850. Liturgical and other Reforms in the Catholic Aufklärung*, Missoula: Scholars Press, 1978.

Tackett, Timothy, *Priest and Parish in Eighteenth Century France. A Social and Political Study of the Curés of the Diocese of Dauphiné, 1750–1791*, Princeton University Press, 1977.

Religion, Revolution, and Regional Culture in Eighteenth-Century France: The Ecclesiastical Oath of 1791, Princeton University Press, 1986.

Tüchle, Herrmann, *Von der Reformation bis zur Säkularisation. Geschichte der katholischen Kirche im Raum des späteren Bistums Rottenburg-Stuttgart*, Ostfildern: Schwabenverlag, 1981.

Turner, Victor and Edith, *Image and Pilgrimage in Christian Culture. Anthropological Perspectives*, New York: Columbia University Press, 1978.

Valentin, Jean-Marie (ed.), *Gegenreformation und Literatur. Beiträge zur interdisziplinären Erforschung der katholischen Reformbewegung*, Amsterdam: Rodopi, 1976.

Veit, Andreas Ludwig, *Kirche und Kirchenreform in der Erzdiözese Mainz im Zeitalter der Glaubensspaltung und der beginnenden tridentinischen Reformation*, Freiburg: Herdersche Verlagshandlung, 1920.

Veit, Ludwig and Lenhart, Ludwig, *Kirche und Volksfrömmigkeit im Zeitalter des Barocks*, Freiburg: Verlag Herder, 1956.

Walker, Mack, *German Home Towns: Community, State, and General Estate, 1648–1871*, Ithaca: Cornell University Press, 1971.

Warmbrunn, Paul, *Zwei Konfessionen in einer Stadt: Das Zusammenleben von Katholiken und Protestanten in den paritätischen Reichstädten Augsburg, Biberach, Ravensburg, und Dinkelsbühl von 1548–1648*, Wiesbaden: Franz Steiner Verlag, 1983.

Wunder, Heide, *Die bäuerliche Gemeinde in Deutschland*, Göttingen: Vandenhoeck und Ruprecht, 1986.

Zika, Charles, "Hosts, Processions and Pilgrimages: Controlling the Sacred in Fifteenth-Century Germany" *Past and Present* 118 (1988), pp. 25–64.

Zimmermann, Wolfgang, *Rekatholisierung, Konfessionalisierung und Ratsregiment. Der Prozeß des politischen und religiösen Wandels in der österreichischen Stadt Konstanz 1548–1637*, Sigmaringen: Thorbecke, 1994.

Zschunke, Peter, *Konfession und Alltag in Oppenheim. Beiträge zue Geschichte von Bevölkerung und Gesellschaft einer gemischtkonfessionellen Kleinstadt in der frühen Neuzeit*, Wiesbaden: Franz Steiner Verlag, 1984.

Zu Fuss, zu Pferd . . . Wallfahrten im Kreis Ravensburg, Katalog der Ausstellung im Kloster Weingarten, Biberach: Biberacher Verlag, 1990.

Index